GoingFaster!

Mastering the Art of Race Driving

The Skip Barber
Racing School

Written by **Carl Lopez**

Foreword by **Danny Sullivan**

RB

ROBERT BENTLEY, INC.
AUTOMOTIVE PUBLISHERS

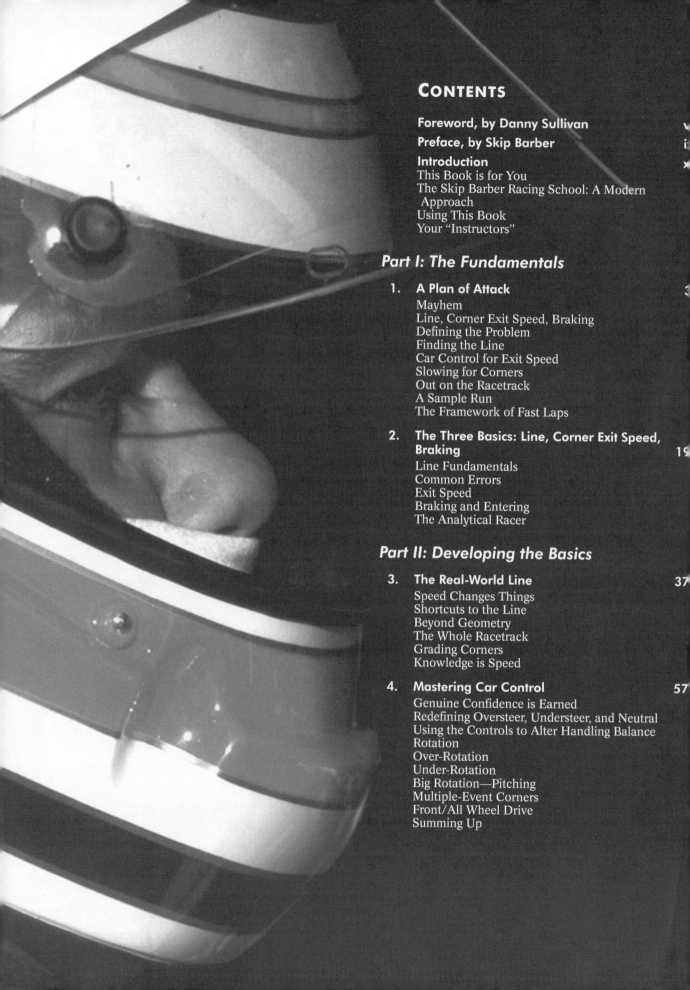

CONTENTS

ROBERT BENTLEY, INC. | AUTOMOTIVE PUBLISHERS

Information that makes
the difference.®

1734 Massachusetts Avenue
Cambridge, MA 02138 USA
800-423-4595 / 617-547-4170
http://www.rb.com
e-mail: sales@rb.com

Copies of this book may be purchased from selected booksellers, or directly from the publisher by mail. The publisher encourages comments from the reader of this book. These communications have been and will be considered in the preparation of this and other manuals. Please write to Robert Bentley, Inc., Publishers at the address listed on the top of this page.

Since this page cannot legibly accommodate all the copyright notices, the Art Credits page at the back of this book listing the source of the photographs used constitutes an extension of the copyright page.

Library of Congress Cataloging-in-Publication Data

Lopez, Carl, 1946–
    Going faster! : mastering the art of race driving: the Skip
Barber Racing School / by Carl Lopez ; foreword by
Danny Sullivan.
        p.   cm.
    Includes bibliographical references (p.) and index.
    ISBN 0-8376-0227-0 (alk. paper)
    1. Automobile racing. I. Skip Barber Racing School. II. Title.
    GV1029.L57 1997
    796.82—dc21   97–48026
                                                              CIP

Bentley Stock No. GDBA

01 00 99 98 10 9 8 7 6 5 4 3 2

The paper used in this publication is acid free and meets the requirements of the National Standard for Information Sciences-Permanence of Paper for Printed Library Materials. ∞

Front cover: Photo courtesy of Mike Powell/Allsport
Back cover, clockwise from top left: 1) Photo courtesy of Don Heiny, Skip Barber Racing School; 2) Art courtesy of Carl Lopez; 3) Art courtesy of Carl Lopez; 4) Photo courtesy of Sidell Tilghman; 5) Photo of Bryan Herta courtesy of R. Dole; 6) Photo courtesy of R. Dole.

This book is dedicated to all those, here and gone, who have been to that place where only a racecar can take you.

FOREWORD

BY DANNY SULLIVAN

WHEN CARL FIRST SPOKE to me about writing the foreword for this book, I couldn't help but think back to how much time has passed since we worked together teaching racing schools. Since 1980, I've been concentrating on my racing career, all the while keeping in touch with Skip, watching his operation grow.

Skip Barber and the organization he's created have made a big impact on the sport over the years. When I was teaching for Skip, we had one group of Formula Fords putting on programs in the East and a few more in Florida during the winter. Now there are four permanent bases, more cars than you can count, and schools and Race Series events are going on coast to coast, year round. Then there's the Pro Series, which Skip started in 1986, adding another 30 cars to the fleet. Now I get to see Skip often when the Pro Series and Indy Cars are running at the same event.

With all this activity, Skip gave drivers the opportunity to learn and prove themselves: first in an amateur series, and then on a professional level. These series are important, and different than the way many of us started racing. Developing and showing your talent by driving against other drivers in equal cars was unheard of when I started. You can see the results with the success of guys like Bryan Herta, Robbie Buhl, Jim Pace, and Jeremy Dale, among many others.

Beyond these things, he did something less obvious, but even more important. He got drivers talking to each other about how they drove race cars fast. Then he shared the information. This was more of a revolution at the time than many people might think. The sharing of information about driving, especially serious driving beyond entry-level basics, was very uncommon. Skip opened up that door.

I feel like I was an early part of the process. I first got involved in the school in 1979 after six years of racing in England and Europe. I called Skip to see if, while pursuing my options in the States, I could help him by teaching in the racing school. My original intent was to keep busy and stay involved with the sport while working to get into a good race team. It didn't take long to realize that the teaching experience would be different than I expected.

I'd been racing for a while by then and had done well but, like many experienced drivers, a lot of my attention was focused on the things you had to do out of

the car to keep going. I'd been to racing school—that's how I started in Formula Ford—but the basic lessons were far behind me. It was difficult at first to take the things you were doing in the car instinctively and explain them clearly to novices, but it helped my driving a lot. Teaching forced me to think more about what I was doing and how I was doing it. Everyone who was instructing contributed their own twist about race driving, and every day we bounced ideas off each other and stole each other's best material.

You've got to remember that we didn't just work together all day at the racetrack. When you're on the road, you bunk together, go out to dinner as a group, and generally talk racing whenever you aren't sleeping. Even in the relatively short time I was there, you could see that this sharing of information and points of view was expanding the understanding of what worked in race cars—well beyond the basics.

I see this book as the same process. It would have been easy for Carl to create a book just by transcribing the lectures on the basics from the Racing School, but I'm glad he went further than that. He's covered all the fundamentals and has then gone on to talk to many of us who are out there dealing with cars and situations that are a long way down the line from a Three-Day Racing School. The end result is a book on race driving that is more thorough, and useful, than any out there.

Now the information is available to everybody—current race drivers, folks considering getting into racing, and the fan who has no plans of going racing but wants to get a better appreciation of what's going on in the cars. The Skip Barber Racing School is doing what it has always done: take the information that race drivers take years to learn and make it accessible to everybody. Seems to me that it's just another natural step in the process Skip began 25 years ago.

PREFACE

BY SKIP BARBER

WHEN I STARTED RACING in the early sixties, drivers were self-taught, and hard-acquired knowledge was rarely shared. The only schools were weekend club programs that dealt with flags and being on time for the drivers' meeting. They featured walking tours of the track with the braking and turn-in points noted as determined by that particular self-taught volunteer instructor. There was no significant pool of knowledge, and the knowledge being shared was often incorrect or misleading. "It's flat out in fifth" meant you'd better brake hard and use third gear.

I had a pretty frustrating racing career, starting while in college (and while heavily in debt to that college—doesn't everybody use their student loan to buy their first racecar?). You can probably see the excuses coming already. At that time, road racing was primarily amateur and road racers didn't associate with the oval track pros. It was also more difficult to enter then without money (excuses piling higher). Consequently, I ended up driving a lot of strange cars (early on, those that were free; later, ones I was paid reasonably well to drive) and was rarely able to measure myself against good drivers in equal cars.

Some people thought I was really fast, but I felt I had achieved less than I should have, with no significant results. Having no resources or connections and being painfully shy didn't help.

See, you're already in school—racers invented the word *excuse*. I beat Jim Clark in an identical car in my first professional race; I also set over 30 lap records and did some Formula 1 races on merit, but never put it together. For me, it is ironic that our school has become the largest, most successful, and, we believe, far and away the best of its kind in the world.

As my racing career was winding down, I backed into the racing school business. I had a friend who had just started a racing school and I put my name on the door. The theory was that he and his wife would do all the work: I would show up on weekdays to teach, work on my tan, have fun, meet lots of people who would want to buy me new racecars, and make some extra money.

Well, so much for planning. Besides coming out of that first year in debt, without new racecars, and probably with future skin problems, I had learned two important lessons. First, and most importantly, you could teach someone how to drive a racecar; and once you had to explain to novices how to race, you thought a lot more about what you, as a racer, did intuitively. There was no reason for racing to be different from other sports, all of which had coaches.

Secondly, I thoroughly enjoyed teaching, and I liked the problem-solving aspect of making the school work both from a teaching perspective and as a business, not to mention the fact that driving a racecar well is high-speed problem-solving.

The school grew, spreading across the country, and the numbers and variety of our programs increased as we added more base locations, race series, a defensive driving school, and the Pro Series. All of this brought more and more instructors into the fold. We currently have more than 150 full- or part-time instructors and many, many more have worked for us in the past. All are or have been good racing drivers.

These guys have created a great culture of working together, learning from each other, sharing information, and helping your buddy get a ride. Some instructors move in and out of this home for racing drivers as their careers rise and fall. This group does their own recruiting, training, and, on occasion, disciplining. The pool of knowledge they have created is what this book is really about.

Just as you would expect at a good university, our accumulated racing knowledge keeps expanding. In this book, Carl Lopez, one of our long-time instructors, attempts to share this vast store of knowledge with you, the reader. It is not a simple collection of war stories. Rather, it is a reference book from which you can choose the sections that particularly interest you. Whether you are a fan or a racecar driver, we hope that you will take something valuable from our collective experience and use it well.

Skip Barber

INTRODUCTION

THIS BOOK IS FOR YOU

This modern racing technique book is unique; its breadth and depth of information make it indispensible for both the novice and experienced race driver.

All of us in the sport of auto racing started out as car-nuts first, then took our enthusiasm and applied it to competition. Some of us started out as kids, fiddling around with coasters, Karts, mini-bikes, ATVs, anything with wheels. Others were late bloomers: drivers who once thought of cars as transportation appliances but have suddenly experienced an automotive awakening. They start to nibble at the edges of the car-nut world and the more they try the more they like. Before they know it, they're hooked.

And once you meet others of like mind any chance of escape from the addiction is gone. Dinner conversations drift toward cars. Trips get planned because a long drive is involved. Budgets get stretched to ac-quire cars that provide high performance and eye-pleasing design. Driving becomes enjoyable, a skill that involves serious thought, a skill in which you take pride.

If you feel this way about cars and driving, regardless of how and when your interest in cars started, this book is for you. We are going to take a detailed look at the knowledge you must acquire and the skills you need to develop to drive a racecar at a lap-record pace, safely. We are going to hold back nothing.

Spectating

If you just want to watch, you can follow along and learn about the skills your favorite racer uses to chase a championship. This book will give you a more accurate idea of what's involved in driving a racecar. In ad-

For both drivers and fans, learning the hows and whys of racing technique increases the enjoyment of the sport.

Beyond the noise and spectacle, educated race fans appreciate the difficult problems racers solve under intense pressure.

dition to becoming a well-informed spectator, you will find in this book that the skills a racer uses to go really fast are the same skills that can make you an excellent road driver.

Go On, Do It

You'll find that the skills required to drive a racecar are not superhuman abilities. There are people out there who don't necessarily want to drive at Indy at 230 m.p.h. but who are getting out on a racetrack from time to time and having a ball without huge expense or unreasonable risk to their cars. The techniques you will learn from this book can open a new and exciting outlet for your enthusiasm for automobiles.

There are plenty of track events where you can run alone, at your own pace, driving the family car only as hard as you feel is prudent. It doesn't matter whether your vehicle is a Ferrari, a Neon, a vintage TR3, or one of the dozens of modern sports cars on today's mar-

You don't need a fancy, expensive racecar to enjoy the thrill of driving on a track.

ket—you can get it on a racetrack near you and exercise it, without the worry of twirling blue lights flashing in your mirror.

In order to do this without damaging your car or scaring yourself, you have to give some thought to how running on a racetrack is different from driving on the public roads.

One aim of this book is to give you an honest understanding of what you are trying to accomplish on the racetrack and to give you a framework you can use to improve your skills. We will give you an understandable explanation of the fundamentals of driving a car over a twisty road at speed. At the same time we will show you how the best and quickest professional drivers have to adapt and develop the fundamentals to put the fastest and most sophisticated machinery at the front of the pack.

THE SKIP BARBER RACING SCHOOL: A MODERN APPROACH

Our racing technique book is different from the old standards.

The first and most fundamental difference is that it doesn't represent one person's opinion of how racecars should be driven. Our Racing School is more like a Racing University, with a large, expert faculty, each of whom contribute to the body of knowledge in their own way. Skip is the Professor Emeritus.

We are going to draw on the total of hundreds of years of racing experience that our instructors have acquired in order to get to the nitty gritty of what it takes to win.

Technique and Technology

The second fundamental difference is that today's technology allows us to look at driving technique in a way that previous authorities on driving technique—people like Piero Taruffi, Paul Frère, and Alan Johnson—could never have done.

We have a data acquisition system that can dissect the racetrack into segments that can be closely scrutinized. We can put instruments in racecars to see where and how a driver uses the throttle, brakes and steering wheel. We use real cars on real racetracks and take a close look at what the driver does with the controls to reduce lap time—what works and what doesn't. Sure, we have an overall philosophy that tries to tie together racing theory and practice, but we don't want this book to be a statement of philosophy; we want it to be an investigation of skills that separate the best from the rest.

Good Information—At the Right Time

We teach people how to drive racecars at over 100 three-day schools per year. As in any specialized field, the closer one looks at the subject, the more complex it gets—it's easy to get bogged down in the complexity.

Modern data acquisition systems replace theory with hard fact.

This is especially true in auto racing, where we deal with both athletic ability and a complicated piece of equipment.

And let's face it: novices come into the sport with preconceived ideas about what is involved, with both good and bad driving habits. They are enthusiasts. They read the car magazines, the racing newspapers, and watch races on TV. They have picked up information about racing from a variety of sources. Some of this information is accurate and useful. Some of it is preposterous and, if acted on, dangerous.

We prefer to start with a clean slate and build the understanding of how to drive well by simplifying the process first and, over time, expand a driver's knowledge in bite-size pieces so that the new information can be applied to driving faster.

One of the most valuable skills our instructors develop when training beginners is knowing what information to leave out. This is especially hard to do when you're five to twenty years into a racing career, as most of our instructors are—it's a challenge to try to remember what it was like on your first day in a racecar when everything seemed so foreign. At the beginning it is important to focus on the fundamentals and not confuse the beginning racer with how the fundamentals can change in more complicated circumstances. Sometimes it's a battle to keep things simple.

It's easy for people who have a little bit of knowledge to shrug off the basics, thinking that the fundamentals are somehow beneath them because of their existing knowledge or their "natural talent." This attitude always turns out to be a mistake.

Over the years we've found that it's tremendously helpful for you to think about each and every aspect of your driving. It's common for drivers, even very good drivers, to have problems on the racetrack and solve them at that moment by moving the pedals and steering wheel, meanwhile ignoring what may be the underlying cause of their difficulties. "Experienced" drivers, we've found, can benefit greatly from going back to basics from time to time in order to get a clear answer to the question, "What am I trying to do?"

USING THIS BOOK

This book is divided into four parts. The first presents the entry-level basics of driving on racetracks, defining fundamental problems, and laying out a plan of attack for going progressively faster. Novices will

From the start, Skip Barber's school meant in-depth training in a well-paced format.

> *"Having to teach had a staggering effect on the way I looked at my own driving. I learned so much the first year just trying to explain it. It's not that I saw things that I didn't understand, it's that if you never try to articulate it you just haven't thought about it as much as you can. Light bulbs went off all that first year. I discovered why I was doing the things that I was doing in a racecar.*
>
> *"I wasn't a real thinking, analytical driver at all. Ironic that I ended up in the school business, because I wasn't that way. I was tremendously disciplined—because I couldn't afford to crash anything—but not analytical.*
>
> *"I remember so many times at Thompson that first year thinking to myself "Oh, you idiot, that's why that happens." It gave me an appreciation for how you could use the car closer to its limits and how I could have solved problems that I never thought about."*
>
> —Skip Barber

certainly want to start here. Experienced racers could skip Part I, but a review will remind you how a grounding in the fundamentals leads to faster laps.

Part II expands on the basics, digging more deeply into the skills of choosing the optimal path around the racetrack, controlling a car at its cornering limits, and slowing for corner entries.

Part III takes the skills and concepts covered in the first two parts and applies them to real race courses and racing situations.

Part IV covers some of the technical information about racecars that can help you put your skills to their most effective use. The final part of the book explores the world of racing as well as how you must adapt your driving technique to faster and faster cars.

We intend to go into great detail. If you have just a casual interest in racing, the sheer bulk of information might seem daunting. But if you're planning on going road-racing, the many techniques and perspectives will not only get you started, but also will remain a storehouse of information that you can go back to and use throughout your career.

YOUR "INSTRUCTORS"

Our instructors, both present and past, have contributed heavily to the information accumulated here in this volume. Ten of them have endured long interviews and will be quoted from time to time. They are, alphabetically:

Skip Barber. Three-time National Champion and one of the few Americans ever to compete in Formula 1. He was considered to be one of the quickest drivers of his era, once beating the legendary Jim Clark in identical cars. Skip's driving experience includes nearly every type of racing vehicle from Bugeye Sprites to Can-Am, Indy Cars, and Formula

1. Since setting his professional racing career aside in 1975, he has built the largest and most comprehensive race training organization in the world, which encompasses the Skip Barber Racing School, the Skip Barber Formula Dodge Series, the Dodge/Skip Barber Driving School and the Barber Dodge Pro Series.

Robbie Buhl. Robbie began racing in 1984, is a graduate, instructor/coach and test driver for Skip Barber Racing. He has won not only races but championships in one class of racecar after another. He has been Sports Renault Champion, 1989 Barber/Saab Champ, 1992 Indy Lights title holder, and in 1993 won the 24 Hours of Daytona in the GTS class. In 1995 Robbie returned to the Indy Lights Series where he was runner-up in the championship. Robbie's first Indy 500 came in 1996 where, driving for Beck Motorsports, he finished 9th. He continues to pursue his goal of a top level Indy Car ride, bringing with him experience in both Indy Car racing and IRL.

Jeremy Dale. Jeremy's winning ways began in the Skip Barber Formula Ford Series where he won 13 races and was named rookie of the year in 1984. Moving up to Barber Saab, he won 9 races, broke six track records, and made a remarkable 18 top three finishes in two limited seasons. He has been IMSA Firehawk Champion, IMSA GTU and GTS Factory driver for Nissan, and has had back-to-back victories in the 24 Hours of Daytona in IMSA's premier World Sports Car class. Jeremy has had to endure one of the cruel realities of auto racing: his career was sidetracked in 1995 by a horrific accident at Road Atlanta where he sustained serious injuries to his legs.

Terry Earwood. Terry is one of the winningest Showroom Stock racers in the U.S. and a five-time national drag racing champion. In 1985 Terry ran into an old drag racing buddy by the name of Paul Rossi who invited Terry to drive with his new team at the 12 Hour race at Road Atlanta. They won first time out and over the next five seasons went on to win three manufacturer's championships, finishing second in the seasons they didn't win. Terry continues to race Showroom Stock as the 1996 IMSA Endurance Champion, a breakthrough after finishing second in the championship five times, four times to a teammate.

Terry was instrumental in designing the curriculum for the Dodge/Skip Barber Driving School and functions as the school's Chief Instructor.

Bryan Herta. Bryan began racing Karts at the age of 12 and, before he moved on to full sized racecars, had won four consecutive Karting points championships, finished third in the World Karting Championship, and in his final year was runner-up in World Karting Association Points. After completing the Skip Barber Racing School in 1989, he won the Skip Barber Race Series Western Formula Ford Championship, recording 14 victories in 18 races. Bryan moved on to win the Barber Saab championship, then the Indy Lights crown in 1993. He finished ninth in the Indy 500 in 1994, driving for A. J. Foyt. Bryan has focused on single seat racecars throughout his career and presently drives for Bobby Rahal in the PPG CART World Series.

David Loring. David has worn many hats in the racing industry since he began as an 18-year-old in Canada in 1969. He dominated Formula Ford racing in the early seventies, winning four championships in Canada and one in the U.S. He always worked on his cars as well as driving them; over the years this ability has kept him involved in the sport on a variety of levels, giving him unique insight. In 1977, for example, Dan Gurney picked David to build, develop, and drive his Eagle Formula Ford and David responded by driving the car to a national championship win in 1978.

He has won the 24 Hours of Daytona in the Camel Lights class and the 12 Hours of Sebring three times in the GTU class as well as winning the GTU driver's championship in 1992.

Jim Pace. In 1987 Jim decided to leave medical school to pursue his passion for racing, starting with a Skip Barber Racing School. By 1988 he was crowned Barber Saab Pro Series Rookie of the Year, then moved on from the single-seaters to build a career in IMSA endurance racing. He first won the 24 Hours of Daytona in 1990 in the GTU class, the 12 Hours of Sebring in GTP Light in 1991, and the IMSA Exxon Supreme GTU Championship in 1994. He moved up to WSC in 1995, where he drove for eight different teams. In 1996, paired with Wayne Taylor, Jim won both Daytona and Sebring. He teaches at the Skip Barber Racing School, test-drives the Formula Dodge for the Florida and Midwest Race Series, and coaches at Barber Dodge.

Dorsey Schroeder. Dorsey has been racing competitively for 24 years. He started at age 18 in an 850 Fiat and has won in every type of racecar he has driven. His experience includes Sports Renault, Formula Atlantic, Showroom Stock, IMSA GTU, GTO and GTS, Trans Am, IROC—even NASCAR and ARCA stock cars. He has won both the 24 Hours of Daytona and the 12 Hours of Sebring as well as overall championships in the Trans Am in 1989 and IMSA's GTS Series in 1990. He is a front-runner in the Trans Am Series, driving Mustangs for Tom Gloy Racing. When his schedule allows, Dorsey instructs and coaches at the Skip Barber Racing School and Barber racing events.

Danny Sullivan. Danny has been from the bottom to the top of the sport throughout his career. Determined to be a successful road racer, Danny went where the hottest action was—Europe—at the age of 21. He quickly distinguished himself in Formula Ford in England against future Formula 1 Stars and stayed with the pursuit of a Grand Prix career in the traditional crucibles of Formula 3 and Formula 2 for six years.

In 1978 Danny returned to the States, worked as an instructor with the Skip Barber Racing School, and tried to rekindle his career. The crucial turning point was his connection with Garvin Brown, who formed a team with whom Danny raced in Can-Am through 1982. In 1983, Danny drove for Tyrell in a full season of Formula 1, returning to the States again to run Indy Cars for Doug Shierson the following year. Danny was hired by Roger Penske in 1985, a six year association that led to an Indy 500 win and a PPG Indy Car World Series Championship in 1988.

Danny has driven the best and worst machinery in the sport and has experienced the highs and lows that a career as a professional racer can provide. While not retired from the sport, Danny has an entirely new vocation as a racing color analyst for television.

Brian Till. Brian began racing informally in Karts and, following graduation from Baylor University, moved up to Sports Renault, qualifying for the National Championship in his first year. He won the inaugural Barber Saab race at the Meadowlands in 1986, going on to finish second in the Championship.

Brian worked at Skip Barber's as an instructor, test driver and Midwest Race Series coordinator. During this association he met Bob Liebert, with whom he would plot his progression toward Indy Car racing. Along the way Brian has won in the Barber Pro Series, Formula Atlantic (where he won the 1990 Championship as well as Rookie of the Year), Mid Ohio in Indy Light, and fulfilled his dream of competing at the Indy 500 where, in 1994, he qualified 21st and finished 12th.

Part I

The Fundamentals

CHAPTER 1

A PLAN OF ATTACK

MAYHEM

At first glance racing looks like mayhem; your first ride in a car on a racetrack even more so. The straights go by in a blur as the car bounces around and the wind blasts past the open top. As you approach the end of the straight your instinct screams that there is *no possible way* the driver's going to make this turn unless he brakes *now*!

> There are three basic problems to solve in racing: 1) driving on the best path, 2) carrying speed away from corners onto straights, and 3) efficiently slowing the car at the entry to corners.

But the driver continues on, foot to the floor on the throttle, unconcerned. You briefly wonder if he has had a coronary when *wham*, you get slammed forward on the belts as the driver applies the brakes and a second later thrown sideways as the car is committed to the corner. *It's sliding, it's sliding!* you scream to yourself, convinced the driver has lost control. But no, a few twists of the steering wheel and some magical inputs on the pedals and you scream off onto the next straight. This happens again and again as you proceed around the course. When it's finally over, you climb out of the car slightly limp, exhilarated, and not quite sure what just happened.

It seems like chaos because the novice isn't clued in to the thinking and planning that is going on inside the helmet of the driver. To have any chance of doing well at the task of driving a racecar, you have to take it out of the realm of mystery and bring it down to earth. You need to develop a clear idea of what you need to do, and why, at every point around the racetrack. It is also important to avoid blind alleys, to find out which aspects of driving hold the biggest potential reward in terms of speed, and which skills lead to smaller gains.

LINE, CORNER EXIT SPEED, BRAKING

We have found that in the quest for fast laps there are three main areas that you need to focus on to reap the most rewards on the racetrack. The first is to find the most advantageous path around the racetrack. You'll find that where you drive the car has a profound impact on both cornering speed and straightaway speed.

The second priority is to learn the skills required to drive on this best path, getting closer and closer to the limits of the car's ability, and carrying optimum speed through the corner, onto the following straight.

The third area is to develop skill in slowing the car from straightaway speed to the appropriate speed for the upcoming corner.

Fig. 1-1. A quick tour of the Sebring 12 Hour course with '96 Champion Jim Pace. "What just happened?!"

In this first chapter you will learn why this three-tiered approach works, and you'll develop a clear understanding of how a talented race driver juggles a car's ability to accelerate, brake, and corner in order to minimize lap time.

DEFINING THE PROBLEM

To start this process, let's first define the fundamental goal of a racer: Confronted with a twisty piece of asphalt, you need to figure out how to drive around it in the shortest possible time. That's it. It's a problem of *minimizing time*.

A Basic Racetrack

Figure 1-2 depicts the simplest possible road circuit, made up of six corners, five rights and one left. To start to figure out how to minimize time, let's divide the track into sections: straightaways and corners.

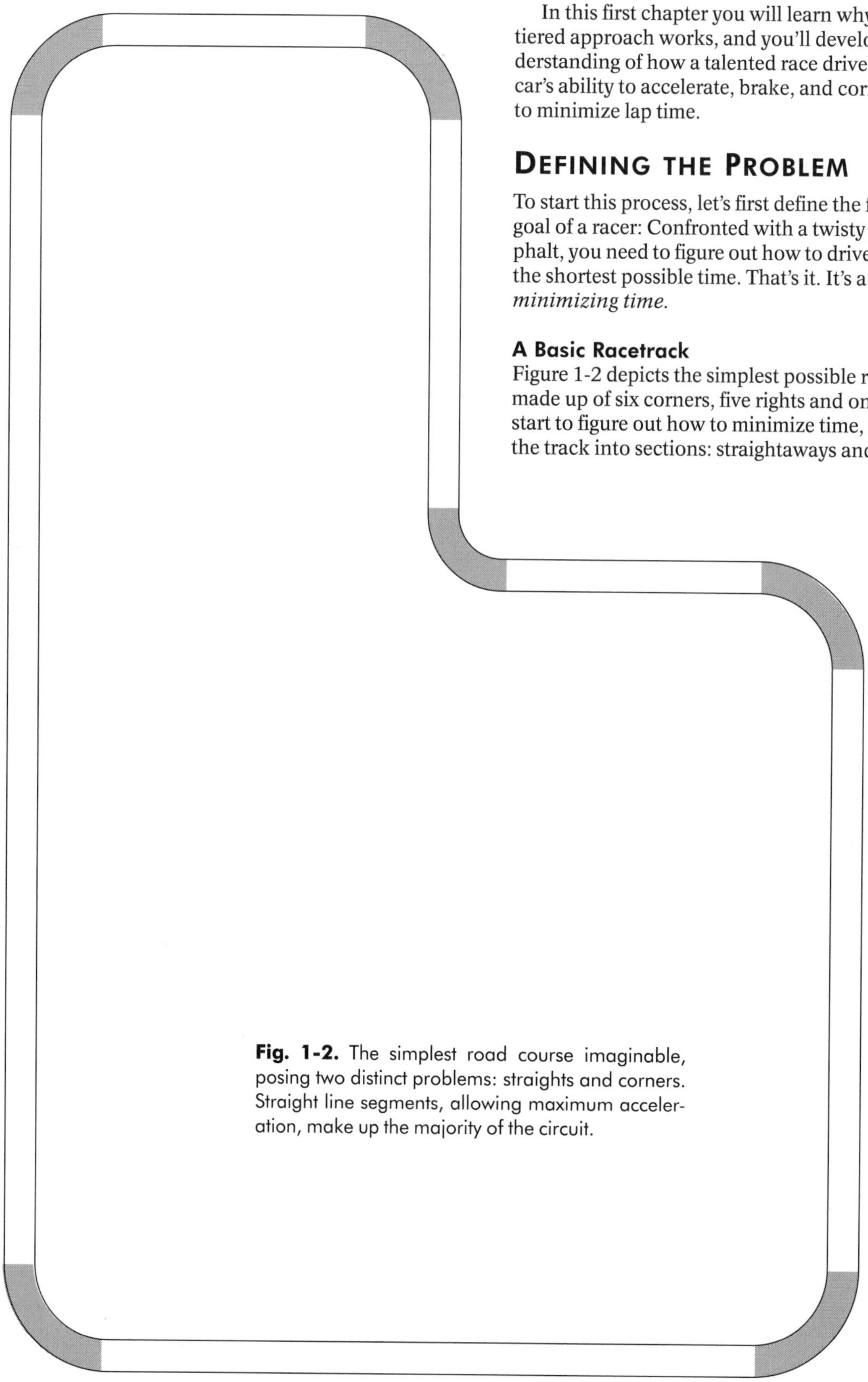

Fig. 1-2. The simplest road course imaginable, posing two distinct problems: straights and corners. Straight line segments, allowing maximum acceleration, make up the majority of the circuit.

Straightaways

How do you drive down the straight in the minimum amount of time? *As fast as possible.* (The questions *do* get harder.)

In all seriousness, you minimize time spent on the straight by accelerating as hard as possible, right foot to the floor on the accelerator, every moment the car is on the straight. You want to use all the horsepower the motor can develop to accelerate the car's mass.

In Fig. 1-2, the unshaded portions of our track map are the areas where you'll do this; and you'll discover that this area covers 70% to 80% of the racetrack, an important point to remember. A racecar typically spends much more time on straightaways at maximum acceleration than anywhere else.

Sadly, there are complications, and they crop up rather quickly (see Fig. 1-3).

Let's say that our racecar has sufficient horsepower to gain 100 m.p.h. between the beginning of the main straight and the corner at the end of the straight. This means that even if you drive onto the straight at 10 m.p.h., the car will end up at Turn 1 going 110 m.p.h. Now, there's no way you are going to make Turn 1 at 110 m.p.h.—Michael Schumacher himself couldn't drive faster than 55 through Turn 1 with our car.

So, somewhere toward the end of the straight you'll have to use the brakes to slow the car down to around 55 m.p.h. in order to turn right and continue your lap rather than go off into the weeds.

Now your straightaway looks like an acceleration zone for most of its length, with a deceleration zone, or braking zone, at the end, represented in Fig. 1-3 by Xs. For now, let's leave the discussion of the braking zone until later. First, you need to figure out how to spend as little time as possible on the straight getting to the braking zone.

If you devised some way to drive through the corner leading onto the straight faster than 10 m.p.h.— say, 20 m.p.h.— it's obvious that you would be faster through the corner. More importantly, however, you would end up at the end of the straight going 120, thus the elapsed time down the straight would be lower.

Corners Are Part of Straights

Now you can see that the average speed down the straight is directly affected by the speed through the corner leading *onto* the straight. So, to minimize the time spent on the straight, you need to work on increasing your speed through the corner.

It's easy to go faster at low speeds—you just use a little more throttle and the car drives easily through the corner 10 m.p.h. faster. Eventually, as you try to go faster and faster, the car will have to work harder and harder to change direction.

We've already touched upon using the car at its maximum, or its "limit," when we said you were going to accelerate down the straights using 100% of its

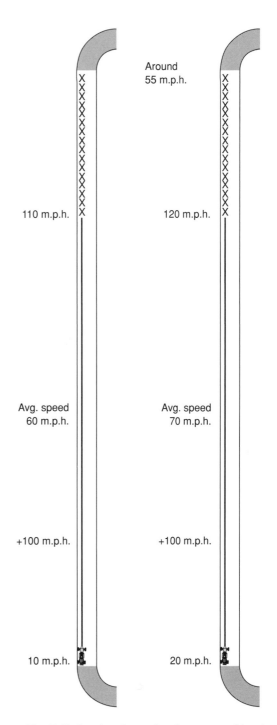

Fig. 1-3. Accelerating as hard as you could, using all the horsepower available, this car would gain 100 m.p.h. from the exit of the turn to the point at which braking would have to begin. Changing only the speed at which you exit the previous corner, the average straightaway speed increases 10 m.p.h.

ability to accelerate. To minimize the time it takes to drive through a corner, you would like to be able to use 100% of the car's ability to turn.

"Limit" Cornering

If a car is moving and you take your hands off the steering wheel, the car will go straight. If you want to change the car's direction, you turn the steering wheel. This uses the grip of the tires against the road to force the car to change direction. Remember, it wants to go straight, and the tires are *forcing* it to turn. When going slowly, or turning the wheel slightly, it doesn't take much force to make the car turn. But raise the speed, or tighten the turn, and the tires will need to work harder.

Using the Skidpad

In your everyday driving you seldom use more than 40% of the tires' ability to work. If you want to experiment with how tires behave at their cornering limits, you need to be in a safer environment where there are no oncoming cars or giant oaks nearby, waiting to turn a mistake into a disaster. The public roads are definitely *not* the place to do this.

We use a skidpad, which is a fancy name for a wide-open flat piece of asphalt devoid of any solid objects to run into. You could use a specially constructed pad at a racetrack or a big empty parking lot.

Take the car to the "pad," turn the steering wheel 45 degrees (right *or* left), and drive away—slowly at first. If you keep the steering wheel in that one position the car will travel in a circle. Now gradually increase your speed.

You can't go faster indefinitely. At some point, you'll be using *all* the grip the tires have—100% of their cornering traction. At this top speed, the tires are working terrifically hard. They're screaming, literally sliding over the surface of the road. If you're driving a

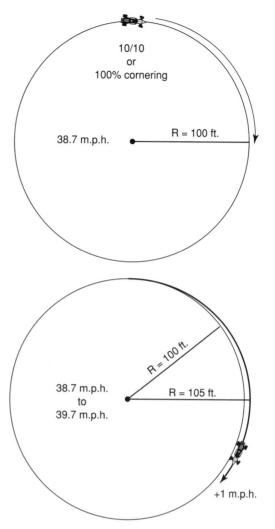

Fig. 1-5. Once the tires are at their cornering limits an increase in speed results in an increase in radius.

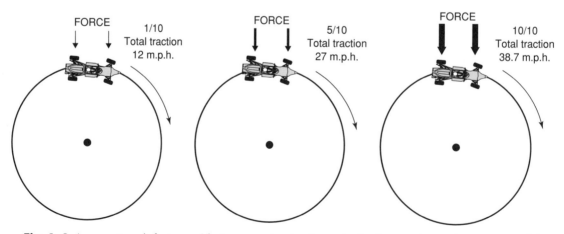

Fig. 1-4. As a car travels faster and faster around a circular path, the tires use increasing amounts of their potential traction to force the car to continue to change direction.

street car, it will have rolled substantially toward the outside of the turn and your body will be pushed to the outside of the circle with a force equal to at least 75% of your body weight. The car is at its cornering "limit" using 100% of its cornering ability.

If, at this point, you add more speed, surprisingly enough nothing terrible happens. The car continues to turn, but it turns on a bigger arc (See Fig. 1-5). At the limit of a car's cornering ability, the speed it can attain is directly related to the radius of the arc it's on. So, in cornering, if you want more speed, drive on an arc with the biggest possible radius. Sounds simple, doesn't it? Yet, it's amazing how many active racers fail to make use of this basic law of physics as it applies to racecars.

All of this information applies to our quest to minimize time around the racetrack. So far we've concluded that:

- To minimize time on the straight, use 100% acceleration on the straight—wheel straight, flat out;
- You need to exit the corner leading onto the straight as fast as possible;
- In cornering, the biggest radius yields the highest speed.

FINDING THE LINE

If you want to drive through a corner at the highest possible speed, then you need to find a path through the corner on an arc with the biggest radius. You need to find *the line*.

Driving up to the corner, you have a lot of choices about how to drive through it. See Fig. 1-6. You can drive around the inside of the corner, but if you do you're restricted to the smallest radius, R1. You can make the radius through the corner bigger by driving around the outside of the corner—the radius R2 *is* bigger than R1, so the maximum speed *will* be higher.

The best bet, however, is to start the arc before the corner, touch the inside edge of the road halfway through, and touch the outside edge of the road again at the exit. If you do this, you can use radius R3, clearly the biggest and best choice.

Why "The Line" is Step 1
When you drive a car at its cornering limits, it's the line you choose (the radius of the arc the car is on) that determines maximum speed through a corner. And the speed you carry out of the corner determines maximum speed on the following straightaway. Since the line ultimately determines both cornering *and* straightaway speed, it's obviously the most important place to start.

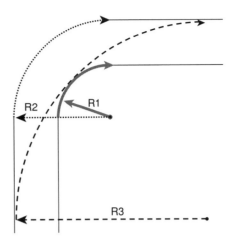

Fig. 1-6. You can choose various paths through a corner, but only one yields the biggest radius: "the line."

Remember, the process of finding the optimum line—the best combination of arcs through corners and paths down the straights—is a tool to use to put yourself in a position to post the fastest possible time around the racetrack.

Charting a Lap
Let's take another look at our typical track map to see what you're going to do with the controls in order to get around the place (see Fig. 1-7). You might not get all this exactly right on the first try so, at the start, you won't try to go as fast as you know you ultimately will when, through practice, you earn the right to go faster.

Coming out of Turn 6 onto the main straight (the longest), you'll accelerate in a straight line toward Turn 1. Again, the acceleration zone is designated by a solid line.

Somewhere toward the end of the straight you'll use the brakes to slow the car down to an appropriate speed for the next corner. The braking zone is designated by a series of Xs.

At a point on the left-hand side of the straight you'll turn the steering wheel to the right, initiating an arc that touches the inside edge of Turn 1 and finishes at the outside edge of the road at the exit. The cornering zone is designated by double lines.

Exiting Turn 1 and heading toward Turn 2, you'll repeat the same routine. You can continue to follow the car's progress around the course, referring to the coding to see which phase of the car's ability is being used at any particular point on the track.

As you can see from this simplification of your lap, a car has only three fundamental abilities: 1) Acceleration, 2) Braking, 3) Cornering.

CAR CONTROL FOR EXIT SPEED

If you drive on the line with the biggest radius and, over time, do it faster and faster until you're using 100% of the tires' traction to corner, you won't be able to begin your acceleration down the straight until cornering is over, at the corner exit: When 100% of the tires' traction is used to corner, there is zero traction left to be used for acceleration.

For example, in Fig. 1-8 the radius of the corner allows you to reach 55 m.p.h. at the limit of cornering. Then, accelerating as hard as you could, you'd reach 155 m.p.h. at the end of the straight. Not bad.

But, if you *averaged* 55 m.p.h. in the second part of the corner, starting at 53 m.p.h. for a while but ending up at 57 m.p.h. at the corner exit, you'd reach the end of the straightaway at 157 m.p.h., averaging 2 m.p.h. faster down the entire length of the straight. If this straight were 1/4 mile long, this 2-m.p.h. difference would represent a lap time .16 seconds lower than the previous try. (See Fig. 1-9.)

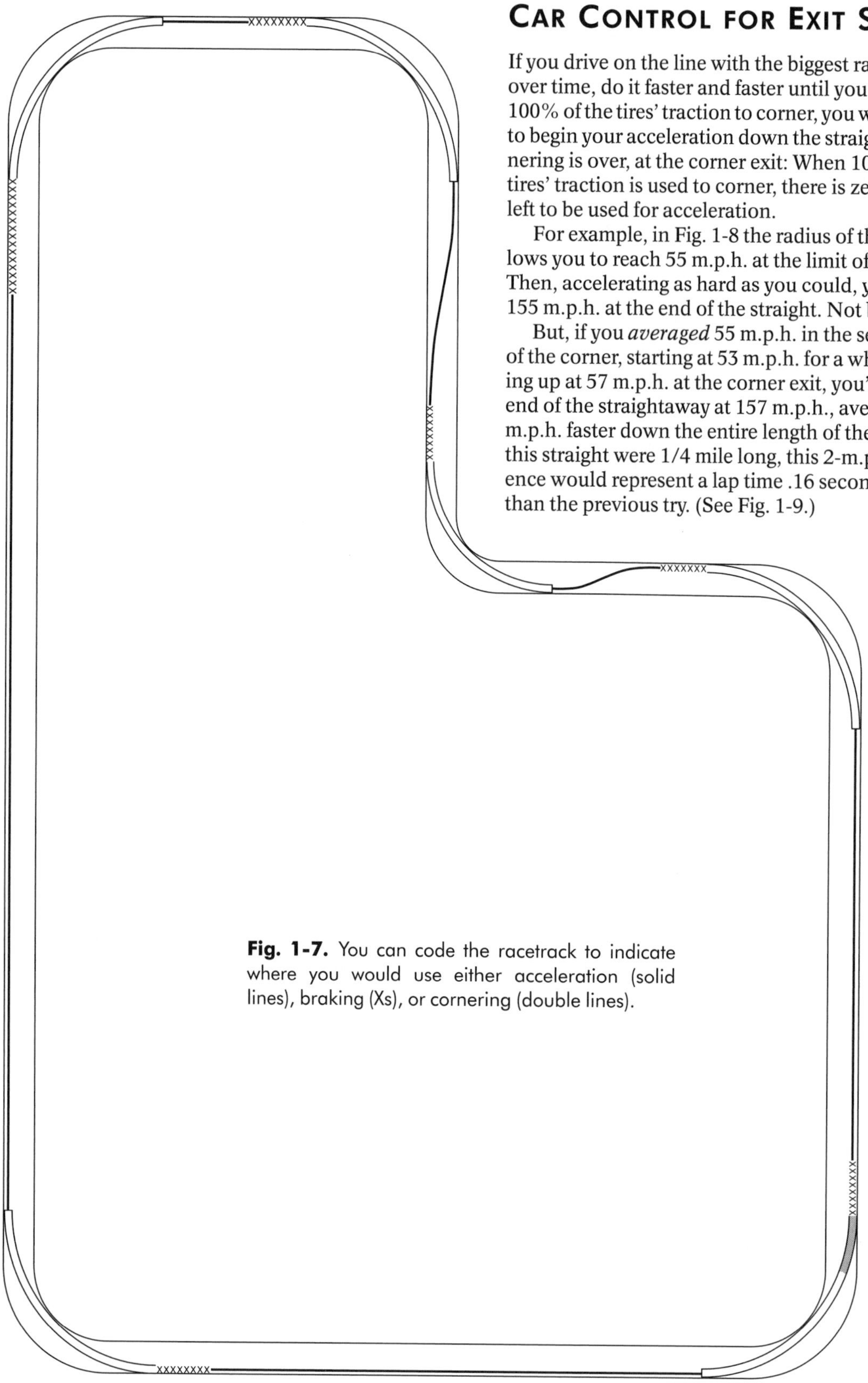

Fig. 1-7. You can code the racetrack to indicate where you would use either acceleration (solid lines), braking (Xs), or cornering (double lines).

Mixing Abilities

We've so far described "the limit" as using the tires' grip in *either* acceleration, cornering or braking. In reality, you can combine these abilities. If you decide to use some acceleration while cornering, the car will do it, with a compromise. If you want to use 20% of the tires' traction for acceleration, you only get 80% of the traction for cornering.

In coding the racetrack, you now need another icon to represent a mix of acceleration and cornering. Starting with Fig. 1-9 we're using a shaded area.

This loss in cornering traction affects your path through the corner: the car will still change direction but, because of the reduction in turning force, it will change direction on a bigger radius arc than before. Additionally, as you accelerate away from a turn, the speed is getting higher and, as you know from your skid pad experience, the higher the speed, the bigger the radius required. See Fig. 1-10.

So, as you're accelerating and cornering you need to increase the radius of the arc you're on. You do this by gradually unwinding the steering wheel as you exit the turn.

Since the greatest part of a lap is spent on corner exits and straights, any speed improvements on this portion of the course, which typically represents 70% to 80% of a lap, would have the greatest effect on decreasing lap time. This strategy takes the focus off

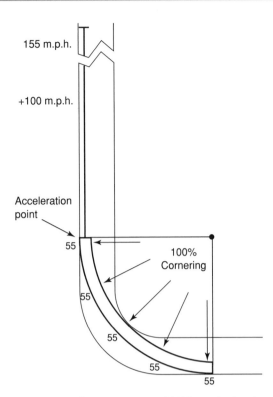

Fig. 1-8. If you corner at 100% from the beginning to the end of the turn, you can't begin accelerating until you complete cornering.

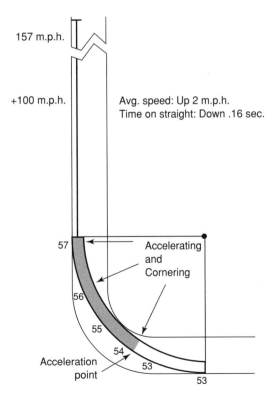

Fig. 1-9. If you combine acceleration and cornering, the higher speed at the exit of the corner reduces the time it takes to drive down the straight.

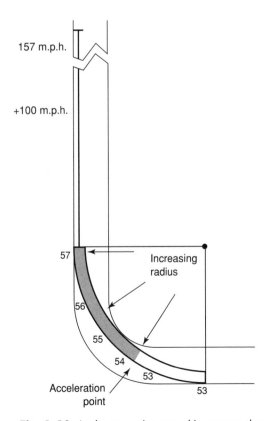

Fig. 1-10. As the cornering speed increases, the arc's radius at the corner exit must also increase.

braking: don't be tempted, as many drivers are, to go immediately to late-braking when you decide that it's time to go faster. It's much more important to get to your throttle application point at the appropriate speed and experiment with driving the car faster and faster through the last half of the corner, under power.

The Order of Effort

Both the line and corner exit speed are extremely important, and just as important is their order of priority. You need to first determine the correct path on which to drive and *then* work on increasing your speed on that path.

Learning the line is easier than many of the other things you'll have to learn to do in a racecar, so indulge yourself at the beginning and concentrate on getting the car spot-on the best path. It's exhilarating to learn the car control skills required to maximize your exit speed, but you have to be careful to not let the kick of sliding the car around get in the way of your ultimate goal: lower lap times.

SLOWING FOR CORNERS

The third basic skill is learning how to slow the car for a corner and how to drive it from where the turn begins to the throttle application point. We call this phase of driving racecars "braking and entering."

Let's go back and consider Turn 1 on our hypothetical racetrack. You exited the corner onto the straight accelerating through 57 m.p.h.; down the following straightaway, the car gained 100 m.p.h. so that you were approaching Turn 1 at 157 m.p.h. At some point on the approach to Turn 1, you'll feel the need to slow down for the rapidly approaching corner. You're going straight here, so you can use 100% of the car's potential braking ability. We call it "threshold braking": threshold, because to get to the 100% level of stopping power, you're at the threshold of wheel lockup, right on the edge.

It seems obvious that slowing the car in a straight line using 100% of its braking ability will reduce the speed of the car to the level you want it in the shortest possible time and distance. No argument. However, let's take a closer look at this situation.

Brake and Turn

Let's say that Turn 1 is just like the corner that leads onto the straight: that is, its cornering limit speeds are in the neighborhood of 55 m.p.h. You could use the straight to slow the car from 157 to 53 m.p.h. by the time you turn the wheel into the corner. In fact, for decades the prevailing thinking was that any time the car was braking, it *had* to be going straight.

The truth, however, is that a car will *decelerate* and turn just like it's able to accelerate and turn. But, just like mixing acceleration and turning, braking and turning requires that you make some compromises.

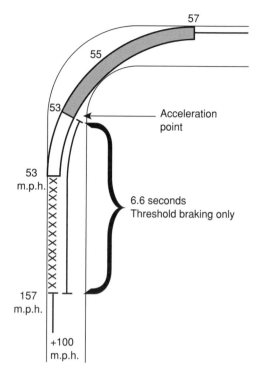

Fig. 1-11. Slowing the car only in a straight line requires that you drive at a constant speed from the point where you begin to turn up to the point where you begin to mix acceleration and cornering.

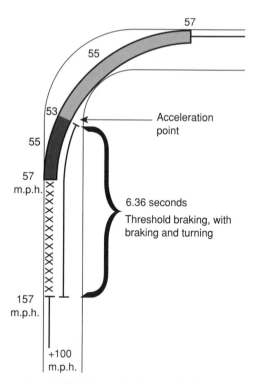

Fig. 1-12. By continuing to decelerate as you turn into the corner, your speed at corner entry can be higher.

Under threshold braking you're using 100% of the traction in the tires to brake. If, while threshold braking, you turn the steering wheel and ask for cornering force, the front wheels will point toward the corner, but the car won't change direction because there is no traction left for cornering.

But, if you reduce some of the braking effort, say, to 80% braking, you get 20% of the tires' traction available for cornering. With the steering wheel turned, that 20% bends the car into the turn.

Gains from Braking and Turning

We have already concluded that you're going to mix acceleration and cornering at the exit of the turn, by starting at 53 at your throttle application point and ending up at 57 at the exit—averaging 55 m.p.h. So the basic aim is to slow the car from 157 to 53 m.p.h. by the throttle application point.

If you restrict yourself to braking on the straight, you'd have to slow the car to 53 by the time you turn the steering wheel into the corner. You'd then drive from the turning point to the acceleration point at a constant 53 m.p.h. In a car with the braking capabilities of our school Formula cars, that would take about 6.6 seconds (Fig. 1-11).

By continuing to brake and turn into the corner, starting at 57 at the turn-in and continuing to decelerate to 53 at the acceleration point (represented by the darker area in Fig. 1-12), you can average 55 across the same stretch of track, rather than 53 when you were only braking on a straight line. The time it would take you is about 6.36 seconds—.24 seconds less.

The lap time, by the way, is not insignificant. While a difference of .24 seconds may not seem like a lot on first glance, if you gain this advantage in four corners you're talking about .92 seconds per lap. In a 20 lap race this gain represents 18.4 seconds—and 20 laps is a short race.

Are these tenths of a second worth the effort? Maybe not at the beginning of a career when you are ten seconds off the pace. Using the braking and turning ability of the car won't get you the ten seconds, but, as you'll see in later chapters, lap time is just one of many reasons to develop this skill.

> "I think that experimenting with your braking is very important, but after you get your line and after you get comfortable with the car coming off the corner. The last area is braking where you're going for that last little bit."
> —Danny Sullivan

Charting a Lap, Take Two

Let's take an updated look at how to proceed around the entire racetrack using our latest code scheme. See Fig. 1-13.

On the straight, you'll use flat out 100% acceleration, designated by the solid line. When you reach the braking zone, designated by Xs, you'll use the maximum, 100% threshold braking. You'll decelerate into the corner, mixing the car's braking and cornering force, designated by the darkly-shaded area on our map. When you accelerate out, you'll mix the car's ability to accelerate with its cornering abilities, shown on our map as a lightly-shaded area. When you reach the next straight, you'll start the process over again, using 100% of the car's acceleration power.

Our coding of this hypothetical racetrack is, admittedly, very general at this stage, leaving out considerable detail. It's not meant to be a 100% accurate representation of exactly what you do on every inch of the course—rather, it's meant to get you thinking about what controls you are likely to be using as you lap the circuit.

OUT ON THE RACETRACK

If your only point of reference is driving on public roads, your first sense of excitement about driving on the track is that you can drive as fast as you like. You can roar down the straight at 90 m.p.h. and nobody complains. At first it's exciting to keep your foot to the floor as your car goes 30 to 40 to 50 m.p.h. faster than the legal speed limit. In fact the most common question we get about our school racecars is, "How fast will it go?" The surprise is that straight line speed is not all it's cracked up to be. It doesn't take much talent to hold the steering wheel straight and press the gas pedal to the floor, so there's no challenge in it. The speed is invigorating at first, but the thrill wears off quickly as you get accustomed to the scenery whizzing by.

The real excitement comes at the end of the straightaway where you need to slow the car down to negotiate a corner. This is where the newcomer to racing, all flushed with excitement from the straightaway speed, starts to fall apart. There are a lot of questions to be answered. Where do I put on the brakes? How long? How hard? What gear should I use for the corner? How and where do I downshift? Where should I steer into the turn? How fast can I go through it? Will the car spin? Will I crash?

Just *driving* around the racetrack, as opposed to a *lap record pace* around the racetrack is an entirely different way of covering ground in an automobile. You can start driving around a racetrack in your street car without much training or knowledge of racing technique as long as you use the same pace that you use in your street driving. You should have no trouble judging when to brake or when to shift.

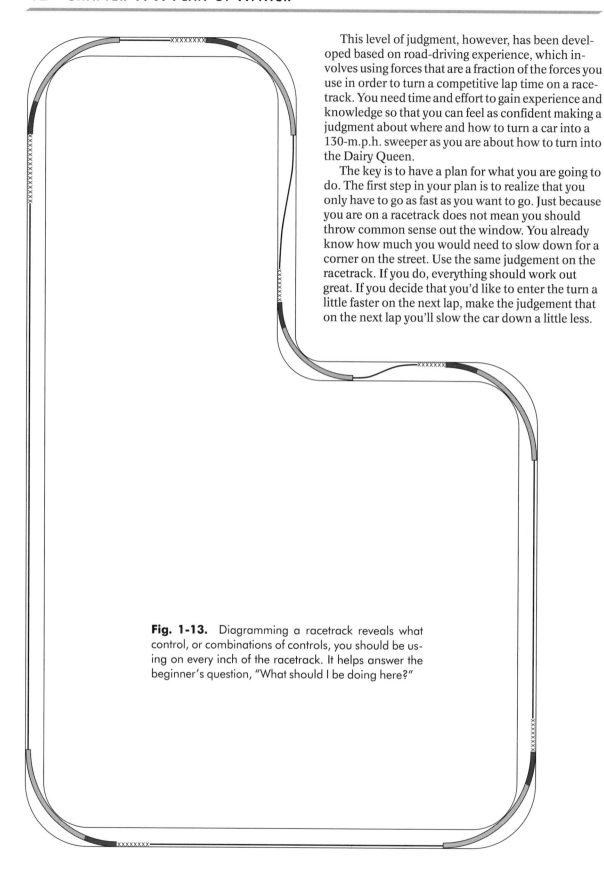

This level of judgment, however, has been developed based on road-driving experience, which involves using forces that are a fraction of the forces you use in order to turn a competitive lap time on a racetrack. You need time and effort to gain experience and knowledge so that you can feel as confident making a judgment about where and how to turn a car into a 130-m.p.h. sweeper as you are about how to turn into the Dairy Queen.

The key is to have a plan for what you are going to do. The first step in your plan is to realize that you only have to go as fast as you want to go. Just because you are on a racetrack does not mean you should throw common sense out the window. You already know how much you would need to slow down for a corner on the street. Use the same judgement on the racetrack. If you do, everything should work out great. If you decide that you'd like to enter the turn a little faster on the next lap, make the judgement that on the next lap you'll slow the car down a little less.

Fig. 1-13. Diagramming a racetrack reveals what control, or combinations of controls, you should be using on every inch of the racetrack. It helps answer the beginner's question, "What should I be doing here?"

Fig. 1-14. Spinning is never good, but once you know the common causes you can avoid them, and help take the anxiety out of approaching the car's limits.

"There's reaction time involved in everything you do in sports, but I think one of the reasons race drivers can continue to be good at older ages than other athletes is that experience has so much to do with it. You don't need 'young legs,' you just have to anticipate what's going on and think about it, looking that one step ahead.

"In racing, like many other sports, you have to get to the point where everything comes to you in slow motion. If you tried to return a serve from Agassi or Sampras, you wouldn't even be able to get the racket into position before the ball would be by you. If everything is coming at you in what seems like a normal fashion, a slower motion, you can deal with it. Experience plays its role in getting to that point. That's why stepping stones are so critical—that you go through the process of getting the experience."

—*Danny Sullivan*

The key word is "little." You'll find that the best bet is to increase your speed a little at a time, not to make a giant leap on faith alone.

Frequently Asked Questions

Now, let's answer some of the questions you might have about driving a car around a racetrack.

Where do I drive the car? The line. Regardless of whether it's Midget racers in Indianapolis or Formula 1 racers at Monaco, drivers go from the outside of the road at the beginning of the corner to the inside of the road in the middle, then back to the outside again at the exit. When you're on the track you should try to

do the same. Turn the steering wheel smoothly; no jerking the wheel to-and-fro like you see in the movies. Expect that you won't do it perfectly on the first try, but keep at it.

What gear should I use? Try a gear and see how it works. You want to be driving through the corner with the car in a gear and your right foot on the throttle—how heavily on the throttle is up to your judgement. If the engine is at low revs and the car feels like it's bogging, try a lower gear next time. If you try the corner in a gear where it reaches the engine's redline RPM before the end of the corner, you'll have to try a higher gear next time to avoid hurting the engine.

How and where do I downshift? If you're driving a standard shift car, which you are likely to be doing on a racetrack, you're stuck with downshifting, like it or not. You'll likely be in a higher gear on the straightaway than the gear which will work best, at lower speed, in the corner. The aim is to downshift without upsetting the car by chirping the rear tires when the clutch comes out in the lower gear. This is as true in your street car as it is in an Indy Car, and it requires you to learn how to tap or "blip" the throttle while still having part of the right foot on the brake pedal. This "blip" just before the clutch comes out in the lower gear is something you'll have to learn how to do for the racetrack. It's a skill that will also make you a smoother driver on the street. Besides, it sounds zoomy.

Where to downshift is a much easier problem. If you put it in a lower gear too soon you might over-rev and damage the motor, so you'll have to wait until the car is going slow enough. On the other hand, you can't downshift too late. You need the car to be in the right gear by the time you decide to go back to the throttle to drive through the corner. Downshifting anywhere between these two points is okay.

Fig. 1-15. Reference points, like these braking markers at Lime Rock, replace guesswork as a means for going faster.

Will my reaction times be fast enough? While it's often impossible to improve reaction time, the good news is that racing is much more about *anticipation.* Sure, there are times when something unexpected happens and you have to react. But far more often you need to use your ability to consistently plan ahead and take some action at a specific place and time. Believing that reaction time is all-important tends to make you move the controls violently and sharply. Violent maneuvers on the brakes, steering wheel, gear lever, clutch or throttle are a hindrance to fast laps, not a help.

> *"I think having good reaction times can get you out of trouble in certain situations, but thinking ahead, having enough foresight to know what you and the car are going to do, allows you to avoid getting yourself in situations where you need quick reactions. I find in a good normal lap in an Indy Car that I'm never reacting. You're making adjustments and corrections but things aren't surprising you. You're not thinking, 'Whoa, I didn't think the car was going to do that.'"*
>
> —Bryan Herta

Will I spin or crash? You don't have to. One of the biggest fables in the sport is that you have to spin to know where the limit is. It's not true. By approaching the limits of the car's capabilities cautiously, you will get plenty of warning that it is nearing a spin. Still, racing is different from street driving in that you're likely to operate a car closer to its limits on the racetrack. When you're close to the limit, you have to pay attention to the details. Actions which, in your everyday driving, may be just sloppy or choppy can mean big trouble on the track. Fortunately, the most common mistakes which cause race drivers to lose control fall into just a few major categories.

The Four Most Common Mistakes

1) Running Off the Road Exiting Corners. As you drive more, you'll find that once you turn into the corner, you hold the steering wheel at pretty much the same angle all the way through the turn. Instead of jerking the wheel to and fro, you should keep constant steering pressure on the wheel, slowly releasing this pressure as the car drives onto the straight.

At the approach to the corner, if you turn the steering wheel toward the inside of the road too early, it may force you to turn the steering wheel even tighter as you reach the end of the corner. If you're going slowly, the car will respond to this second turning motion; but if you're going faster, you could get to the point where the car won't respond, and it will run wide coming out of the corner regardless of what you do to persuade it not to.

You need to control your desire to go fast until you know exactly where you want the car to be on every inch of the racetrack—you have to know "the line"—before you can safely go fast.

2) Going Hopelessly Late Before Braking For A Corner. Most professional racers use an easily recognizable marker at the approach to a corner as a cue to start braking. Novices need "brake points" too. You can easily avoid going too late by starting with a conservative brake point and, if you like, move it in toward the corner in small increments.

> "Let's say you're braking at the 300 mark with no problem. Do you move the next spot to the 200? If you make that, do you jump to the 100? No way. You've got to take small steps to find out where that limit is. My way of doing it is to go just past the 300, and the later I go, I'm going to start taking it in much smaller steps, because if I know I'm fairly close, I don't want to screw everything up by going impossibly late."
>
> —Danny Sullivan

3) Bad Downshifts. Chirping the rear tires on a downshift as you turn into a corner can spin you around very quickly. Practice smooth downshifts in your everyday driving and make sure to downshift before entering the corner.

4) Carelessly Lifting Off the Throttle. When a car is cornering fast, its behavior depends on keeping a nice balance between the grip of the front and rear tires.

An abrupt snap off the gas upsets this balance and can steal traction from the rear tires, causing a spin. Small, smooth, and subtle changes of the controls are the best bet on the racetrack.

A SAMPLE RUN

Let's go wring out a quick piece of machinery to get an idea of what a good driver does with the controls in a typical run around a track. Our winter operations are run out of our facility in Sebring, Florida—100 yards from the famous 12 Hour course. For starters, let's run a Viper around part of the test circuit, the part where you'll experience the highest and the lowest speeds the car will attain on a lap. See Fig. 1-16.

As you exit Turn 8 and approach Turn 9 (Fig. 1-17), you're getting the car positioned on the extreme right side of the road so that you can form the gentlest arc possible through this long left-hander. On the approach you have slowed the car to a speed that you're comfortable with, about 65 m.p.h., and you've left the car in second gear.

At a precise point near the edge of the road you turn the steering wheel to the left, aiming for a point on the inside of the turn that you feel will put you on an arc that will end on the outside edge of the road at the exit off the corner (Fig. 1-18).

After you turn the wheel, you gently relax the pressure you have been exerting on the brake pedal. As your right foot comes off the brake, it immediately moves over to the throttle and begins squeezing on the gas very lightly (Fig. 1-19).

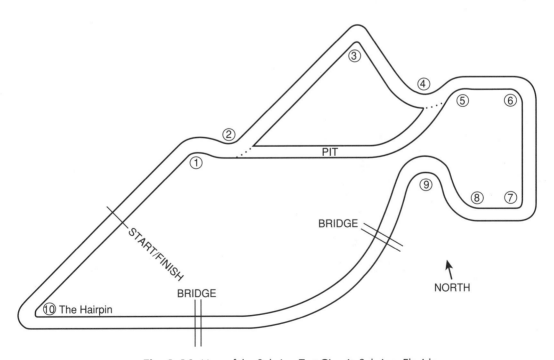

Fig. 1-16. Map of the Sebring Test Circuit, Sebring, Florida.

Fig. 1-17. Coming up to Turn 9, the "Carousel," you keep the Viper right, looking ahead for your turning point past the second curb.

Fig. 1-18. Relaxing the brake pedal, you transition over to the throttle and begin squeezing it on.

Fig. 1-19. The initial turn of the steering wheel hopefully puts the car on a path that touches the inside edge of the road.

Looking ahead, past the inside edge of the road, you're trying to judge whether the path to which you have committed is going to end up where you want, on the asphalt, but right on the outside edge of the road at the exit. You're trying to keep the car on a smooth arc so you're trying to avoid turning the steering wheel any more or any less than you did when you first turned into the corner.

Your eyes tell you that you're doing fine so you continue squeezing the throttle down past 30%, 40%, 50% of full throttle, concentrating on being smooth on the application and not being so greedy about it that you'll have to change your mind and reduce the throttle while still in the turn. The line for this lap looks good, so the throttle continues toward the floor, 60%, 70%, 80% (Fig. 1-20).

Fig. 1-20. Exiting the corner, you continue to squeeze the throttle toward the floor as you relax the steering wheel.

Leaving the corner, you start to relax the amount that you have the steering wheel turned in order to smoothly exit the turn. You finish the corner on the right-hand edge of the road with the engine revs moving through 5300 RPM, around 65 m.p.h.

You have to shift at 5800 RPM and the V10 engine sounds great screaming up toward the redline. You have a half-mile of full throttle acceleration ahead of you and you're through 80 m.p.h. (Fig. 1-21) as you shift to third gear and mat the accelerator once again.

The Sebring straight bends to the right for the first quarter-mile of its length and the Viper is gaining speed rapidly at full throttle. In many cars, this portion of the course is easy, but the Viper holds your attention. At 105 m.p.h. (Fig. 1-22), you're swinging out to the left hand edge of the straight a few hundred feet before the pedestrian bridge, with its protective concrete wall six feet or so from the edge of the racetrack.

Fig. 1-21. The second to third shift at the bridge comes at 80 m.p.h.

Fig. 1-23. Your eyes are focused on the brake point, not the speedometer.

Fig. 1-22. Foot on the floor, the Viper sweeps to the left side of the road and the shift to fourth comes at 105 m.p.h.

Fig. 1-24. With the brakes on hard, the process of selecting the proper gear for the upcoming corner begins.

You're straight for an instant before shifting up to fourth here, so you peek at the speedometer one last time to see that you're at 110 m.p.h. with the car accelerating as strong as before in the new gear. You think for a second that there are two more gears to go—if only the straight were long enough.

The hairpin is coming up and you start looking for your brake point, foot still on the accelerator, squeezing it into the carpet. You're going faster than 125 m.p.h. but your eyes are outside, focused on the brake point, marked by the first of four pylons (Fig. 1-23).

As you approach the first cone you quickly lift off the throttle and go immediately to the brake pedal, which you squeeze on hard (Fig. 1-24). As the car slows in a straight line, you go down through every gear, blipping the throttle with the right half of your right foot just before the clutch is released in each downshift. Fourth to third, blip, clutch out. Third to second, blip, clutch out. You judge how much to blip by the smoothness of the engagement of the next lowest gear. If the car leaps forward against the brakes, you blipped it too much. If the nose of the car dives lower as the rear tires try to speed the engine up, you blipped too little.

Next up, it's time to turn into the corner. The curb on the left-hand verge of the track has reflectors glued to the edge of the road for use at night in the 12 Hours; you know from experience that turning at the second pair of reflectors will put you on a path through the corner that touches the inside and outside edges—the gentlest arc through The Hairpin (Fig. 1-25).

You turn at your reference point, the car already in second gear at about 35 m.p.h., ready to begin accelerating away from the corner. An instant after you turn the wheel right, you begin to relax the braking pressure, just as you did in Turn 9. From here on out of the corner it's the same routine—relax the last bit of brake pedal pressure, squeeze on the throttle, and relax the steering pressure as the car's path looks good.

Fig. 1-25. The focus now becomes the turn-in point, the second pair of reflectors glued to the track surface.

> "I think that the idea that you have to be fearless to be a good racer is the biggest misconception that anybody has about racing. I'm the world's biggest chicken. I am not brave at all. I've won a lot of championships and a lot of races over 25 years and I consider myself the biggest chicken out there. Sure, you can win some races on bravado but what looks to be bravery, later on, is knowing what you can and can't get away with. I would take one ounce of brains over two pounds of bravado."
>
> —David Loring

What is "Fast"?

It's remarkable how something so repetitive can be so much fun. As fast as it seems to the uninitiated observer, this run down to the Sebring hairpin was not fast in terms of the way a racer defines fast: time.

Through Turn 8 to the exit of the hairpin was done in 38 seconds. The total lap time was just over 1 minute, 30 seconds. The same car, driven closer to its limits, would be some four seconds per lap faster. It would be very hard to convince your first-time passenger that you could possibly go faster at all, let alone four seconds a lap, but the time is there to be gained.

Some drivers will choose to make the effort to get there. Some will be perfectly content to drive around the course at a slower pace, getting their enjoyment and satisfaction by going much faster than they would ever have a chance to in the highway environment. The techniques they would use to do this well and safely should be the same techniques that the driver on the lap-record pace uses. The primary difference between the two would be how closely each driver is willing to approach the limit of the car's ability, knowing that the closer one gets to the limit, the smaller the margin for error.

Bravery

We urge you all to not confuse skill with daring. Unfortunately, some auto enthusiasts are more willing to take risks with themselves and their cars than they are willing to exert the effort it takes to learn how to drive well. All drivers, especially drivers who make claims that they are better than the norm, have a responsibility to not endanger others in the pursuit of what is, after all, a sport.

We feel this responsibility keenly. Every week of the year we expose new enthusiasts to an area of speed and control they have never before explored.

As each school draws to a close, we hope that we have given the students skills that will have a positive effect. But beyond specific skills, the most important lesson is that in order to drive extraordinarily well, you have to use your head much more than your guts.

THE FRAMEWORK OF FAST LAPS

In this chapter, your goal has been to understand the framework in which you'll operate. You need to get a sense of which subjects related to driving racecars should be covered first so as to build a thorough understanding of what you'll try to accomplish in each of the areas that will help you turn fast, safe laps. The time-tested framework we use in our schools is to first concentrate on learning what it takes to turn a fast lap alone.

On the track as well as in the classroom, the first subject a racer needs to learn about is "the line," since it has such a great effect on both cornering speed and straightaway speed.

Big chunks of lap time will come off by learning to maximize the exit speeds coming off the corners, by mixing acceleration and cornering, closer and closer to the car's limits. Learning about and practicing "corner exit car control" will be the logical next step.

On the racetrack, you can't have been practicing the previous two subjects without using the brakes at the entry of the corners, and just because we leave the concentration on the subject for last doesn't mean that you shouldn't use the brakes. It's just that, when it comes to lowering lap time, mastering braking yields smaller lap time increments than developing the first two skills.

Still, once you've mastered the line and corner exit car control you'll find that the skill of transitioning the car from the straight to the throttle application point is the skill that separates the fastest from the fast. Braking and Entering will be our final area of concentration in dealing with the process of turning a lap in the minimum amount of time.

CHAPTER 2

THE THREE BASICS: LINE, CORNER EXIT SPEED, BRAKING

LINE FUNDAMENTALS

There are three basic problems to solve in race driving: 1) driving on the best path, 2) carrying speed through corners and onto straights, and 3) efficiently slowing the car at the entry to corners.

We know that the fundamental aim of driving through a corner is to drive on an arc with the largest possible radius. Let's put some numbers to the problem, using a simple, straightforward corner like the 90-degree right-hand turn in Fig. 2-1. The dimensions of the corner are a close representation of Turn 7 at the Sebring test circuit. Each of the possible paths has an radius dimension attached to it. The path along the inside of Turn 7 has a radius of 103 feet. The arc around the outside edge of the corner has a radius of 130 feet. The radius of the arc that represents the racing line through the corner is a whopping 195 feet. That's 89% bigger than the inside arc, 50% bigger than going around the outside.

Predicting Corner Speed

To find out how much faster you can go through Turn 7 on the right line, you have to attach some speeds to these arcs. To do this, you have to describe the rela-

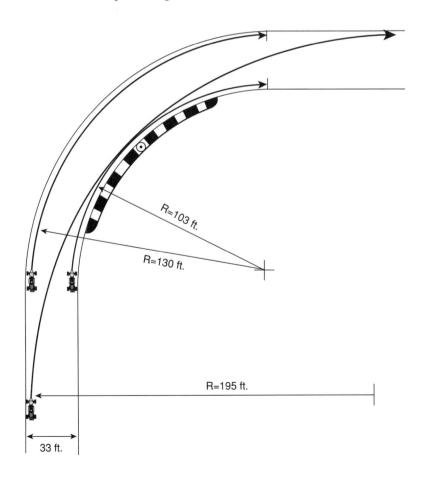

Fig. 2-1. The increase in radius available by driving outside, inside, outside is formidable. In this case the large radius is nearly twice the size of the arc that hugs the inside of the road.

R=103 ft.

R=130 ft.

R=195 ft.

33 ft.

tionship between the size of an arc and the maximum speed a vehicle can attain on that arc. From the skidpad, you know that the bigger you make the radius, the higher you make the potential speed. In addition, you have to take into account how well the car corners. A car with greater cornering force will reach its limit at a higher speed.

The equation that ties these two interrelated facts together is $15GR = m.p.h.^2$. G represents the car's maximum cornering force, where G is the force of gravity. R represents the radius of the corner in feet.

To compute the maximum cornering speeds on different arcs through Turn 7, let's simplify things and call our car a 1G car. (For comparison, a street sedan might be able to exert 7/10ths of 1 G of cornering force at maximum. An Indy Car can develop between 1.4 and 4.5 Gs.) Then plug in the radius numbers and solve the equation. For example, to figure out how fast the car could drive around the inside edge of the corner, substitute 1 for G, and 103 feet for R:

$15 \times 1 \times 103 = m.p.h.^2$

$1545 = m.p.h.^2$

$39.3 = m.p.h.$

As you can see in Fig. 2-2, driving around the outside of the corner on the 130-foot radius would allow you to go 44.1 m.p.h. Driving on "the line," with a radius of 195 feet gives you 54 m.p.h., almost 15 m.p.h.

> "Nelson Piquet, three-time World Champion, was telling me about him being invited by BMW to do a Pro Car race at the old Nurburgring—14 miles and 176 corners. He'd never driven it before so he said, 'Okay, but I tell you what I want to do—I want three cars and I want to go there for a week.' He took the three cars, blew the motor in one, crashed one, and one he just wore out. But, in the week he did 400 laps of the 14-mile circuit just to learn the racetrack. Nelson won the race, by the way."
>
> —Danny Sullivan

faster than hugging the inside of the road, *and* 10 m.p.h. faster than the outside route. You can see why it's a good idea to find the line and to drive on it.

You will also notice that the distance you have to travel on the line is longer than around the inside edge of the corner. Though you would think there'd be an advantage to driving the shorter distance, the tighter arc required serves up a big speed penalty: Although you drive almost 5% further on the line, you do it 37% faster, which is a good trade-off.

Putting the car exactly on the optimum path is not something you strive for because it looks pretty. You

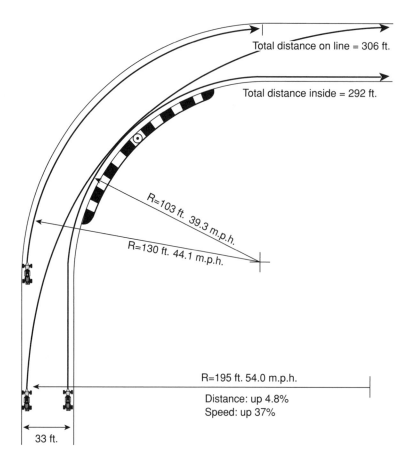

Fig. 2-2. Driving on "the line" results in driving further than taking the shortest path, but in this case, you drive roughly 5% further at 37% greater speed—a good trade-off.

Total distance on line = 306 ft.

Total distance inside = 292 ft.

R=103 ft. 39.3 m.p.h.

R=130 ft. 44.1 m.p.h.

R=195 ft. 54.0 m.p.h.

Distance: up 4.8%
Speed: up 37%

33 ft.

do it because it's fast: it minimizes the time it takes to drive through the corner and maximizes the entry speed onto the following straight.

Turn-in, Apex, and Track-out

For the balance of the discussion in this book, we'll be using specific terms for the reference points of the arc through a corner. It begins at the "turn-in" point, comes closest to the inside edge of the corner at the "apex," and comes closest to the outside edge of the road at the "track-out" point. See Fig. 2-3.

In our example, we've created an arc that starts at the turn-in point, touches the apex and ends at the track-out. You could go out to Turn 7 at Sebring, get to the turn-in point and turn the steering wheel once and hold it there, placing the car on an arc that touches the apex with the right tires, then touches the track-out with the lefts. When you start working on the line, this is exactly what you're looking for, although as you try to get going faster, it's not quite so simple.

The Constant Radius Arc

An arc like this that doesn't change is called a constant radius arc. While you could handle all corners this way—after all, this arc gives you the biggest radius so therefore must allow you the highest speed—it doesn't take into account that in most corners, you are interested in carrying speed *away* from the corner and down the following straight. This requires acceleration, most commonly begun before the apex of a corner. Remember, if you're accelerating in the corner and your speed is rising, the radius of the arc you're on has to increase.

The difficulty is that it is much harder to draw increasing radius arcs than constant radius arcs. An accurate drawing of the arc a racing car is on as it leaves a corner near the limit would be one with an increasing radius. But at the start, you can learn more about identifying the right line by using the simpler version, the constant radius arc. Remember, too, that as you're working on finding the line you'll be driving the car under its limit to start. Only after finding the line—and proving that you can stay on it—will you start adding speed and approach the car's cornering limit.

Reference Points to Keep the Line Consistent

In our racing schools, we place bright orange pylons at the reference points for each corner. The drill looks simple: Get to the turn-in pylon and turn the steering wheel just the right amount to get to the apex pylon—hopefully this arc will end up at the track-out pylon.

The pylons are, at first, a great help in locating reference points, but what each driver eventually needs to do is to find indicators other than pylons around

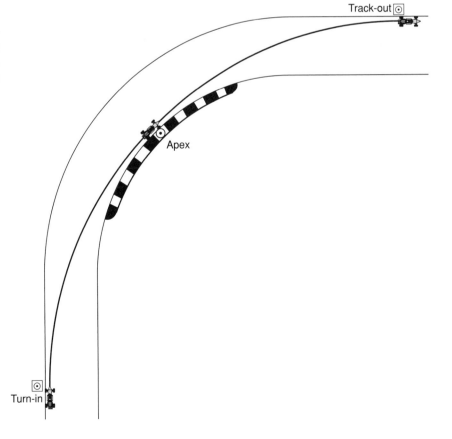

Fig. 2-3. Every corner has at least three distinct reference points: the turn-in, the apex, and the track-out.

> "I absolutely use reference points around the track to keep on the line. If they're there, by God, I'll find them. It gives you consistency, and I think that's the difference between consistently running up front and winning races."
>
> —Robbie Buhl

the racetrack that help show them the way. You want reference points that help you consistently turn the car into the corner at the same spot every lap, that help you clip the same apex time after time.

At first, the racetrack may look like a uniform strip of black asphalt. You'll find that you have to look much closer than you might have thought to accurately find your way around. Any kind of irregularity near the turn-in point will do—a gouge in the racing surface, a crack in the pavement, a paint line on the edge of the racetrack, changes in pavement or patches made in the racing surface, curbing at the corner entry.

The further away from the road the reference point is, the more potential for distraction, but, at courses with walls, you can frequently use advertising banners as reference points. Turning in "five feet past the Bosch sign" often works.

It's a mistake to be rigid. The process of finding the line is continuous. If you've never seen the racetrack before, never driven a racecar before, it's going to take a considerable amount of mental energy. You'll go round and round, picking reference points, adjusting them lap by lap until at some point you feel you really have it down, right on the edges of the road, smooth arcs through every corner.

And it's never over. It's difficult to hit marks right on the button every time and you will find that you're

> "You have to be willing to experiment. Once you find a line that works you still have to keep looking for something better. Even during a race I'll change lines if I feel I can find a little more grip on another part of the racetrack. I make small changes. I might change my entry to a corner a little bit on one lap and if it's better I might try it a little more the next time. No big jumps. I don't go from the 3 marker to the 1 marker.
>
> "I think that's part of the art of racing—something that all the really good racers do. I think it's one of the things that Al Jr., for example, is really good at. He just keeps plugging and plugging away and keeps working on it and he gets there in the end."
>
> —Bryan Herta

constantly fiddling with reference points in the pursuit of the perfect lap. As you'll see in later chapters, there are other variables, beyond your own inability to be perfectly consistent, which will change your corner reference points.

Common Errors

Inaccuracy
When we set up our pylons in our racing schools, we want to see our drivers get within 6 inches of the turn-in and track-out points; we like to see them touch the apex with their inside tire.

> "I was lucky enough when I was a kid to be able to practice all the time. We would go to Thompson in Connecticut in the middle of the week and you could run all day for $5. I just drove and drove and drove—not fast, but I was just logging time, getting experience behind the wheel.
>
> "[We] would go out and put quarters at the apexes, because [we] read somewhere that grand prix drivers could hit a coin at the apex every lap. I got so I could be very precise with the car and when it was time to go fast I was ready."
>
> —David Loring

In racing, inches and tenths of miles per hour matter. For example, if you are one mile per hour faster than your competition, you gain approximately 1.5 feet every second you do this. A 1-m.p.h. advantage in a half hour race represents 2600 feet. At Indianapolis, a race that's close to three hours, a 1-m.p.h. advantage represents a three-mile lead. You find that elusive mile per hour by using every inch of road available. Let's take a look at what happens when you don't.

You've been working on Turn 7 at Sebring, so let's stick with it. If you did it just right, you could drive through Turn 7 on a 195-foot radius at 54 m.p.h. (earlier Fig. 2-2). If you were 12 inches off the edge of the road at the turn-in, missed the apex by 12 inches, then held the car off the edge of the road at the track-out by 12 inches, your radius would be 189.5 feet. Plug this into our m.p.h. equation and your cornering speed is down to 53.3 m.p.h. Seven-tenths of a mile an hour difference doesn't sound like much, but in terms of the distance lost to a competitor, it's a bunch.

Say you made this mistake at the Keyhole at Mid Ohio, a corner that, in one of our racecars, leads to a straight where you accelerate for 20 seconds. Seven tenths of 1 m.p.h. is still over a foot per second of velocity. Lose a foot per second for 20 seconds and you've been beaten by almost two car lengths. Make these one-foot line mistakes in every corner and you're out of contention.

How close you get to the edges of the road will vary by circumstance. You might not choose to apex as closely to the wall at a street circuit like Long Beach as you might at a benign course like Topeka. But you should be making the *choice* not to get too close, not missing the apex because you *can't* get there.

You can use every inch of road, and then some—we've seen drivers clout curbs and track right out into the dirt at the exits. It *does* make the radius bigger, but radius is not the only part of the equation. If your line is seriously upsetting the car's grip on the road surface, or increasing the likelihood of damaging the suspension, the extra radius is probably not worth it.

Turning Too Early

Let's take a look at Turn 7 again and see what happens when you keep the car on the edge of the road at the corner entry, but initiate the turn too soon.

The entry phase of this corner works just fine with an early turn-in. You're driving into the corner on an arc with a much bigger radius to it. If you're going about the same speed you were going on the last lap, the car would feel better, that is, it wouldn't take as much force to turn the car on a more gentle arc. It may feel good, but at some point it becomes obvious that you're heading off the road. Your sense of self preservation urges you at this point to turn the steering wheel more to keep the car on the racetrack.

The key question here is whether the car can do it or not. If you're going slowly, not using all the traction that the tires have available, the car has the surplus turning power available for you. You turn more and the car responds, turns on the tighter arc, and stays on the road.

But, if you made this mistake at the limit of the adhesion of the tires with a 1 G-cornering car, and your ideal arc is 195 feet, this early arc would scale to 300 feet. At the car's cornering limit, you could carry 67 m.p.h. into the corner on the 300-foot arc—13 m.p.h. more than if you turned in at the later turn-in point.

The problem is that to stay on the racetrack, you have to negotiate a tight arc late in the turn. The radi-

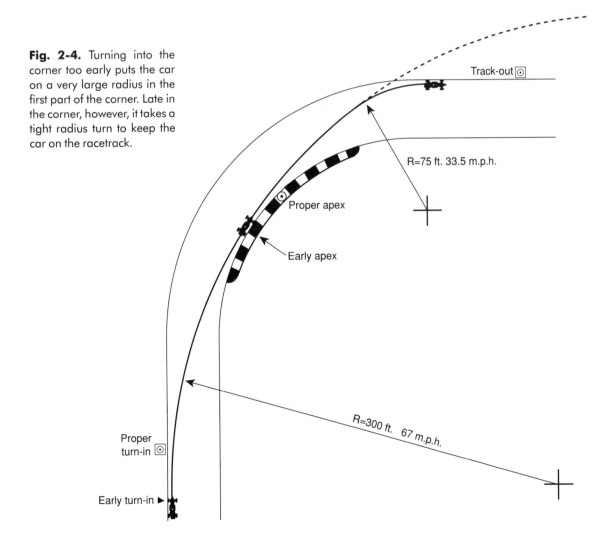

Fig. 2-4. Turning into the corner too early puts the car on a very large radius in the first part of the corner. Late in the corner, however, it takes a tight radius turn to keep the car on the racetrack.

Track-out ⊙

R=75 ft. 33.5 m.p.h.

⊙ Proper apex

Early apex

R=300 ft. 67 m.p.h.

Proper turn-in ⊙

Early turn-in ▶

"I've got a great picture at home of the GTO Cougar I used to race. It's a picture of the front wheels around an angled wall at Del Mar where you'd swear the door was touching the wall. It was so close to touching that the reflection off the orange paint is on the wall and you can't see any light through. The car had bulbous fenders and the door went in a little bit between the front and rear wheels and I used the indentation in the door between the fender flares to get closer to the apex."

—Dorsey Schroeder

us of that arc scales to 75 feet: using the cornering equation, you get 33.5 m.p.h. as the maximum speed on this arc. You can't negotiate a 33.5 m.p.h. corner at 67 m.p.h.

If you turn the steering wheel more, the front wheels will point more to the right but since the car is at its cornering limit, it will continue on its way on the 300-foot arc you started back at the beginning of the corner. Sadly, that arc leads off the racing surface. What becomes of you and your racecar is at the mercy of the laws of physics.

The Early Apex
This unfortunate chain of events is known as the "early apex." By turning into the corner too early, you have formed an apex that is significantly earlier than the proper one. The two are naturally tied together: turning in too early will lead to an early apex; an early apex leads to an early exit.

An early apex is by far the most common mistake that gets both novice *and* experienced race drivers off the racetrack. The next time you are at a racetrack look for the areas where no grass has ever or will ever grow—at the corner exits. Why? Because everyone continues to drop wheels, or entire cars, off at the exits because they early apexed.

Primary Symptom of Early Apexing
If you're driving through a corner and feel the need to increase the amount of steering effort past the apex, it is probably because you turned into the corner *too soon*. This is the single most reliable symptom of early apexing; you can use it from your first day in a racecar until the day you hang up the helmet.

Correcting the Early Apex
Recognizing the symptom means you need to do something different the next time you drive up to the corner—namely, turn later. In order to do this you need to firmly establish your reference points *and* develop a sense for where you are on the racetrack.

One other thing you need to do is to examine your perspective or attitude. You *guaranteed* that your car would go off into the boonies because you asked it to do something it was flat incapable of doing: take a 33.5 m.p.h. arc at 67 m.p.h. If you had driven into the corner at 33.5 m.p.h. and late in the turn realized that you needed the tighter arc to stay on the road, you would have gotten away with the mistake. The car would have turned on the 75-foot arc you wanted. You made the same mistake but it cost you less. And the reason it cost you less was not that you didn't screw up, you still early apexed but you had a cushion. You were operating under the limit, using less than 100% of the car's capability, keeping a reserve in hand in case of foul-up.

You can't operate with this reserve forever. A racecar driven at lap-record pace is being used with no reserve. But you're not qualifying now. You're looking for the proper path around the racetrack. You can afford to leave yourself a cushion, especially if it points the way to the proper line and keeps you on the racing surface.

The Late Apex
Using our Turn 7 example, let's look at what happens when you turn into the corner too late. If you turn 20 feet past the geometric turn-in point, the first thing you'll find is that you clip an apex 20 feet further around the curb: a later turn-in will lead to a later apex.

At the track-out, if you held the steering wheel in the same position from turn-in until you're facing down the following straight, you'd have almost 20 feet of racetrack left to the outside at the exit of the corner! From a safety standpoint, that's terrific. You make a mistake and you don't go off the track—you have extra road left. Therein lies the beauty and value of the "late apex."

There are, however, disadvantages. Compute the potential speed you could carry into the corner on an arc that starts 20 feet later than perfect. By scaling it you find that your 20-foot later turn-in requires that you use an arc with a radius of 160 feet to make the apex. Plugging 160 feet into our cornering speed equation yields a maximum speed of 49 m.p.h. That's 5 m.p.h. slower than the geometric line. So the late apex line is a safer but slower path through the corner.

"Absolutely, you need reference points. You can't do it all by feel. You have to find your own marks on the track—that's how you'll be able to go fast consistently. There are lots of places where it's hard to find markers. At a place like Cleveland that's flat and featureless, you have to try even harder to find your spots."

—Danny Sullivan

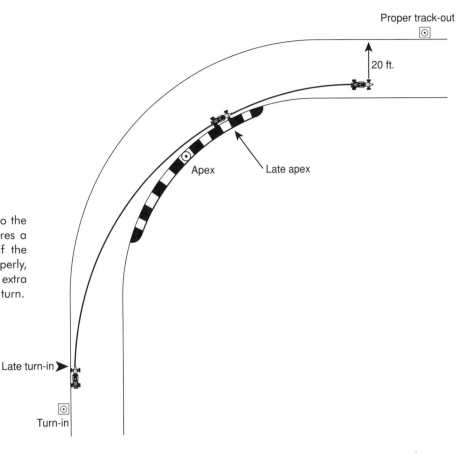

Proper track-out

20 ft.

Apex

Late apex

Fig. 2-5. Turning into the corner too late requires a tighter radius than if the corner were done properly, but it results in having extra room at the exit of the turn.

Late turn-in ▶

Turn-in

Primary Symptom of Late Apexing

If there is road left at the exit of the corner, you have chosen a turn-in and apex that were *too late*.

Now, this assumes that you're driving at less than the limit. You know by now that any racer would naturally unwind the steering wheel when he or she realized there was 20 feet of road left at the corner exit. As you get closer to the limit, the symptom becomes more like the suspicion that driving away from this corner is too easy. You're able to essentially drive straight out to the edge of the road.

At line-finding speed, the late apex is an advantage since you're looking for reference points and not lap time. You're much better off erring on the side of turning in and apexing too late than too early.

Line-Finding Strategy

Since the late apex is a safer path to take through the corner, it's a very useful tool to use in the effort to find the right line around the racetrack. When you are at a circuit that's new to you, intentionally turn into corners later than you think you should. You'll have a sense (a combination of hand-eye coordination and experience) for when you should initiate a turn.

When you feel you should turn in, overrule your instinct and turn later. Aim for an apex point that's later than you expect it eventually will be, then hold the

steering wheel in the same position and see what happens at the exit. If the apex was too late, turn a bit earlier on the next run up to the corner, and aim for an earlier apex. Continue the process lap after lap, adjusting the turn-in and apex until the car is using all the road coming out of the corner. All along you should be picking up reference points for the turn-in, apex, and track-out and working from them, adjusting your line. After many repetitions, you'll develop the knowledge of where the car should be, every inch of the way around the course.

> *"At a new racetrack I look closely at the course and try to find references for turn-ins and apexes and start out, just as you learn in school, later than you might think. You always start later, then back it up earlier and earlier, fine tuning the line."*
>
> —*Brian Till*

Make Time

Those of you who are active racers may say, "Who's got the time. Practice is only a half hour, then we have to qualify." There is always time pressure. Just remember that to get the car on the pole you'll have to be driving the optimum line.

Make time. Almost all tracks have open practice days. If they don't, take your family sedan and enter a car club time trial event. Use the track time to drive around and find the line. Don't feel like it's Mickey Mouse. Guys like Emerson Fittipaldi will drive around a new circuit for hours in a rental car just getting a feel for the place. The line you take at 40 m.p.h. in your street car may not be the exact path you'll take in your racecar, but you'll have reference points to work from and when you finally go racing, the racetrack will feel more like an old shoe than a foreign planet.

> *"When you go to a racetrack for the first time, you just have to go there early and drive around it. I've done everything from driving it in a rental car to riding it on a bicycle or a motorbike. If you don't, you're stuck using the first practice session in the race car, driving slowly, learning it, and getting the line down without doing it at breakneck speed."*
>
> —Danny Sullivan

EXIT SPEED

Close to the Edge
Once you're confident of your ability to put the car on the line, you can more safely move up toward the car's cornering limit with less fear that you're making a commitment to the corner that the car can't keep.

In the earlier Turn 7 example, you started out looking for the line by driving through the corner in the 40 m.p.h. range. This is 14 to 17 m.p.h. slower than the speed you can expect to reach at the limit. Being this conservative on speed means that the tires only need to use up 55% of their cornering traction to negotiate the proper line.

To maximize the speed at the corner track-out, you'll eventually have to use everything the car has got. To do this, you have to develop some familiarity with how the car behaves and how you can affect its behavior when it's being driven near its limit using a combination of *throttle* and *steering*.

Neutral
We said originally that as the car went faster and faster it used up more and more of its 100% of available traction, and that there was a specific speed where it would have to use 100% of its hold on the road to stay on its cornering arc. We assumed in this example, for the sake of simplicity, that the front pair of tires and

the rear pair of tires on the car reached this 100% level of traction at the same instant.

This *does* happen in the real world, but not often. Usually, one end of the car reaches its limit of traction a bit before the other end and this affects what we refer to as the "cornering balance" of the car.

However, in the case of a car that reaches the limit at both front and rear simultaneously, we call it a neutral handling car: both front and rear tires contribute their maximum traction to the cornering effort.

Understeer
If you were on the skidpad with a car which reached 100% of the tires' cornering capabilities at the front tires before the rears, the front end of the car would slide first, leading you nose-first away from the direction the front wheels were pointing. This cornering state is called "understeer."

Oversteer
At the other end of the spectrum is the case where the rear tires reach the limit first and slide out wider than you intend. This tail-out attitude is called "oversteer."

How Throttle Influences Understeer Or Oversteer
Different cars, owing to their particular design and set-up, have built-in tendencies to either oversteer or understeer at the cornering limit. In most cases, however, the car isn't grossly biased toward one extreme, and you can use the controls of the car to dial up whatever cornering balance is needed. To do this you have to have some effect on the traction of the front or rear pair of tires. It would be nice if you had a dial on the dash to do this, but you don't. The next best thing is to use the control you have down in the footwell of the car, the throttle.

You can load or unload the front or rear tires (change their traction) by applying or backing off the throttle. You can also steal cornering grip from the rear tires (assuming a rear wheel drive car) by applying the throttle and demanding acceleration, or by backing off the throttle and demanding engine-braking traction.

In a rear wheel drive car, applying the throttle creates two opposing tendencies: first, it transfers load onto the rear tires, which helps them grip, but at the same time it uses up part of the traction, which hurts cornering grip. Whichever of the two has the greater effect will determine the result.

For example, if you're driving an underpowered car with sticky rear tires, those tires don't have to surrender much grip to deal with the level of acceleration the motor creates. The increase in grip from the transfer of load, combined with the loss of grip at the front is likely to produce understeer.

If, on the other hand, you're driving a car with skinny rear tires and a King-Kong motor, you can use

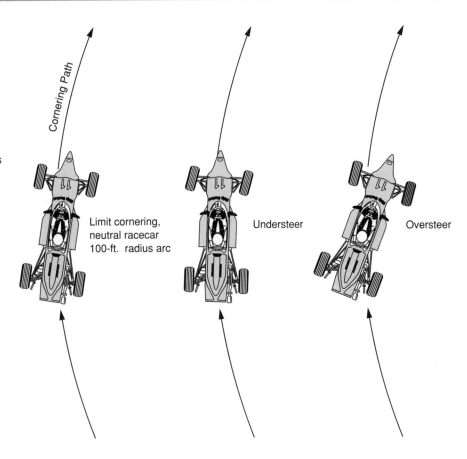

Fig. 2-6. When both front and rear tires are contributing proportionately to the cornering effort of the car, its cornering balance is *neutral. Understeer* occurs when the front tires reach their limit before the rears. When the rear tires reach their limit before the front tires, *oversteer* occurs.

Cornering Path

Limit cornering, neutral racecar 100-ft. radius arc

Understeer

Oversteer

up a giant percentage of rear tire grip with the same level of squeeze on the throttle, producing oversteer.

To pin it down to a fundamental rule (remember, this is a guideline, not a guarantee):

A gradual increase in throttle will tend to create understeer. An abrupt application of throttle will tend to create oversteer.

Trailing Throttle Oversteer

Now let's look at throttle release. When you release the throttle, relaxing pedal pressure, there is a point where you're using just enough engine power to maintain speed, neither accelerating nor decelerating. The front to rear loading is constant.

If you back off further on the throttle, engine compression slows down the driven wheels and the resulting deceleration shifts load off the rear tires onto the front. Along with the change in loading, the engine compression uses some of the rear tires' grip for braking, further reducing traction at the rear.

If you're cornering near the limit, these changes will cause the rear of the car to slide out onto a bigger arc—into oversteer. This is known as "trailing throttle oversteer," oversteer caused by trailing off the throttle. The more abrupt the throttle lift, the more violent the oversteer. A slight breathe off the throttle would result in a smooth transition to oversteer, while

a snap off the throttle can snap the car around faster than you can react to it.

To pin it down to another fundamental rule (remember, this is a guideline, not a guarantee):

Lifting off the throttle while near the cornering limit will create oversteer in direct proportion to the severity of the lift.

Using Throttle to Correct Understeer

As you work towards raising your exit speed out of corners, you'll experiment with squeezing the power on earlier and earlier. As you get closer to the limit, you're likely to experience understeer since your application of power unloads the front end of the car. Behind the wheel, the sensation is one of the car running wider than you intend it to.

The most common reaction is to turn the steering wheel more: after all, past experience has taught that the more you want to turn, the more you turn the steering wheel. But when you are over the front tire's cornering limits, more steering angle is *not* going to make the front end turn more.

The front tires need more download in order to provide more grip. The dilemma is that you don't want to give up pushing on the throttle coming off the corner since it's going to hurt your exit speed. At times like these you have to remember that going off the road hurts exit speed even more.

In the case of developing understeer at the exit of the corner, the right thing to do is to surrender some throttle—often not much—to transfer a little load back to the front tires and get the nose of the car pointed back toward the inside.

Dealing with understeer frequently is done by adjusting the throttle, not the steering wheel. It's probably the easiest car control to develop, since it parallels your instinct to slow down when things aren't going well. Dealing with oversteer typically takes a little more practice.

Steering to Correct Oversteer

On the racetrack it's called oversteer, but most people call it a skid. The street driver is interested in stopping the oversteer before it develops into a loss of control, and doesn't care if the car stops in the process. The street driver is best advised to use only the steering wheel to correct an oversteer slide.

On the racetrack, you certainly don't want to lose control either, but you also don't want to lose very much speed or time. These slightly different goals affect the way you use the steering wheel *and* the throttle to keep oversteer from developing into a spin.

The slide starts somewhere. For some reason—trailing throttle, too much throttle, a missed downshift, whatever—the tail end of the car moves out onto a bigger arc than the arc the front wheels are on. What is the first thing you do?

Back in Driver's Ed., most of us learned to "steer into a skid," and this advice is correct—up to a point. As the rear end comes out, you turn the steering wheel toward the direction the rear end is heading. You're trying to lessen the amount that the front end is being drawn toward the inside of the corner, exaggerating the effect of the rear coming out. By turning the wheel toward the direction the rear is going, you're trying to put the front end of the car on the same arc that the rear is heading for, which will bring the oversteer situation back closer to neutral.

Correction, Pause, Recovery

Turning the steering wheel is the "correction" phase of the slide. If you've corrected enough, the motion of the rear end toward the outside will slow and stop at some point, then begin a swing back toward the inside. This point is called the "pause," and is the signal to begin the "recovery," where you unwind the steering wheel, taking the correction back to zero as the rear of the car comes back from its slide

Note that as the rear end begins its swing back, toward the inside of the arc, it builds up momentum. If you're slow to take out the steering correction that halted the first slide, this momentum will snap the car around in a direction opposite the first slide.

Every tail-out slide should be dealt with by making a correction, then using the pause as a cue for begin-

Fig. 2-7. As the rear of the car slides wide, the driver steers the front wheels toward the direction the rear is going. Here the "Correction" is over 270 degrees.

Fig. 2-8. At the height of the slide, the rear end pauses for an instant before coming back the other way. This "Pause" is the cue to begin the "Recovery'— bringing the steering wheel back to straight, quickly.

ning the recovery. While these phases primarily define what you should do with the steering wheel, the throttle can come into play.

Combining Steering and Throttle for Control

Exactly how you use the throttle depends on what initially caused the oversteer. If the tail came out because you abruptly lifted off the throttle in the middle of the corner, causing trailing throttle oversteer, you can contribute to restoring traction to the rear of the car by applying some throttle.

If the oversteer began because you got greedy on the throttle and created power oversteer, you can help solve the problem by breathing back on the throttle, which should restore some cornering traction to the rear of the car.

Using the throttle correctly takes a tender touch. A majority of both beginning and experienced drivers over-use the throttle in these situations. The most common misuse is full power to solve any situation. You need to remember that small changes in throttle can have a huge effect on the car, especially when it's dancing through a corner on the limit of adhesion.

So far the concentration has been on car control in the part of the corner where you combine turning and accelerating, the area where beginning drivers should first experiment with the cornering limits of the car.

You'll soon see that the car is also driven at its combined limit of braking and cornering on the way from the turn-in point of the corner to the throttle application point. You have to use car control to keep the car balanced at its limit in this part of the racetrack as well, but you'll find that it's harder to creep up on this limit than it is to flirt with the limit of combined acceleration and cornering. You'll also find that there is less overall lap time to be gained by being right on the limit at corner entries than there is to be gained being on the limit coming out of corners.

> *"Using both your hands and the throttle is something that is totally feel. The first thing is opposite lock—turn into the slide. Then you balance the throttle to help get the car as straight as you can, but it's like dancing on the throttle—little changes either more or less according to what the car needs."*
>
> —Danny Sullivan

BRAKING AND ENTERING

The final step in lowering lap time is developing braking skill. This aspect of driving skill is often referred to as "braking and entering."

Lose Speed Quickly

At corner entry there are two fundamental goals. The first is to minimize the time it takes to go from the brake application point to the throttle application point. The assumption here is that spending less time on the brakes means more time on the throttle, which *has* to be faster. This approach would mean using all of the braking power available so that you can lose the speed required in the shortest amount of time.

Lose the Right Amount of Speed

Just as important as the rate of speed loss is the total amount of speed you choose to lose. If you slow too much by either braking too early or too hard or too long, this speed is lost not only on the corner entry but on the acceleration zone following the corner.

Not slowing enough can put the car off the racing surface. Arriving in the corner too fast will, at the very least, delay the beginning of the acceleration away from the corner as you struggle for control on the way to the apex.

Braking Fundamentals

It's helpful to know some of the forces at work when you use the braking system, and what will be required of you to approach the limit under braking.

As with cornering and accelerating, it is tires' grip against the road surface that provides you with the force to slow the car. Put a better set of tires on the car—tires that have a greater capability for grip—and the car's braking performance will improve.

Tires create traction in direct proportion to how hard they are pushing down on the surface of the road. If, for example, a tire is pushing down on the road surface with 500 lbs. of force, a typical race tire will provide you with 500 lbs. of maximum resistance against the road surface.

You can use this potential 500-lb. force however you choose. You can use it to corner the car or to accelerate it. As you've seen earlier, you can use a combination of accelerating and cornering, or braking and cornering. Braking in a straight line, you can use all of this 500-lb. force exclusively for braking.

Pressing on the brake pedal creates hydraulic pressure in the brake lines and calipers, pressing the brake pads against the brake rotors which are spinning around at the speed of the wheel and tire. The brake system resists this rotation. The force exerted by the brake system is in the opposite direction from the rotation of the tire, illustrated by the clockwise arrow at

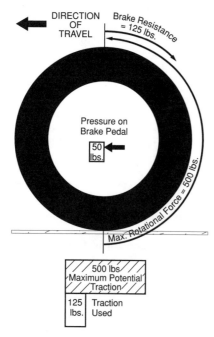

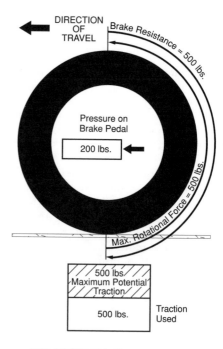

Fig. 2-9. With light brake pedal pressure the resistance to the tire's rotation is less than the tractive force that the tire could exert at the limit of its grip on the road.

Brake Pedal Pressure (in lbs.)	Brake System Force (in lbs.)
50	125
100	250
150	375
200	500
220	550

Fig. 2-10. Higher pedal pressures use proportionately more of the potential grip. Here, the brake resistance equals the maximum rotational force, signifying threshold braking.

the top of Fig. 2-9. You control the amount of this resistance by the pressure exerted on the brake pedal.

If you push lightly, with 50 lbs. of pressure on the brake pedal, it would only take 125 lbs. of the potential 500 lbs. of force to turn the tire counterclockwise, leaving 375 lbs. of potential traction in reserve. Doubling the pedal pressure to 100 lbs. forces the tire to use 250 lbs. of force to rotate the wheel.

As the brake pedal pressure goes up, the force countering the rotation of the tire goes up proportionately (Fig. 2-10). You'll notice too that the force on the pedal is multiplied by the design of the hydraulic system. 100 lbs. of force on the pedal, for example, creates 250 lbs. of force at the tire.

As you push harder on the brake pedal, more and more of the potential 500 lbs. of traction has to be used to counter the resistance to rotation. You can see from the chart that there is a specific pedal pressure at which it will take *all* of the tire's grip to keep the tire turning. If your aim is to slow down in the shortest possible time and distance, this is the place you want to be. At around 200 lbs. of pressure on the brake pedal, you're using all 500 lbs. of potential force to slow the car.

Threshold Braking

The goal is to stay at this maximum traction point. This occurs when the tire is revolving at a rate 15%

slower than it would be if it were freely rolling over the surface. This is a very tender balance point. Any less pressure on the brake pedal, and less than the full 500 lbs. of braking traction would be used, making the speed loss take more time than necessary. At a particular level of pressure on the brake pedal you're right there at the peak. We call it the *threshold.*

Lockup

If you go beyond the maximum and increase the pedal pressure past 200 lbs., the resistance to the tire's rotation is greater than the force acting to revolve the tire and the tire stops turning. When "tire lockup" happens, things go from bad to worse.

When the tire stops rotating, it typically loses 30% or more of its grip. Your original potential of 500 lbs. of force drops to 350 lbs. It takes longer to slow down, not to mention the damage you're doing to the tire by grinding the rubber off the spot in contact with the pavement.

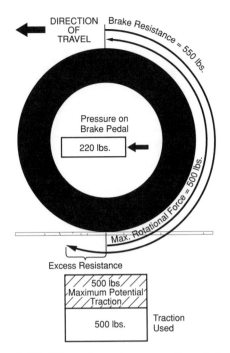

Fig. 2-11. When the resistance to the rotation is greater than the maximum tractive force of the tire, the wheel stops rotating.

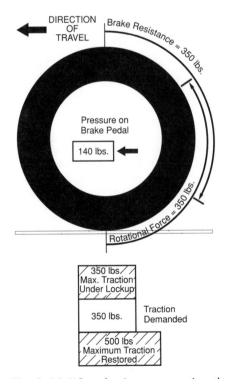

Fig. 2-12. When the tire stops rotating, the tractive force falls by some 30%. By relaxing the brake pedal pressure, you eliminate lockup and restore full braking traction.

Brake Modulation

In order to get the tire rotating again, you need to reduce pressure in the braking system enough so that this 350 lbs. of drag against the contact patch will start the tire rotating again. That is not to say, "take your foot off the brake pedal" (the most common beginner mistake). Pressure on the brake pedal needs to be reduced but not eliminated. Once the tire begins to roll again, its full traction is restored and you can increase pressure again in search of that level that puts the tire back to its threshold, yielding the maximum braking grip available.

From a theoretical standpoint, threshold braking is matching the appropriate brake pedal pressure to the maximum grip of the tire. In the real world things get complicated since you're dealing with not one, but two pairs of tires on opposite ends of the car.

Brake Bias

It's rare to have all four tires doing an equal share of the braking. When cars change speed and direction, inertia transfers load from front to rear and side to side. These loading changes alter each tire's traction.

Take a look at Fig. 2-13, a diagram of one of our Formula cars as it sits motionless in the pit lane. Its 1000-lb. mass is distributed as follows: 600 lbs. on the rear set of tires and 400 lbs. on the front pair. This is its static weight distribution which, once the car moves, is almost never seen again.

As the car accelerates, inertia (which wants the car to stay at rest and resists attempts to change its velocity) transfers load off the front tires onto the rear tires. The amount transferred depends upon the center of gravity of the car, its wheelbase, and the level of acceleration. When a car decelerates, the load is transferred off the rear tires onto the fronts. The greater the level of deceleration, the greater the load transfer off the rear tires to the fronts.

Under maximum deceleration, one of our Formula cars may transfer 250 lbs. of load onto the front tires, making the download 650 lbs. on the fronts and 350 lbs. on the rears; under hard braking 65% of the traction is at the front pair of tires while only 35% is at the rears. It would seem appropriate, then, that the front brakes exert 65% of the total braking effort while the rears take care of the remaining 35%. This difference in the proportion of braking effort afforded the front vs. the rear is called "brake bias."

Most street cars have this proportioning done by the designers of the car and the bias is figured on a particular loading and target range of deceleration. For racecars which are pursuing the maximum available performance, this kind of "ballpark" brake bias isn't good enough.

All real racecars will have a brake bias adjustment on the car (Fig. 2-14). Some are easily driver-adjustable, while others require a stop at the pits and a mechanic's help. The aim is to get both ends of the car

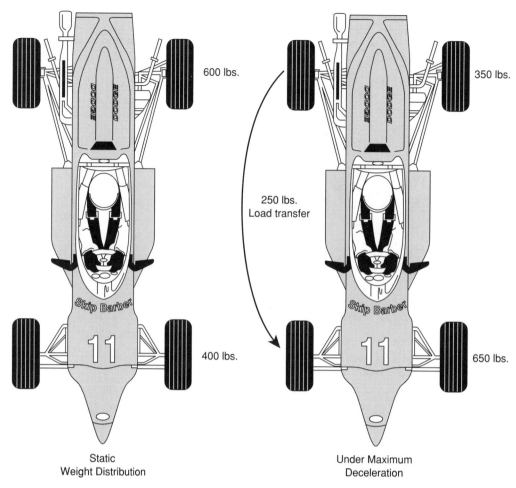

600 lbs.

350 lbs.

250 lbs.
Load transfer

400 lbs.

650 lbs.

Static
Weight Distribution

Under Maximum
Deceleration

Fig. 2-13. Sitting stationary in the pit lane, the static loading on the tires is different than it will be when you put the car into motion. Under deceleration the loading of the front versus the rear tires changes, transferring load from the rear to the front.

doing their fair share of the braking. If the front tires have 65% of the traction yet they have 75% of the brake effort, the rear tires aren't doing their full share and the front tires will tend to lock prematurely. The same holds true for the rears.

Of the two, front bias is easier to deal with than rear bias. If you inadvertently lock a front wheel, the car at least will continue to go straight. The car won't turn because the locked tire can't deliver a lateral force to change the car's direction and the rears, with the drag of both brakes and engine drag, will act like the feathers on an arrow, keeping the rear wheels obediently behind the fronts.

Lock the rears, however, and things like road crown or crosswinds or the slightest steering wiggle will get the rear sliding. It's not fun, especially at the end of a straightaway where you'd like to be thinking about getting the car slowed for the rapidly approaching corner, not catching an oversteer slide.

How Much Different from the Street?
You know that braking on the racetrack is going to be different than normal street driving because you're going to use a lot more force than you're accustomed to. Other than the level of force, there is nothing new here in the basic process.

Be forewarned that you will never be able to come up with a corner entry routine that covers all cases. In some instances, you arrive at the end of the straight at 180 m.p.h. and need to slow for a 25 m.p.h. corner. In some cases the approach is at 70 m.p.h. and the corner requires 68 m.p.h. It should be no surprise that different techniques are required for these two extreme cases, and for the others that lie in between.

Components of Corner Entry
Even with the wide variety of corner entries in racing, there are basic components which are common to most speed-loss situations. We can break the whole process down into four major blocks which might all

Fig. 2-14. Brake bias adjusters allow the driver to alter the brake bias of the car while it's underway.

> "I check the brake bias just about every time I get in a race car. Stuff always changes. Some cars are wildly sensitive to brake bias and some aren't, but you have to check. It also depends on the racetrack as well. If I go to a place like Road America where there are four or more hard straight-line braking zones, I'm going to try more rear brake bias in the car to absolutely maximize the car's straight-line braking potential. At a place like Lime Rock where there is no straight-line braking zone and you are braking and turning a lot, I'll run more front bias so that I can carry more brake power into the corner with more confidence."
>
> —Jeremy Dale

get used. But, as you'll see, there are corner entry situations where you will choose to use just one of the four blocks. For now, a simple explanation will suffice. Later, we will look closely at each of these blocks and see what types of skills you need to develop in order to excel in this aspect of the racing game.

Block 1: The Throttle-Brake Transition. Taking your foot off the throttle and putting it on the brake pedal can be done in very many different ways. Here, you're covering the range of techniques from a slow, cautious, lift off the throttle and onto the brakes, to the lightening-quick transition from full throttle to hundreds of pounds of brake pedal pressure.

Block 2: Straight-Line Deceleration. When the car is going straight it has no other demands on the tires than braking. You can decelerate at the car's maximum rate in this segment of corner entry. There are frequently cases when you will want to exercise the option to brake at less than the "threshold" level.

Block 3: Brake-Turn. Here you can both decelerate and change direction. In brake-turning, you can use a constant level of pressure on the brake pedal, yielding a constant level of cornering force, or you can reduce the braking pressure over time, creating increasing cornering force as the car approaches the throttle application point.

Block 4: Brake-Throttle Transition. At the very end of deceleration you leave the brake pedal and pick up the throttle to accelerate away from the corner. You can do this quickly or slowly, with or without a pause between the last bit of braking and the first bit of throttle.

THE ANALYTICAL RACER

In this chapter, we have introduced some of the most basic information a good race driver should understand in order to do well. As you can see, there is a lot to it, and performing well has a lot less to do with instinct than with planning.

A good driver knows what needs to be done at every point on the racetrack and takes the time to develop the skill needed to make the proper moves. There is a plan: brake there; shift there; turn in at that spot; take a specific apex; apply the power just so; clip the edge of the road at the exit.

Early in a career many of these decisions take a good deal of conscious thought. As you get more experience and develop the physical skills necessary to drive a car fast and smoothly, less conscious thought is required for these decisions, and more can be applied to advanced subjects that will affect your level of success.

Part II
Developing the Basics

Chapter 3

The Real-world Line

WHEN WE LOOKED AT THE basics of racing we outlined the fundamentals for driving on the best path around the racecourse. But in the real world of racing, the line is more complex. There are a number of variables you have to consider as you plan your way through the real-world line.

Real-world situations go beyond the basics of the line. There are many variables that will affect your choice of the best path through a given corner.

Speed Changes Things

Even with the simplest corners the primary symptom of an early apex changes as speed rises. At lower speeds, well below the car's cornering limits, you could tell that you've early apexed by the need to turn the steer-

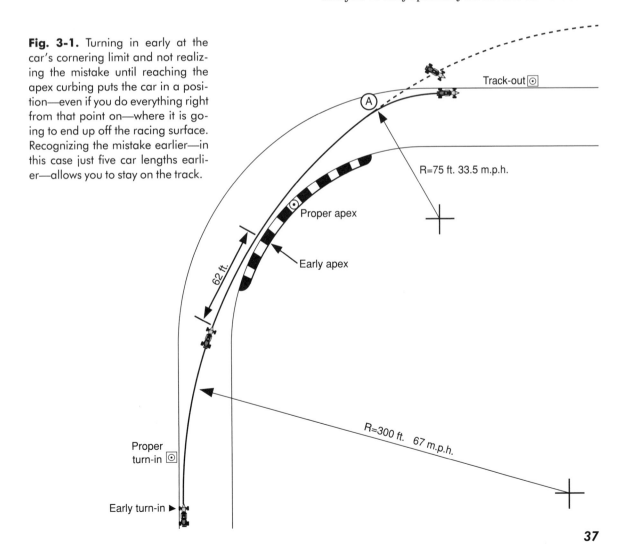

Fig. 3-1. Turning in early at the car's cornering limit and not realizing the mistake until reaching the apex curbing puts the car in a position—even if you do everything right from that point on—where it is going to end up off the racing surface. Recognizing the mistake earlier—in this case just five car lengths earlier—allows you to stay on the track.

Track-out ⊙

Ⓐ

R=75 ft. 33.5 m.p.h.

Proper apex

Early apex

62 ft.

R=300 ft. 67 m.p.h.

Proper turn-in ⊙

Early turn-in ▶

ing wheel more in the second part of the turn. But as you become more aggressive about adding power through the apex and corner exit you'll find that you need to identify and cure the early apex much earlier.

Early Apex Diagnosis

Let's look at Fig. 3-1 to define the problem. If you did this corner perfectly you could drive through it in the range of 55 m.p.h.

If you turn three car lengths early, your arc into the corner is very broad, allowing you to corner at 67 m.p.h. on the way to the apex. If you reach point A before realizing that you've early apexed, you're in deep trouble: you're now going to ask the car to take a 33.5 m.p.h. corner at 67 m.p.h. It should be no surprise that the car continues on the big-radius arc right off the road. The initial problem was the early turn-in, but what guaranteed a bad outcome was realizing the mistake too late in the turn.

If you make the same initial mistake, but realize it earlier, the results are less severe. If you caught the mistake 62 ft. before the apex, straightened the steering wheel, and used the brakes hard, you'd be able to slow the car to 33.5 m.p.h. by point A, allowing the car to stay on the road at the corner exit.

This is a critical fact to keep in mind about driving race cars: The faster you go, the earlier you have to identify and cure mistakes. In this example you would have to identify and begin to cure the early apex over 90 feet before the proper apex of the corner.

When Mario Andretti was winning the World Championship in 1978, he had to give hundreds of interviews. In one, the interviewer, gushing superlatives, asked how it was to achieve perfection behind the wheel of a racecar. Andretti's reply was that no-one is perfect in a racecar. "The difference between the world class driver and the average racer," he said, "is that the champions recognize their mistakes sooner."

This type of skill calls for two things: one, knowing where the correct line is; and two, knowing where your car is on the racetrack, within inches, all the time. You obviously need reference points for your turn-in, apex and track-out. Also make yourself identify other reference points on the way into the apex, especially in long, fast corners where it may be a con-

siderable distance between the turn-in and apex. Notice where the car is in relation to these spots when you're going slowly on the right line. Then, as you go faster, any excursion *inside* these reference points on the way into the corner will clue you in to an impending early apex.

I Know It's Coming—Now What?

If the signs point to an early apex, you have to instantly switch your concerns from driving through the corner faster to driving away from the corner with the car in one piece.

You'll need to do two things. First, you need to admit to yourself that by going in early you have obligated the car to do more turning in the second half of the corner than it did in the first half—in short, you'll have to run a smaller radius in the second half. In order to do this, you'll need to be going slower. Job number one is to slow the car down.

If you're braking and turning into the corner, you could just rest your foot on the brake pedal a second or so longer than usual. If it's not a corner where you do a lot of braking and turning you could be more conservative on the application of power, providing balance for the car with some throttle application, but not accelerating up to the slowest part of the corner. If the situation were desperate, you could relax the steering effort, thereby asking for less cornering force, and use some braking to lose the speed required.

Second, you have to try to get the car back on the proper racing line as soon as possible—no later than the apex. If you succeed in having the car back to the right apex and at the right attitude at the apex, the second part of the corner will not be a tighter radius, and you can start picking up normal speed again.

What do we mean by the "attitude" at the apex? When the car hits the apex properly, not only is it close to the apex point but it's also pointing in the right direction. It is possible to make it close to the apex, yet not have changed the car's direction enough by this point in the corner. In Fig. 3-2, Car 1 is close to the apex but hasn't done enough change of direction for this point in the corner. The result will be the same as the early apex—more turning needs to be done later in the corner, requiring a tighter radius. Car 2 has got the apex and the attitude right.

Getting a reference point for the attitude of the car is a little more complicated than simply driving from dot to dot, but driving the proper arc over and over develops a mental image of what the apex and the corner exit should look like.

Using A "Sight Picture"

Many of our instructors refer to it as a "sight picture." After many repetitions through a corner, your mind develops a picture—a transparency, if you will—of the general scene in the corner. If the scene is different than normal, the car's position and attitude are

> "If you're any good, the instant you turn your hands into the corner you know if you've made a mistake. You don't wait for the apex and say 'Oh gosh, I'm early or, I missed it by two feet'—way too late! When you see it early you have all that time to get out of the throttle a little and get the car headed in the right direction. If you're any good you make mistakes constantly but you never go off the road."
>
> —Skip Barber

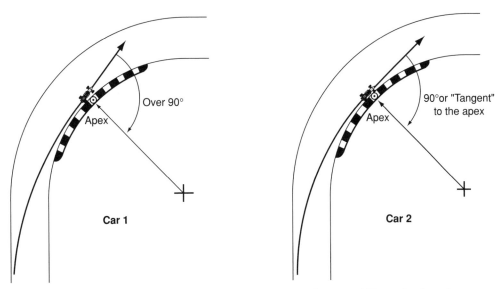

Fig. 3-2. Both these cars are near the apex but the car in the second illustration is at the correct attitude for its location in the corner.

wrong. The trick is to define how it's wrong and to decide on your next course of action.

Think of it as the same mechanism that is at work when six-year-old kids first try to catch a baseball. They know nothing of ballistics and trajectories, and their first attempts to predict where the ball is going to end up are futile. But as they do it more and more, their eyes and brains work together to make some predictions about what is likely to happen the next time the ball comes at them. After years of practice and thousands of repetition, good fielders start running to where the ball is going to be the instant the ball leaves the bat.

Through repetition, coordination, and athleticism, you can develop a sense of where you are in space versus where you need to be and how to coordinate your actions to get into the position you visualize.

Reference Points vs. "Feel"
While we've recommended orienting yourself on the racetrack using concrete reference points, it's worth knowing that some top-level professional racers don't. After 15 years of driving racecars, a racer is more equipped, with this level of experience under the belt, to use a sight picture approach to location on the racetrack. With less experience and fewer repetitions, the beginning racer is more likely to drive point-to-point. Starting with this approach and developing sight pictures over time is a common progression, but one is not necessarily any better than the other—it's all what works for you.

Early Apexing at Speed
When you get cooking, running through the corners very close to the limits of the car, the symptoms of early and late apexing change. We've looked at the kind of trouble an early apex can cause using some gross examples. Most drivers can get close to the right path, yet they always seem to make small line mistakes. An experienced driver is less likely to turn into a corner 30 feet early than the novice is, but in the process of refining the line at the limit, it's still possible to adjust the turn-in point too much.

Just like at lower speed, any need to turn the steering wheel more when past the apex is an obvious no-no. Mark Donohue always put a 1" strip of bright tape at the top of the steering wheel so that he could clearly see which way the steering wheel was heading on the way out of the corner. If it was heading toward the inside of the turn, the turn-in and apex were too early.

At racing speed, you should always be unwinding the steering wheel at the corner exit. If not, try a later turn-in and apex. There are, of course, exceptions. If the car is at terminal velocity, that is, there is no acceleration going on, then it's okay to have a stationary

> *"I start with fixed reference points, which I think you need to identify the line, but, as the weekend goes on and you've been through the corner more and more, the visual picture becomes implanted in my mind and the fixed points start to go away. You end up at those same points but you are not concentrating on them, per se, any more."*
>
> —Brian Till

steering wheel at corner exit. In the vast majority of cases, if you can't unwind the wheel, you're too early.

Throttle position is another good indicator. If you have to breathe off the throttle coming out of the corner you may not have left yourself room enough to widen the arc at the exit. Solve it by turning later and apexing later.

Late Apexing at Speed

At racing speed the late apex provides you with a dilemma. The later you turn, the more change of direction you accomplish in the first part of the turn—and the less you have to change the car's direction at the exit. This makes putting the power on easier and makes it easier to unwind the steering wheel: both are goals you'd like to accomplish.

The catch is that when you turn later, you have to go slower at corner entry. In our earlier Turn 7 example, turning one and a half car lengths too late (20 feet) cut your potential speed to the apex by 5 m.p.h.

Some cars will make up that 5 m.p.h. loss and then some by the track-out point. Some racecars take *forever* to gain back 5 m.p.h. You could be late apexing the corner, but since you're unwinding the wheel and the car is ending up at the edge of the road at the track-out point, you think you're doing fine. In fact, you could be losing time because, for your car, the late apex costs both cornering and exit speed.

How do you tell? It should be a bit of a struggle, even though the steering wheel is being unwound, to exit the corner without dropping a wheel off. If it's too easy perhaps you're giving away too much entry speed by taking too late an apex. A valuable technique to get into the habit of using is to check the tachometer (or speedometer, if your car has one) at the exit of every corner. In trying to decide the turn-in and apex to use, start with a late apex, then begin turning slightly earlier and look for an RPM improvement at the track-out. If the exit speed is improving, keep moving the turn-in earlier until symptoms of the early apex show up.

SHORTCUTS TO THE LINE

It would be wonderful if we all could have unlimited track time to practice, practice, practice. We don't. Luckily, there are things you can do *off* the racetrack to make yourself a better driver. When it comes to finding the line, you can make some generalizations that can help you find the right path around the course in less time.

Constant Radius Corners

A corner which can be defined by one radius, like Turn 7 at Sebring, is a constant radius turn (Fig. 3-3). Here, the inside edge of the road has a 100-foot radius which doesn't change from the beginning of the corner to the end. In such a corner the apex is close to the mid point, around halfway from turn-in to track-out.

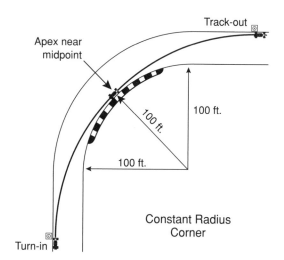

Fig. 3-3. In constant radius corners, start looking for the apex around the midpoint of the turn.

When you first go out on the circuit, don't waste your time starting with a late apex 7/8 of the way around the corner. Look for the apex slightly later than the midpoint and use your knowledge of symptoms to refine your reference points.

Constant radius turns aren't restricted to 90 degrees. They can be from 10 degrees to about 120 degrees (over about 120 degrees, a corner becomes a hairpin turn).

Decreasing Radius Corners

A decreasing radius corner is one where the radius of the later part of the turn is smaller than that of the entry (Fig. 3-4). In these types of corners the apex is further along than the halfway point—a later apex. If you

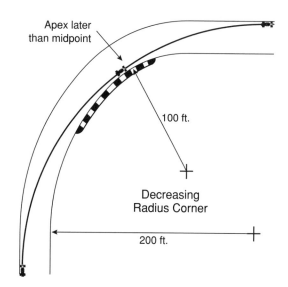

Fig. 3-4. If the corner has a decreasing radius, look for the apex later than the halfway point.

thought it was easy to early-apex constant radius corners, wait till you try one of these.

Increasing Radius Corners

If the radius of the first half of the corner is smaller than that of the exit, you've got an increasing radius corner on your hands (Fig. 3-5). The apex will be earlier than halfway through the corner and the turn-in will be earlier than you might guess.

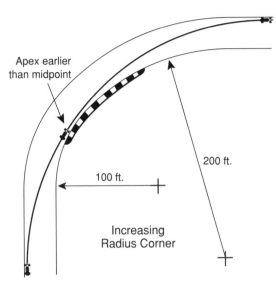

Fig. 3-5. In increasing radius corners, the apex is earlier than halfway through the turn.

Hairpins

When faced with a corner like this, you've got plenty of choices. You could apex it at the midpoint. If you did just that, 90 degrees into a 180-degree corner (Fig. 3-6) with a 100-foot radius, you could get a 130-foot arc good for 44 m.p.h.

The primary problem here is not so much the speed but that with a single constant radius, you can't increase speed at the corner exit. Consequently, exit speed is the same as entry speed: 44 m.p.h.

You could create a bigger radius if you treated the corner less like one 180-degree change of direction and instead divided it into two 90-degree corners. You could create a fast (over 55 m.p.h.) arc into the corner and another fast one out (Fig. 3-7).

The problem here is that you need to "park" the car in the middle part of the corner to get its direction changed. "Park," in this case means slowing to 30 m.p.h. or so. If the big arc can support 55 m.p.h., you could come out of the corner 11 m.p.h. faster than your first approach of apexing the corner in the middle. To take advantage of this approach, you need a car that's capable of going from 30 m.p.h. to 55 m.p.h. quickly. The longer the car takes to accelerate from 30 to 55, the less likely it is to gain an advantage from apexing the hairpin twice.

A good Indy Car car, for example, can accelerate at over 1G—that's 22 m.p.h. per second. It will go from 30 to 55 just fine, thank you. A Formula Vee, on the other hand, powered by a 65-hp motor wouldn't be able to gain back speed at nearly the same rate that it lost it. The wiser thing for the driver of a low-horse-

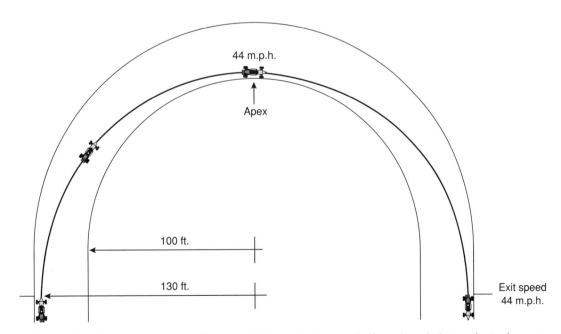

Fig. 3-6. Hairpin corners create dilemmas. Taking a single apex halfway though the turn limits the car to a long period of constant speed cornering.

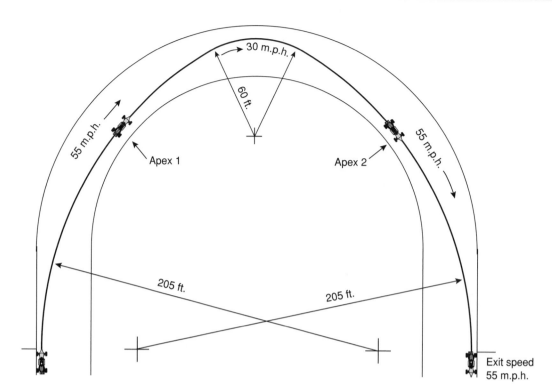

Fig. 3-7. An alternate approach to hairpins is to form two apexes, resulting in potentially higher entry speeds and exit speeds, but often creating a mid-corner section where speed is limited by a tight radius.

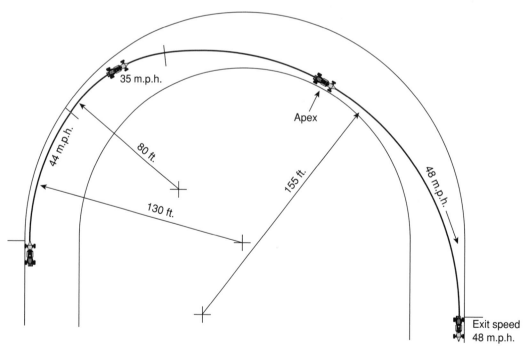

Fig. 3-8. The most common approach to hairpins, especially tight ones, is to form a single late apex that allows higher corner exit speeds, critical if the corner leads onto a long straight.

power car would be to avoid any extreme tightening of the arc. Instead of double apexing the corner, it would be better to begin the hairpin on an arc that would keep the speed up but still allow for an increasing radius arc out of the corner.

The most common approach to hairpins, especially tight hairpins, is to take a single late apex about 3/4 around the corner (Fig. 3-8). Some speed is sacrificed at the entry of the corner but not as much as is lost by using the double apex. The concentration is put on maximizing exit speed and starting the run out of the corner as early as possible at a higher initial velocity.

That doesn't mean you don't double apex 180-degree corners unless you've got more than 600 hp on board. If the 180 is broader, with a radius of several hundred feet and up, the change in direction in the high side of the corner is more subtle, requiring less of a speed loss. Cars other than great accelerators can then take advantage of the entry speed advantages of the double apex without putting themselves at a great disadvantage coming out.

In the 450-foot radius corner pictured in Fig. 3-9, the speed difference required to change the car's direction back toward the second apex is down to 18 m.p.h. compared to a 25 m.p.h. change required in the 100-foot radius example we used earlier. As hairpins get bigger and bigger radii, they begin to fall into the category of "carousels," and the speed change required to get turned down to the second apex gets smaller and smaller.

> "The size of the radius of a hairpin is probably the biggest part of the decision to single or double apex. I can make up my mind pretty quickly by reading how sharp or broad the corner is. If it's fairly tight, I'm going to assume it's a single apex. If it's broad and fast, you try two and see how it works.
>
> "The way I handle a hairpin sometimes depends on the car I'm driving. If the car doesn't have a problem with the direction change in the middle of the corner then I'll try to blast the entry a little bit and slow down in the middle—treat it like an oval where you come in hard, gather it up in the middle, and then come out hard. The Group C car, for example, was not very nimble and didn't respond well to a mid-corner line change so, with that car, you avoided double apexing a hairpin."
>
> —Jeremy Dale

Notice in this illustration that the line in the high part of the corner doesn't go all the way to the outside of the road. The further into the corner you take the original broad arc, the more drastic the change of direction necessary to get the car headed toward the second apex and consequently this portion of the corner has to be slower.

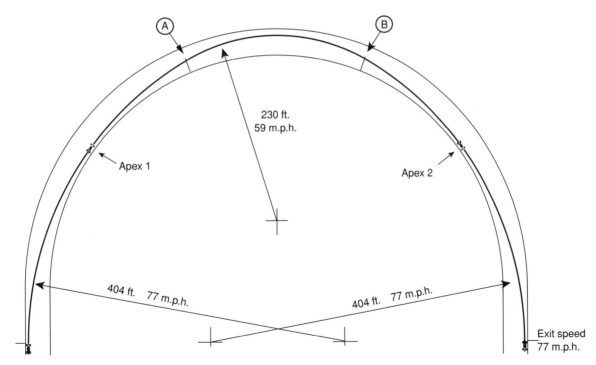

Fig. 3-9. As the radius of the hairpin gets larger, a more subtle radius change in the middle of the corner between point A and point B makes the double apex approach more sensible.

In these diagrams we've been giving radius and speed numbers just for illustration purposes. Clearly, the car doesn't lose speed instantaneously as it moves from one radius to another. What's really going on is that, depending on how you're using the controls, the speed and radius change simultaneously and gradually. On the way into the corner, the speed is going down and the radius is decreasing. At the corner exit, the opposite is happening—you're accelerating and the radius is expanding.

BEYOND GEOMETRY

The shape of corners is going to give you hints about approximately where the apexes are going to be but, especially at speed, the line complications don't end here. When looking for the optimum line, you need to determine where in the corner the car is going to change direction best.

Changing Traction

Generally, in a constant radius corner you'd like to do half of the car's direction change before the middle of the corner and the other half of the direction change after the apex.

This works out fine if the car changes direction as well in the first part of the corner as it does in the second part (Fig. 3-10). In our chalkboard corner, where you can only see the corner as a space between two lines, this seems like a reasonable assumption to make. In real life, however, it's not that simple.

If, for example, the car generates twice as much cornering force in the second part of the corner than it did in the first (Fig. 3-11) it allows you to turn in earlier and carry more speed into the corner on an early-apex line: you can use the superior turning ability late in the corner to change the car's direction and keep it on the road, all at a higher speed than you might think possible.

If, instead, you take the constant radius arc that *appears* to be right based solely on the shape of the corner, you have to go slower at the entry of the corner because of the smaller radius arc that's required to get to the apex— in this case, 13 m.p.h. slower! Turning too late in this instance obligates you to a 54 m.p.h. arc as opposed to a 67 m.p.h. arc if you read the corner correctly.

Here's the general rule for variable cornering force turns: If the car corners better in the *second* half of the corner than the first, the turn-in and apex are likely to be *earlier* than the shape of the corner would dictate. If the car corners better in the *first* half of the corner (see Fig. 3-12) than the second half, the turn-in and apex are likely to be *later* than the shape of the corner would dictate. In this situation you would use the additional grip to get more of the car's direction changed early and to reduce the amount of turning required in the later part of the corner.

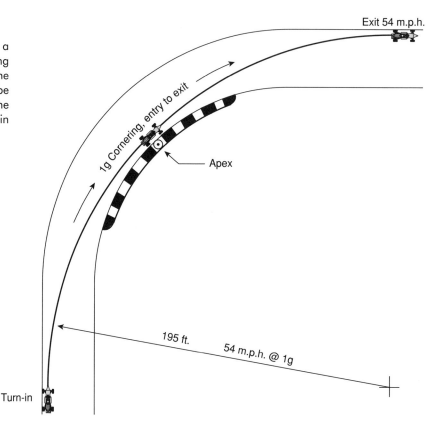

Fig. 3-10. If the car has a consistent level of cornering force, roughly half of the change of direction can be done in the first half of the corner and the other half in the second half of the turn.

1g Cornering, entry to exit

Apex

Exit 54 m.p.h.

195 ft.

54 m.p.h. @ 1g

Turn-in

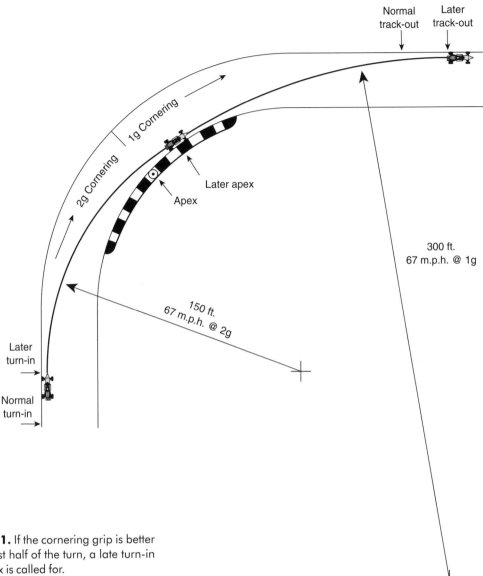

Fig. 3-11. If the cornering grip is better in the first half of the turn, a late turn-in and apex is called for.

There are many things that can change the car's cornering force *during* the corner. Anything that affects the tires' grip on the road qualifies as an influence and has to be considered in choosing the best line through the turn. A short list of factors includes the composition of the racing surface, debris, track temperature, bumps, elevation, and banking.

Racetrack surfaces are seldom perfectly horizontal and any variation from level is going to affect how well the car corners. Let's look at the cornering forces at work on a flat road and then look at how they change when the road is banked.

Fig. 3-13 shows a 1,000-lb racecar turning to the right at its cornering limit. If this were a perfect 1 G racecar, all four tires would be exerting their maximum sideways force, a total of 1,000 lbs, to the right (represented by the bold arrow). Resisting this turning force

is the force of inertia, which essentially wants everything to remain at constant speed or direction. When you force your car to alter its direction, inertia, in the form of centrifugal force, resists that change with an equal force in an opposing direction (represented by the fine arrow pointing left). On a flat road, 1,000 lbs of force generated by the tires is resisted by 1,000 lbs of centrifugal force—everything is in balance.

Banking
But when you change the surface of the road to a banked surface, the balance of forces also changes. Let's put the same 1,000-lb car in a corner where the road is canted 5 degrees toward the apex (Fig. 3-14).

The first thing you need to determine is how hard the tires are now pushing down on the road. As you'll learn in detail in the chapter about tires, there is a di-

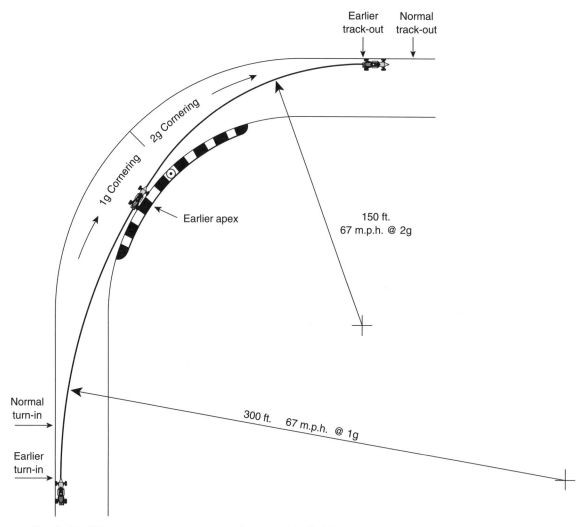

Fig. 3-12. If the cornering grip is better in the second half of the corner, an earlier turn-in and apex can result in higher speed.

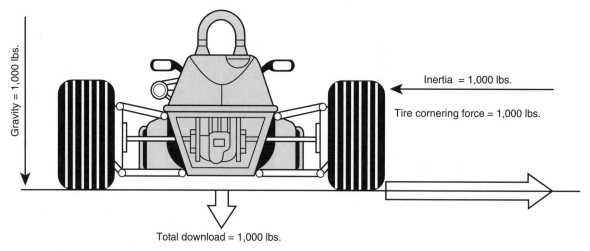

Fig. 3-13. On a perfectly horizontal track surface, the downforce on the tires is purely a function of gravity (excluding aerodynamic effects).

rect relationship between download on the tires and cornering force.

On a flat road, the four tires on this car had 1,000 lbs of download on them and delivered 1,000 lbs of cornering force—a realistic expectation. On 5-degree banking, the car's 1,000 lbs is no longer *all* going toward loading the tires. Using a little trigonometry, you'll find that at 5 degrees, only 996 lbs of the car's mass is loading the tires. Another part of the thousand-pound load, the part represented by the arrow parallel to the road's surface, will actually contribute to the forces acting to change the car's direction.

When you set the car in motion things change again. If the car goes through the corner at a speed which creates 1 G of cornering force—54 m.p.h. in our 195-foot radius of Sebring's Turn 7—the centrifugal force no longer acts in direct opposition to the turning as it did on a perfectly horizontal road surface. Part of the centrifugal force (represented by the bold arrow in Fig. 3-15) is diverted into loading the tires. This force has two components: the downward component perpendicular to the road, which increases grip and limit speed; and the component resisting the change of direction parallel to the road.

On a 5-degree banking in a corner like Turn 7, centrifugal force eventually contributes over 100 pounds of downforce to the tires of a 1,000-lb racecar, providing over 10% better cornering force. That's a lot. Race

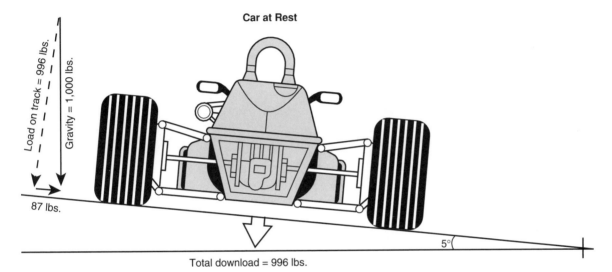

Fig. 3-14. When the road surface is banked, even subtly, the download changes, affecting cornering ability.

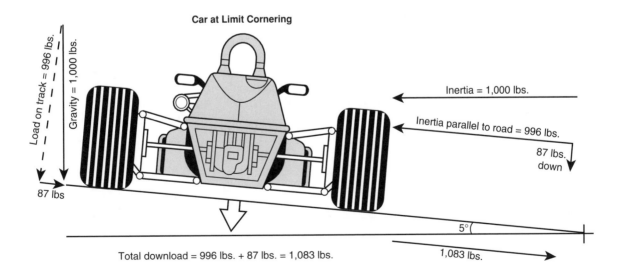

Fig. 3-15. On a banked track surface, a number of effects combine to increase the car's ability to change direction.

car designers would sharpen their mechanical pencils with their teeth for 10% more cornering force. Advantage Number One of banking is that it creates more traction by loading the tires more.

Advantage Number Two is that gravity is helping the car change direction. With a 1,000-lb car, 87 lbs of force is acting parallel to the road surface to help pull the car toward the apex. Picture the road covered with ice. That 87-lb force would move the car sideways from the top of the banking right down to the bottom.

Banking, even subtle degrees of banking (or "road camber"), has a significant effect on the car's cornering limits and the speed at which you can negotiate portions of the circuit. For instance, in our Sebring example, if the corner were banked 5 degrees in the later portion of the turn, your 1 G car could go 59 m.p.h. there as opposed to 54 m.p.h. on a flat corner.

By changing your line so that you could arrive late in the corner at the higher speed, i.e. by turning in early, you could improve both the corner time and the exit speed onto the straight. There are potentially great advantages for noting even subtle changes in road camber. Even one degree of road camber can improve cornering grip by over 3%.

So far we've focused on the positive aspects of road camber, but it's quite common for road courses to have banking that goes the wrong way: what's commonly called "off-camber." If this happens, the double gain that makes banking so wonderful becomes a double loss as the car loses significant traction. The car won't become uncontrollable: it just acts like a car with a lot less grip and will slide around more than expected and consequently use up more road.

Multiple Camber Changes

Sometimes you'll end up with multiple changes in road camber in the same corner. While ovals and some purpose-built road courses are very carefully laid out and surveyed by engineering crews, many older courses were simply paved over the lay of the land. There may or may not be consistency to the road camber from entry to exit of the corner.

The classic example of this is on street circuits where the roads are laid out to accomplish different goals. Most public highways are crowned, higher in the center than on the edges, to help drain rain water toward the gutters. This creates problems for racers that have to negotiate a corner where a cross-section of the road surface looks like it does in Fig. 3-16.

At the turn-in point, the road is off-camber, reducing cornering force at the entry. As the car crosses the middle of the road, the situation improves until at the apex everything is wonderful. Coming away from the apex, the car loses grip as the road camber goes away, ending up at the track-out with a lot less grip than it had just seconds ago at the apex. It's your job to be aware of the different factors that will affect the racecar's performance. Noting road camber changes is part of that job.

Many drivers don't make the effort and the following scene is played out far too often at circuits that have crowned road surfaces. Driver and team set out for a practice day at the unfamiliar circuit to "set the car up." The driver goes out and in ten laps comes in and gives the crew chief the following report: "I dunno. On the corner leading onto the pit straight I can't seem to get the car turned in—it just won't point. Once I manage to get it across the road it's just great at the apex but as I come off the corner on power it skates to the outside and it wants to fly into the weeds at the exit." The crew chief who makes chassis adjustments to solve this "problem" engineers his way to the back of the grid.

On public highways, the typical crown in the road is 4 to 6 inches higher at the center than at the curbs. This would represent at least 1-1/2 degrees off-camber at the turn-in and track-out and 1-1/2 degrees of positive camber at the apex. With a 1 G racecar, the apparent cornering force would vary from .956 G to 1.044 G over the course of the corner. This initially doesn't sound like a big difference but it means that you have 4.5% more traction at the apex and 4.5% less at the turn-in and track-out. That's a 9% spread—something that needs to be considered.

Even permanent circuits need to be considered closely. On "The Downhill" at Lime Rock, a fast right-hander leading onto the straight, the road has 1 degree of road camber at the turn-in. What complicates things is that the turn-in is at the base of the hill. The car becomes heavily loaded, creating gobs of grip—

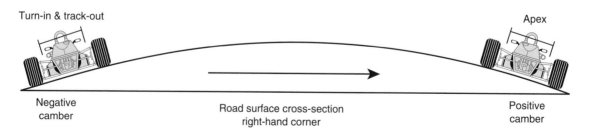

Turn-in & track-out

Apex

Negative camber

Road surface cross-section right-hand corner

Positive camber

Fig. 3-16. Multiple road camber changes throughout the course of a corner can substantially change the car's cornering ability and the driver's choice of line.

"The line can be a difficult thing to teach because it gets complicated, and there's a lot of feel to it. The standard geometric line might not be best because the surface may be bad or the camber is wrong, or there's a crown in the road.

"You've got to go where the grip is. In the Keyhole at Mid Ohio, for example, you'd think you should start out wide, then come in on the apex. We all tried it like that to start, but there was no grip out wide—it was off-camber—so what worked there was just to stay down on the inside to the apex. Doesn't look right, but you've got to be able to learn the line, then adapt to what the track gives you."

—Danny Sullivan

for the moment. The road camber increases as you approach the apex, reaching a maximum of +4-3/4 degrees. Coming onto the straight, the banking falls away to +1-1/4 degrees at the middle of the road to -1-1/2 degrees off-camber at the track-out.

Road Surface Changes

It is easy to assume that the entry of the corner is made of the same stuff as the exit, but you really have to look. Asphalt is expensive, so when it's time to repave, often the racetrack will do the worst sections of the circuit first, sometimes resulting in a corner that has one type of asphalt at the entry (aged, weathered and leaked on) and brand new stuff from the apex out. If the pavement surface will affect the car's traction, it will affect the line. Drivers run into this consideration more often these days with the proliferation of street circuit races. I can recall counting eleven different pavement surfaces at the Meadowlands one year—four different types in one corner alone.

"There's different amounts of grip on different types of pavement surfaces and a lot of it depends on the conditions. The best example, I think, is Mid Ohio where the track is asphalt but there are several cement patches in the middle and exits of corners. Depending on the weather conditions, there's different amounts of grip on those different surfaces. When it's very cold, the asphalt generally has more grip than the cement, so I might take a later, wider, entry in order to get to the asphalt quicker or to spend more time on the asphalt. When it's hot, the asphalt loses grip, where the cement, because it's a lighter color, stays cooler and so it has more bite."

—Bryan Herta

Bumps

For the tires to deliver traction they need to be in contact with the road surface. If the surface of the road at the geometric apex of a corner is terrifically bumpy, causing the tires to be in the air half the time, perhaps staying out of the bumps would create more potential cornering speed than the extra few feet of radius would. Similarly, if the exit of the corner is bumpy, making it difficult to accelerate and turn off the corner, getting more of the direction change done earlier in the corner may help.

Elevation Changes

Changes in elevation during the course of the corner have much the same effect on the line as banking. As a racecar runs into a hill, inertia creates a download on the tires, increasing the tires' traction phenomenally. At our home track at Lime Rock we have one of the classic elevation change corners in the United States in "The Uphill."

To give you an appreciation of the downforce that the Uphill can create, we could have four of our mechanics stand on the rear bulkhead of one of our Formula cars, and their combined weight of 700 lbs would not make the car bottom. But, because of the compressive force of the road going steeply uphill, we have been forced to put skidplates on all of our cars to keep from grinding the bottom of the chassis away.

This downforce creates substantial grip late in the corner and changes the line. As you can imagine, the opposite effect is just as critical. If the car comes over a crest, as it does before the exit of the Uphill, it will reduce traction to nil in some cases. You'd better not be trying to turn the car, and you'll sometimes find that getting the steering wheel dead straight over the crest of a rise may be required.

Slippery Conditions

In most of the situations we have been dealing with you can anticipate the change in the line through the corner by doing some advance homework—looking for road camber changes, differing pavement surfaces, varying shapes of corners. Often, however, the need to make an alteration to your standard line comes up rather suddenly. Anything that can make the racetrack slippery can affect the line. The list includes sand, mud, dirt, leaves, water, anti-freeze and—the worst—oil. Rain is a special sort of slippery condition which we'll cover in detail in the chapter about rain driving.

Say, for example, you are coming up to Turn 7 at Sebring and, looking to the left as you approach your braking point, you catch out of the corner of your eye an unusual motion followed by a cloud of dust. You have four seconds to gather the facts, plan and execute your response. Clearly, you have to be prepared to alter the line through the corner, but before you even turn the steering wheel, your response should be

Fig. 3-17. Elevation changes can increase or decrease grip dramatically. Here, Jeremy Dale lifts the front tires off the ground at the top of the "Uphill" at Lime Rock.

to slow down. It sounds almost too obvious to mention, but it's a fundamental truth about racing. Racers are intent on maximizing their speed at every opportunity and tend to forget that sometimes it's wise to slow down when things start to go badly.

Many novice drivers overreact and slow the car to a crawl, often creating more havoc behind them as other drivers stack up accordion-style. A car that can brake at 1 G (a pretty common racecar) can lose 2.2 m.p.h. per tenth of a second, so braking just a tenth of a second earlier can put you at the turn-in point over 2 m.p.h. slower than a normal lap. Two tenths of a second earlier gives you almost 5 m.p.h. of cushion.

Sometimes you don't see the incident that caused the traction change. Here's where good corner workers can save you. A yellow and red striped flag displayed at the entry to the corner means that there is either debris or a slippery condition in the corner. Don't second-guess the flag. It's not a command to slow down, but it's valuable information and you'd be a fool to ignore it.

Once you've handled the braking, you have to decide how to modify your line. If the traction is affected more in one half of the corner than another, the alteration of the line would follow the same guidelines you used in variable cornering force turns. The only difference is how fast you need to decide.

Most of the time, the line change in these situations is to apex the corner later. Most spins have their conclusions at or past the apex, so you're more likely to see sand and dirt and lose traction late in the corner. Occasionally, drivers *will* spin under braking, mucking up the first part of the corner. The correct re-

sponse would be to stay inside the muck if you can, early apexing. Going in early is going to require more turning late in the corner, so slow down.

In conditions where the track "lubricant" has come from another car (anti-freeze, oil, or a combination), how it affects the line depends upon whether the car dumped all its fluids in one place or dribbled it out a bit at a time, coating the entire racetrack (on the line, of course).

If it's all in one corner, you make a line adjustment based on where the spill is. If it's all over the racetrack, you'll need to alter not only the line in the corner but also the braking zones on the approach to the turn. Either way, you have to switch from maximizing your radius to maximizing your grip.

You'll want to slow for the corner on dry pavement, and the greater the speed loss required for the corner, the more important in terms of lap time this will be. At some point you'll have to cross the greasy stuff, but you'd like the crossing to be as quick as possible, so you may drive diagonally toward the outside, making as perpendicular an intersection as possible. Expect that the first turn of the steering wheel into the corner may not change the car's direction much—the tires will pick up some coating as they cross the slick. As it wears off, the car will bite better and better.

The next task is to get the car's direction changed and accelerate away from the corner, knowing that you'll have to cross the slick again. This is one of those times when reading the tach at the corner exit becomes a big help as you try different paths to see which yields the greatest exit speed. Use the dry, abrasive pavement to get the turning done, straighten the wheel as much as possible, and get across the greasy stuff as quickly as you can, modulating the throttle all the while to avoid excessive wheel spin. It ain't pretty.

Changing Back
Once some substance makes the racetrack slippery, it doesn't necessarily last forever. Dust and dirt blow away quickly, especially if there is a big field of cars racing, so your alteration to the dry line may last only a few laps.

Water and coolant tend to stay around longer, but on a hot, sunny, windy day, it too may have a short-lived effect. Oil is pretty persistent: it hangs around for a long time. However, we've seen racetracks that were undrivable get back within one to two percent of their pre-spill lap times within a half hour. As the conditions are changing, the good drivers are gradually working their way back to the dry line using the symptoms of early and late apexing and reading their exit speeds to define what the best line is under present conditions.

THE WHOLE RACETRACK

So far we've been looking at each corner as if it were the only turn on the course. You can't afford to make this assumption. In fact, not all corners were created equal. A particular corner's placement on the course, where it leads to and what precedes it, may also affect the line you choose to drive through the corner.

In Fig. 3-18, you have two simple constant radius 90-degree corners. Choosing the biggest radius arc through the first would make it impossible to take the biggest radius arc through the second. What to do?

Compromise Corners
In order to answer the question, you need to decide which of these corners, the right or the left, has the greatest effect on your total lap time when driven on the biggest radius arc.

The first thing you need to know is where the second corner leads. If it leads onto a long straight, you would like to carry as much speed as possible away from the corner and minimize the time it takes to get to the braking zone for the next turn. This is the case here. Given the choice to drive on the big arc in the

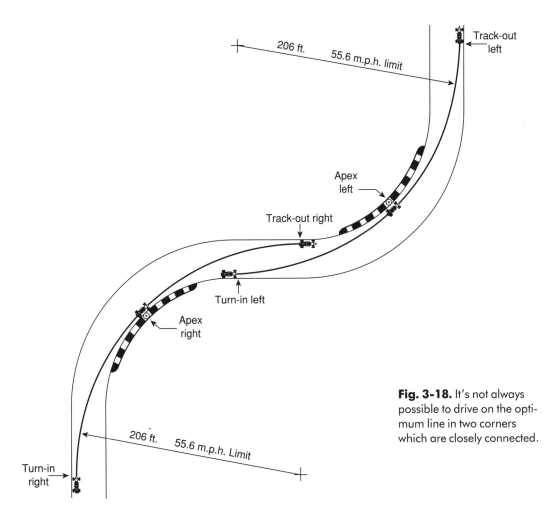

Fig. 3-18. It's not always possible to drive on the optimum line in two corners which are closely connected.

> *"Once you realize a corner is a compromise corner, then it turns into a discipline corner. I almost always find that it's easier to go faster on the wrong end. The fact that you could do the first corner really fast will make you feel like you're quick—but then you blow the second corner and subsequently you're down the straightaway slower."*
>
> —Dorsey Schroeder

right and a smaller arc in the left or a smaller arc in the right followed by a big arc onto the straight, the latter choice is the best.

In this case, you make a conscious decision that, for the sake of a better overall lap time, you make a compromise—you drive on a tighter (read slower) arc through the right-hander so that you can position the car at the right side of the road at the entry of the left and get the biggest radius (read faster) arc through the left and onto the straightaway.

This series of corners, the right closely followed by the left, is called a "compromise esse." Any corner where you would make a decision to drive a line different from the optimum big-radius line in order to ac-

commodate another corner is called a compromise corner. In this first example (Fig. 3-19), the first corner, the right, is completely compromised in order to place the car in position to take the left.

Incomplete Surrender

You don't *always* completely surrender one corner in favor of another. Let's extend the straight between these corners (Fig. 3-20). Now there's enough room between the turns to let the car come out from the inside edge of the road a quarter of the way and still get back to your turn-in point for the left hander.

By using more road, you've increased the radius of the right, allowing you to take the right a little faster—in this case, at 49 m.p.h. rather than at 47 m.p.h. As the straight between these two corners gets longer, the right has to be compromised to a lesser and lesser extent. At some point you'd be able to run the normal line through the right and still be able to hustle the car over to the turn-in point to the left—the series of corners would no longer be a compromise situation.

The important point here is that some corners are strategically more important than others. We'll discuss this soon in more detail but, before we leave this compromise esse, we should explore other facets of the compromise corner.

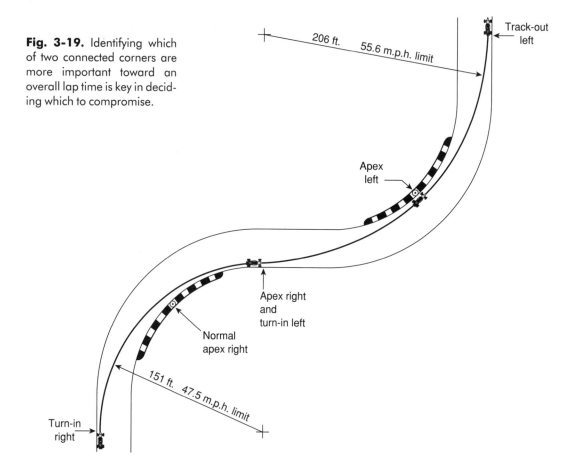

Fig. 3-19. Identifying which of two connected corners are more important toward an overall lap time is key in deciding which to compromise.

Track-out left

206 ft. 55.6 m.p.h. limit

Apex left

Apex right and turn-in left

Normal apex right

151 ft. 47.5 m.p.h. limit

Turn-in right

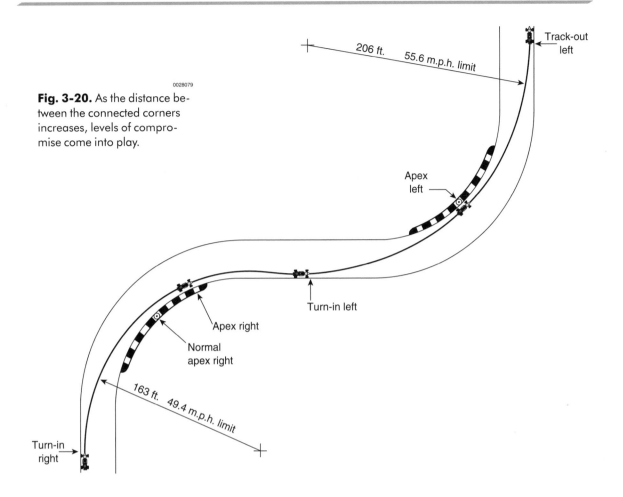

0028079

Fig. 3-20. As the distance between the connected corners increases, levels of compromise come into play.

206 ft.   55.6 m.p.h. limit

Track-out left

Apex left

Turn-in left

Apex right

Normal apex right

163 ft.   49.4 m.p.h. limit

Turn-in right

One Line Fits All?

We're often asked whether the line is the line—whether the arcs at low speed in a school race car are the same arcs Indy Car drivers use on the same circuit. The answer is generally yes, with an explanation. All racecars have their strengths and weaknesses. The primary variable, though not the only one, is the ability of the car to accelerate. Let's go back to the compromise esse again to see how horsepower can change the line you'd choose.

If you fully compromise the right-hander by taking a very late apex, you would have to run a small radius to get there—in this case, a radius that would have a maximum speed of 47.5 m.p.h. By doing so, as you saw in Fig. 3-19, you make it possible to drive through the left on an arc that would support 55.6 m.p.h. A car with a lot of horsepower will go from 47 m.p.h. to 55 m.p.h. pretty quickly. Herta's line through this esse with his Indy Car would be this kind of compromise.

This path wouldn't necessarily be the best for a racecar like a Formula Vee, a single seater powered by a 65 hp four-cylinder Beetle engine. If you slowed to 47 m.p.h. for the right-hander and accelerated as hard as you could through the left the car would only gain, say, 4 m.p.h. because of its limited ability to accelerate

(as in Fig. 3-21). Although the arc through the left would support 55.6 m.p.h., the car can't get there.

The better compromise for the acceleration-limited car would be to move the apex for the right hand part of the esse *earlier*. This would increase the radius of the right and decrease the radius through the left. This might be a 49 m.p.h. right followed by a 53 m.p.h. left, as in Fig. 3-22. This approach would be 2 m.p.h. faster at the exit of the left than simply appropriating the Indy car line.

GRADING CORNERS

In deciding which corners to compromise, you made a judgment that the corner leading onto the straight was more important than the preceding turn. It's crucial to identify the relative importance of corners on the racetrack.

The first thing to do is to take an overall look at the racetrack and identify the most important corner. Ask yourself where you would most like to have one more mile per hour. One more mile per hour would do you the most good entering the longest period of full acceleration. If you start that acceleration one m.p.h. higher, you'll carry a 1.46 foot per second advantage every second the car is gaining speed.

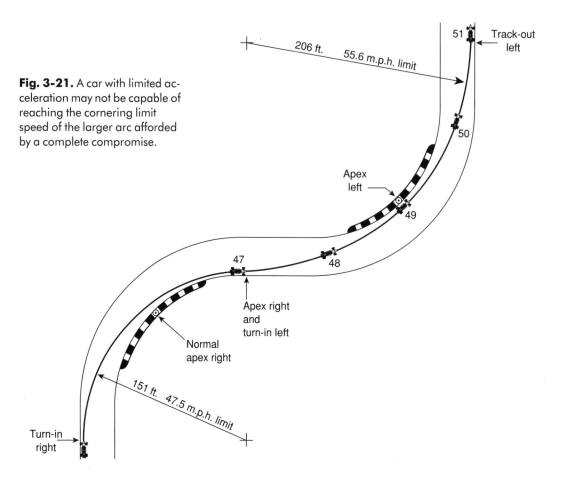

Fig. 3-21. A car with limited acceleration may not be capable of reaching the cornering limit speed of the larger arc afforded by a complete compromise.

Onto the Longest Straight

When trying to decide which corner to concentrate on most, the corner that leads onto the longest period of effective acceleration is a good starting point. Next is the corner that leads onto the second longest period—next, the third—on and on until you identify the least important corner in terms of exit speed. This grading system is a way to help put your effort in a place where it is most likely to be rewarded.

Fast Corners

There is also a very good argument for putting a high value on fast sweeping corners. The logic involves a number of considerations. The first is that a fast, 90+ m.p.h. turn is a much more intimidating corner to do right on the car's limit. It is much more comfortable sliding through a 50 m.p.h. corner than it is to be on the brink of control at over 90 m.p.h. Consequently, fewer drivers in the field will do the faster corner at its limit. If you are one of the ones that works at generating the confidence it takes to do fast corners at the limit, you'll gain an advantage over the rest.

The second argument is that, since the speed is higher, any percentage loss in potential speed through the turn will represent a higher number. If you can drive at 99% of the car's potential cornering speed,

you are .5 m.p.h. below the peak in a 50 m.p.h. corner. In a 90 m.p.h. corner you will be close to a full 1 m.p.h. slower than you could be. Also consider that faster corners are longer than slow corners and if you're right on the limit, carrying that extra 1 m.p.h. over your competitors, you carry that speed over a longer distance than you would in a slower, shorter corner.

Type I, II, Or III

Another system of grading corners is one used by Alan Johnson in his book entitled *Driving in Competition*. Alan points out that there are really three types of turns: turns that lead onto straights, turns at the end of straights, and turns that lead to turns. Turns that lead onto straights he calls Type I turns—turns where exit speed is the most important consideration and therefore would more likely be driven with a later apex to allow for the aggressive acceleration needed to enter the straight at the highest possible speed.

Type II corners are corners at the end of straights and, in order to keep your straightaway speed as long as possible, can frequently be driven with an earlier apex. That way, you can aggressively brake and turn the car down past the apex, not worrying about throttle application and exit speed. If a corner can be a

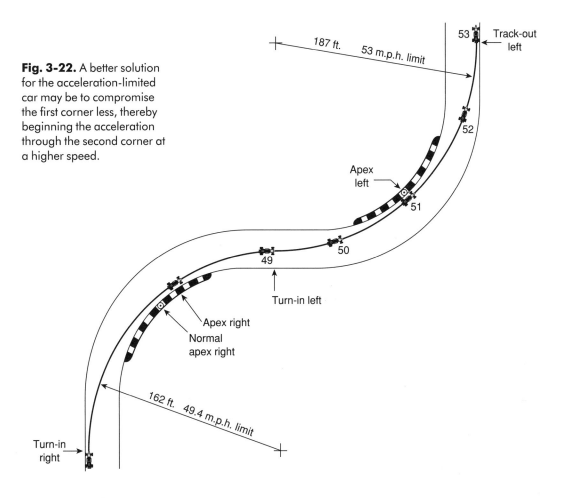

Fig. 3-22. A better solution for the acceleration-limited car may be to compromise the first corner less, thereby beginning the acceleration through the second corner at a higher speed.

Type I *or* Type II, it should be treated as a Type I because there is a lot more time spent accelerating from the corner out than decelerating from the braking point in.

The Type III corner is one that leads to another turn. In our example of a compromise esse, the right-hand corner, even though it came at the end of a straightaway, would be considered a Type III, one that needs to be sacrificed for the benefit of a Type I.

KNOWLEDGE IS SPEED

This system of analyzing the corners of the racetrack and making decisions about their relative importance can help prepare you for finding the optimum line *without pushing the starter button of your racecar.* Bill Prout, one of our first instructors and a long-time competitor in a variety of road racing classes, once made the foolish mistake of dividing his annual Formula Atlantic budget by the number of times during the year he pushed the starter button. The resulting dollar-per-start figure was depressingly high, but it's a good reminder that anything you can do to improve

your driving performance without pushing the starter button is valuable indeed.

We've covered many details having to do with the racing line and how to find it. The line, especially if you're fascinated by geometry and mathematics, can be an intriguing subject to play around with. For the sake of clear understanding, we've made some simplifications in the diagrams we've presented. We've drawn constant radius arcs where we've admitted that an absolutely accurate illustration of the car's path through the corner would be on paths with constantly changing radii.

We were tempted to create a computer model that would draw arcs of both decreasing and increasing radii depending on a car's specific braking and accelerating ability and how the driver was using a particular combination of braking and cornering or accelerating and cornering. But for what? In real life you drive a car on a particular path because there are sound logical reasons to choose one route over others. You temper that logic with what the car is telling you as you drive it. What's important is to have the available knowledge and to use it to find a route around the course that takes the least amount of time.

The Key Points

The key points to remember about the line are:

1) The path the car takes determines the limit of both your cornering speed and, since it affects your corner exit speed, your ultimate straightaway elapsed time.

2) Unless there is a good reason not to, use all the road at the turn-in, apex and track-out.

3) There are symptoms for both early and late apexing. Know them and respond to what the car is telling you about the righteousness of your path.

4) The best line can change from moment to moment, from day to day, and from car to car.

5) The line is seldom a constant radius arc but such an arc is an adequate approximation, especially when you're at the very beginning of the process of finding the line.

"I find that I'm not always right when, ahead of time, I pick what I think are going to be the most important corners—the ones that hold the most potential time in them. Traditional theory has it that the corner leading onto the longest straight is one of the most important. But my experience has found that there are definite exceptions to that. I end up concentrating more on corners leading onto straights initially to find lap time, but as I start driving the circuit I find that certain corners hold more time in them, even though they don't lead onto straights—sometimes a lot more than you would think. Faster corners in general, I find, have the most time in them.

"The way I pick up on it is when we make a change to the racecar and it improves the car in a certain corner more than others and we make a big jump in lap time. I know that the car felt better in only a couple of corners and maybe those corners weren't the ones where I thought there was a lot of time to be gained. Suddenly you realize that there was more time in those corners than you gave them credit for. If I can get better through these corners I'm going to find even more time.

"It's a constant process. Human nature is that you try the hardest in the corners you think you're doing the best in. The corners that you think you're getting through well, you feel comfortable and confident in trying different things and pushing harder. I think it takes a little more of a conscious effort in corners where you're having problems, to look outside of yourself and ask yourself if there's something different you need to do with the car. Is there something different I need to do with my approach to the corner?"

—Bryan Herta

CHAPTER 4

MASTERING CAR CONTROL

Y OUR BIGGEST WORRY IN racing is losing control of the car. It comes slightly in front of "being bog slow." And, being slow is bad enough, but being slow and out of control is worse.

To be competitive, you have to be willing, even eager, to flirt with the car's limits. The excitement begins when you turn the steering wheel, because you know that if the car isn't sliding you're probably not going fast enough. But once the slide begins, there is always a measure of doubt in your mind as to whether this slide is one that will go too far or is just another of the thousands of perfectly manageable ones that have gone before. With a veteran driver, one with good car control, the doubt is small, the confidence that every slide is controllable is high.

With a novice the doubt is greater, especially if you've spun in the recent past, and greater still if you don't know the reason for the previous spin. Without knowing why it happened and what you might do next time to keep the car under control, spins become random, unexplainable, events. It's like driving around with a bomb in the car that might go off at any moment—or might not.

GENUINE CONFIDENCE IS EARNED

Driving around the racetrack with this doubt hurts your performance in the car. You're going to be slower since you don't dare do anything that makes the car go faster, lest it fly off the road. Some would call this prudence and, while some people live quite happily with the motto "don't take a chance" they are not often successful racers.

This is not to say that cautiousness is all bad. A worse response to the anxiety is to pump up your confidence unrealistically—to use bravado to urge yourself to go faster. It doesn't work. If you don't have the skill required to control a sliding car, feigned bravery will only result in more spins, more loss of control.

> Racers use steering, throttle, and braking to keep a racecar in control at its limit. Data collection can help pinpoint solutions to car control problems.

Confidence in your car control comes from having the experience of sliding the car and bringing it back from the edge of loss of control by making the right moves. By practicing and getting good at it, even if you're inclined to be timid, you will be more willing to stretch the limits. If you're overly brave, you will do better by learning that it is skill that lowers lap time and not the willingness to sacrifice your car and yourself to the barriers.

> "You've got to take small steps to find out where the limit is. You have to learn that fine line of where the car starts to break loose and learn to control it. But, to spin to find the limit? Not on a damned oval, you don't."
>
> —Danny Sullivan

The "Necessity" of Spins

There is an attitude in the sport that spins—losses of control—are a necessary, even a beneficial, part of driving racecars. We strongly disagree. Any loss of control puts you in a position where what happens to you and your car is purely a matter of luck. With good luck the car spins down the middle of the road and you don't hit anything and nobody hits you and you drive away unscathed. With bad luck you hit something solid at high speed, and the results can be fatal.

Don't kid yourself. Although motor racing has gotten much safer in the last decade, you're driving lightweight vehicles at high speed and bad things do happen. Bad things happen less often to drivers who maintain control of their cars.

When it comes to driving faster than the rest, under complete control, it would be good to use Rick Mears as a role model. When Rick retired in 1993 he had run 15 years at Indianapolis, qualified on the pole (faster than 32 to 40 of the country's fastest drivers) six times, was on the front row eleven times, won the race four times, and, in all that time, spun and hit the wall twice—both times because of a mechanical failure. Spinning is not necessary for success—just ask Rick.

Spinning is evidence of failure to accomplish the most basic role of a race driver: keeping the car on the road.

> "I just don't think spinning the car trying to find the limit works. How do you measure the limit? If you're going backwards into the wall you've exceeded the limit, okay, but what do you learn from that?
>
> "I understand how it feels in the car when you've overstepped the amount of traction or grip you've got. That's how I know you've passed the limit. I don't get what revolving gets for you. I don't get it. Some guy goes flying off the road, then says "Well, that's too fast." What's he do, go back and look at where the speedometer needle stuck on impact?"
>
> —Skip Barber

Finding the Limit
Some would say, "You can't find the limit is if you don't go over it from time to time and spin." Nonsense.

You find the limit by taking small bites, experimenting with a little higher entry speed, a little earlier throttle application. Carrying more speed on the same arc will create a greater angle of slide, which might be faster, or might scrub off speed, making you slower. You don't need to spin to find this out.

Perhaps more entry speed makes the car wander wide of the best line and you need to give up some throttle on the exit of the corner to keep the car on the course. Again, you found the limit without losing control. When your car control is good you don't worry so much about spinning as you do about doing something in the corner that will cost you speed. Control is never in doubt.

> "The mistake, going over the limit, makes the car go too far sideways and you correct it, and the car comes out of the corner slower. You blew the corner, but not the car. To lose it you're taking too big a bite, or you don't have the skill to recognize a mistake and fix it. You've got to know you have a problem then know how to solve it. If you have to be going backwards to know you made a mistake, you're not too smart."
>
> —Skip Barber

Redefining Oversteer, Understeer, and Neutral

In our chapter on the three basics we introduced the fact that cars cornering at the limit of adhesion can do so with three different attitudes: understeer, oversteer, and neutral. In understeer, the front tires reach their cornering limit before the rears; in oversteer, the rear tires reach the limit first. In cornering a neutral car at the limit, both front and rear tires operate at their cornering limits and the car as a whole, since all four tires are contributing their fair share of the cornering load, generates its best cornering force.

Each of our illustrations of understeer, oversteer and neutral steer had one thing in common: the nose of the car was pointed in a direction *inside* the line defining the arc the car was traveling on.

Yaw Angle
When the car is pointed in a different direction than its direction of travel it is developing "yaw." Yaw is a phenomenon we see whenever cars change direction, whether it's at the cornering limit or in everyday street driving. Sometimes this yaw angle is relatively small, especially when dealing with low cornering forces, but sometimes, as with sprint cars on a dirt track, the car is pointing in an entirely different direction than the direction it is traveling. This can be entertaining to watch, and either exciting or terrifying when you're behind the wheel.

In Fig. 4-1, the car is turning right on an arc with a 100-foot radius. At any given instant its direction of travel is represented by a line tangent to the arc at the car's center. This line is called the car's "instantaneous direction of travel." The "yaw angle" of the car in this diagram, 10 degrees, is simply the angle between the direction of travel and the centerline of the racecar.

While it's impressive to watch cars being driven at large yaw angles, racers need to use just enough yaw angle to help the car go faster; spectacular slides, although they look so, aren't necessarily fast.

Slip Angle
"Slip angle" is the direction the wheel rim is pointing versus the direction the tire is traveling. The simple distinction is that slip angles refer to tires while yaw angle refers to the whole car.

Take a look at Fig. 4-2. This race car is cornering at its limit on a 100-foot radius arc. At the particular instant that this illustration captures, the driver has the steering wheel straight ahead. It might have been turned more to the right an instant before, or it might have been turned more left—not important. Now it's dead straight.

Let's draw a line in the center of each tire representing the direction each wheel rim is pointing. Here we'll say that each wheel is aligned perfectly with the

Fig. 4-1. A vehicle's yaw angle is the angle between the direction it is pointing versus the direction it is traveling.

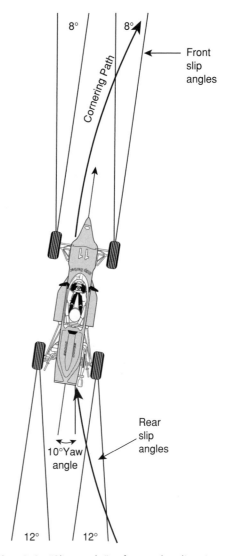

Fig. 4-2. "Slip angle" refers to the direction the wheel rim is pointing versus the wheel's path over the surface of the road.

centerline of the car, although with real cars this is often not the case due to toe-in or toe-out of the wheels.

To measure the slip angle of the tires, compare the direction the wheel is pointing to the direction the tire is traveling. The direction of travel of the tire is a line tangent to the 100-foot arc of the corner *at the tire*.

When you measure the difference between the tangent (the direction it is traveling) and the centerline of the wheel rim (the direction it is pointing), you find that the slip angle of the rear tires is 12 degrees.

At the front, the slip angle turns out to be eight degrees. It is slightly different from the rear because the front tires are eight feet further around the corner, and so the tangent lines differ by four degrees.

You can also see from this illustration that if you really wanted to be accurate about the slip angle of

each tire, you would have to draw radius lines to each tire's contact patch and take any toe changes into account in your measurements.

For our purposes, it is enough to know that slip and yaw are different and that, for a given amount of yaw, the front tires need to add angle to the inside of the turn to match the yaw angle, and that the slip angle of the rear tires is slightly larger than the yaw angle.

Slip angle also varies with corner radius. The deflection of the fronts inward needs to increase as the radius gets smaller and decrease as the radius gets larger. The slip angle of the rear tires will be proportionately larger than the yaw angle in tight radius turns than it will be in large radius turns.

Redefining Attitude

Up to now we defined understeer and oversteer in terms of which end of the car "slides" first. While this is an okay conceptual way of describing the sensation, it's not really true. A car doesn't need to slide to exhibit understeer or oversteer. A tire doesn't necessarily have to be at its cornering limit to encounter slip angles.

Even at low speeds and cornering loads, cars develop slip angles at the front and rear tires. Consequently the car as a whole develops a yaw angle. At low loads the slip and yaw angles are small, but they're there. A more accurate way of defining a car's cornering attitude at both low speeds and high is to compare the slip angles of the front and rear tires.

New Definition of Understeer

If the slip angles of the front tires are greater than the slip angles of the rears, the car is understeering. The sensation you'll get is that, relative to previous experience, the front wheels are pointing further into the corner than they should be considering the direction the car is pointed. In Fig. 4-3, the first car is in a classic state of understeer. The slip angle of the front tires is at 14 degrees, and the slip angle of the rear tires is at 6 degrees. The overall yaw angle is a modest 4 degrees.

New Definition of Oversteer

In the middle of Fig. 4-3, the same car is oversteering. The slip angles of the rear tires is at 16 degrees, the yaw angle of the car is at 14 degrees and, typical of this

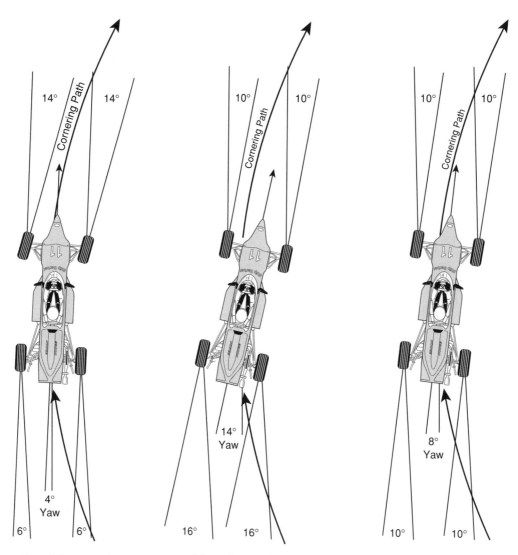

Fig. 4-3. An understeering car will have larger slip angles at the front tires than at the rear. An oversteering car will have larger slip angles at the rear tires than at the front. A neutral handling race car will corner with all four tires operating at the same slip angle. For maximum cornering force this slip angle will be in the range where the tires create maximum grip.

oversteer attitude, the front wheels are turned slightly left with a slip angle of 10 degrees.

Neutral Yields the Best Grip

Of the two cornering attitudes, the oversteering car certainly *looks* faster than the understeering car. The best cornering speed, however, doesn't come from either of these setups.

In the chapter on tires, you'll find that the ultimate cornering grip available from a tire comes in a narrow range of slip angle. The best slip angle will vary from tire to tire and car to car but, for now, let's say that you get the best traction when the tires operate at a 10 degree slip angle. In Fig. 4-3, the car with the most total grip, and consequently the highest potential cornering speed, is the car on the far right. The front and rear tires are operating at 10 degrees of slip, at their peak cornering traction, and since the slip angles are the same, the car is said to be "neutral."

Remember, though, that the car is neutral but it still has some yaw. Many drivers mistakenly think that a neutral car simply tracks around the corner with zero yaw. It doesn't. Neutral simply means that the front and rear slip angles are matched, hopefully in the range where the tires deliver the most traction.

Cornering Balance Is Fluid

A frequent mistake is to use one of these terms to sum up a car's cornering behavior. Pronouncements like "Porsches oversteer," or "front wheel drive cars understeer," or "mid-engine cars are neutral" are too generalized. The same car can exhibit understeer, oversteer, and neutrality under different conditions, often in the time it takes to drive through one corner. The process is a fluid one where you get a feeling for the right vehicle attitude and manipulate the controls of the car to keep cornering with just the right amount of yaw and slip.

USING THE CONTROLS TO ALTER HANDLING BALANCE

The key is that, although cars have designed-in tendencies toward oversteer, understeer or neutrality, you can change the car's characteristics by using the controls in different ways.

It's always dangerous to generalize, but the following guidelines show the handling effect of different control actions. These rules are for the most common racecar arrangement, rear wheel drive. Front wheel drive cars have some special handling considerations and we'll take a close look at this type of racecar later.

Braking Control

First, let's look at the corner entry, the portion of the turn between the turn-in point and the throttle application point.

> *"I think that the level of slide you use, the amount of yaw that works best, is specific to the car. For example, on a Formula Ford with street radial tires you can get away with a lot of slip angle in the tire without scrubbing much speed, but if you were to put slicks on the car you would have to use a lot less slip angle, or yaw, through the corner.*
>
> *"I think that the tire and the amount of grip determine that. But I haven't changed what I do much. I never used big angles on the car—I just don't throw the car around a lot. I've stuck with that approach and I think it's been more of an advantage as I've moved up.*
>
> *"There are examples of guys who have driven cars crossed up all the way through their careers—Gilles Villeneuve, for example. It's exciting to watch and sometimes I wish I drove more that way because it makes you look spectacular, but I don't think a lot of good things come out of that. You're using your tires more, you're heating your tires more and you're putting the car in an unnatural position. Especially with a ground effects car, when you start changing the angle of attack of the car to the airstream, you start losing downforce. Once you start to slide and you're losing downforce too, you're just compounding your own problem.*
>
> *"In an Indy Car, unless it's a very slow corner and the driver's got wheelspin at the exit, you very rarely see big angles on the car. It doesn't help the car go fast."*
>
> —Bryan Herta

A properly biased braking system should have a neutralizing effect on the balance of the car past the turn-in point, reducing the cornering traction of both front and rear tires proportionately. Experience has shown, however, that this general rule can vary widely. Cars with slightly too much front brake bias will tend to understeer at corner entry while cars with slightly too much rear bias will tend to oversteer.

In either case, if the relaxation of brake pedal pressure is gradual; the balance you had when you first turn in will continue to the throttle application point. A snap off the brake pedal will make the car's balance go toward oversteer. Any pause between the brake release and the throttle application will also move the balance toward oversteer since the pause essentially causes trailing throttle oversteer.

Throttle Control

At the corner exit, where you're trying hardest to accelerate the car away from the corner and onto the following straight, gradual applications of throttle tend to create understeer. Abrupt throttle applications, especially with powerful cars and/or limited grip, tend to create oversteer. Lifts off the throttle change the handling in the direction of oversteer. The more abrupt the lift, the more dramatic the effect.

> *"The tires give you the G and it's the driver's job to find how much pedal—either one— he can put down at the time for what he's asking the car to do. It's like asking from second to second, 'Can you take this?'*
>
> *"In real life we have to make up for our errors by adjusting the controls to keep the car on the racing line at close to the best angle."*
>
> —Terry Earwood

Steering Control

Done perfectly, your initial turn of the steering wheel at the turn-in point should initiate a rotation of the car around its center to the point where the vehicle's overall yaw angle is in the range of the tires' optimum slip angle. Ideally, once the car is at this angle, you barely move the steering wheel again as you maintain this perfect angle using the braking and turning ability of the car on the way into the corner, and the accelerating and turning ability on the way out. It can actually happen this way. Honest! Every now and then you do it just right, and it's the stuff grins are made of.

Often you use both the throttle *and* the steering wheel to fix a car control problem. Often you use the brake *and* steering wheel together as well.

ROTATION

As a car enters a corner, it is turning, that is, changing the direction it is traveling, but it is also rotating: as the car goes from zero yaw to whatever yaw angle it's going to operate at in the corner, there has to be some rotation around its center.

Let's use a model to make this phenomenon more clear. First, think of a vehicle that would corner with zero yaw. The best example is a railroad train negotiating a turn. When it is doing so, the centerline of the train and each of its cars would be perfectly aligned with the direction it's going at any instant. As the train enters a corner, it changes direction, but it doesn't develop any yaw. See Fig. 4-4.

Cars are different. To picture how a car both changes direction and rotates into yaw, let's mount a lazy susan on one of the train flat cars and put a racecar in the center of the lazy susan.

If the car were taking the corner without any yaw it would stay perfectly aligned with the train's centerline. Since all cars develop some yaw when cornering,

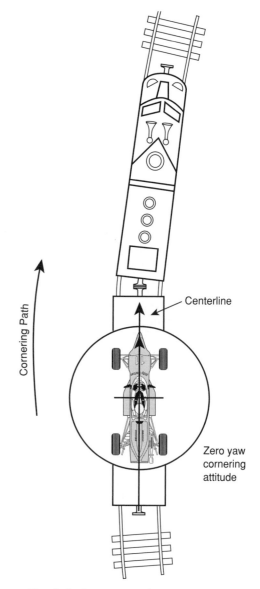

Fig. 4-4. Cornering with zero yaw is akin to taking a corner on rails.

however, the car on the lazy susan will rotate clockwise some time after the turn has begun.

In our race car example we want it to rotate 8 degrees, up to the range where the tire slip angles will be in the area where they make the most traction. At the exit of the corner, the rotation back to zero yaw will be back 8 degrees counterclockwise (Fig. 4-5).

This rotation has magnitude (the size of the angle we rotate to) and velocity (how fast the car rotates).

Your aim is to rotate the car to the best yaw angle at a rotation speed that makes it possible to tightly control the yaw. Cars that rotate fast are typically harder to control than cars with a slower rotational speed.

The struggle is to not over-rotate or under-rotate. Rotation, done right, is a thing of beauty. As the steer-

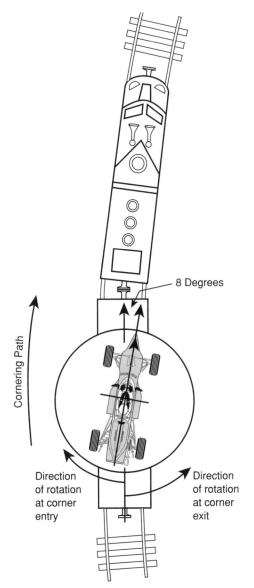

Fig. 4-5. At corner entry the car not only changes direction, it rotates around its center, creating a yaw angle. At corner exit, the rotation is in the opposite direction as the car goes back to zero yaw entering the following straight.

ing wheel is turned, the car not only changes direction, it rotates up to its best yaw angle in a gradual, manageable fashion. The initial steering input frequently has to be adjusted to maintain the proper angle as does the pressure on the brake pedal or throttle.

The control you adjust and the amount of the change depends on whether the car has over-rotated or under-rotated and where in the corner the understeer or oversteer occurs.

OVER-ROTATION

Your aim is to allow the car to slide up to some optimum yaw angle, then hold it there for the duration of the corner if you can. By doing so, you'll be operating the car in a range where the tires deliver their maximum grip; more grip allows you to raise your cornering speed, the ultimate aim of car control. Let's go a step beyond theory and look at some real-life car control problems you'll face when you get going quickly on the racetrack.

Over-Rotating the Corner Entry
On the entry to Turn 7 at Sebring, you turn in a tad too late and pop off the brake pedal just past the turn-in point. The net effect is that the car not only rotates around its center the 7 to 10 degrees it should for optimum grip, it continues to rotate 10 degrees more into severe oversteer (Fig. 4-6). The nose of the car is pointed inside the apex and if you don't do something fast, the car is going to continue rotating until it arrives at the apex backward.

Fig. 4-6. By suddenly releasing the brakes at the turn-in point you create a rotation bigger than needed to maximize the tires' grip.

Sensing the Oversteer
The good driver is already looking at the apex when the steering wheel is first turned, and the first indication of oversteer is the recognition that the nose of the car is pointed too far in for this stage of the corner. The other indicator is the seat of the pants feel, the kinesthetic sense that the motion of this car around its center is too rapid.

Correction
The first reaction is with the hands—dial in opposite lock, steering in the direction that the rear end of the car is trying to go. This is the "correction" phase of skid recovery.

Fig. 4-7. After correcting with opposite lock steering and settling the rear of the car with a subtle application of power, the "pause" at the peak of the slide is the trigger to recover by getting the steering wheel back toward straight.

Settle the Rear

The second, almost simultaneous action should be to settle the rear of the car by transferring weight onto the rear tires. You do this with throttle application—a *little* throttle application. A common mistake here would have been to instinctively jump on the power to save the slide. If you did that, you would have *lost* cornering traction at the rear by asking for too much acceleration traction.

By squeezing on the power, applying 30% throttle or so, you move load to the rear and cancel the engine braking effect of the abrupt snap off the brakes.

The Rotation Stops

The car begins to recover. The rotation around the center slows, then stops from the steering wheel correction and the throttle application. You're in the eye of the storm. The rotation has paused at its peak. This is the "pause" phase, your cue to start taking out the opposite lock.

The Need for Recovery.

Now the rotation starts back the other way, counterclockwise, reducing the car's overall yaw angle. If you don't take the left steering out fast, you'll get caught with the car back at zero rotation, a lot of load on the right tires and the steering wheel turned left. You'll have saved the clockwise slide but gotten caught by the reaction of the rear rotating counterclockwise—you'll end up spinning in the opposite direction

This time you do it right and quickly get the wheel back to center following the pause: you successfully dissipate the rear end's momentum back toward the right. The car settles down with an overall yaw angle less than you would have liked, but you didn't spin.

Back to Business

As it settles you take the throttle on toward the floor, feeling just how much it will take without getting the rear out again. Total time of the event: 2.1 seconds from turn-in to recovery. Total time lost relative to your best job through Turn 7 is .15 seconds slower, with a corner exit speed 1 m.p.h. lower.

Saved But Not Forgotten

You saved the situation on this pass by using good car control skills, but you don't want to do this on every corner. First, it's slower, and second, you don't want

Fig. 4-8. The car is back to a sensible yaw angle at the apex and what might have been a spin is merely tenths of seconds lost on this particular lap.

to go to the well too often. The bucket only has to come up empty once.

Driving away from Turn 7, a good driver would be doing a quick analysis of what went wrong so that something different can be done on the next lap to avoid the mistake: in this case, turn earlier and relax the braking pressure more slowly so that the car doesn't over-rotate.

There's pressure to squeeze in this self-analysis in a short period of time. You don't want to be preoccupied with the Turn 7 error as you enter Turn 8. We see it all the time. A driver has a "moment" in a corner, gets rattled or preoccupied with the mistake, and goes off in the next turn. You have to put the mistake behind you. Try to figure out what went wrong, when time allows, but crank up the concentration for each corner. Of course, the pressure and the potential for choking vary widely.

> *"It's always the case that when you make a mistake, it's over, it's done with, you have to put it behind you. It's hard to do. I actually find it easier to do if I'm racing with someone rather than alone. Little mistakes are like warning shots for me: 'That was a close call—you've got to pay attention—be alert.'"*
>
> *—Danny Sullivan*

Choke Etiquette

If this were a practice session, the amount of time you lost would be no big deal. But on the last lap of a race with a competitor on your gearbox, it's a whole different story. The frustration level can go through the ceiling when, through a simple mistake, you've given away a race.

This situation calls for emotional self-discipline. You've got to concentrate on driving and avoid the temptation to punch the steering wheel or hit yourself in the helmet. There is always time in the race to do something even dumber than you just did, and you don't want your agitation to get you into another mistake. You have to remind yourself that it could have been worse. You could have spun or crashed. You could have been running 14th. Try to be mature, at least until you park the car in the pits. Then you can throw your gloves at the dashboard and kick rocks around the paddock.

A Closer Look at Over-Rotation

In this example the causes of over-rotation were a late turn-in coupled with a violent snap off the brake pedal. Either could have caused the oversteer, but the pop off the brake pedal guaranteed that oversteer would be the end result of the late turn-in.

> *"If someone hits you and puts you off, you get really pissed. If you spin by yourself and miss your opportunity, then you're pissed at yourself. One is more anger, the other is more frustration. But either way, you have to take the energy you get from that and focus it on driving the car."*
>
> *—Jeremy Dale*

In a late turn-in, you sense that it's going to be tough getting to the apex, so you instinctively turn the steering wheel more than normal—and more abruptly than normal. What makes the situation worse is that the late turn-in requires an arc of a smaller radius than the proper turn-in; a tighter arc requires lower speed.

If you were ever going to be on or over the limit, this is it. The pop off the brake pedal suddenly relieves the front tires of any braking loads, and since the front tires are still heavily loaded from the weight transfer, they have gobs of cornering power. The snap off the brake also leaves the rear lightly loaded and high in the air. To top it off, unless you go immediately to some power, the engine compression acts as a rear-end brake, which, coupled with the rest, guarantees a sudden rotation toward oversteer.

This certainly is not the only way to get oversteer on the corner entry. Trailing throttle will tend to create many of the same problems: there's load up front to help the front bite, an unloaded rear, and drag on the rear tires from engine compression.

A sudden turn-in can also provoke over-rotation. The load transfer off the inside tires to the outside has an element of impact rather than a smooth transfer. This speeds up the rotational velocity, giving you less time to catch the rotation at a reasonable yaw angle.

A mismatched downshift will really get the rear out, especially at or after the turn-in point. If you chirp the rear tires just when rear end traction is needed for the correct handling balance, the tail may come out too fast for you to catch.

There are also causes other than improper technique. The front-to-rear handling balance of the car, whether it be chassis related or aerodynamic, might be too much in the direction of oversteer. Or perhaps the problem involves too much rear brake bias reducing the cornering grip of the rear tires.

Whatever the reason for the over-rotation, correction, pause, and recovery define the steering solution and transferring load with light throttle handles the footwork.

Over-Rotation by Power Oversteer

Sometimes the entry is just fine but something happens on the way out that gets the car sliding more than you want it to. For example, in your eagerness to begin your run onto the straight as early and as forcefully as possible, you might open the throttle too soon or too abruptly. Let's take a look at Turn 9 at Sebring, the carousel leading onto the longest straight.

On this lap your approach to the corner is routine, decelerating down to about 70 at the turn-in. You continue to decelerate using braking and turning down to 63 m.p.h. at the throttle application point, then you're on it hard, going from zero throttle to full throttle in 30 feet. There was adequate rotation on the

way into the corner but the sudden application of throttle kicks the rear end out to the right, threatening to spin the car.

Correction

Your first reaction is to turn the steering wheel right to try and get the rear back in line. It works at first and you don't lift the throttle as the steering wheel comes back for the recovery. Often this will do the trick and you don't have to use throttle to save the oversteer.

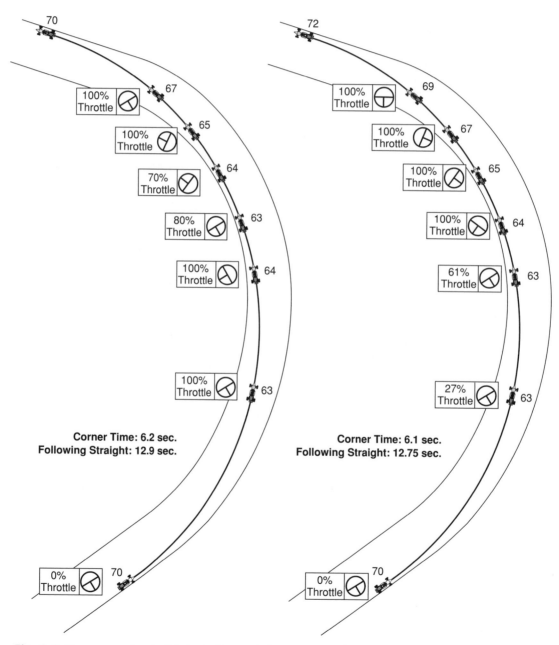

Fig. 4-9. Two approaches to Sebring's Carousel, the one on the left looking spectacular with big opposite lock corrections of power oversteer. The run on the right is more subtle and faster, both in the corner and down the following straight.

Add a Throttle Adjustment

In this particular case, though, the rear end pops out again. This time the countersteer goes past 90 degrees to the right. With a long straightaway to follow, you don't want to surrender any throttle, but at some point it becomes obvious that it's the only recourse.

You've got to be careful here. If you snap off the throttle, instead of restoring grip to the rear tires you would use even more of the rear tires' traction by engine braking. Combine this with unloading the rear tires by lifting, and it's a guaranteed spin. Happens all the time—a big rotation started by too much power, then taken beyond controllability by overreacting and snapping off the throttle.

With the correct amount of breathe, say, to about 70%, the rear tires get better bite, the rotation counterclockwise stops, the pause occurs, and you can start the recovery, getting the steering wheel back to straight, then to the left as the oversteer settles down.

This oversteer run through Turn 9 looked spectacular, but the elapsed time through the turn was a tenth of a second slower than a subsequent run where the throttle was fed in gradually but, once at 100%, stayed there.

More significantly, the interruption of throttle application reduced corner exit speed by 2 m.p.h., which hurt the elapsed time down the following straight and up to the entry to Turn 10 by another .15 sec.

Comparing these two passes also shows you that what looks fast and spectacular is not necessarily the fastest way around. Especially coming onto the longest straight, drivers tend to get greedy about starting the application of power. You can see here that getting the power on early and aggressively, especially in a long corner, has its limits if it forces you to reduce power later in the corner to keep from spinning.

UNDER-ROTATION

As you learned earlier, understeer is an easier car control problem to solve than oversteer. Typically, understeer is caused by the front tires either being overused or underloaded.

The Overused Fronts

"Overused" means that the front pair of tires are often asked to do more of their share of the cornering of the car than the rears.

The majority of cars intended for street use are intentionally designed to understeer at their cornering limit. The thinking is that if an indifferent driver stumbles upon the car's cornering limits they are likely to lift off the throttle, which is exactly the right thing to do to restore grip to the front tires.

This setup is less than ideal for the racetrack, where you'd like the front and rear ends of the car to do their appropriate share of the direction change, allowing your car to get up into its ideal slip angle range.

Even with true racecars with their adjustable suspension systems, the cornering bias frequently ends up toward the front. Oversteer can be intimidating for racers as well as for street drivers, so the car is often adjusted to dial out the sensation of the tail of the car being further out than the nose.

What some drivers don't realize is that a neutral car (one where the front and rear tires are operating in the same range of slip angle) corners with the rear slightly further away from the inside of the corner than the front (refer back to Fig. 4-3). You shouldn't mistake this for oversteer. Many people do and, consequently, there are a lot of racecars out there that suffer from overused front tires and inherent understeer.

Underloaded Fronts

Even if the car does not have built-in understeer, you can provoke it by unloading the front tires: that is, using the controls in a way that reduces the download on the front tires.

The classic way to do this is to turn into the corner and simultaneously apply lots of throttle. If you do it right you can get the steering wheel turned to full lock and *still* not make the apex. Of course, doing this sort of thing routinely will generate tire temperatures off the gauge; the hotter they get, the worse they grip, the more they understeer, the hotter they get—on and on.

The trick is to turn into the corner with some load still on the front of the car, preferably by using the brake pedal past the turn-in point, trying to get the needed rotation up to the car's best slip angle.

In relatively fast corners where there isn't much speed loss required on the entry, the most common problem is getting understeer early in the turn. Two things seem to cause this problem most often. The first is that in a long fast corner, the throttle application point is typically closer to the turn-in than the apex. Drivers, in their never-ending attempt at maximizing exit speed, get greedy about putting the throttle down, unload the fronts and generate understeer.

The second cause is that aggressive throttle application, especially in a low powered car, doesn't have the same traction-robbing effect in higher gears as it does in lower gears. Experience has shown that in the higher gears, this early, abrupt throttle application more often results in unloading the front tires.

Sebring Chicane

A good place to look at this type of problem is in the second turn on the Sebring Test Circuit, the left hand swerve of the chicane. The chicane is made up of a third gear right, Turn 1, immediately followed by a left, Turn 2. You need to compromise the right—that is, take a later apex—so that at the exit of Turn 1 you're on the right side of the road, allowing a big radius through the left.

In our school race cars, you approach Turn 1 at the very top end of third gear, around 98 m.p.h. You brake

> *"After all these years, I was having trouble at Turn 6 in Miami and Roberto Lorrenzutti, who was driving with us, said, 'What a hard corner! you have to be so patient with the power—feeding, feeding, feeding, feeding.' I was trying to turn in and go immediately to lots of power, like a jerk. I teach this stuff every day of my life and still my right foot got the best of me. Next time out I tried just feeding it in, just short of wheelspin, and it was perfect, no correction, no late lifts, no nothing. So now, every corner I'm saying to myself 'feeding, feeding, feeding, feeding.'"*
>
> —Terry Earwood

down to 80 m.p.h. at the corner entry and get right back to full throttle through the apex, up to the turn-in point to the left, Turn 2. You swear you could turn in to Turn 2 without giving up full throttle, but if you do, the front end washes out into understeer and the apex becomes just a fantasy.

The technique that results in the quickest run through Turn 2 is to breathe the throttle just an instant before the turn to the left toward the apex, just enough to settle a little load onto the front tires. If you breathe the throttle back from 100% to 60% or 70% the car actually turns when you commit to the apex. Once it commits, you feed the power back on to full as you judge how much it will take without tripping the car back into understeer.

What's So Bad About Understeer?

A lot of drivers will say, "Wait a minute, I *like* understeer. The car's nice and stable. You're not constantly worried that the rear is going to take that big step out to uncontrollability. It gives the rear tires an additional measure of acceleration traction because you're using less of their cornering grip."

All true, but like everything else there's a compromise, depending on the degree of understeer. Subtle understeer may be overusing the fronts one percent more than what would be their fair share of the front/rear cornering balance. Overusing the fronts by 70% creates understeer of another magnitude, one that is so far off the optimum balance of the car that it will suffer from both a lack of total cornering grip and a resistance to acceleration due to tire scrub.

Each driver who fools with the cornering balance of the car can decide what balance is most comfortable. Some drivers will get very close to neutral, then bias things just slightly, that one percent, toward the front. Others will get very close to neutral and end up just a shade to the rear. Others, who are not so good at either setup or technique (or both) tend to end up *way* off of neutral, normally in the direction of understeer.

"Never Lift"

In some fast corners where the approach speed is almost the turn-in speed, you can get caught up in the pursuit of turning into the corner without giving up any throttle, trying to take the corner "flat out." The problem comes if turning in "flat" creates enough understeer that the car never makes the apex, or if the plowing of the front tires creates extra resistance to acceleration away from the corner. In these cases "flat out" might be slower than doing a slight lift to help the car rotate into the corner.

The "never lift" philosophy is frequently seen in drivers who generate understeer in a corner: everything seems okay, but then they spin at the corner exit. They "never lift" early in the corner where a breathe off of the throttle could get the car out of its understeer and help it turn more. Instead, they put in more and more steering lock, hoping that increasing the angle of the front wheels will get the nose of the car pointed down the following straight. Still, the right foot stays planted as the car understeers its way off the road at the track-out of the corner. *Then*, with dirt and rocks flying, you hear a big throttle lift and, as often as not, the car spins off the road to the inside.

> *"I've tried to get through Turn 1 at Mid Ohio flat out in a lot of cars and you can't quite do it, not faster than a lift anyway. You can turn in flat but then you have to give it up. If anything could do it would be a Super Vee and I tried it in one of those—couldn't do it."*
>
> —Robbie Buhl

Corner Exit Understeer

The "corner exit" is where you're trying to deliver as much power to the ground as you can, keeping the cornering speed up to maximize exit speed. Power oversteer can be a problem in this phase of the corner, and so can power understeer. It depends upon the car and situation. The same throttle application that produced oversteer in a high-powered, low-grip car will produce understeer in a high-grip, low-powered car.

It's impossible to make one statement that covers all cars. What you do know is how to solve the handling problem once you're in it: Oversteer is handled with the steering wheel by using the correction, pause and recovery technique; and by using throttle control to improve the bite of the rear tires.

Corner-exit understeer is corrected with throttle, but *not* steering. Adding more steering lock will most likely not deliver any more cornering ability to the front pair of tires. In fact, it will most often *reduce* the cornering force at the front by increasing the slip angle of the front tires into an area where they lose grip.

The answer is to lift off the throttle to keep from unloading the fronts as badly. Sometimes just a slight breathe is enough, sometimes you have to really come out of it, but beware of the snap off the throttle. With a violent lift you can turn a subtle understeer into a monster oversteer in a snap.

BIG ROTATION—PITCHING

Especially with experienced racers, it's a common notion that "pitching" the car early in a corner—that is, over-rotating it at the corner entry— allows you to do less cornering later in the turn. This is false. Doing more *cornering* early—steering the car on a tighter radius—is the only thing that allows you to do less cornering late in the turn where you would like to do more accelerating. Pitching, running the car at a higher yaw angle, only moves the tires away from their optimum slip angle.

Let's use a 90-degree corner as an example. The fundamental goal of driving through this corner is to change the direction that the car is travelling. In this case you have to change the car's direction 90 degrees.

Some would argue that if you rotate the car from zero degrees of yaw at the turn-in point to 8 degrees of yaw approaching the apex, you've reduced the amount of direction change needed by 8 degrees. But yaw and direction change are different.

Consider an extreme example (Fig. 4-10) where the driver has exercised brilliant car control and pitched the car sideways 90 degrees at the turn-in point. It's now pointed down the following straightaway, but this does not mean that all of the cornering is done. The driver still has to change the direction the car is *traveling* 90 degrees. The direction of travel (arrow A is tangent to the arc the car is traveling on (arrow B) *regardless of the direction the nose is pointing*. Remember, it's the radius of the arc on which the car is traveling that determines how fast the car changes direction.

There are valid uses for big rotation. In corners that are very slow and of long duration, it doesn't hurt to rotate the car more than you might in a fast sweeper—especially if they have following straightaways. This rotation gives you a cushion against the car falling back into understeer, which will force you to get

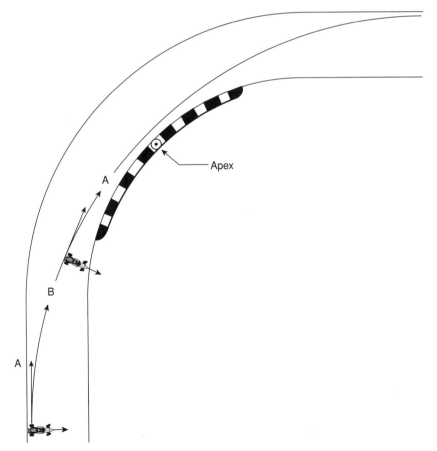

Fig. 4-10. "Pitching" the car seems like a valid way to change the car's direction rapidly, but on analysis the radius of the car's path relates to changes of direction, where yaw angle only represents the direction the nose is pointing.

out of the throttle to get the yaw angle back.

As cornering speeds get under 40 m.p.h. the rate of direction change per foot traveled increases rapidly. Tightening the radius of the first part of the corner by turning slightly later increases the rate of change of direction at double the rate that speed is sacrificed.

In looking at the data, it seems that pitching a car is less the reason that the approach is faster than an effect of the late turn-in—which really is the reason that acceleration can begin sooner, harder.

Generally, the cornering job is spread more uniformly across the corner as the corner gets bigger and faster. In slower corners, proportionately more cornering is done sooner in the turn than later, at least with the fastest drivers. As the turn gets tighter and slower, the spread between the amount of first-half cornering and second-half cornering gets bigger. In a fast sweeper, especially in an entry level car with limited horsepower, the balance of the change in direction between the first half and second half of the corner gets closer to 50/50.

Hand Brake Turns

Truly big rotation, often set off by using the handbrake to lock the rear wheels, can be useful in autocross, often to reverse the car's direction at the end of a slalom.

In this case the speeds are very low and a big, quick, rotation of 180 degrees, followed by acceleration essentially from a stop, can be faster than waiting for the car to turn through 180 degrees.

MULTIPLE-EVENT CORNERS

You will often have to deal with multiple problems in the same corner. Let's use Turn 7 at Sebring again for an example. On this particular lap you brake early, and at the turn-in point, the car is going 2 m.p.h. slower than normal. You turn in with very little rotation since the tires aren't at their limit. You get on the throttle at the same spot and with the same gusto as normal, and the car goes into understeer. You realize it and lift off the throttle. Weight transfers onto the front and off the rear, the car goes into trailing throttle oversteer and rotates up to an angle you like.

You stop the rotation with a touch of throttle and opposite lock. As the angle looks good, you continue the throttle's progress on toward the floor, keeping the slip angle within bounds. Just past the apex the road goes to reverse camber and the loss in traction causes the rear to slide wider. You react with opposite lock and a slight breathe off of full throttle to around 80%. The rotation stops, you recover the car and squeeze back down toward wide open. As the car moves toward the corner exit you gently unwind the steering wheel and accelerate at full throttle to the edge of the road at the track-out. You check the tach.

All of these moves on the steering wheel, throttle and brake are very typical of the way a car is driven at

its limit through a corner. The essence of car control is taking the car's cornering state at a particular instant and changing it to accomplish what you want—keeping the car in a range of yaw angle that lets the tires deliver the best grip on the road surface.

Despite the myths, car control is not a skill you're born with. The ability to keep a car accurately on the line as it's sliding through a corner requires that you know what to do and that you *practice* enough to develop the physical skills to do it.

PRACTICE

Professional schools offer programs that introduce you to the handling limits of street sedans. The lectures and exercises are invariably interesting and useful, but the skid pad is where the fun is. Most often, a car is intentionally driven in a circle at obscene yaw angles and the student has to practice the right moves to keep the car from spinning.

If you're considering a school of this type, ask about the nature of the skidpad or the skid car. If the pad is greased or the car you'll use is a specially built "skid car," the traction is so low that you won't experience the kind of loading sensations that you'll encounter in real life and, while the practice is useful, everything seems to happen in slow motion.

In our Skip Barber Dodge Driving Schools, which use a skidpad for part of the training, we simply wet down the skidpad to help the cars slide and to make the tires live for up to a day. The cornering forces are more realistic, and the sliding and recoveries occur over a time period which is more like real life. You're coached and encouraged to practice for hours.

The problem is that you can't afford a school every week of the year, and a couple days practice a year isn't enough to get good at any sport. Imagine practicing baseball two days a year and then expecting to be able to compete on a par with a Minor League player. Won't happen.

For practice, your racecar doesn't have to be a fancy, expensive one. Many road courses have open practice days, time trial events, or club races where the entry fees are low and the track time is abundant. Pick out the corners with the most runoff room so that if you make a mistake it would be hard to hit anything, then experiment with your limits. Slide the car more than you normally would in these corners and work on your car control. Don't just let things happen. Review the techniques you want to perfect and the car control problems you want to solve and work on them. Forget lap time and use each session as your own private clinic. It will pay off when you go racing in earnest.

Racing Karts is good practice, but just because they're small doesn't mean that they're cheap. Also realize that their response time and typical time spent in corners is significantly quicker than a full-size race-

> "As far as spinning the car to find the limit, there are really a few ways to look at it. A driver has to learn just how far to go in cornering—you've got to know what the car can do. Although you don't want to lose control of the car, on the practical side, a driver without a lot of experience is going to overstep the bounds a few times. The thing is you have to pick your spots. There are places on each racetrack where there's a lot less risk if the car goes off and these are the places you'd play around with the limits with less risk of hurting the car or yourself.
>
> "But once you're past the beginner stage you can't think that losing the car is OK. Two or three spins a weekend is way out of line. One every thirty days might be barely acceptable. The only use for the early spins is to learn from them—learn how not to do it again."
>
> —David Loring

> "The eyes are the single most important partner in driving the race car. If we were writing a book on baseball, the first sentence would be, 'The most critical thing you can do is to keep your eye on the ball.' In the sport of driving, we're sitting in the ball. We should be looking where we want to go....
>
> "The first time you read that sentence, you think, 'Of course I'm looking where I want to go,' but it's not guaranteed—you slide the car and you tend to look where the car is sliding, not where you want it to end up. When you come up to a corner, it's easy to stare at the turn-in point and not look into the corner soon enough. We think we look where we want to go but often we don't unless we concentrate on it."
>
> —Terry Earwood

car. A lot has been learned about car control, inexpensively, in shopping mall parking lots after a snowfall. Don't tell the officer we sent you.

Using Your Eyes

You've heard the advice from your parents and maybe you even pass it on to the next generation: "Will you *please* watch where you're going!" It's good advice for a ten-year-old sprinting through the den, bouncing off end tables. It's even better advice for a racer.

When you're in a slide, it's very tempting to focus your eyes on the thing you're concerned about hitting—the oak tree, the lamp post, the AArmco barrier next to the racetrack. We've found that concentrating on looking where you want the *car* to go increases the probability of getting there. It's a matter of keeping the connection between the eyes and the hands.

From day one you develop the coordination to turn the steering wheel or handlebars just enough to get you where you're headed (where you're looking).When things get dicey and you're likely to act reflexively, you want your eyes focused on where you want to be, not on what you want to avoid. In racing you want your eyes on the apex or the track-out and your hands will tend to move the steering wheel to get you there. It sounds like a minor hint but looking where you want to go is a significant aid for finding the racing line and staying on it, even when the car is sliding wildly.

FRONT/ALL WHEEL DRIVE

With the advent of showroom stock racing in the 1970s, more and more front wheel drive cars were showing up at racetracks. With more than a decade of road racing experience you still don't see front wheel drive being employed by many racecars that are built specifically for racing. Teams race them if they must, but there is no competitive advantage in the front wheel drive configuration.

The problem with front wheel drive is that the driven wheels become unloaded under acceleration, reducing the tires' traction just at the time you need it. As a general rule, front wheel drive cars create power understeer in circumstances where a conventional drive car creates power oversteer. Where an aggressive burst of power robs traction from the rear of the car in a conventional setup, the same burst robs cornering grip from the front of a FWD car. This traction loss is worse than it is in a conventional layout.

If you were starting from scratch designing a racecar, you would much rather have the driving wheels on the end of the car that will gain tire loading under acceleration: the rear pair of tires. Nonetheless, if you're racing showroom stock and your car of choice happens to have front wheel drive, you have to learn to deal with it.

Braking Control

A properly biased braking system is even more important on a FWD car. Many FWD cars which start out with a small percentage of their weight at the rear of the car will transfer almost all of it forward under braking. Once the car is turned into the corner and load transfers off the inside tires to the outside tires, you may end up with the inside rear tire in the air.

You're now cornering with the two front tires and the outside rear. If there's a little too much rear brake bias, the rear end will swing wide, creating substantial oversteer on corner entry.

Just like RWD, the front drive car will go toward oversteer if you snap off the brake pedal while cornering. The fronts, relieved of their braking requirements and loaded heavily from weight transfer, will dart toward the inside; the rears, high in the air and unloaded, will slide toward the outside of the turn.

The pause phase of trail braking that can help rotate a RWD car by allowing engine braking to help the rear end slide doesn't affect the FWD driver. You can still use the pause as a time to wait for the rear to reach the yaw angle that you like before stabilizing it with throttle. FWD doesn't have the tendency toward oversteer that engine drag on the rear tires gives to the RWD car.

Throttle Control

Brake bias-induced oversteer is not altogether a bad thing. If the rear comes out to even a quite lurid angle, the built-in understeer that will take over once you apply the throttle will bring the car back toward neutral.

In a FWD car, oversteer is solved with the same correction, pause, recovery routine used in a RWD car, but it also responds eagerly to throttle application. In the RWD car, you had to be careful about not overdoing the throttle application, losing rear tire traction and making the oversteer worse. In FWD, adding power and opposite lock drives the front end of the car over in front of the rear. If you overdo it and add too much power, the front loses traction and slides out onto a bigger arc, reducing the angle of the oversteer. Either way you win by adding power and opposite lock in a FWD oversteer slide.

Like the rear wheel drive car the FWD tends to create understeer with gradual throttle application. Again, just like the RWD, lifts off the throttle will change the handling of the car away from understeer and toward oversteer.

We haven't experimented with all-wheel drive on the racetrack. Generally, they share a greater similarity with FWD cars than rear drivers. They tend to create more power understeer than conventional racecars. One common comment by racers who frequently drive all wheel drive cars is that, in rain races, the additional traction from two more driving wheels is a huge advantage.

Summing Up

The role of car control is to keep the car on your intended path at a yaw angle in the range that creates the best grip from the tires, increasing the speed that you can negotiate the cornering arc.

Controlling the car from the turn-in point of the corner to the throttle application point involves mixing braking loads with cornering loads. Gradually reducing braking loads will tend to maintain the car's steady state cornering balance: oversteer will stay oversteer, understeer will stay understeer and neutral will tend to stay neutral.

Suddenly popping off the brake pedal while cornering will move the car's handling toward oversteer. A pause between brake release and throttle application will tend to move the car toward oversteer.

Gradual increases in throttle moves the car in the direction of understeer. Abrupt throttle applications move the car in the direction of oversteer. Lifts off the throttle change the car's balance toward oversteer.

Correction, pause and recovery are the three phases of the steering solution to oversteer skids and slides.

Rotation is the process of the car going from zero yaw to the cornering yaw angle necessary to develop the optimum slip angles and thereby the ultimate grip of the tires. Even "neutral" handling cars develop yaw angles.

Looking in the direction you would like the car to go can help by using your developing coordination between your eyes and extremities.

Car control is not an inborn skill any more than hitting a golf ball is inborn. Understanding what you want to do, and practicing the physical moves required, develops car control.

CHAPTER 5

BRAKING AND ENTERING

IN THE CHAPTER ON THE three basics, we introduced the idea that you could break down the corner entry process into four main blocks, and that you could use some or all of these blocks, depending on the corner entry situation.

> There's more to corner entry than the simplistic "brake late, brake hard" approach. Four "building blocks" make up the corner entry process. The speed loss required for the corner determines when and how you use these blocks.

cars at the Sebring hairpin, you don't want to waste any time getting off the throttle and onto the brake pedal. You'll carry the straightaway speed at full throttle right up to your chosen braking point and instantly get off the throttle and onto the brakes—hard. There's nothing gentle about it.

- Block 1: the throttle-brake transition. To use the brakes you have to take your foot off the throttle and put it on the brake pedal.
- Block 2: straight-line deceleration.
- Block 3: brake-turning.
- Block 4: the brake-throttle transition, where you switch from the brake pedal back to the throttle.

In terms of reducing lap time, this last of the three cornerstones of a fast lap has less to contribute since it represents a much smaller segment of the course than the other two. Nonetheless, the braking and entering section of the race lap is typically where the best drivers find the last second of lap time.

You know that one technique does *not* fit all, but how do you choose between the alternatives? By using the building-block approach to closely analyze skills, you can determine the type of corner entry technique you should use for a particular setting. This is especially helpful when you're faced with a new racetrack and have to decide on how to approach each corner entry. Let's start with Block 1.

BLOCK 1: THROTTLE-BRAKE TRANSITION

Coming off of the throttle and onto the brakes at the end of a long straightaway is a vastly different process than you're accustomed to using in your everyday driving. On the street, you're trying to be smooth with the car and sensitive to your passengers, so you don't move your foot from the throttle to the brake with much speed or force.

In a racecar approaching a 35 m.p.h. corner at 110 m.p.h., as you would be in one of our Formula Dodge

No Slams

You go to a lot of braking force in a very short period of time in racing. In our Formula cars at Sebring, a good driver will go from full throttle to over 130 lbs. of foot pressure on the brake pedal in 3/10 second. You would think that you could only describe this as "slamming on" the brakes, but that's not the case. Slam implies impact. Here, you're moving your foot from the throttle to the brake pedal *fast*, but the build up of pressure is a hard squeeze as opposed to a "slam."

Slamming on the brakes is a common mistake. Some drivers hit the brake pedal as if driving a nail with a hammer. This often results in instantaneous front wheel lockup. This lockup occurs because the front brakes start slowing down the front tires before load transfer can help deliver extra grip.

Fleet Feet

In straight-line threshold braking, there is going to be little variation in the move from throttle to brake. You want to spend as little time as possible getting off the throttle and into significant brake pressure to avoid wasting time coasting. When the speed loss requires less than threshold, it still makes sense to go to the brakes as quickly as possible.

There are exceptions. If the car you're driving is very sensitive to pitch changes—for example has idiosyncrasies that exaggerate the loss of rear wheel traction in a throttle lift—you might breathe the throttle back more gently before going to the brake pedal.

> *"In braking a Formula car, you have almost instantaneous feedback through the tires and suspension—also visually. In a showroom stock car it's a little softer—everything takes more time. It's like night and day, really. In a Formula car you just get with it. In the Saturn I raced, you settle it, then go at it."*
>
> —Robbie Buhl

Throttle-Brake While Turning

In some corners, the first application of brakes comes *after* you've turned into the corner. In these cases you have to be careful about snapping off the throttle on the way to the brakes. If the car is cornering hard, the sudden loss of rear tire traction caused by an abrupt lift off the throttle can cause a spin. As you'll see later, the throttle-brake transition under these circumstances has to be done more gradually, and with a good degree of sensitivity and anticipation.

BLOCK 2: STRAIGHT-LINE DECELERATION

Going from the throttle to the brake is just the start of the straight-line deceleration braking block. As you've seen, you don't want to *impact* the brake pedal but you do want to squeeze the brakes on hard, quickly.

Not Too Delicate

We see our share of gorilla brakers, but a far more common mistake for beginning drivers is to underestimate just how hard you can push on the brake pedal without locking up the tires. A good street sport sedan like a Dodge Stratus requires only 40 lbs. of pressure on the brake pedal to generate 80% of its maximum braking force. This level of braking would be considered quite aggressive for normal street driving. A driver transitioning into racecars understandably has to relearn the pedal pressure effort required near the limit.

Whoops!

To locate the limit, you're going to have to push harder and harder on the brake pedal until at some point there is too much pressure and the tire locks.

In our racing school we devote a considerable amount of time, and a lot of Michelin's rubber, to allowing fledgling racers to experiment with the limit under threshold braking. You can intellectualize all you like, but there is no substitute for putting the brakes on hard 100 times to learn something about what's required.

In these exercises the side benefit is plenty of practice in unlocking a locked tire. You know that a locked tire has 30% less traction than one at its brak-

ing limit, so you need to relax enough pedal effort to get the tire turning again. The difficult talent to develop is the feel for just how much pressure to relax.

Learning to Modulate

Brake modulation involves both increases and decreases in brake pedal pressure. You should be adjusting pedal pressure to compensate for changes in traction between the tire and road surface, constantly flirting with lockup—adding pressure to probe the limit, relaxing pressure at the hint of lockup. That's when it's done perfectly, but there are lots of ways to fall short of perfection.

The gross mistakes fall into two categories. The first is when you overreact to a locked tire and leap off the brake pedal. The car—which, because of the locked tire, has been slowing at 70% of its potential—now loses *all* of its braking force. Think of the logic here— giving away *all* your braking in an attempt to recover 30%. Normally this total release of pressure is followed by another application of brakes and another lockup, soon followed by another total release.

This pumping of the pedal is playing havoc with the car's load distribution. First the nose is down, then it leaps up as the brakes are released, then down again as the brakes go back on.

When it comes to brake modulation changes in *pressure* rather than changes in *dimension* are required. For example, to unlock a locked tire in the latest version of our Formula Dodge, the brake pedal pressure needs to be released from approximately 140 lbs. down to 100 lbs. The foot motion required to effect this 40 lb. change in pressure on the face of the pedal is barely perceptible to the naked eye. So, instead of changing the brake pedal pressure by moving your entire leg, try changing the level of pressure by changing the tension of the muscles in your lower leg and ankle. The changes are more likely to be subtle, which is exactly the type of change needed.

The second gross error is the tendency to respond to wheel lockup by continuing to increase brake pedal pressure on up to the point where you could create

> *"No one, absolutely no one, is proof against panic. More than 20 years ago, the late Graham Hill, twice world champion racing driver and one of the most expert and experienced drivers alive, stuffed one of our Ford GT40s into an earthen bank at Le Mans, doing considerable damage. When I asked him what happened, he replied, 'I went into the corner a little too fast, realized it, called upon my legendary skill and years of experience, panicked, locked up the brakes and slid into the bloody bank—sorry!'"*
>
> —Carroll Smith

Fig. 5-1. The deceleration rate of a race car with ground effects, like the GTP Intrepid pictured here, can approach over 80 m.p.h. per second.

diamonds from coal. This seems to happen with greater frequency when there is a barrier or other solid object in your line of sight at the end of the braking zone. There's an element of panic in this mistake. It is also the kind of error at which experienced drivers might sneer. But beware smugness—no one is ever immune to these kinds of errors, no matter how experienced they are.

Gaining Time In Long Braking Zones

When you are driving a racecar as fast as it will go in a long straight-line braking zone, it's at the absolute limit of braking, at the threshold of lockup. As we mentioned earlier, this is only half of the aim of minimizing time in this section of the racetrack. The other, equally important part is arriving at the turn-in point of the corner at just the right speed—neither too fast for the car to be able to turn into the corner on the right line, nor so slow that you're not using all of the grip available.

Easy to say, but it's not reasonable to expect a relatively inexperienced driver to reach this goal right out of the box. Even a skilled racer doesn't get it perfectly right on the first few attempts.

You need to come up with ways to approach the limit in heavy braking in a way that can whittle the time down without taking too big a bite, risking an excursion off the racetrack.

> *"I have to use specific brake points. You just can't be consistent enough using any other method. At least I know I can't."*
>
> —Jeremy Dale

Brake Points

You spent a good deal of time finding reference points to help keep you on the proper path through the corners. In braking you need to develop reference points to cue your application of the brakes. Racetracks are generally cooperative about putting number boards up in the obvious hard braking zones, but, more often than you would like to think, there are no clear markers to help you apply the brakes at the same spot every lap. Nonetheless, you have to seek out a brake point at the entry of every corner that will require braking.

The main difficulty is that brake points are variable. If you're taking it easy, learning the line around the racetrack, your straightaway speeds are going to be lower. Consequently, you can put the brakes on *later* than you will when you start flying. On the other hand, you'll tend to be on the brakes *earlier* because most of your concentration is on getting the line and corner exits right before trying to get the last bit of lap time from braking skills. The key is to establish a brake point for every corner and then work off of that point to suit the circumstance.

Don't Start By Going Deeper

The most common mistake that drivers make when they turn their attention to getting the last bit of lap time available at corner entries is to drive closer to the corner before braking—going deeper.

Going deeper, first of all, should be reserved for high-speed-loss corners where threshold braking will be used. It is very seldom that threshold braking will be the appropriate technique to use in every corner entry situation on the track. At Lime Rock, for example, there are six corner entries for every lap; only one involves threshold braking, and there's some active discussion about that one.

Identify the Threshold—"The Procedure"

In a threshold braking zone, it doesn't make sense to start going deeper before you are certain that you're using maximum braking. The first step in a procedure for making up time on corner approaches is to push harder and harder on the brake pedal to identify where the threshold is. Once you get to the point where you lock up a tire occasionally, you can start to move the brake point closer to the corner.

By starting out the process using more braking force, you actually lower the speed at the turn-in since you're braking over the same distance but with more force. Once you've identified the right level of force, you raise the speed at the turn-in point by moving the brake point closer to the corner—a little at a time. At some point you will have gone too far; your entry speed will be such that the car won't turn on an arc that will get it to the Apex. The car will still turn: it just won't be able to run on the best line. You'll probably need to continue the brake-turning portion of the corner entry to the point where it interferes with the throttle application, hurting your corner exit and the following straightaway.

> "I don't brake at the absolute possible last moment every corner of every lap because to do so, you're going to give up a bit at the exit by virtue of the fact that you can't pick up the throttle where you might otherwise be able to.
> "If you're braking at the last possible moment, that means braking to, or slightly past the apex. To do that, you sacrifice the exit. "
>
> —Bryan Herta

"The Procedure" for working your way up to a quicker corner entry of a threshold braking corner is straightforward:

1) Identify the level of threshold braking available by braking harder and harder on successive laps.
2) Once you're in the vicinity of threshold braking, move the brake point down toward the corner in small increments (three feet at a time is a good rule of thumb).
3) If entry speed gets so high that the car begins to be forced off-line or the throttle-application is delayed, you've taken the braking *too deep*. Move the brake point back to where it allowed you to do the line and corner exit properly.

> "I absolutely use 'The Procedure' we teach—all the time. I can't see that there's any other way to approach it. If you try to brake late before you've ID'd the brake level available, you're wasting time. You start by braking a little early and working on the level that's available to you. Once you've ID'd how much is there you can start working it down. As you get more experience and confidence you can do both—you can step the brake level up and move it down toward the corner at the same time. "
>
> —Jeremy Dale

Always Start With Threshold?

In a long braking zone, threshold braking from top speed down to the maximum speed the car will take at the turn-in point is the fastest way. No argument. But this isn't necessarily true in all braking zones.

The deceleration from threshold braking is formidable. In one of our Formula cars, the deceleration is over 1 G: at least 22 m.p.h. per second. Some racecars with slicks, wings and downforce-producing underbodies can see deceleration as high as 4 Gs, or 88 m.p.h. per second! In a car such as this, a corner entry situation requiring an 8 m.p.h. loss of speed would take under .1 seconds of threshold braking. Many drivers are tempted to use threshold braking under all situations, but this outlook is a little too simplistic.

Words of Advice

When Mario Andretti was competing on the Formula One circuit for Lotus, the team for which he won his World Championship, he was asked by an interviewer to talk about his driving technique. His response was that his technique was his livelihood and something that he might discuss with his sons but not a subject for public comment. "I will say one thing." he volunteered, "It is amazing how many drivers, even at the

Formula One level, think that the brakes are for slowing the car down."

The enigmatic quality of that statement is priceless, and there's an underlying message that the braking process does more than just slow you down. It also has a significant effect on the attitude and balance of the car as it works its way to the throttle application point.

The Effect of Short, Sharp Braking

In a car capable of 4 Gs of braking force (an Indy Car), think of what a threshold brake application does to the loading and attitude of the car in this situation—full throttle to maximum braking to brake release then turn-in—all in a tenth of a second. You might as well hit the car with a sledgehammer. The better move would be to not use everything the car had available in braking and instead concentrate on losing just the right amount of speed. Using lighter braking over a longer period of time allows the car to be more predictable and stable as you turn into the corner.

You're shooting for a specific target entry speed. By using the brakes forcefully for such a short period of time it's hard to get the speed just right. The tendency would be to over-slow the car, losing speed that may never be recovered on the following straight.

One rule of thumb is that you should consider abandoning threshold braking when the speed loss at the corner entry requires less than a full second of braking. If the corner is one which doesn't require a downshift, think of using a level of straight-line braking less than threshold in order to balance the car at the corner entry at the precise maximum entry speed.

What Does Lighter Braking Cost?

For those die-hard threshold brakers out there, let's do some lap time comparisons of threshold vs. 75% braking.

In Fig. 5-2, you can see that at 75% of threshold it takes 66 feet to slow the car from 80 m.p.h. to 70 m.p.h. by the turn-in (you will do additional slowing *after* the turn-in point and before the throttle application point, but your target entry speed is 70 m.p.h.). It takes the car .6 seconds to cover this distance.

If you go to threshold braking, it will only take you 50 feet to lose the 10 m.p.h. and you'll cover the last 66 feet up to the turn-in in .572 seconds. That's just over a quarter of a tenth of a second difference.

By braking more lightly, you're gambling that the slight time sacrifice on the way into the corner will be made up by doing the 75% braking more consistently, giving you better control of the entry speed and car. With the car more in control you'll be more consistent with your throttle application point.

Comparing Different Strategies in Long Braking Zones

You've seen that using "The Procedure" is an established way to work on improving at high-speed-loss corner entries. In this approach you increase speed at the turn-in by braking later and later. Another way to accomplish the same goal is to keep the brake point consistent and alter the level of braking force. Let's take a look at some real life runs through the last 400 feet approaching the turn-in point of the Sebring hairpin to see how the time in the straight line braking zone varies using different approaches. See Fig. 5-3.

On the quickest run, the driver approaches the braking zone at 104 m.p.h. The driver lifts off the throttle, and it takes .15 seconds before the first bit of brake pressure. .1 seconds later the pressure on the brake pedal is at 65 lbs., peaking at 122 lbs. in the next tenth. Threshold braking begins 339 feet before the turn-in point. It has taken .35 seconds to go from full throttle to maximum braking. During the decelera-

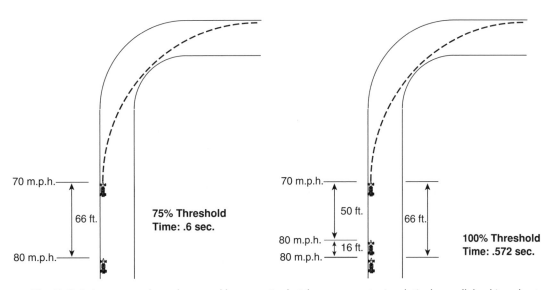

Fig. 5-2. In instances where the speed loss required at the corner entry is relatively small, braking short of threshold has a minor effect on potential lap time.

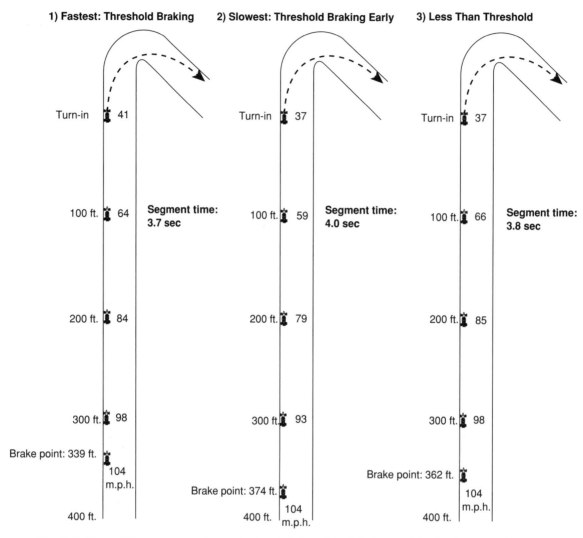

Fig. 5-3. Three different approaches to the last 400 feet of the Sebring straight, leading to the hairpin.

tion, the brake pressure varies from 90 to 130 lbs. The driver gets to the turn-in point at 41 m.p.h., 3.7 seconds after braking begins. The average speed loss is 19.7 m.p.h. per second—nearly .9 G.

On the slowest run, which takes .3 seconds longer, braking started 374 feet from the corner, 35 feet earlier than in the fast run—in other words, about three car lengths earlier. The time it took to go from full throttle to maximum brake pressure was identical to the first run, as was the maximum brake pedal pressure. The rate of deceleration was likewise very similar, around .9 G. The biggest differences were where the braking began and the speed of the car at the turn-in point.

The surprising thing is that the .3 seconds were not lost by braking 35 feet early; in fact, the lap time differential in the first 35 feet is imperceptible. The difference in lap time comes from the run being from 3 to 4 m.p.h. slower over the last 339 feet of the braking

zone, culminating in being 4 m.p.h. slower at the turn-in point.

The problem here isn't a matter of not slowing the car fast enough—the deceleration rates are nearly identical—but that the driver started the process too soon. When the driver stayed with this hard level of braking all the way to the turn-in point, the car had the same speed shortfall at the corner entry. Actual data shows that, during the quicker run, the driver reduced the level of braking pressure in the last 100 ft. of the braking zone. One conclusion is that the slower run is the ideal type to gain from following "The Procedure."

There is another way to work the time down. Let's look at the third run and see how much of the three tenths of a second deficit our driver can make up without driving 35 feet closer to the corner before going to the brakes.

In this pass, the braking starts 362 feet from the turn-in, and isn't as aggressive, running 15 to 30% lighter than the fast run. But the lighter braking keeps the car's speed, foot by foot, equivalent to the faster pass for about 3/4 of the braking zone. The time difference between these two runs is down to one tenth of a second.

That last tenth comes from the last 100 feet before the turn-in where the driver's slow build-up of braking pressure finally surpasses that of the faster run and the speed begins to fall below the target, ending up 4 m.p.h. slower at the turn-in.

What does all this mean? Hopefully, it can give you tools you can use to improve in hard braking zones. The fastest way to handle threshold braking situations is, just like the theory says, to find the absolute maximum level of braking force available and use it to slow the car from straightaway speed to the maximum possible turn-in speed for the corner entry.

In our examples, 41 m.p.h. is the fastest speed we have seen at the turn-in point with a skilled driver over a multitude of laps, so we can safely call this the limit—the fastest the car can be going at this point and still make the apex.

If your driving is less than perfect and you are losing time in the braking zone, you can see in this illustration that 2/3 of the time deficit can be made up by actually being below the braking threshold and braking earlier than required. The lighter level of braking keeps the car at a speed, foot by foot, on the approach to the corner, close to what the car would be doing with a later, harder brake application.

It's important to realize that this driver, in one of the hardest braking zones to be found anywhere, was just a tenth of a second off the peak performance while being 15 to 30% under the threshold. This reinforces the tactic of concentrating on line and exit speed first, and leaving the effort at braking at the absolute limit until later when that tenth of a second is an improvement you need.

Modulation—Not Just for Lockup
There are potential advantages to choosing not to brake at one consistently hard level from the time you touch the brakes all the way to the turn-in point. In the fastest run in the above example, the driver modulates away from threshold braking to a lower level about 90 feet short of the turn-in. It's an effective way of boosting the speed at the turn-in, while experimenting with the maximum speed available at the corner entry. This allows you to get acclimated to the sensation of speed at the turn-in point so that when it comes time to get every bit out of the corner entry, you have an appreciation for the speed potential at the turn-in point without the distraction of the effort it takes to be right on the threshold braking limit.

> "A lot of drivers forget that you are not locked into one level of pressure on the brake pedal. Even though you feel that you may be a little early on the brakes, there's nothing wrong with that because you can always pull back five per cent on the pedal and kind of float the entry speed into the corner. The pressure can always be modulated."
>
> —Jeremy Dale

Lighter Braking for Smaller Speed Losses
The last ten miles per hour of speed difference between approach speed and corner entry speed is best handled with progressively less and less braking force over approximately the same time and distance. You've seen how small a difference in lap time there is in situations where the speed difference is 10 m.p.h. The time spread is even smaller when you're in the 4 m.p.h. to 1 m.p.h. range. Look at Fig. 5-4 to sketch out how you might deal with the last 10 m.p.h. of straight-line speed loss.

Speed loss	Control input
10 m.p.h.	75% braking
9	60% braking
8	50% braking
7	30% braking
6	20% braking
5	Full-throttle lift
4	Shorter full-throttle lift
3	Partial throttle lift
2	Shorter breathe
1	The kind of lift only you and God know about
0	No breathe—full throttle

Fig. 5-4. Small speed losses at the corner entry can be accomplished with a variety of methods from light braking to a tiny lift off the throttle.

Using the Breathe
Just lifting off the throttle will slow the car down more gently than the brakes, and is often used to make small speed adjustments at the corner entry. Coming part way back from full throttle reduces the car's speed by removing some of the thrust that accelerates the car against the resistance of inertia and mechanical and aerodynamic drag. Lifting further creates de-

celeration as the motor creates a drag of its own on the rear tires.

There is a difference in these two types of throttle-related deceleration that is worth noting. The light breathe—one that reduces thrust—reduces the car's speed without making any demands on the tires. Lifting enough so that engine compression aids the slowing demands a portion of the traction available to the rear tires (in a rear wheel drive racecar). Normally, this is not a problem when the car is in a straight-line braking zone. As you've seen earlier, however, the car can be biased toward oversteer if the throttle is lifted while the car has cornering loads on it.

As the speed loss requirements go down, the full breathe will get shorter and shorter until, rather than a short, sharp lift, a partial breathe over a longer period of time will accomplish the same speed loss without detrimental effects on the balance of the car. And, as breathes get lighter and lighter, they enter the realm where they're doing more for your psyche than they are to solve an entry speed differential.

> "One thing that has always amazed me is that the difference between running a fast corner flat out and running it with just the tiniest lift, is remarkable. Just a little breathe on the throttle puts enough weight on the front of the car so that it turns in really well, whereas without the lift it just doesn't want to turn."
>
> —Jeremy Dale

BLOCK 3: DECELERATING WHILE TURNING (TRAIL-BRAKING)

As stated earlier, there has been, and still is, a philosophy that *all* slowing for corners should be done on the straight. We disagree. Since the Skip Barber Racing School began in 1975, we have trained drivers to use not only straight-line braking but also the brake-turning ability inherent in every vehicle. Our philosophy is that it is easier in the long run to learn the skill and sensitivity required to brake and turn right from the beginning rather than learn a technique that will then have to be modified at a future date. If you choose to continue braking past the turn-in point, be it 150 feet or two feet, we call this "trail-braking."

In reality, all the argument over whether to trail-brake or not is a bit over-blown. Using the braking and turning ability of a car is just another tool in the effort to lower lap time. You don't use a hammer for *every* repair, but it's the perfect tool for some jobs.

No one is sure who coined the phrase, but the first well-known driver to talk publicly about braking and turning was Mark Donohue. In the late 1960s, Mark

> "This whole issue of trail-braking or not trail-braking is bullshit because every quick driver trail-brakes, whether they talk about it or not. On fast racetracks, like you find in Europe, you might do it less, but in the States you have more tight turns where you have to carry the brakes in there to help point the car and to gain an advantage by going deeper. There should be no question about it. That's that."
>
> —Robbie Buhl

and other members of the Road Racing Drivers Club held seminars on racing technique and car preparation; it was in these seminars that Mark first began the heretical public discussion of using the brakes beyond the straight-and-narrow confines of conventional racing technique. The prevailing wisdom was that one was courting disaster by mixing the steering wheel and the brake pedal. Mark, a Brown University-trained mechanical engineer, based his premise on a graphic conceptualization of a tire's traction capabilities, which he called the "friction circle."

The Friction Circle

Let's build a friction circle graph. For the sake of simplicity we'll graph a 1 G tire. Under acceleration, this tire could create 1 G of accelerating force. Under braking the force would be the same, 1 G, but in the opposite direction. Cornered at its maximum, the tire would create 1 G of cornering force.

In Fig. 5-5, we graph acceleration on the vertical axis below the point where the two axes meet. The tire's braking ability is shown on the vertical axis above the 0 point. To the right of the origin is the tire's right cornering force; to the left, left cornering force. Since this tire's maximum is at 1 G, you can pinpoint on the graph the maximum abilities of this tire at four points. As the driver, you can choose to use the tire at less than its maximum if you like. At point A, for example, you would be using a portion of the tire's braking potential. By pressing harder on the brake pedal, your level of force would travel up on the graph, closer to the tire's maximum limit. The same is true of cornering. You could choose to use a portion of the tire's cornering ability, represented by point B; or by driving faster or cornering on a tighter arc, you could use more of the tire's cornering ability, up to the maximum available.

You can, however, mix abilities. Tires can develop a combined accelerating force and cornering force. Still, they won't provide you with cornering force if you are using maximum acceleration. At point A on the graph in Fig. 5-6, you would have zero potential for cornering. If you accelerated at a point short of maximum, the tire would have some traction left over to provide some cornering potential.

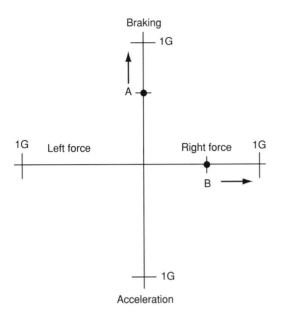

Fig. 5-5. A "friction circle" graph identifies the tire's maximum capabilities in the three forces it is capable of producing: accelerating grip, decelerating traction and cornering force.

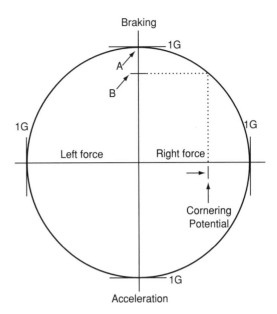

Fig. 5-7. By graphing all of the combinations of braking and cornering effort the tire can produce, you form a friction circle.

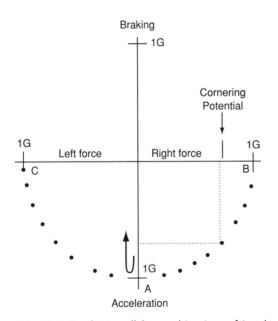

Fig. 5-6. By plotting all the combinations of Acceleration and Cornering force a tire is capable of, the lower half of the graph becomes a semi-circle.

If you graphed all of the combinations of accelerating and cornering force available, those points would form a semicircle, starting at point B, going through point A, and ending up at point C.

Using the Friction Circle

The friction circle allows you to think about what happens to one ability of the tire as you increase or decrease the demands for another ability. A lot of this is intuitive, but the graph helps you visualize what is happening with the tire. The bottom half of the circle in Fig. 5-6 represents the accelerate-turn combinations. The braking and turning forces available from this tire are represented in Fig. 5-7, as another semicircle above the x-axis.

What you now have in Fig. 5-7 is the complete friction circle, a graph of all the potential combinations of ability available to you. For a moment, take a look at the brake-turn part.

Under threshold braking, at point A, there's no cornering force available. But if you relax the brake pedal effort so that your demands for braking force are reduced, say, to point B, you can trace a horizontal line out to the circle and see that, with this reduced demand on the tire's braking force, you get a considerable amount of cornering potential. The key, again, is not to identify specific points but to understand how you can affect the cornering potential of the car by the pressure on the brake pedal.

More Than Just a Concept

The friction circle is a real thing, not just some conceptualization in a text book. Our data collection system has the capability of drawing graphs which plot lateral G vs. longitudinal G—in essence, drawing friction circles for a real car on a real racetrack. Fig. 5-8 is a direct copy of one of these graphs drawn for the

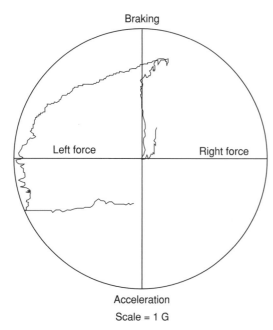

Fig. 5-8. An actual 1 G friction circle graph of a Formula Dodge pass up to and through the Sebring Hairpin.

braking entry of the Sebring hairpin. The traces are exactly as Mark Donohue theorized.

How Much Braking and Turning?
Corner entry technique as taught at many other racing schools would not include the topic of carrying braking past the turn-in point. We have found that in most racing situations, it is advantageous to do so. The question is not *if* you're going to do it, but *how*.

There is a wide range of brake-turning efforts. At one extreme there is the aggressive brake-turn right down to the apex, which you might use either at the end of a long straight leading to a compromise corner or in a passing maneuver. At the other extreme there is the light modulation off the brake pedal that you might use just past the turn-in for a fast sweeper.

Significance of the Throttle Application Point
When trying to choose the appropriate degree of brake-turning, an important variable is the location of the throttle application point. The later you apply the throttle, the more you'll use brake-turning.

As discussed earlier, you should begin the acceleration through the apex and onto the following straight as early as possible. This yields higher corner exit speed and consequently greater straightaway speed. The end result is improved segment times from the apex of the corner to the entry of the following turn.

If this is the case, why not begin accelerating *at* the turn-in point—you can't get any earlier than that! The problem is that, depending on the acceleration potential of the car and the radius of the corner, starting the acceleration that early may create so much speed that you can't make the second half of the turn. As a rule, the throttle application point is where you can begin acceleration *and still make the corner*. If you have to feather the throttle at the exit of the corner to stay on, then you've begun acceleration too early.

You will find that, for the same corner, lower powered cars will have earlier throttle-application points than cars with more horsepower and greater acceleration potential. The speed range of the corner also affects the throttle application point since the car's ability to accelerate changes with speed.

In one of our Formula Dodges, for example, the car can gain over 5 m.p.h. per second in the 60 to 70 m.p.h. range, but this falls off to less than 2 m.p.h. per second between 90 and 100 m.p.h. The primary reason for this drop-off is an increase in aerodynamic drag as speed increases. As the car goes faster, more horsepower is used just to push the air out of the way, leaving less for acceleration. As a result, the throttle application point will move earlier as the speed of the corner rises.

> *"The amount you trail-brake into a corner really changes with the type of car you're driving. With a low powered car with a lot of grip, like a Formula Vee on slicks, there's not a lot of braking and turning because in most corners you're on the power so early in the corner. In the WSC car, for example, you use it a lot because with so much horsepower you can't get to the power early so you decelerate deeper into the corner."*
>
> —Jeremy Dale

How Corner Angle Affects Brake-Turning
The total amount of direction change required in a corner affects the throttle application point and therefore the extent of the brake-turn. Take a look at the three 55 m.p.h. corners in Fig. 5-9. The radius of the arc required to negotiate each corner is in the 200 foot range and a 1 G car can reach 55 m.p.h. on this arc. As usual, the radius would expand at the exit, as would the speed, but the constant radius arcs we've drawn will be fine for illustration purposes.

In each of these three cases, let's say that the *earliest* you can manage to begin acceleration away from the corner is 225 feet from the exit. Any earlier and the car falls off the road; any later and exit speed is lost.

In corner A, a 75-degree corner, you'll find that the 225 feet takes up 65 degrees of the change of direction. The car only needs to change direction 10 de-

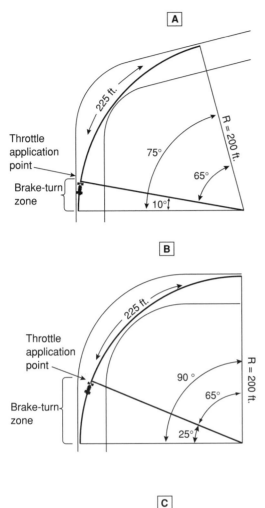

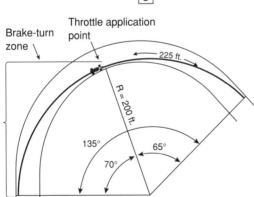

Fig. 5-9. The throttle application point varies with the total amount of direction change required in a corner.

grees before the throttle application point. The brake-turning portion of the corner entry is going to be brief if not non existent. Since the throttle application

point is barely 30 feet into the corner, you may choose to go directly from straight line deceleration (Block 2) to the brake-throttle transition (Block 4). In this case, in the 55 m.p.h. range it takes barely .4 seconds to go from the turn-in to the throttle application point, so you can skip the brake-turn phase.

In example B you have a 90-degree corner. The throttle application point is still 225 feet from the track out, but the difference is that the distance from the turn-in point to the throttle application point is now 86 feet. It would be wise to use some brake-turning to cover this distance at the highest possible average speed.

In corner C, as the corner angle increases to 135 degrees, the throttle application point moves further into the corner, right down around the apex. The length of the arc from the turn-in point to the throttle application point is over 240 feet. In the 55 m.p.h. range the car will be in the zone between turn-in and throttle application for around three seconds. The way you balance the car on a combination of braking and cornering will be very different than the braking technique used in the other two corners.

Pedal Force During the Brake-Turn
There are two basic ways of using the brake pedal in brake-turning. The first is to constantly relax the pedal pressure as the car approaches the throttle application point.

Let's say, for example, that at turn-in pedal pressure is at 140 lbs., and the brake-turn portion of the corner entry is going to take .7 seconds, as it does in this run into the carousel in Fig. 5-10. In a uniform brake modulation, you would release 20 lbs. of pressure each tenth of a second, going from 140 lbs. to 0 lbs. in a steady progression. When you take a detailed look at the brake pressure graphs of different drivers and different cars, you'll most commonly see this kind of brake-turning. In fact, the term "trail-braking" undoubtedly comes from explaining the process of trailing away the braking loads as the car decelerates while turning.

The second general way you can use the brakes while turning is by relaxing the brake pedal effort to a certain level and holding it there. In the example shown in Fig. 5-11, the driver turns in with 140 lbs. of pedal force and, over the first .3 seconds, relaxes the pressure to 70 lbs., then holds it there for a bit before relaxing the last 70 lbs. We have found that in corner entries where the brake-turn segment is longer (as in the 135-degree corner we looked at earlier), you try to find a specific combination of braking and cornering effort that slows the car *and* puts it on the right path for the apex. Once you've found the level of pressure that results in good speed loss and a solid cornering balance, you stick with it up to the point where the brake-throttle transition needs to take place.

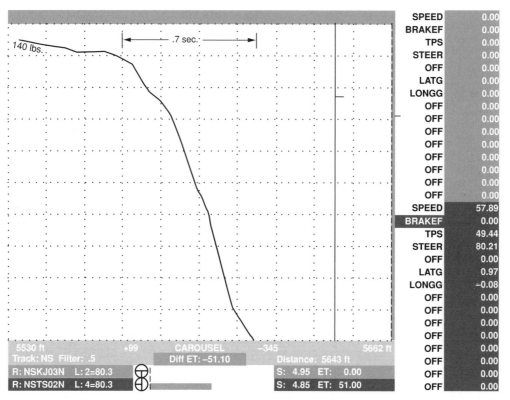

Fig. 5-10. This graph of brake pedal pressure depicts a uniform relaxation of braking pressure, decreasing braking force and increasing cornering potential.

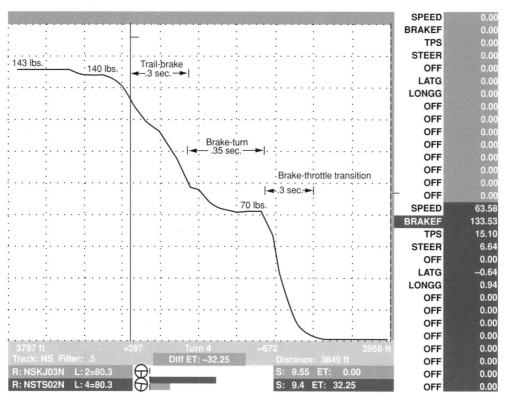

Fig. 5-11. When the brake-turn segment is longer, a constant level of braking pressure, below threshold, provides a balance of deceleration and cornering.

Connected Corners

Another corner entry where you see this kind of brake-turning is where there is little or no opportunity to brake the car in a straight line approaching the corner. Since most or all of the slowing is done while turning, you try to brake at a level that accomplishes the speed loss but still leaves enough cornering force.

These situations are often found where there is a string of two or more corners, and the last corner is slower than the previous one. In Fig. 5-12, the left-hand corner leads to the right hander without an intervening straight. The curved braking zone will require braking and turning at a constant level of pressure.

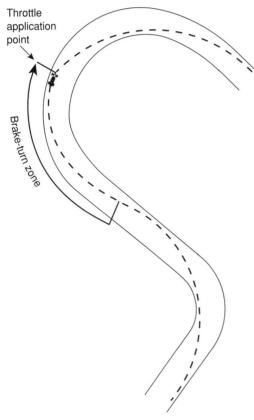

Fig. 5-12. Where there is no straight line braking segment, a constant level of brake-turning, subtly done, mixes deceleration and cornering.

This type of corner entry is tricky. At the beginning of the braking zone the car is already turning right. If you snap off the throttle on the way to the brake pedal, it is likely that the tail of the car will slide out toward the left. The throttle-brake transition needs to be done smoothly and over time to reduce this tendency.

The same goes for the initial brake application—smooth and progressive is the key, building to a con-

stant level until it's reduced in the brake-throttle transition. This slowing-down process is going on quite close to the edge of the racetrack, and if, for one of any number of reasons, you get in a little fast and the car wants to go straighter than you intend, you have to modulate the braking loads to create some cornering force to keep the car on the road. This is a standard part of braking and turning—being able to control the degree of cornering force available by increasing or decreasing the brake pedal pressure.

Ovals

Although we're concentrating primarily on road racing, drivers progressing up the ladder toward Indy Cars will encounter oval racetracks and their special demands. Entering long corners like those on ovals is very much like the situation in Fig. 5-12. The throttle application point, especially with more powerful cars, is relatively late in the corner, and there is significant lap time to be gained by carrying straightaway speed into the corner entry. The transition off the throttle onto the brake has to be done delicately, and many drivers smooth out this transition by learning to use their left foot on the brake pedal. For those of us accustomed to braking with our right foot, this is a skill that takes time to develop, but one worth learning if oval track racing is in your future.

> "On ovals, most of the time, you drive the car down into the corner on power, then slow it down, then pick up the throttle for the exit. The car is already light down in the middle of the corner, so it's a delicate deal—I had to learn to use my left foot on the brake and, until you do it for a while, you find that you have a lot less feel with your left foot. It took a while to get good at it."
>
> —Danny Sullivan

Shape of Corners

In decreasing-radius corners that *are* at the end of straights you are most likely to see constant-level braking and turning. This is because the more gentle arc in the first part of the corner often puts the turn-in point past the point where the road curves.

In Fig. 5-13, the car is first turned to match the arc of the edge of the road (point A), well before the turn-in point where the car is committed to the apex (point B). Since it is a long way between turn-in and the throttle application point, it is likely that you'll use constant-level braking and turning. Whether this will follow straight-line braking depends upon the total speed loss required. If the speed loss requirements are high, the process will likely start with threshold brak-

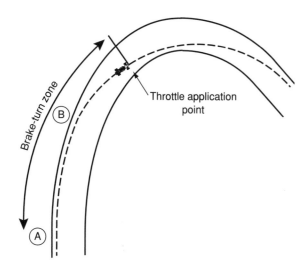

Fig. 5-13. Constant level brake-turning is more likely used in decreasing radius turns.

ing. Then, at the first turn of the steering wheel, reduce the brake pedal effort to a level that allows the car to negotiate the arc between A and B. At the real turn-in, the level may have to be reduced again to accommodate the tighter arc of the line toward the apex. In both segments, though, the pressure is likely to be constant-level rather than a bleed-off.

As speed loss requirements decrease, the braking point gets closer and closer to the corner. Especially in decreasing radius corners, the initial braking point may end up *in* the corner. If so, the cautions and requirements of starting the deceleration process while turning are the same as we outlined in the "connected corner" situation.

When Not To Use Brake-Turning

Starting to slow for a corner *after* you have turned into it is not the most common corner entry procedure, but it *is* one you should have in your repertoire. But there are times, even if you can do it well, when you might choose not to. The cases I'm thinking about are those which we dealt with when looking at small corner entry speed losses.

> *"I don't think I ever, ever, release the brake before the point of turn-in, but sometimes it's not so much to save time in braking. On fast sweepers, you don't want rotation, you don't want big weight transfer, you just want stability. So you knock off the speed before you get to the corner and have it as stable a platform as possible at the entry. It's a balance deal."*
>
> —Dorsey Schroeder

For example, if you only need to lose two m.p.h. of speed, why do it with a breathe on the straight when you could drive into the corner, brake-turn lightly, then transition back to power? The reason not to do this has more to do with handling considerations than with chasing the latest possible braking point. The sticky point is the throttle-brake transition.

When speed loss requirements are low, there isn't much time available to do a smooth throttle lift after the turn-in and, smooth or not, the initial lift off the throttle is going to tend to create oversteer. If the brake-turning process is going to be a long one, the application of the brakes settles down the oversteer by substituting a proportionately balanced loss of cornering traction, front to rear, for the unbalanced situation of using engine braking at the rear tires while the fronts are at full potential cornering traction.

For now, let's agree that you are going to carry some deceleration past the turn-in point of all corners where speed loss is required. In fast corners and small speed losses, this may mean the continuation of a throttle breathe ten feet past the turn-in. In some cases you will be losing 60 or 70 m.p.h. between the turn-in and throttle application point.

Using Throttle Before the Turn-In

As you've seen in the chapter on car control, simultaneous inputs of steering and throttle most often create understeer. This is the fundamental disadvantage of a throttle-then-steer entry. Once the understeer is created how is it defeated? Most often, a lift off the throttle, which comes *after* what would have been the throttle application point, takes care of this problem. The down side is lower exit speed caused by the delayed throttle application.

Brake-Turn vs. Corner Type

Your decisions about how much brake-turning to do are also affected by whether you're dealing with a Type I, Type II, or Type III corner. As you no doubt recall from the chapter on the racing line, we said that the line could change depending upon whether a corner led onto a straight, came at the end of a straight, or led to another corner.

In corners leading onto a straight, exit speed is king. You want to bias the throttle application toward the early side, so you would tend to do a shorter brake-turn in Type I corners.

In Type II corners where exit speed is not the prime consideration, you could make use of the braking and turning ability of the car and decelerate up to or past the apex, making up time in the braking zone.

In Type III corners, you are more likely to not only extend the brake-turning zone but to find yourself in situations where the slowing down process will have to begin while the car is still turning.

> "Late in my career I drove a Porsche Carrera RSR at Watkins Glen and it was a beautifully balanced car—you could do anything with it.... My habit on the approach to the 90 at the Glen was to pitch the car at the entry, get a lot of opposite lock and try to be really aggressive with the power trying to get the best shot up the back straight. On one lap—I think I was passing someone—I really carried the brakes down toward the apex. The car was much more stable than usual and I found since it was more stable that I could apply more throttle sooner and the speed at the trackout was much better. "
>
> —Skip Barber

Car Capability Affects Brake-Turn

The handling predispositions of your car affects how aggressively you choose to brake and turn. If the car's setup is biased toward the oversteer side, whether intentional or not, the brake-turning aspect of corner entry has to be de-emphasized. This oversteer tendency may be generated in any of number of ways. It could be that the rear sway bar is too stiff, the rear ride height too high, the front sway bar broken or missing—any of a number of chassis-related thrillers. It

could be the rear tires going off or the brake bias proportioned too much to the rear. If the car can't be changed back toward neutral handling, you have to adapt. One of the adaptations for driving an oversteering car is to reduce the level of aggressive braking and turning, if not abandon it altogether.

In these situations you're trying to reduce the braking traction demands on the rear tires so that they can supply more cornering force, settling down the oversteer. You'll find that, likewise, the accelerating and turning ability of the car is going to suffer and that more sensitive throttle application will be necessary to keep the rear end behind the front.

BLOCK 4: THE BRAKE-TO-THROTTLE TRANSITION

The "brake-to-throttle transition," a fancy way of describing how you take your foot off the brake and put it back on the throttle. Let's look at the variables.

Time

The first variable is how long the process takes. You can take your own sweet time going from your initial braking level (be it threshold or not) down to zero brake pressure. You could also pop your foot off the brake pedal in a nanosecond.

Sometimes, as you can see in Fig. 5-14, you gradu-

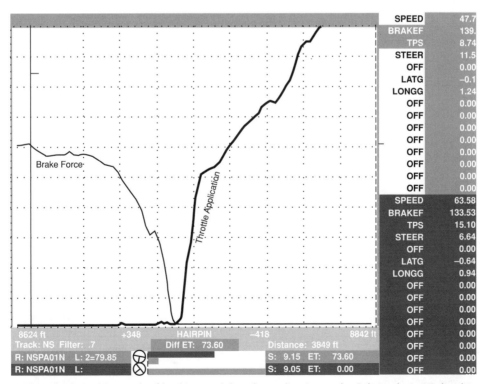

Fig. 5-14. In this graph of braking and throttle application at the Sebring hairpin, the driver gradually reduces braking force from 140 lbs. to zero over 1.1 sec. then makes an instantaneous switch from the last bit of braking to the application of throttle.

ally reduce braking effort down to zero and the right foot instantly picks up the throttle and begins to squeeze it on. This is exactly the same motion as a brake-turn done in the bleed-off style—that is, with a progressive reduction in brake pressure. It's the same as a slow, deliberate brake-throttle transition. The two are interchangeable.

If the brake- process is one where brake pressure is more or less constant, the brake-throttle transition can be slow and gradual as it is in Fig. 5-15, where it takes 1.25 seconds to go from roughly 80% braking down to zero. You *could* do it suddenly, as in Fig. 5-16, where everything else is similar but the brake-throttle transition is more abrupt.

Effects On Handling

The length of the brake-throttle transition will affect how the car sets its cornering slip angle. A slow brake-throttle transition allows the reduction in braking effort to keep in sync with the changes in front-to-rear loading. These changing forces work together over time, maintaining (or at least not upsetting) the overall cornering balance of the car. A sudden, sharp reduction in the braking effort delivers instant cornering traction to the front of the car by suddenly giving *all* of the front tires' grip over to cornering force. The car is likely to point aggressively toward the apex, increasing the car's yaw angle. Sometimes you want this to happen, sometimes you don't.

In a sharp, slow corner, having the car rotate an extra 5 to 10 degrees might be helpful—it keeps the car out of understeer. In a 95 m.p.h. sweeper, however, you might not enjoy the kind of excitement that 10 degrees of extra yaw angle provides.

The Pause

The second element you can use toward the same end is to choose to go directly to the throttle to stabilize the yaw you have created, or you can pause before picking up the throttle.

The "pause" is an intentional trailing-throttle oversteer maneuver. If the car has some rotation going, but not enough for your liking, a pause before going to throttle will help the car increase its yaw angle. If you like the extent of the slide you've got going, go immediately to enough throttle to stabilize the yaw angle. Once at this point, you're now playing the corner exit game of squeezing on as much power as you dare, trying to maximize your speed coming onto the straight.

Assumptions We've Made

The type of car you're racing will affect your braking choices. Many racecars, especially the ones that a beginning racer is likely to start with, have excellent brakes. On a purpose-built racecar like a Formula-Ford, Spec Racer, Ford 2000, Formula Atlantic, or Sports 2000 car, the brakes should be able to work at their maximum level every time you go to them, from

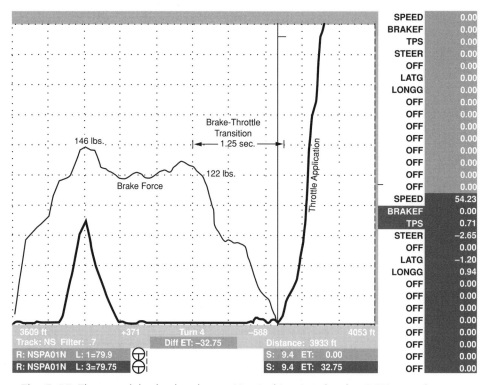

Fig. 5-15. The smooth brake-throttle transition in this example takes 1.25 seconds.

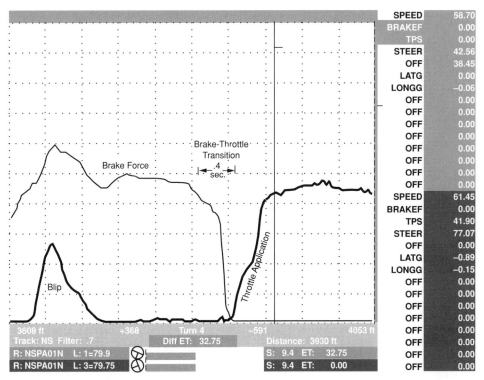

Fig. 5-16. Similar to Fig. 5-15, but the transition from brake to throttle happens in .4 seconds, which affect car rotation at the corner entry.

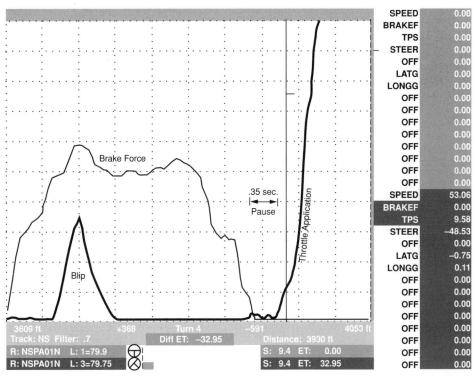

Fig. 5-17. Here the driver apparently didn't like the amount of yaw and paused for .35 seconds between the brake release and the application of plenty of power. Note the position of the lower steering wheel on the graph—it's turned significantly left in this right hand corner. The "pause" worked.

beginning to end of your race.

Expecting a showroom stock car to perform like a Formula car under braking is a big mistake. In a car designed primarily for around-town use, the brakes are not up to the task of stopping a heavy vehicle time after time for hours on end. Although threshold braking may be desirable and achievable for a few qualifying laps, the faster and heavier the car, the more likely it is that you will have to modify your approach to braking to compensate for deterioration in the braking system.

Remember, during a long race, the pursuit is not for the single fastest lap but for the fastest *average* lap time over the race distance. An intelligent racer has to make the distinction between the technique which is usable in a sprint race in a bulletproof car and the driving required in order to save a car which has deteriorating performance in one or more of its systems.

> "Sure, you'd like to try and go into every brake zone as hard as you can, but in a long race you can't drive every one at 100%—98% is more like it. If something changes, and it always will, or if you run into problems, you have a one or two percent margin. It doesn't have to cost you speed. "
>
> —Jeremy Dale

The Key Points of Corner Entry

Corner entries are exciting—more exiting than corner exits, to be sure. Coming out of a corner, you feel more fully in control, squeezing on the accelerator. If anything unusual or threatening takes place, you just don't push the throttle down as aggressively. Coming into the corner you feel a bit more like a passenger.

You've made a commitment at your braking point that your technique this lap has to be very close to the last lap's or you'll arrive at the corner going too fast to make it. Consistency in brake point and the level of pressure used on the brake pedal is critical.

It's important to keep in mind what you're trying to accomplish at the corner entry. Remember that taking the speed off in the shortest amount of time is only part of the goal. Slowing down to the right speed—the maximum speed the car can support on an arc that makes the apex— is even more important because, especially in entry level cars with limited horsepower, this speed frequently determines the cornering speed and your speed down the next straight.

Different corners present different speed loss situations and you can count on the fact that you won't use the brakes the same way in every corner. A little thinking and planning before you go out in the race-car can help you prepare for improving your corner entry performance.

> "A lot of people jump on the brakes very hard. I was always a guy who braked, for the most part, very easy. I didn't use up the brakes at all since I tended to roll off the throttle and onto the brake more easily.
>
> "To put it in perspective, at Laguna Seca, which is hard on brakes, Rick Mears and I were teammates at Penske and Rick finished the race with only 70 thousandths of an inch of brake pad material left. I only used 70 thousandths of the pad in winning the race. People brake differently but can still run the same lap time, especially in a race."
>
> —Danny Sullivan

Chapter **6**

Shifting

IF RACECARS OPERATED IN a very narrow speed range there would be no need for a gearbox. If the speed varied very little, it would be easy to choose the overall gearing of the car so that at racing speed the engine would always be operating in the RPM range where it makes its best horsepower: what we call its "powerband." In road racing, cornering speeds may vary from 30 m.p.h. to 170 m.p.h., and the gearbox is the device that allows you to operate the motor in its powerband at widely different speeds.

In our experience of teaching over fifteen hundred Three-Day Racing schools over the last 20 years, we have found that the single most frustrating skill for a fledgling racer to learn is proper downshifting.

The main difficulty is that, in racing, the downshift comes at a time when the car (and driver) is busy slowing for an upcoming corner. It's easy for one activity to impose on the level of concentration required for another.

Downshifting

The downshift in racing is not as simple as it is on the street: clutch in, shift, clutch out. To illustrate the differences, let's start with the case of a single downshift

"Double-clutch heel-toe" downshifting, the classic racing technique for going down through the gears, has many variations. Upshifting, while simple, requires speed and consistency.

in a street sedan. Refer to Fig. 6-1, a cross-section of the drive line of the car.

The engine (A) spins the flywheel/clutch assembly (B). When the clutch is engaged—with your foot *off* the pedal—the engine is directly connected to the input shaft of the transmission (C). When the transmission is in gear, a pair of gears are working together—one on the input shaft and one on the output shaft—so that for a particular RPM of the input shaft a different RPM comes off the output shaft side (D). In most transmissions this difference is true for all the gears but top gear. Top, whether it's fourth in a four-speed or fifth in a five-speed, is often a 1 to 1 ratio—that is, for every revolution of the input shaft the output shaft turns once. In all of the lower gears, the input shaft would turn faster than the output shaft. The lower the gear, the faster the input shaft spins relative to the output shaft.

The differential changes the direction of the rotation to one you can use to propel the car forward. At the same time, it changes the RPM of the wheel and tire relative to the RPM of the output shaft. Normally, the ratio of this change is between 3 to 1 and 5 to 1. If the differential ratio were 3 to 1, the wheel would revolve once for every three revolutions of the output shaft.

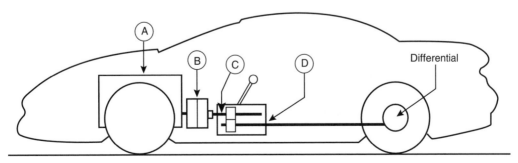

Fig. 6-1. Simplified cross-section of the basic mechanical pieces involved in shifting: A) the motor, B) the flywheel/clutch assembly, C) the transmission input shaft, and D) the output shaft.

RPM Differences

Let's take a look at Fig. 6-2, which shows the RPM of all of these bits when you're attempting a downshift. At 60 m.p.h. the average tire is revolving at 900 RPM. At a 3 to 1 differential ratio the output shaft of the transmission would be spinning around at 2700 RPM. If you were in top gear at 60 m.p.h. in a car with a typical transmission (1 to 1 top gear ratio), the input shaft (C) would be turning around at 2700 RPM as well.

Okay, now you're going to slow the car to 50 m.p.h. to negotiate the upcoming curve. Before you get to the corner you're going to downshift to third gear. You take your foot off the throttle and squeeze on the brake, slowing the car to 50 m.p.h. As you can see in Fig. 6-3, the rear wheels are turning over at 744 RPM, the output shaft is spinning at 2232 RPM, and you put in the clutch. When you do this, the engine is no longer connected to the input shaft—the clutch has broken this connection. With your foot off the throttle and the engine disconnected from the transmission (thereby disconnected from the rear wheels), the engine falls to idle speed—say, 1000 RPM.

Now you move the gear lever out of fourth gear toward third. In this lower gear, the input shaft, when you're done with the shift, is going to be revolving faster than the output shaft. The increase in RPM differs

from transmission to transmission, but it's in the range of 25% faster than it would be spinning when fourth is engaged. In order to get third gear engaged, the input shaft will have to spin up to 2790 RPM at 50 m.p.h.: that's over 500 RPM faster than it was spinning when you put the clutch in. In a street car, synchronizers in the transmission speed up the lower gear so that when the teeth on one come into contact with the teeth on the other, they are going at the right relative speed so that there isn't a god-awful *graaaunchh* when the gear lever gets shoved into the third gear.

The bad news is that the transmissions in most racecars *don't have any synchronizers*. You'll have to face the music on this one soon, but for now, let's finish this street car downshift.

In Fig. 6-3, you muscled the transmission into third gear; now the input shaft is turning at 2790 RPM and the output shaft is at 2232 RPM—the appropriate RPM for your 50 m.p.h. road speed. The engine is still at idle: 1000 RPM. If you engaged the clutch like a steel trap—*boom*—it would instantly slow the input shaft to 1000 RPM which, in third gear, translates to only 18 m.p.h. of rear wheel speed.

Since you're going 50 m.p.h. while the rear wheels are only turning over at 18 m.p.h.—that's like locking up the handbrake at 50 (Fig. 6-4). Fortunately, the

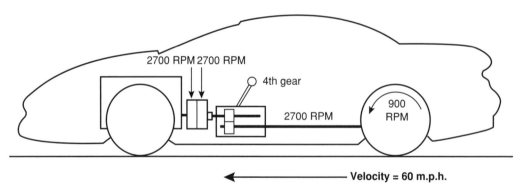

Fig. 6-2. At 60 m.p.h. in top gear the relative RPM of the rear wheels, the output and input shafts, and the engine are displayed above.

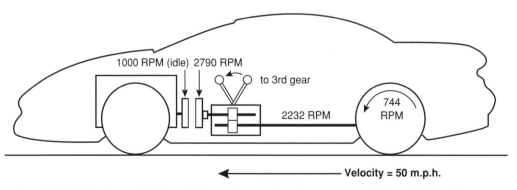

Fig. 6-3. Shifting from 4th to 3rd at 50 m.p.h., synchronizers speed up the input shaft of the transmission to 2790 RPM: the appropriate speed for 50 m.p.h.

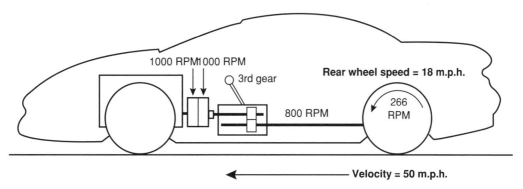

Fig. 6-4. If the clutch were engaged with the engine at idle speed, this converts to just 18 m.p.h. of road speed at the rear wheels. At 50 m.p.h. this is quite a shock as the rear tires have to speed up the engine from 1000 RPM to 2790 RPM.

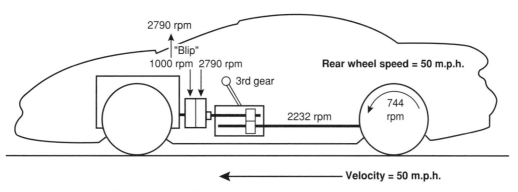

Fig. 6-5. If you "blip" the throttle, bringing the engine's RPM up to about 2790, *then* engage the clutch, the shift will be smooth and not overtax the rear tires' grip on the road.

clutch will slip when you engage it so that the shock to the driveline is minimized somewhat, but just dumping the clutch after doing a downshift is brutal on the balance of the car.

The Blip

Properly done (see Fig. 6-5), you should use the throttle to raise the engine RPM to about 2790 before the clutch is engaged again. You don't squeeze on the throttle and hold it; you tap it. You give it a quick, sharp burst. "Blip" is the perfect word for it. The blip should take place just before re-engaging the clutch so that there is no shock to the drive line when going from a higher gear to a lower gear. On the street this is done to keep the ride smooth. On the racetrack where you're operating close to the tires' limit of adhesion, a downshift without a blip can use up *all* the traction of the rear tires and spin the car in the straight-line braking zone. Even for a car with a synchronized transmission, a blip before clutch release is mandatory.

Heel-and-Toe

Since your left foot is on the clutch, and your right foot is on the brake pedal, you have to make some adjustments in order to blip the throttle. The way to do it

is to adjust the pedals in the car so that with the ball of your foot pressing on the brake pedal there's a few inches of right foot left over to roll your foot to the right and tap the throttle, blipping the engine up the required RPM so that when the clutch comes out everything will be smooth and gentle.

Fig. 6-6. A proper brake/throttle relationship locates the throttle close by and just slightly below the brake pedal when the brakes are on hard.

This downshifting method is called "heel-and-toe-ing," although, as we've just described it, it doesn't involve your heel or your toe. The phrase was coined more than forty years ago, when many racecars had the pedals arranged so that the brake pedal was on the right, the clutch pedal on the left, and the throttle was between them and about six inches lower. Under braking, the driver had the ball of his right foot on the right-hand pedal and when the "blip" was needed, pushed down on the throttle with his heel—hence, heel-and-toe. Pedal arrangements have changed but the term lingers on.

The pedals in most street cars aren't set up to facilitate heel-and-toeing, so drivers are forced to go through some real contortions to be able to touch the brakes and throttle at the same time. To do it right you have to do more than just be able to reach both pedals with the same foot. You need to accurately control how hard you're pushing on the brake pedal, a skill that's lost to many drivers who twist their feet into deformed postures to accommodate the awful pedal positioning in their cars.

What Downshifting Is Really For

We ask this basic question of every racing school class. The most frequent (and incorrect) answer is, "to help slow the car down." In a racecar with good, durable brakes (the majority of modern racecars), downshifting to help the car slow down is unnecessary. The *brakes* slow the car down. You downshift to get the car in the proper gear to exit the corner.

There *are* cars with marginal braking systems, most notably showroom stock racers which have brakes designed for the demands of the street environment. Their brakes, especially in an endurance event, may fade away to nothing, at which time you use whatever you can to slow the car for the corners. In this case you certainly *do* use the downshifting to slow the car down—but it's a last resort.

Choosing Your Gear

You decide which gear is the proper gear for a corner simply by picking one and trying it. If the engine is turning over too slowly—that is, it's operating in an RPM range below where it makes its best power—the gear you've chosen is too high. Next time, try a lower gear.

At the other extreme, if the engine hits its redline RPM before the exit of the corner, the gear you've chosen is probably too low. Try the next highest gear next time. When in doubt, use the higher gear since it's less likely to damage the motor, and in the future you'll be more likely to take the corner faster than slower.

Where To Downshift

Rather than drawing an X on a track map, we try to help the driver make the decision based on avoiding shifting too soon or too late. Take a look at Fig. 6-7 to see the range of choices.

For simplicity's sake, let's say that this is a third gear corner, approached in fourth gear. You certainly can't downshift the instant you go to the brake pedal. At this speed the car would be going too fast for the engine to be under the redline RPM in the next lowest gear. You need to let the car lose enough speed so that when the clutch comes out in the next lowest gear you don't over-rev the motor. In this case let's say that the earliest point at which you can downshift comes at point A.

If the throttle application point in this corner is at point B, that would be the latest possible point for the downshift: shifting anywhere between point A and point B is OK—a wider range of choices than you might have guessed.

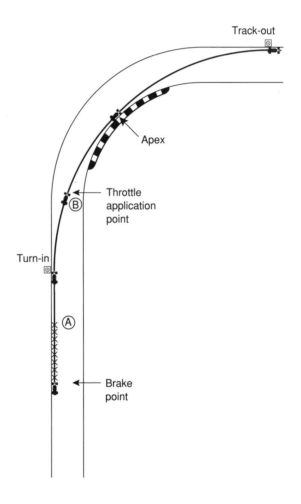

Fig. 6-7. There is an earliest and latest point at which the downshift can be done. Anywhere between point A and point B is fine, keeping in mind that, given the choice, it's less risky to downshift while the car is going straight.

There is one other potential restriction. If you have the choice, downshift while the car is going straight rather than when the car is turning. If you blow it and chirp the rear tires when the clutch comes out in the lower gear, the car is much more likely to spin if it's under cornering load than if it's not. There will be times when you're forced to downshift while the car is turning, and you'll have to do it well, but given the choice, you take less risk by downshifting on the straight.

Double-Clutch Downshifting

In shifting gearboxes with synchronizers, the function of the blip is to smooth out the clutch engagement after moving to the next lowest gear. Since most racing transmissions do not have synchronizers, the blip not only cushions the clutch engagement, it also allows you to synchronize the speeds of the input and output shafts. Here's how it's done.

With your foot on the brake you push in the clutch and shift to neutral from a higher gear. You let the clutch out, and then, still in neutral, you blip the throttle.

Since, with the clutch engaged, the motor is directly connected to the input shaft, your blip easily spins up the shaft to the higher RPM. The instant after you blip, push in the clutch and move the gear lever into the third gear position. Once it's there, let the clutch back out again. This last bit has to happen fast before the extra RPM created by the blip falls away.

By performing this series of maneuvers, you've synchronized the gears, going from fourth to third without grinding. The secondary benefit is that since the clutch re-engaged in third gear with the engine turning over at the right RPM for the road speed, you shifted into third gear smoothly without lurching off the drive-line.

Use Figs. 6-8 through 6-18 as a visual guide:

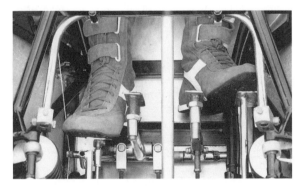

Fig. 6-8. Full throttle on approach to corner.

Fig. 6-9. Come off the throttle.

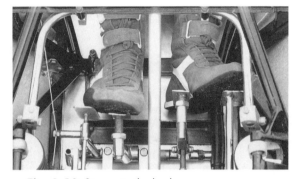

Fig. 6-10. Step onto the brakes.

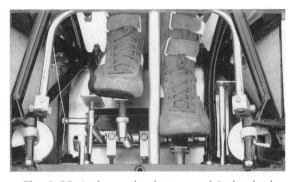

Fig. 6-11. As the car decelerates, push in the clutch.

Fig. 6-12. Move the gear lever down to neutral.

Fig. 6-13. Then let the clutch back out.

Fig. 6-14. Blip the throttle.

Fig. 6-15. Push in the clutch pedal.

Fig. 6-16. Move the gear lever into the lower gear.

Fig. 6-17. Let clutch out, turn in, then relax brake pedal pressure.

Fig. 6-18. Apply throttle through apex and away from corner.

Be Clear About The Routine

When you first try to double clutch, it seems like your hands and feet just won't work together. it's very easy to get flustered, especially if, like most of our Three-Day Racing School Students, you're sitting in a real race car for the first time.

It helps to think of the process as doing two normal shifts to accomplish one—a shift to neutral, and a shift to the lower gear. Think about it. The shift to neutral is like any other shift—clutch in, move the gear lever, clutch out. The next half of the double-clutch is simply another normal shift—clutch in, move the gear lever to the next lowest gear, clutch out.

The only difference is that when you stop in neutral you give the motor (and the input shaft) a blip.

Dorsey Schroeder invented the downshift jingle which he'd perform at every drivers school he would teach, and he swears it helps. Using the same meter as your basic samba dance, it goes:

Verse 1,4th–3rd
clutch in, neutral, clutch out
blip
clutch in, next gear, clutch out
Verse 2, 3rd–2nd
clutch in, neutral, clutch out
blip
clutch in, next gear, clutch out
Verse 3, 2nd–1st
clutch in, neutral, clutch out

blip

clutch in, next gear, clutch out

If he'd had his way, he'd have everybody in a samba line getting the jingle down before trying it in the cars.

> *"Double clutching is important to me— it's my balance. I always do it, and always use the clutch. I've had times when the clutch broke— a pushrod or a hydraulic line—and I'd still use the clutch pedal for a timing deal. I've learned not to release brake pressure when blipping the throttle and if I change my routine I get segmented and throw the timing off. It just didn't work right without double clutching."*
>
> —Dorsey Schroeder

MISTAKES

Keeping the Clutch Dipped

The most common error when trying to learn to double clutch downshift is forgetting to let the clutch back out when you stop in neutral and give the motor a blip. When the engine isn't directly connected to the input shaft of the transmission, which would be the case if you let the clutch out, the blip isn't as effective at speeding up the input shaft. There is some drag going on between the motor and the input shaft, and a blip, even with the clutch depressed, will speed up the shaft some. The blip is much more effective, however, if you positively connect the engine and input shaft by letting the clutch back out in neutral.

Slow Move to the Next Gear

Once the throttle is blipped and the input shaft spun up to speed, the shift to the next lowest gear has to be done right away. If you wait too long, the motor and the shaft slow down and the synchronization is lost, resulting in a more difficult (and louder!) downshift. If for some reason the lever doesn't go into the next lowest gear following the blip in neutral, you need to blip the throttle again before trying again.

Trying to Shift Too Fast

Just because you're driving a racecar does *not* mean that every motion you make behind the wheel has to be fast. Most downshifts come at a time when you're decelerating the car for an upcoming corner and there is more time available to do it than you might think. You don't have to perform like "The Flash," especially if double clutching and heel-and-toe is new to you. Avoid trying to move the gear lever from the higher gear to the lower gear in one motion, hoping that the clutch will come out and the blip will occur at the precise instant the lever passes through neutral. Move the lever twice: once to neutral and then again to the next lowest gear. You can take as much time as you like doing the first half of the downshift—clutch in, lever to neutral, clutch out. But, as mentioned above, once you blip, you need to complete the shift quickly.

GETTING GOOD

There's no secret to developing the ability to downshift smoothly, instinctively. You need to do three million heel-toe double clutch downshifts. Well, maybe not that many. If you drove an hour a day, every day of the year, and did three downshifts for every minute on the road you'd do 60,000 a year. That would do it.

If you're serious about it, get a standard transmission street car and set up the pedals so that you can heel-and-toe it. From that day on, *always* heel-and-toe double clutch downshift. In a year, you'll never have to consciously think of downshifting again.

To Clutch, or not to Clutch

A lot of people ask us if top-level professionals go through every step of this downshifting process. The answer is that some do, some don't. The biggest variable is when and if the driver uses the clutch.

> *"I never double clutched in my life. I always blip on the downshift and use the clutch to go down, even with the sequential gearboxes, but I don't necessarily let the clutch out in neutral. I've always been very gentle with gearboxes and when I taught racing with Skip's, it was the one thing I didn't do that we taught. Guess I just give bigger blips than the average driver."*
>
> —Danny Sullivan
>
> *Author's Note: We never could get Danny to buy into double clutching, but the single clutch works if you blip higher than you would if you engage the clutch in neutral. Blipping higher spins the input shaft up the same amount, even without the direct connection between engine and input shaft that engaging the clutch in neutral provides.*

At the very beginning of the process, when you lift off the throttle and go to the brake pedal, there is a moment when the tension on the gears is released as the car goes from driving the rear wheels with the motor to the motor being forced to turn by the rear wheels. In this little transition period, you can easily pop the car out of the higher gear into neutral without using the clutch and without any strain on the gear box. Now you're all set up to do the blip without having used the clutch. The second phase of the shift would be to push in the clutch, shift to the lower gear, and let the clutch out—unless of course you choose to do this part of the downshift without the clutch too. If the blip was perfect, not too high or too low, the gears should be perfectly synchronized and the gear lever should just fall into the next lowest gear without any grinding from a mismatch.

Many experienced drivers who are very good at matching the input and output shaft revs, shift without the clutch as a routine. Blipping the throttle as they pause in neutral allows them to do this without harming the transmission.

If, however, your technique is less than perfect, using the clutch takes the shock out of the inevitable mismatches in gear speeds that occur when you blip too much or too little. Using the clutch provides a little slip in the system and a minor mismatch just wears a little more off the clutch plate—a much less expensive part than gears and dog rings.

> *"I have used the clutch on upshifts and downshifts all the way up to the point where we started using sequential gearboxes in the Indy cars. I used the standard double clutch downshift technique I learned in my Three Day School all the way through, F/Ford, Barber/Saab, Indy Lights—everything. Not using the clutch risks hurting the car. You've got to have some mechanical sympathy."*
>
> —Bryan Herta

A lot of inexperienced drivers rush into trying to shift without the clutch, mostly to be like the big guys. We think it makes much more sense to learn how to do the double clutch heel-toe downshift using the clutch and leave it up to the individual to decide when they, (and their transmission maintenance budget), are ready to move on to clutchless shifting.

Keep in mind that in downshifting there is no lap time advantage in shifting without the clutch. Downshifts come when the car is slowing down and it's the brakes that determine how quickly the car covers this section of the course. Getting the car into the lower gear a tenth of a second faster than the competition doesn't necessarily mean that the braking process is going to take a tenth of a second less. In most cases, there's more than enough time to get the downshift done, regardless of the method you use. One thing is for sure: you want to end up at the end of the race with a gearbox that works as well as it did when the race began. Grinding gears on every shift uses up the gearbox and results in defeat by your own hands—and feet.

Inside a Racing Gearbox (Or: Why Bother to Double Clutch)

A common explanantion for matching the speeds of the input and output shafts of the transmission is that when you change gears you're forcing a gear on the input side to come into contact with the gear on the output side. This is not true.

Although the above makes for a more vivid mental picture, the gears, or more properly, the *pairs* of gears, are constantly intermeshed with each other. Moving the gear lever selects which pair of these intermeshed gears you choose to use. When the gear lever is in neutral, none of these pairs of gears are hooked up to the input shaft of the transmission.

The gear lever moves into place a device called a dog ring. The dog ring spins at the same speed as the input shaft, and when the gear level is in neutral they spin freely, out of contact with any pair of gears.

When you move the gear lever into the first gear position, that slides the input-shaft dog ring along until its teeth (called dogs), engage the dogs on the pair of gears that make up first gear. At this point, power that is delivered from the engine through the clutch to the input shaft is transferred to the input shaft half of first gear, to the output shaft, and from there through the differential to the driving wheels.

All of your double clutching and blipping is an effort to make the dog ring on the input shaft spin at the same RPM as the gear into which you plan to shift. When it all goes wrong, those horrible noises you hear coming from inside the gearbox are from the dogs on the dog ring clattering into the dogs on the gear you're aiming for.

Skipping Gears

You can either go down through the gears one at a time, or you can go from fourth to first rather than stopping at third and second along the way, but like everything else, there are pros and cons for each method of downshifting.

The defense for skipping gears is the argument that doing one shift is less distracting to the braking process than three. In our data collection we have found that even very experienced and talented drivers tend to release some brake pressure when they blip the throttle for downshifts. Three downshifts would mean three variations in brake pedal pressure, so it stands to reason that you'd want to do just one to minimize braking changes.

The difficulty with skipping gears comes in timing the shift. If you drive the same racecar a lot, you get accustomed to the amount of time you need to wait in order for the car to slow down enough so that engaging the next lowest gear will not over-rev the motor. it's a matter of internal timing. You don't consciously count "one thousand one, one thousand two," but you develop a sense for when the clutch can come out in the next lowest gear.

If you decide to skip gears and go directly from fourth to first you have to remember to triple the amount of time it takes before you can let the clutch out at the end of the downshift. Yet in the heat of battle, you're apt to revert to the single gear timing for the clutch release, which would do serious over-rev damage to the motor. If you're confident you can keep the timing right, there's no disadvantage to skipping gears other than the fact that it isn't exactly the subconscious routine you'd like your downshifting to be.

In some cases you're forced to skip gears in downshifting. Some cars slow down so fast that you simply can't move the gear lever fast enough to go through every gear. A Formula Atlantic car, for example, can lose over 60 m.p.h. per second under braking. You might choose to go fifth to third to first instead of directly to first, but stopping at each gear along the way is out of the question.

> "I skip gears downshifting in situations where it's, like, a fifth gear straight and a second gear corner. I skip because I find the braking more stable that way. Going through every gear, if you're perfect with the blips, the car isn't going to notice but, in practice that's difficult. Skipping keeps the car more stable for me."
>
> —Jeremy Dale

Shifting to Help Braking

In most entry-level racecars, the brakes are durable enough to slow the car repeatedly without much help from engine braking. In cars with marginal brakes, this engine braking may contribute a critical amount of braking help; and choosing to skip gears on the approach to corners may end up overtaxing the braking system. It's not uncommon in racing to lose some or all of the braking ability of the car—the only way you can continue in the race is by using the engine and gearbox to get the car slowed down for the corners. In this case you back off early (sometimes even shutting off the ignition), let the car slow to a speed that won't over-rev the motor in the next lowest gear, and shift it down. it's not an ideal situation but, especially in endurance racing, many of the finishers are the walking

wounded, and the ethic is to get the car to the finish no matter what it takes.

UPSHIFTING

The shift up to a higher gear in either a racing gearbox or a stock transmission is the same—clutch in, move the lever up a gear, and clutch out. There is absolutely no need for a blip in the middle of the shift. In the upshift situation the input shaft needs to slow down somewhat in order to synchronize with the next highest gear ratio and this happens naturally as you back off the throttle and depress the clutch. Blipping between upshifts only makes the mismatch worse.

Unlike drag racing, you don't power shift—that is, keep your accelerator foot to the floor while you operate the gear lever and clutch. You should lift off the accelerator, taking the strain off the gear set, and dip the clutch quickly as you move the lever up. You don't necessarily have to push the clutch pedal all the way to the floorboard. You can feel the release point just past the end of the freeplay in the clutch pedal. An inch or so of this hard pressure area is sufficient to create enough slip in the drivetrain to reduce the mechanical shock of the upshift.

> "I don't always get the clutch all the way down to the floor—sometimes you only move it halfway, but you get a little bit of disengagement and it makes the gear change that much softer on the gearbox."
>
> —Bryan Herta

Clutchless Upshifts

Some drivers argue for upshifting without using the clutch at all. Again, it's a matter of how good you are at matching the speeds of the input and output shafts. With a very close ratio transmission, just the act of backing off the throttle between gears slows the input shaft enough that the gears end up perfectly synchronized and the gear lever falls into the next highest gear. An expert driver will develop a sense of timing of how long to pause before going back to full throttle to accommodate the synchronization. But, if you don't get the timing right you can really damage the transmission.

We feel that you should use the clutch on upshifts. We've tried it both ways and found that there is no time saved by upshifting without using the clutch. It takes a good driver around .2 seconds to go from full throttle to zero throttle and back again to full during an upshift. If your right foot can move the distance from full throttle to off and back again in two tenths, your left foot can surely do the same thing with the clutch. The benefit is that the clutch cushions the impact of dog against dog and the shock of sudden full power on the driveline. If it were faster, it might be worth the risk, but in test after test we can find no lap-time advantage in not using the clutch on upshifts.

> *"Everybody seems to want to speed shift. It's not any faster. I can tell you because we measured it on the computer."*
>
> —Bryan Herta

Bigger Cars

As you move up into faster and more powerful cars, it is possible that you will be faced with the situation where the clutch is the weak link in the driveline—the piece that will wear out first. Each shift and each slip of the clutch plate wears it out a little bit. With big horsepower and a lot of grip, the clutch may wear out before the end of the race due to this slippage, so you may be forced by circumstance to avoid using the clutch for upshifts. In this case, you'd better have the synchronization right or you'll save the clutch at the expense of the gearbox.

> *"I always upshift without the clutch, because I find it smoother. I think it also saves the clutch, which isn't the weak link in a lot of cars, but can be in something like a GTS car. I figure if you never push the clutch going up through the gears, you're probably not going to wear it out or break it."*
>
> —Jeremy Dale

Upshifting Speed

It *is* important to develop the ability to upshift quickly. Any time spent between gears is time where the car is no longer accelerating. Minimizing the time spent between gears lengthens the acceleration time, yielding higher straightaway speeds and lower elapsed time down the straights. But here's the catch: the more you rush it, the greater the chance of a missed shift. It takes anywhere from 3/4 seconds to 1-1/2 seconds to recover from a missed shift, and, if the motor blows as a result, it can take even longer.

One of the problems is that as you try to do it faster, you tend to tense up, squeezing the gear lever with a death grip that causes you to lose all sensitivity of the lever's location. You don't have to use more *force* to move the lever faster. You can still hold the gear lever with your thumb and two fingertips: just increase the hand speed (or wrist speed in a formula car). All in all it's the old risk vs. reward trade-off. There are tenths of seconds of lap time in fast shifting, so you try to develop the skill and avoid the pitfalls.

Shift Point

The normal routine when accelerating up through the gears down the straights is to keep your right foot hard on the floor until the tachometer reaches the engine's redline, then shift it up. Much has been written about determining shift points, but taking the motor up to the engine builder's or team manager's recommended redline before shifting pretty much covers it. In powerful cars, especially in the lower gears, the engine is accelerating so quickly that you may need to anticipate the redline by several hundred RPM in order to keep from overshooting.

Rev Limits

There are very few constraints in driving racecars. You're pretty much free to make independent decisions about most driving-related issues. A major constraint is that you have to drive quickly without abusing the motor by taking it over its RPM limit. This constraint is there all the time, whether you're racing your own car or driving for a team.

There is nothing artificial about the redline. Some engines are relatively durable: you can over-rev them from time to time and they don't blow up immediately. But there are some that are real hand-grenades, and one missed shift creates an oily, expensive mess. Shifting is the biggest danger area for motors.

Automatic Shifting

If the current trend toward automatic and semi-automatic gearboxes continues, most of this chapter becomes moot. The computer and the engine management system together select the right gear for the situation. But before you get to Formula 1, you'll have to spend years dealing with non-synchro transmissions. Becoming a good shifter, even though it's not the most fun part of driving racecars, is indispensable in learning to be a talented racer. It's a skill worthy of your attention and effort.

Part III

Honing Your Skills and Strategies

CHAPTER 7

WORKING UP A TRACK: FROM MAP TO LAPS

ARMED WITH THE INFOR-
mation from the preceding
chapters, you should be all
set to get on the racetrack
and try driving a racecar.
When the day arrives, you're going to be emotionally
charged, which is great—it's one of the reasons we
drive racecars—but you can't let the excitement interfere with your performance.

We have often seen drivers with considerable talent rely on adrenaline rather than knowledge and
skill when they move from the everyday world onto
the racetrack. They lock into being aggressive and in-
ordinately brave, and are often fast—briefly. They try
too hard and think too little.

> "Natural talent is so rare. In the years I've
> been teaching, maybe one or two drivers, out
> of hundreds, had wonderful natural talent.
> And part of that was not appreciating the con-
> sequences of their actions—and being lucky.
> It's possible to be fast for a while by just react-
> ing to what happens to you, but in terms of
> winning a championship, they're not the guys
> to put your money on. The analytical, method-
> ical, technical approach is going to get you to
> run up front more, complete more laps, and
> be in a better position to win a championship.
> You see it all the time—drivers who win an oc-
> casional race but crash out of a lot of them."
>
> —Jim Pace

When it's your turn to get on a proper race course,
don't get caught in this trap. The professional approach is to recognize and take risks, when you need
to, but to finish races. You've got to *finish* to finish
first. Fastest laps are good and pole positions are
great, for sure, but ultimately, you'd like to be known
as a series champion.

> The value of racing theory lies in its ap-
> plication to real problems. An analysis of
> the Sebring Test Circuit reveals a plan-
> ning method that works at all racetracks.

"WORKING UP" THE RACETRACK

Let's go through the process
that a good race driver uses
when planning how to outperform the rest of the
field. We'll take all the knowledge you've acquired
and apply it to a real racetrack: the 1.8-mile Sebring
test circuit in Sebring, Florida. Sebring is used
throughout the winter months as one of the most popular testing sites for professional teams from CART,
IRL, Indy Light, and Trans Am , to mention a few.

Details, Details, Details

The analysis we're about to start goes well beyond
what many race drivers would do. But to succeed in
racing—to be the fastest of the crowd—means that
you have to leave mediocrity behind. If you're content
to do what the "average" racer would do and leave it
at that, you will limit your success.

Our experience with the type of racing we do at
Skip Barber's colors our approach. Unlike many other forms of racing, the competition in both the Formula Dodge Series and in the Barber Dodge Pro Series is
among drivers competing in identically prepared,
equal cars. If you're going to get an advantage over
others, it comes from looking within—to driving skill.
This fundamentally changes your approach from trying to get the car to go faster to making yourself, as the
driver, the focal point. The competition at the front of
any of our series events is so close that the difference

> "One of the great challenges of driving a
> racecar is that nothing is ever exactly the
> same. You always learn. You're almost never
> thinking, 'Oh, this is exactly how I did it last
> time.' You always have to be ready to adapt
> and change."
>
> —Danny Sullivan

between winning and not is a matter of a tenth of a second or two per lap. This fact drives us to turn over every rock that may yield a lap time improvement.

A Plan that Works

Our intention here is not to make you a Sebring expert but to show you a process that will increase your chances of success. Our analysis process is the same regardless of the racetrack: you can use it whenever you go to a circuit you've never driven before. It's also a good idea to go through these steps at a track you know, just to confirm that there haven't been any changes since your last visit. It's a plan that works.

Start by getting a general, broad view of the racetrack to see which way it goes and to identify its obvious highlights. Once you have an overall familiarity with the course, you can hone in on the details by applying the following steps.

1. Look closely at the line. Consider whether the corner stands alone or whether another corner will force a compromise in the classic line. By walking, pedaling or slowly driving around the course, you can begin to identify likely reference points that will help you keep the car on the best path.

2. Next, consider how you would maximize the corner exit speed by determining where and how you would begin the acceleration through the apex and away from the corner.

3. Finally, focus on each corner entry to identify the likely braking process you'll need to use.

Simply put, you're trying to decide in advance what you'll do with the steering wheel, the throttle, and the brakes in each corner. To do this, look at each turn in great detail and think about the likely choices

> "A lot of what I do today is drawing on 25 years of experience, but still when I get to a new racetrack, I'll start with the basics. I'll first of all break it down into the most important corners and think about what I'm going to have to do to get the car to work there. And then I'll work back from that and start to work on subtleties. I'll really take a close look at each corner to see if there's track features that can help, things like a camber change or a pavement change I may have missed and can use."
>
> —David Loring

and the potential complications that will affect your line, throttle application and type of braking.

All of this is work you can do without driving the racecar. Getting access to the racetrack in order to drive around it slowly in a street car is easy if you're polite and diplomatic. Don't abuse the privilege by driving quickly and scaring the track management and staff. Ninety percent of what you need to learn can be accomplished at less than 30 m.p.h.

Ultimately, however, some problems can only be solved behind the wheel of the racecar. Specific reference points for braking, turn-in, apex and track-out are constantly being developed and refined in the racecar at speed, starting with the general references you found in your early tours around the track at a slower pace. Before you set out in the racecar, you should have a clear idea of the unanswered questions you'll need to work on through experimentation.

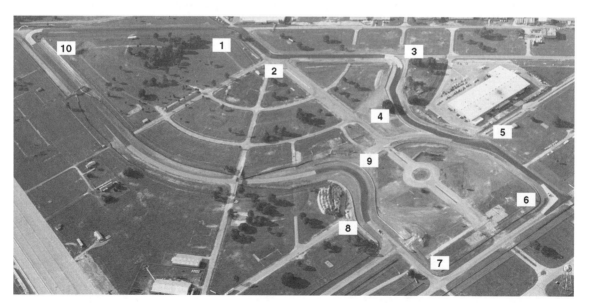

Fig. 7-1. The Sebring test circuit, part of the 12 Hour course, offers a variety of challenges. An excellent training facility, it has a wide variety of cornering speeds, braking approaches and compromises.

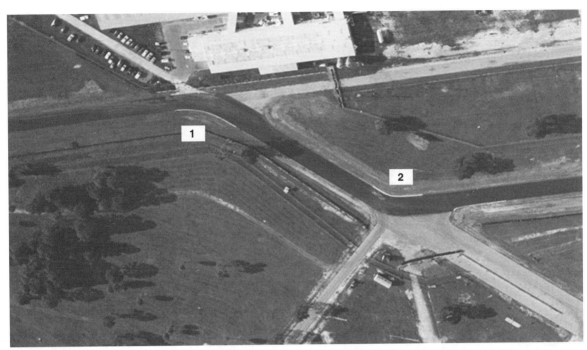

Fig. 7-2. Turns 1 and 2 make up a high-speed compromise esse: you'll determine the extent of the compromise when you're in the racecar.

Having a list of alternate approaches that you will try helps you arrive at the best conclusion more quickly.

FIRST IMPRESSIONS

The aerial photograph of the Sebring Test Circuit in Fig. 7-1 will give you an accurate idea of which way the road goes. Follow along and learn the turn numbers. They will be important in how you communicate to your crew, describing the car's, and your, behavior around the circuit. Everybody has to speak the same language to avoid miscommunication.

The first thing you will notice about Sebring is that, like most of Florida, it's absolutely flat. Changes of elevation won't be a big factor here. You'll start the lap crossing the finish line, between Turns 10 and 1.

Turns 1 and 2. It's almost a 1/4 mile run from The Hairpin up to Turn 1 so you'll expect to be going pretty fast when you get there. Turn 1 is directly affected by Turn 2 since together, they constitute a gentle esse (see Fig. 7-2). Turn 2 leads onto a straight, so of 1 and 2, it looks to be the more important corner to drive "on line."

Turn 1 may not, however, have to be completely compromised. It looks like you can use some road coming out of 1 and still get back to the right hand edge of the road for the turn-in for 2. These two corners are the fastest on the course—their arcs much more gentle than any of the others. The good news is

Fig. 7-3. Turn 3 is much tighter and slower than Turns 1–2 and leads to a long stretch of acceleration.

that there is a lot of grassy run-off area so, although 1 and 2 are high-speed areas, they are relatively safe.

Turn 3. After tracking out of 2 all the way to the right-hand verge, you have to bend the car back to the left to get set for the approach to Turn 3 (see Fig. 7-3). You want to coax the car left, not horse it over—there should be time.

Turn 3 is a tight right-hand bend with an increasing radius: primarily concrete with lots of reference points available from the painted curbs.

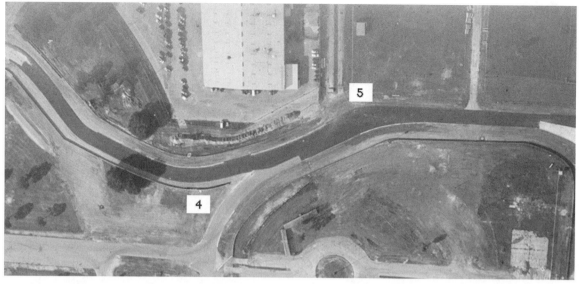

Fig. 7-4. Turns 4 and 5 bend left, then right, but their radii are so large that they may be taken flat out, essentially constituting a straight.

Fig. 7-5. The gentle bend of the inside curbing of Turn 6 can be deceiving, tempting you to turn early.

Fig. 7-6. Turn 7 is a short, classic, 90-degree right.

Turns 4,5 and 6. Turns 4 and 5 look to be just bends in the road, one left, one right, that will probably be taken flat out, accelerating as hard as possible (see Fig. 7-4). The run through 4 and 5 and up to the braking zone for Turn 6 is a long stretch of road, just as long as the straight between The Hairpin and Turn 1. Exit speed out of Turn 3 will be important.

Turn 6, another right-hander, also has entry and apex areas made of concrete but, worthy to note, the concrete ends before the track-out (see Fig. 7-5).

The approach to Turn 6 is very deceiving. The inside curbing angles gently down toward the apex while the outside edge of the racetrack is shaped like a sharp 90 degree corner. Look to the inside and the corner looks more gentle— and faster—than it does if you look toward the outside. All that road down there at the entry will tempt you to turn in too early.

Turns 7,8 & 9. Turn 6 is followed by a very short straight leading to Turn 7, a textbook 90-degree right-hander and a very short corner (see Fig. 7-6). You're in and out quickly, but it will be quite slow—you might consider using first gear.

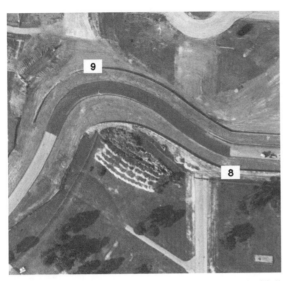

Fig. 7-7. Turn 9 leads onto the longest period of full throttle acceleration so you'll plan on sacrificing 8 to be sure you're on line for 9.

Fig. 7-8. The slowest corner on the racetrack is The Hairpin. If any corner in the world requires threshold braking, this is it.

Turn 8 is just a jog to the right and is going to be important mostly because it leads to Turn 9, the entry to the longest straight.

Turn 9 seems to go on and on, a long corner with smooth asphalt, well over a 90-degree change of direction, with a decreasing radius as well (see Fig. 7-7). You'll need a late apex as well as some device to keep you from getting in early and having to lift coming onto the longest straight.

The "straight" isn't. It bends constantly to the right as the road sweeps gently under the vehicle bridge, then, a quarter-mile later, still turning right, under the pedestrian bridge. This half-mile long curving straight is the section of the course where you are likely to reach the highest speed, accelerating with your foot to the floor up through the gears. The straightaway is a chance to take a breath, wiggle your fingers, check the mirrors and gauges, and let the car do the work.

Turn 10: The Hairpin. Finally, 2,000 feet after you finish Turn 9, you flash by the second bridge and the road straightens for 200 hundred yards or so where you begin braking for Turn 10 (see Fig. 7-8).

The Hairpin is tight and slow—our Formula Dodge racecars, as run in our race series, are in the mid-30 m.p.h. range at the slowest point. The corner is also followed by a 1/4-mile straight, so exit speed and throttle application to deal with wheelspin, are going to be big considerations here.

The entry to this turn is odd. Obviously, there is a lot of braking going on here, from whatever top speed the car can generate down to around 35 m.p.h. Should you have a failure, there is an escape route to

the left, a route many find hard to take since their minds are focused on turning right. Fifty feet before the turn-in point, the track surface changes from asphalt to concrete. In the last 20 yards of braking zone, the road widens to the left with a two-foot wide curbing you could use it to widen the arc of the corner. You can try it later to see if it upsets the handling of the car. The apex curb here is pretty steep and it probably won't help to hit it with the right front tire. The exit is smooth but sandy.

These first couple of laps, driven slowly in a street car, give you first impressions. Now it's time to get out a track map and try to get specific about the problems presented by each corner, thinking about how you're going to solve them.

FOCUS ON THE DETAILS

Take as much time as you need. Remember, problems are much easier to ponder and solve at this stage than they will be at speed. Issue Number One is the line.

Try to decide whether a corner can be considered singly or should be compromised for the next corner; and identify the more important corners—those leading onto long periods of acceleration as well as those that are long and fast. Look at each corner's shape and note changes in banking or road surface that will affect your apex. At the same time, scout out your reference points for the turn-in, apex and track-out of each corner.

Next, consider corner exits—concentrate on where and how you will likely apply the throttle.

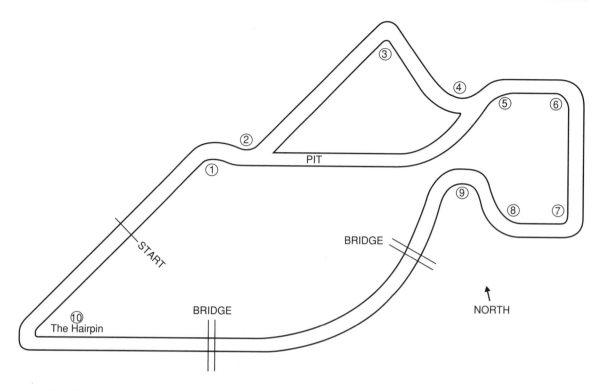

Fig. 7-9. Track maps are seldom to scale but can be useful in making driving decisions before getting in the car.

Finally, on the last 25 laps, consider the type of braking required for each corner based on speed loss and location, all the while looking for your braking reference points.

Let's apply this method to the Sebring test circuit, starting with Turns 1 and 2.

Turns 1 and 2

The Line. The obvious problem here is that you can't drive outside-inside-outside in Turn 1 and be able to get over to the turning point for the classic line through 2 (see Fig. 7-10).

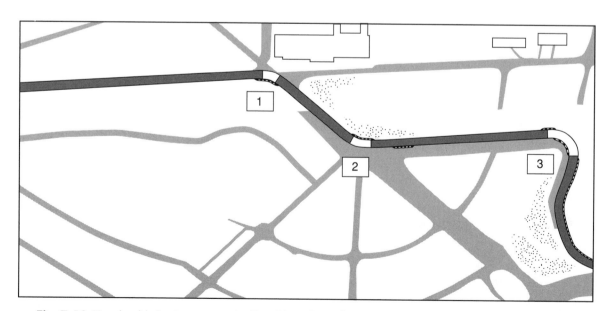

Fig. 7-10. You should plan to compromise Turn 1 in order to drive on the biggest radius through Turn 2, since the track segment from 2 to 3 is longer than Turn 1.

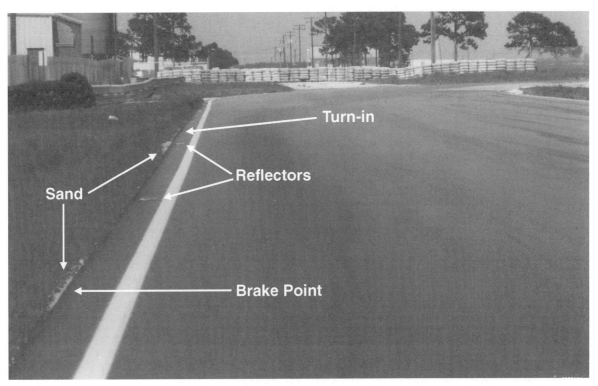

Fig. 7-11. The approach to Turn 1 has very uniform features, so you'll have to find creative reference points.

In choosing which turn is more important to drive on-line, your choice will depend upon the length of the Turn 1 track segment versus the length of the track segment from the turn-in point for 2 to the next braking zone. You'd prefer to carry the extra speed which the classic line will allow over the longest portion of racetrack. The distance from the approximate turn-in of 1, through the apex and up to the turn-in for 2 is about 450 feet. The turn-in to 2, through the apex, past the track-out and up to the braking point for 3 is almost 600 feet. You'd rather carry extra speed for 600 feet than for 450 feet, so the solution would appear to be to compromise the line through 1 to get the best shot through 2.

If Turn 2 led onto a long straight, the choice would be obvious: sacrifice the first corner for the second. When the second corner leads nowhere, you might not choose to sacrifice the first.

When it comes to compromise corners, keep in mind that the big radius advantage of the classic line is most useful when the line determines the speed. The line limits the speed through the corner when the car is operating at its cornering limit. If Turn 1 were tighter, say 30 m.p.h. slower than Turn 2, you might not be able to get the car going fast enough into 2 that it needs the big radius offered by the classic line. In this case you could compromise Turn 1 less, making its radius bigger, and be able to carry more speed through 1 *and* 2.

This isn't the case here. The car will be at its cornering limit in both 1 and 2 so the line through these turns determines the car's speed, as long as you exercise the skill to drive the car at its cornering limits in the 75–85 m.p.h. range.

Another consideration for trying to run on the biggest possible arc, even though you don't need it to accommodate limit cornering, is the plain fact that more steering wheel lock creates more tire scrub, causing drag, which resists acceleration. We'll deal with this consideration shortly.

The line difficulties in these two corners are going to involve picking up a good reference point for the turn-ins for 1 and 2. The approach to 1 has very uniform features, making it tough to pick out a brake point and turn-in point (see Fig. 7-11). The apex for Turn 1 falls in the middle of the short curb, an obvious aiming point.

At the turn-in for Turn 2 (see Fig 7-12), you'll be traveling near 80 m.p.h., just finishing your drift through 1, straightening for an instant, then committing to 2. Getting a consistent turn-in reference is going to be something you need to develop at a conservative pace and pick up with your peripheral vision since, in this especially fast corner, you want your eyes on the apex when you turn. The apex reference for Turn 2 is easier; the concrete patch in the center of the corner makes a good target (see Fig. 7-13).

Fig. 7-12. The white discoloration at the right of the track before Turn 2 looks like it's too late for a turn-in point; vary your distance to these points as you experiment with the turn-in.

The track-out for 2 has a relatively flat, narrow curb and the adjoining dirt runoff is quite level so that, should you drop a wheel, it shouldn't create a big control problem as long as you don't try to horse the car back to the left. It's also worth inspecting how deep the drop-off on the back side of the curb has become. Sometimes, if it's been recently graded by the track maintenance crew, it will be even with the track surface. But if it's a busy race weekend, the drop-off can be like a canyon and has to be avoided at all costs.

At the apex of Turn 2, there is a big, sudden camber change which, even at low speed, feels like a big bump (see Fig. 7-13). It's bad enough that if you had the car at an excessive yaw angle and were just starting to gather it up when you hit the bump, it could trigger a spin. Unfortunately, you can't avoid it as this would

Fig. 7-13. The apex of Turn 2 falls in the center of the concrete patch. Note the sudden camber change at the apex. Track-out is at the very end of the exit curbing.

put you 10 feet wide of the apex. Just remember that if the car is out of shape approaching the apex of 2, it's important to get it settled before the apex bump.

Throttle Application. Since the two are directly connected it makes sense to take them together. Since both are fast corners—probably third gear—you won't have to worry about generating wheelspin with too much throttle. In Turn 1, you'll expect to get back to full throttle right after brake release and carry a lot of speed through the apex of 1. The trick is going to be the entry of Turn 2. You can't tell, until you're in the racecar, how much you will have to slow the car for the entry of 2. Presumably, you won't be flat on the throttle through both Turns 1 and 2. You'll have to slow the car some to get the car turned into 2. In any event, you *do* know that you need to be careful of snapping off the throttle while the car is still turning right, exiting 1.

Expect that, if you need to slow for 2, you can breathe back the throttle while finishing 1, but that any full lift or braking maneuver has to be saved for the period when the car gets straight for a bit between 1 and 2. In high-speed sweepers like these, the car will be more stable with some power on and its yaw can be controlled with small—10–20%—power changes.

Braking. Although Turn 1 comes after a long straight, it's such a gentle bend that it's doubtful that you'll have to lose a lot of speed for the corner entry. Rather than expect threshold braking, you'll most likely want to control the entry speed more accurately with a lighter braking level. This will make the load transfer more progressive and help make the car feel less upset at the corner entry. You're likely to trail the brakes into the corner a bit but, since you're keen to get back on the throttle to stabilize the speed and handling, you'll probably trail less than normal.

You won't know whether the brakes are needed in turn 2 until you try it. If they are, it will be a light application to lose just a touch of speed to enter 2. If braking isn't needed, the speed adjustment will be just a breathe of the throttle. Be careful of TTO.

The bulk of the breathe should come while the car is briefly straight between 1 and 2, and you should expect to stabilize the car with some power just as you turn toward the apex of 2.

Turns 3, 4, and 5

The Line. At first, Turn 3 (see Fig. 7-14) looks as if it can be considered all on its own. It's a tight right-hander, with little road camber to consider and a concrete surface throughout the last 2/3rds of the corner. It leads onto a sweeping acceleration section of the course which is almost a quarter mile long from the exit of 3 to the turn-in for 6, and this can have an effect on the line you choose.

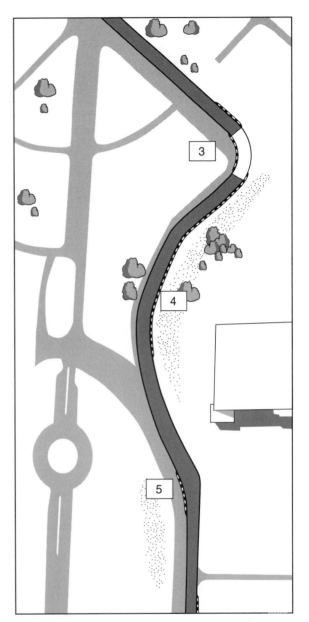

Fig. 7-14. Experimenting in the car at speed in Turn 3 will tell you whether to use all of the road at the track-out point.

The corner entry is not a problem. A curb on the left is going to be helpful in picking out a turn-in point and the striped apex and the complex of seams in the concrete will make it easy to pick an apex mark (see Fig. 7-15). The concrete section starts about halfway between the turn-in and the apex so you'll have to look for changes in grip between the two surfaces to see if it affects your line.

The biggest complication comes from deciding whether to let the car track out all the way to the edge

Fig. 7-15. The apex for Turn 3 is not a problem: the striped curb and the concrete seams will allow you to pick your apex mark easily. Also remember that the change to concrete and then back to asphalt will affect your grip.

of the road at the exit or to take a line that holds it a car width or two toward the middle of the road.

If you let the car all the way out at the exit you will then have to hug the inside edge of the road through the beginning of Turn 4. You can take this section flat out, accelerating as hard as you can, but if you start on the left you'll have to turn the steering wheel more, especially through 4. Using more steering angle will create more scrub against the road, adding resistance to acceleration. Minimizing tire scrub on the acceleration run up to Turn 6 could be worth lap time. If you decide not to track all the way out of Turn 3, the down side is that, because of the tighter radius, your speed out of 3 will be lower. You may accomplish your goal of limiting tire scrub but, since you start the acceleration run from a lower speed, it may all come out even in the end and the elapsed time from 3 to 6 will be the same, or maybe even worse. There's no way to know but to try it both ways at speed. Your plan in this case is to stick with one approach and when it's time to start looking for the last second of lap time, to experiment in Turn 3.

Tire scrub dominates the approach to Turns 4 and 5. As the car accelerates around this long left-hand bend , you want to take the line of least resistance, especially with a car with lower horsepower. Tire scrub will be a bigger factor in limiting the acceleration of a low horsepower car than it will on one with 600 or more horsepower.

In a low horsepower car you want the car to take its own smooth path, never trying to muscle it to turn more, but attempting to unwind the steering wheel— within the confines of the road, of course. Guiding the car through Turns 4 and 5 will be a matter of fingertip control of the steering wheel, letting the car have its head, nursing the car up to speed (see Fig. 7-16). You will have to be careful not to get out too far right as the outside is filled with the sand, grit and bits of used up tire rubber we call "the marbles." It can get very slick on the marbles and, even though you're not on the limit cornering through 4 and 5, the marbles can lower the traction enough to create a real problem.

The actual line through 4 will take you close to the apex curb twice as you try to create a gentle arc up to 5 (see Fig. 7-17). The first curbing is about 150 feet past the track-out of 3 and is very steep, so it's not to be hit. Come close, but try not to hit it. The car floats right, away from the curb, if the steering wheel is held at the same angle, then floats back toward the inside again getting closest about another 300 feet along. You let the car drift right again heading for the apex curbing at Turn 5. As you get to 5, the steering wheel is almost straight. You would have to actually turn the wheel right to get to the apex of 5 so you don't bother. Your path is headed diagonally toward the entry of Turn 6 and there's no reason to drive over to the apex curb for 5 simply because it's there.

Fig. 7-16. The best path through Turns 4 and 5 will be the one with the least steering input. Here, you can see that, coming out of Turn 4 and heading into turn 5, the car does not need to be forced to the apex.

Throttle Application. Turn 3 leads onto a long period of acceleration, so once you get the car turned in, you want to get to full power as soon as you can manage it, well before the apex. Wheelspin may be a problem since it's a slow corner taken in a lower gear. Turns 4 and 5 look to be, essentially, an acceleration zone, so

you'll expect to have the throttle to the floor except for the upshifts.

Braking. Turn 3 is one of the slower corners on the circuit and, since Turn 2 is fast, there will be a lot of speed loss required here—definitely use threshold braking. Since the corner leads to a long acceleration

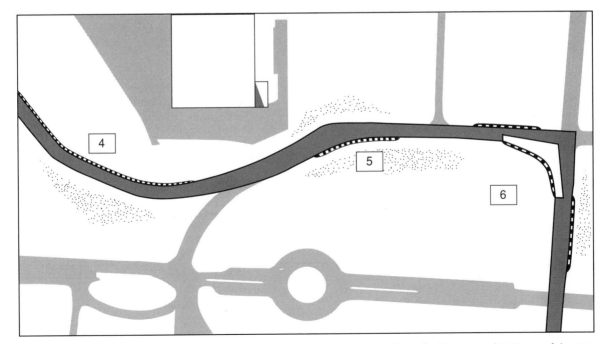

Fig. 7-17. To be on target for Turn 6, there's no need to hit the apex curbing for Turns 4 and 5. Be careful not to drift too far right or, through Turn 4, you'll get into the marbles.

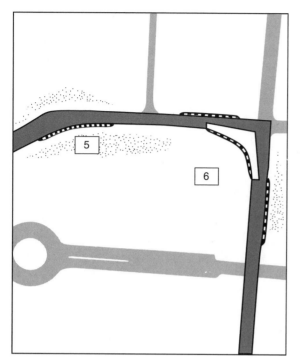

Fig. 7-18. Turn 6 is the first uncomplicated corner on the circuit. The turn-in for 6 may be later than it appears because of the decreasing radius.

zone and it's an increasing radius corner, throttle application will come early, so don't expect to trail the brakes deeply into the corner. Trail-braking about a third of the way or less between the turn-in and apex will probably do.

Experience will tell whether the best approach is to brake diagonally toward the turn-in or to get the car parallel alongside the left edge of the road, depending on the room available, before going to threshold braking. Having the car straight under braking will be the priority, regardless of the direction it's pointing.

Turn 6

The Line. Finally, a straightforward corner. The corner shape has a decreasing radius, so the turn-in may be later than it appears (see Fig. 7-18). Still, it's pretty simple: start on the left, apex on the right, track all the way out on the exit.

You'll need to decide whether you have to drive the car parallel to the edge of the road at the entry or whether a diagonal approach to the turn-in point allows better braking without making the initial turn-in any tighter. You can probably only resolve this at speed. If you let the car go straight past the apex of 5, you can drive straight toward the turn-in for 6 or you can bend the car left, then right again, to align it with

the edge of the road for the braking zone for 6. The advantage of doing this would be to make the total amount of direction change in 6 smaller. If you arrive at the turn-in point with the car pointing more toward the left, it just increases the number of degrees of direction change you need to accomplish.

On the other hand, in order to do this left-right swerve to align the car with the edge of the road, you'll be adding tire scrub and perhaps slowing the acceleration up to the corner. Affecting your decision at this point is just how much additional direction change is involved. Is it 45 degrees more, or less than 10 degrees additional turning? In this case the increase is small, under ten degrees. Another factor is whether you can comfortably align the car with the edge and get it straight before the braking point. For now you'll decide to try a diagonal approach to 6 and, once up to speed, try the alternative approach and see which you like better.

There is a very visible two-layered curbing, striped in blue and white, at the corner entry. You can gauge your turn-in on the clearly visible junction between the low and high curb (see Fig. 7-19).

The inside edge of the road bends very gently toward the apex, making the radius of the corner seem extraordinarily large on the way in. You'll have to make a point of ignoring the temptation to get in early.

At the corner exit, two things happen that may have an impact on your line and how the car will feel at speed. As you cross the middle of the following straight heading for the track-out point, you come over the crown of the road onto a section of negative banking (off-camber) and at the same time the track surface changes from concrete to old asphalt. The apex may be later than you think because the car is going to lose cornering grip when it gets to this part of the road.

There's not much of a straight following Turn 6, so you probably won't play with a later apex, hoping to eke out a little extra exit speed.

Should you get in too early, there's a gently angled curb at the track-out that gives you an extra two feet of road and could catch the car in a pinch. It flattens out past the trackout and you could use this flat painted portion but you'd want to hustle the car back onto the racetrack proper. You want to avoid giving the driveline a shock by dropping the left rear onto the sand where the curbing ends.

Throttle Application . Although Turn 6 has the same angular change as Turn 3, it is a much longer corner. The transition to aggressive throttle will have to come later than in 3, or you'll gain too much speed to be able to keep it on the road at the corner exit. Wheelspin doesn't look to be a problem since 6 should be faster than 3.

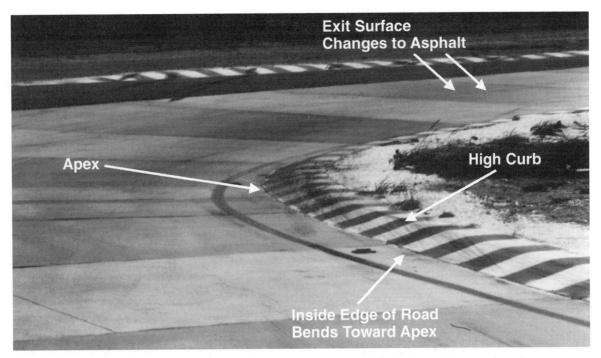

Fig. 7-19. The high curb in Turn 6 makes the apex easy to spot. Watch for surface changes at the exit.

Braking. Coming at the end of a 1/4 mile acceleration zone, the entry speed will be high and, although 6 is not as slow a corner as 3, you can expect to need a lot of speed loss. Threshold braking, or close to it, will likely be required.

Turn 6 is a longer corner than 3 and a decreasing radius corner. It's likely that the throttle application will come on later than in Turn 3 and the braking will go on longer. Expect that you'll trail the brakes deeper into the corner, especially if it helps you carry some of the straightaway speed with you into Turn 6.

Turn 7

The Line. This turn is a textbook right-hander with a well-marked apex curbing (see Fig. 7-20). There is a dark road surface discoloration off the left edge of the road which will help you establish a turn-in point.

There looks to be a good deal of positive road camber (banking) around the apex, so you might be able to add a bit of steering lock to briefly get the car's direction changed more around the apex.

The bad news is that the road goes sharply off-camber as you approach the track-out and, judging from the wide patch of raw dirt to the left of the track-out curb, it forces a lot of cars to go wide on the exit.

It looks as though the curb can be used on the track-out, but there's a deep drop-off on the left that will bottom out the suspension if you drop your wheels in there (see Fig. 7-21).

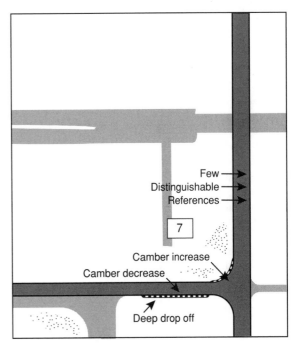

Fig. 7-20. The major difficulty in Turn 7, a textbook right-hander, is its lack of distinguishing features at the corner entry.

Throttle Application. This turn is the tightest 90-degree corner on the circuit, so aggressive throttle should come earlier than the other two. Since it

Fig. 7-21. Watch for the deep drop-off at the exit for Turn 7; you can see here that plenty of drivers have gone wide on this turn and landed in the dirt outside the track-out curb.

might, however, be a first gear corner, you might need to be more progressive on the way to full power to avoid wheelspin.

Braking. The approach speed won't be as fast as 6 but the corner sure looks slow and short. You'll probably use threshold braking but not for as long as in 6. The trail of the brakes into the corner should also be considerably less simply because there isn't much distance between the turn-in and apex—even if you trail brake halfway to the apex, it's still less than three car lengths. The biggest problem in 7 is finding a good braking point since there's no turn-in curb at 7 and there are few road features to help you.

Turns 8 and 9

The Line. Here are another pair of corners that are connected, so you'll have to compromise one for the other (see Fig. 7-22). Since Turn 9 leads onto the longest period of full throttle acceleration on the racetrack, there is no doubt that you compromise the path through 8 in order to get to the right side of the road for the turn-in point for 9.

Turn 8 comes just 100 yds after the very slow Turn 7 so it's conceivable that you may not have to slow for

8, but just drive through it up to Turn 9. Only time on the track will tell.

The turn-in will be easy to locate since it comes slightly past where the intersecting road of the 12 Hour course adjoins the Test Circuit. Plenty of reference points here. In order to get you in position for the turn-in for 9, the apex in 8 will be very late, actually at the very end of the striped curbing on the right. It's easy to spot.

The turn-in for 9 is also an easy landmark. There is another curbing on the right near the turn-in, but you can't let it fool you. The actual turn-in point is beyond it, marked by a dark discoloration of the track surface.

The apex, however, is another matter. The corner is long—it's almost 500 feet from the turn-in to the track out—and the car has to change direction about 110 degrees. This means that the apex is almost a football field away when you turn the wheel at the turn-in. The entire inside edge of the corner is lined with a 4-inch high curb so there's no chance to see the apex until you're halfway to it (see Fig. 7-23). Complicating matters is the fact that, although it looks like a long constant radius corner at first, it's actually a long decreasing radius corner and, therefore, requires a later turn-in. It will be very easy to early apex this turn.

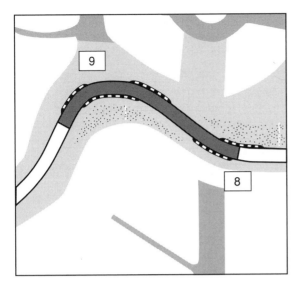

Fig. 7-22. Turns 8 and 9 have plenty of reference points, from the intersecting road of the 12-Hour course at the turn-in for 8 to the turn-in curb for 9. Turn 9 leads to the longest straight on the circuit.

This is the most important corner on the circuit as far as exit speed is concerned. If you get into the apex early, you'll have to lift out of the throttle to keep from running off at the exit; and the last place you want to be decreasing throttle is coming onto the longest straight. It will be crucial to get a reference point so that you can check on your progress toward the apex in time to make an early correction. This is going to take a lot of repetition and a sharp eye for reference points that coincide with the correct path.

Throttle Application. You won't be able to tell until you get out there, but it looks like you might be able to drive through 8 without lifting. If not, you want to plan to lift just before turn-in and squeeze the power back on as you turn in to stabilize the car. You don't want to turn in with your foot on the floor, then lift while the car has heavy cornering loads on it because TTO will get the tail out.

Other than the sweepers, Turn 9 is the longest corner on the racetrack, with almost 500 feet between the turn-in and track-out. Even though you would like to go to aggressive throttle as early as possible in order to maximize the exit speed onto the longest straight, you'll have to be patient here. If you go to a lot of power early—say, in the first 50 feet following the turn-in—the car will gain too much speed by the apex and you'll almost certainly have to lift coming off the corner to keep the car on the track. The throttle application is likely to be a long progressive squeeze toward the floor, being constantly sensitive to whether your throttle application is forcing you off-line. You still want to be hard in it before the apex, but not 100 feet before the apex. Even low-powered cars are likely to take some delicacy here.

Braking. If you do any braking in Turn 8 at all, it should be just a touch before the turn-in. In Turn 9 it looks as though you will be able to get the car straight

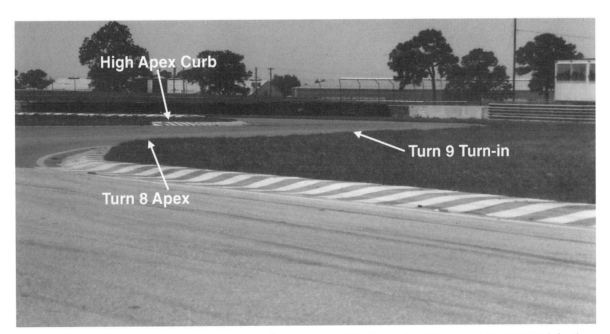

Fig. 7-23. Exit speed is crucial in Turn 9, so you'll compromise 8 for 9, apexing late through Turn 8. Watch for the apex curb in Turn 9, which is hard to spot until you're halfway there because the curb is so high.

long enough at the exit of 8 to begin braking in a straight line for 9. If not, you'll have to focus on taking a line through 8 that makes it possible. It appears that only sloppy car placement in 8 will cause a problem here.

Considering the fact that Turn 9 is such a long corner and that aggressive throttle will come on a long way past the turn-in point, you might be able to make up time at the corner entry by decelerating and turning toward the throttle application point. This is especially true since Turn 9 is a decreasing radius corner. You may want to use the big radius in the early part of the turn to carry extra speed in, as long as it doesn't interfere with the throttle application. For this corner, there might be a lot more brake-turning than straight-line braking.

Turn 10 : The Hairpin

The Line. Turn 10, or "The Hairpin" (see Fig. 7-24), is a classic corner, one driven by motor racing's greats, from Moss to the Andrettis. It is not, however, terribly complicated. It will be a standard out-in-out corner, but since it is both slow and leads onto a substantial straight, you may have to turn later and apex later than it appears. This is especially true since there's a big direction change involved—you change the car's course over 135 degrees. There aren't many corners around that are this slow, yet seem to go on this long.

Reference points are plentiful in this turn. The concrete starts 50 feet short of the turn-in and each

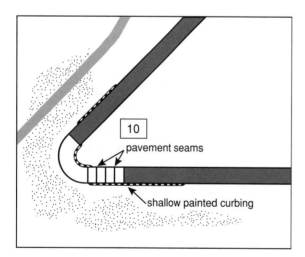

Fig. 7-24. Reference points, especially for braking, are crucial in Turn 10, The Hairpin, since it is the slowest corner on the circuit. The change from asphalt to concrete will be especially helpful for judging your braking point and turn-in.

12-foot section has a seam which can be used for a reference. In addition, there are small square reflectors, useful at night in the 12 Hour, cemented to the edges of the racetrack.

The apex curb, striped in red and white, has a red dot painted on the track surface which can be an aiming point for the apex. The problem is that the dot is so far around the corner that you can't see it from the turn-in. The initial turn of the steering wheel is toward a point beyond your vision so it will help to develop a waypoint—some reference on the track surface—to let you know whether you're inside or outside the proper path (see Fig. 7-25).

There is no road camber to speak of and, although the concrete paving stops 80 feet or so short of the track-out point, it shouldn't be a major traction loss problem like Turns 6 and 7 are.

The concrete track-out curbing is absolutely flat and may as well be part of the racetrack. Of course you'll use it, but it doesn't extend as far down the track as you'd want it to, so there will have to be a little jog to the right to rejoin the racetrack proper, just past the track-out.

Throttle Application. This turn is the slowest corner and the one with the biggest angular change. Since it's followed by a straight almost a quarter mile long, exit speed is important. The corner is very slow, most likely first gear, so wheelspin can be a very real problem. You'll have to squeeze the throttle on, trying to keep a reasonable yaw angle going by feeding on just the right amount of power to keep the car sliding in a range where the tires' slip angles are best. Since the corner is so slow and you have the wheelspin capability of first gear, it's a corner where you can have a lot of fun with big, lurid tail-out slides. Remember to restrain yourself. The key is getting the power down in order to get a good shot onto the straight.

It's going to be easy to get obsessed with getting the power on early here. If you get on the power too soon, before the car gets to rotate into a usable yaw angle, you're likely to trip it into understeer, which you'll have to solve with a breathe or lift late in the corner.

Braking. The approach to The Hairpin can be a little intimidating. A huge billboard is right in your line of sight as you approach the corner and at speed, it seems like it's one foot off the racetrack. A brake failure here would not be good, as your options are limited. There is a makeshift escape road to the left which you could take to avoid driving straight into the tire barrier, but it wouldn't buy you that much time. You should make a mental note to be sensitive to the onset of brake fade in any of the other corners and plan that if you sense it, even a hint of it, you'll give the brake

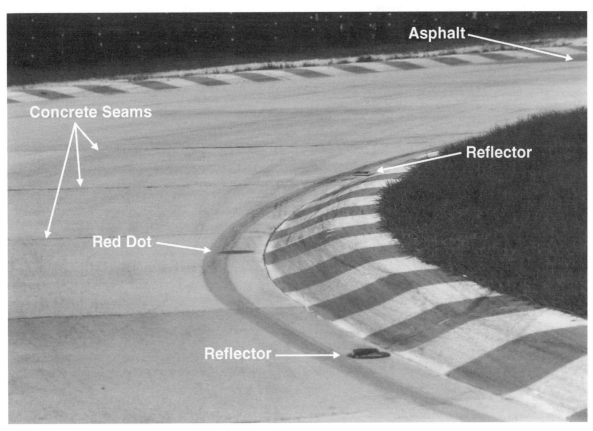

Fig. 7-25. The seams in the concrete section of The Hairpin serve as good reference points. There is also a red dot painted below a white section of the apex curb which, along with reflectors on the edge of the track, help to establish your apex once you've made the turn-in.

pedal a tap or two before the brake point for The Hairpin, just to make sure somebody's home.

If there ever was a threshold braking corner approach, The Hairpin is it. You'll have to go from however fast the car will go—around 110 m.p.h. in our Formula Dodge race cars—to as slow a corner as you'll ever see. Braking points are simple to pick out as there are either number boards or pylons set up at 100 foot increments from the turn-in. Expect to use threshold braking and to work the braking point toward the corner as you practice. Remember that getting to the turn-in point at the right speed is just as important as doing a perfect threshold braking level. Especially in the early sessions on the racetrack, don't be shy about modulating out of maximum braking in the last portion of the braking zone to increase your speed at the turn-in, getting a feel for what turn-in speeds are possible.

Remember that in a tight and long corner such as this one, it's easy to pick up gobs of understeer by going to the throttle before the car has rotated to a usable yaw angle. Continuing the braking past the turn-in, then using a quick release of the pedal pressure, can help get the tail out to where you want it: then it's a matter of holding it there with throttle. Remember, too, that a pause between the relaxation of brake pressure and the application of throttle can also help generate yaw angle.

Gearing

As you may have noticed, we've avoided recommending gear selection for each corner. We've done this because you really won't know which gear is appropriate until you try it. In practical terms, you pick a gear you think will get you from the throttle application point to the track-out without having to shift to another gear. As you first try the course, you'll take your best guess and probably be off by, at the most, one gear. You'll either have guessed a gear too low, in which case the engine will reach the redline before the track-out, or too high, in which case the engine labors through the corner in a rpm range below the best power range of the engine. You adapt by trying a better gear next time.

Most of the corner entries are relatively small speed losses, so you can expect that the downshift will be to the next lowest gear and that it will be a standard double clutch downshift. If possible, you want to do the downshift while the car is going straight on the approach to the corner in order to minimize the chance that a mismatched downshift will lead to a spin. In the corners where you may try to carry extra entry speed—Turns 6 and 9—it is possible that the car might be going too fast at the turn-in point to do the downshift before turning in. In these corners, you'll have to make a note to try to do the smoothest downshift you can manage to keep from upsetting the car.

The Hairpin, however, opens up the possible choice of skipping gears and perhaps choosing to do a fourth-to-first downshift. If you decide to choose this option, you have to remember to delay the shift to a point where, when the clutch comes out in first, the car is going slow enough so that you don't overrev the engine or break the rear tires loose by engine braking.

All Set To Go

If we all went through the preceding analysis of the racetrack before setting out to do battle with the stopwatch, we'd have many fewer surprises in store. You would know, by walking your way through it, which corners are the most important and are therefore most deserving of your attention. You would know which corners are straightforward. You would know which corners are going to require a majority of threshold braking and which will require a more subtle touch. You would begin to have an idea of which corners are

going to call for quick, point-and-squirt type throttle application and which corners may require long, well-modulated control of the accelerator.

Before you set out, you want to have a plan for each corner. Suiting up, jumping into the car and going out on the course, hoping your "natural ability" will solve all your problems, is just dreaming. Knowing what you want to do comes first.

TIME TO DRIVE

Having gone through the off-track homework, it's now time to apply it in the race car and begin the task of become familiar with the course in the car you're going to pace. I'll take you with me through a lap at Sebring: once you're in your equipment and buckled in the car, it's time to go.

I take a good look in the left hand mirror to see if anyone is coming down the pit road, slip in the clutch, and we're underway. The pit lane at Sebring is wide and uncluttered, unlike many pit lanes, but I still take it easy going out, since there are a dozen or so drivers lapping Formula Dodges here today and there is a small crowd milling around the cars near the pit exit. Once clear of the crowd, I accelerate up to 5,000 rpm in first, about 50 m.p.h., before slowing and looking to the left at the pit exit for traffic—a simple street driving action that a surprising number of new racedrivers seem to forget.

The water temperature is coming up on 160 degrees so I can feel free to use the full 6,000 rpm redline without fear of stressing the motor. I enter the racetrack at Turn 4 after having shifted from first to second

"It's all with a person just having a little session with himself going in. Most times, the less experience you have, the more unknowns are going to come at you when you're in there. There's going to be so much confusion and that's when a mistake happens. You just— gosh— it's happened.

So that's the time when you figure, 'I'm going to go in there and I'm going to build up to it. I'm going to go a little bit—the heck with what they're saying back there with the stopwatches—I'm just going to go out there and do it at my own pace.'

If nothing else, it shows a lot of maturity. You'd be surprised how much of that is respected back in an area where you think you're being criticized for being slow. To be patient, slightly patient with yourself, I think, is something that will always work for you."

—Mario Andretti

Fig. 7-26. Turn 6 brake point: I start at the middle of the racetrack between 5 and 6. It will be later as I progress. Don't over-slow. Brake reasonably hard but not like in 3. Use constant-level brake turn so as not to over-rotate. Turn-in: 15 feet past the change in curbing height, the fourth blue stripe on the curb, as a start. The curb is relatively flat and it doesn't look like touching it will upset the car.

Fig. 7-27. Turn 6 apex: yellow line on inside of track turns black at apex and this coincides with a left to right track seam with a change in pavement color. Track out: the very end of the steeper curbing.

Fig. 7-28. Turn 7 brake point: the cone is helpful but the disrupted turf is as easy to see. Trail out of brakes quickly but avoid popping off. Turn-in: the last reflector and some darker eroded pavement on the left. Keep the left tires to the left of the heavy marks.

at 6,000 rpm (60 m.p.h.) and accelerate to 6,000 in second (75 m.p.h.), entering the racetrack proper at the apex of the right-hand sweep of Turn 5.

I'm accelerating smoothly, squeezing the throttle toward the floor in a much more gradual way than I will eventually, but this is a warm-up session, so I can afford the luxury of floating gently around the course. I do an easy upshift to third and accelerate at half throttle up to the entry of Turn 6. I approach the left

Fig. 7-29. Turn 7 apex: I notice that a blob of paint from the apex stripe extends onto the track surface and the stripe itself is darker than the rest. Track out: again, the steep curb turns flat. I'll be able to use the flat section later.

Fig. 7-30. Turn 8 brake point: don't need one. Turn-in: 5 feet past where 12 Hour curbing ends. Look right.

and find that the motor blips eagerly, which is not always the case.

As I approach the curb, I divert my eyes toward the apex, picking up the turn-in using peripheral vision. The steering comes in smoothly; I relax the brakes and pick up the throttle, gently. The arc is right out of 6 and the car naturally uses all the road coming out.

Rather than shift up to third on the short straight between 6 and 7 (the right gear for this section at-speed), I stretch second up to Turn 7, the tight 90-degree right. I get on the brakes early at 7, continuing the warm-up process. The brakes go on easy and early and I wait two seconds as the car decelerates toward the corner before doing a double clutch downshift to first gear.

As I approach the turn-in point, I divert my eyes toward the apex so that when I turn the wheel, I'm looking in the direction I am about to go. At the turn-in point (this track stain is also clearly visible), I turn the wheel to the right, ever so slowly on this warm-up, and the car bends into the turn.

Now I breathe back the braking level and when it's at zero, start squeezing on the throttle. It all feels like slow motion now. The car scoots away from the corner and I shift up from first to second ten yards past the track-out point.

side of the road on a diagonal from the apex of 5 and the change in the two levels of curbing, which I thought would be a good turn-in reference, comes clearly into view. Even on this prelude to a warm-up lap, I'll try to run the racing line and look for reference points to guide me around.

The braking for Turn 6 is light, since the brakes are cold and the first application begins the process of warming them up. I do a quick downshift to second

Fig. 7-31. Apex of 8: aim a little past the end of the curb. Brake point for Turn 9: start halfway between the two curbs. Try smooth, light brake turn. Delicate downshift while turning. Pick up part throttle after trail. Turn-in for 9: discoloration (looks like sealer) 10 feet past the curbing.

I decide to get some temperature in the brakes before we get there. As the car is accelerating up to Turn 8, I move my left foot under the steering shaft and put it on the brake pedal. Initially, I don't push on it very hard—I don't want to shock-heat the braking system, I just want to coax it up to operating temperature. It only takes five seconds or so to go from 7 to 8 and I drag the brakes up to the corner, turning right toward the entry of Turn 9, the carousel leading onto the main straight.

Approaching 9, bending to the right on the way to the turn-in point, I lock up the right front tire. Damn. I didn't want to do that! I'm trying to treat the car well by warming it up and in the first minute of the day I lock up a front, potentially flat spotting it. Fortunately, the street radials fitted to the car are reasonably hard and the total weight of the front corner is only around 160 lbs, so the flat spot, if any, will be small.

As I accelerate out of Turn 9, I keep it in second at about three-quarter throttle, still squeezing on the brakes (more lightly now), dragging them all the way down the .4 mile acceleration zone leading to Turn 10, the Sebring Hairpin. Next lap, we'll be accelerating through the gears on this long sweep to the right. There will be very little time when the car will be going dead straight. As I drift toward the left verge, passing under the bridge, I'll get the car straight for just 2 seconds or so before applying the brakes for the slowest corner on the circuit.

I'm just cruising up to The Hairpin now at about 50 m.p.h. I move my left foot back over to the clutch side of the footwell, brake the car conventionally with my right foot, and do the downshift to first to get a running start out of The Hairpin for the start of the first data collection lap.

Fig. 7-32. Apex of 9 impossible to see. Look as far ahead as possible to inside of road. Hold car right of track seam until beginning of exit curb is visible. Correct, if necessary, in order to guide car to inside.

Fig. 7-34. Straight approaching Turn 10: Hold the car along the right edge until the pavement change, then track left (after checking mirror).

Fig. 7-33. Turn 9, first 1/3 of flat exit curb. Aim just past the change in steepness of the curbing.

Fig. 7-35. Turn 10 brake point: start with second pylon. Save threshold for later.

Fig. 7-36. Turn 10 turn-in: last reflector on concrete. Very black, just 12 feet before the white line turns right.

Fig. 7-38. Turn 10 apex: Once halfway across the straight pick up the second reflector.

Fig. 7-37. Turn 10 apex: aim far around corner. Think of trying to come around behind the curb you can see from the turn-in.

Fig. 7-39. Turn 10 track out: use all flat curb, sneak back at very end.

I accelerate away from the apex of The Hairpin and get full throttle before the exit. The motor feels good and peppy. The tach needle moves quickly in first gear and I let it go to 6,000 before shifting to second. Foot to the floor in second, I'm accelerating through about 70 m.p.h.; then I shift up to third at 6,000 and put my foot back to the floor.

I'm approaching Turns 1 and 2 at 82 m.p.h., and there's nothing fancy about my braking point. I use my judgement (biased toward the conservative) and squeeze on the brakes lightly, slowing the car to 72 m.p.h. by the turn-in point. Turn 1 is a gentle bend, so the steering wheel motion is small and, at this speed range, there is no perception of sliding as the car solidly tracks toward the apex. I carry the light braking past the turn-in point and pick up 50% throttle to keep the car comfortable and balanced through the right-hand portion of this right-left sweep.

I'm down to 74 m.p.h. as I transition the car from turning right to turning left, trying to do this fluidly; easing the steering wheel away from right lock, then easing in steering effort to the left. I can see it's going to be hard switching my vision away from the turning point for 2 over to the apex. It's going to have to be done quickly, especially as we go faster, to get a good sight on 2's apex.

By the time I'm headed for the apex, the throttle is at 70% and we're picking up speed, reaching 80 m.p.h. in third gear at the track out point. All this is solidly under control, no sliding around, no sudden twists of the steering wheel or jabs at the pedals.

As I proceed around the course I start to pick up my reference points, based on what I discovered on the early drive-arounds in a street car. The Formula

Fig. 7-40. Turn 3 brake point: braking pylons here are very helpful. Start at first one, work it down later. Brake reasonably hard, trail it a quarter of the way in. Turn-in: start 5 feet before the striped curb starts.

Fig. 7-41. Turn 3 apex: seam in concrete goes diagonally left to right. Apex where it meets the inside curb. Track out: use all the road, left tires touching curb.

Dodge, in which my eye level is two feet closer to the ground than the Intrepid sedan I first drove around the course, changes the perspective. I look for the brake points, turn-ins and apexes which I scouted earlier and use most, but in the process discover others.

The mental process is one of looking forward, almost straining to see your next marker as you go around the course. This line development goes on lap after lap, always looking for better references and establishing what works best with this car on this day. The work—the challenge of pursuing perfection—is the fun part.

CHAPTER 8

FINDING LAP TIME

ANYONE WHO DRIVES A racecar knows deep in their heart what they really want to hear: "you've got the fastest time by over a second." Whether it's practice, qualifying, or a race, we all live for those precious words. It doesn't happen often.

> A Data Collection System can help find the most common areas where lap time is lost and help you formulate a plan for going faster.

It's much more common, especially when you are just starting your career, to find that you're full seconds off the fastest pace. Finding this out, drenched in sweat after trying as hard as you can to go as fast as possible, can be dispiriting. You ask yourself, "Where am I going to find (fill in the blank) seconds?"

SEBRING—OUR LABORATORY

In this chapter, we'll look at some laps of Sebring and see where that precious lap time comes from. In the preceding chapter, you saw the level of detail we put into the analysis of the course. Here, the detail is in the speeds and tenths of seconds that separate a slow lap from a lap record. We'll concentrate on laps driven in our Formula Dodge race cars which we use in our Racing Schools and in our Formula Dodge Race Series. Since such a wide variety of drivers compete in these cars at Sebring, we have a huge sample of unique laps on which to draw.

In addition to first-hand feedback, we can rely on our data acquisition system to answer very specific questions about a variety of laps. Computers and the data acquisition systems that feed them have become a commonplace tool in the testing and development of modern racecars. There are a variety of systems in use now: some monitor engine systems, some keep an eye on speeds and RPM, and some look at the G forces that the car is generating around the course.

The MRG/Skip Barber Performance Monitor

The system we use was developed by Chris Wallach of Marblehead Racing Group (MRG). Chris's hardware is a combination of a memory unit, a control system and a variety of transducers which provide the raw data. The raw information is made accessible by the MRG Performance Monitor software package, which produces a variety of reports and user-designed graphs that make the car's performance come alive in a usable, understandable format.

In most race teams, the system is used primarily as a car-sorting tool. Changes can be made to the racecar and the driver can do back to back runs while the performance monitor looks closely at the results of the changes. "Closely" is an understatement—the monitor looks at up to 250 samples of data a second, and the type of information available is limited only by the development engineer's imagination. There are sensors available to measure air pressure changes, suspension movement, tire loading, and even tire temperature.

In looking at driving technique, we're looking for simple things. First, we'd like to know where the racecar is on the circuit so that when an event takes place, like the driver applying the throttle, we can say definitively that the throttle came on 50 feet before the apex, or worse, 50 feet *after* the apex.

We use two systems to accomplish this. The first is a series of infrared beams set up at specific measured distances around the racetrack. A sensor on the racecar recognizes these beams and the system makes note of the elapsed time from beam to beam. The computer gives us a running lap time as well as the times for each segment of the course.

The system also gives us the car's speed by counting the tire or driveshaft revolutions, so by knowing the speed and having frequent updates on the car's position, we can locate the car on any portion of the circuit to an accuracy of +/- 4 feet.

Now for the driving part: we want to know how the driver 1) applies the throttle, 2) uses the brakes, and 3) turns the steering wheel. To get the throttle information, we have a transducer that measures the percentage of throttle application from 100% to 0%. For braking, we're interested in how much pressure the driver exerts on the brake pedal, so we have a transducer that gives us pedal pressure in pounds of force at the pedal. In the steering department, we're able to measure the steering wheel deflection in degrees. In order to see the forces that are created by all this motion of the controls, we have sensitive accelerometers on the car that measure braking, acceleration, and cornering force in Gs.

All of this data is time referenced, meaning that the system takes a snapshot, if you will, of all these different channels of information between 20 to 250 times a second (user's choice) as the car proceeds around the course. By integrating the time and speed, we can create distance-based graphs which show where the car is on the racetrack at any time.

When analyzing a driver's performance, our most useful tool is the primary display which shows brake pressure, throttle position in bar graph style, and the position of the steering wheel, represented by a little steering wheel. The primary screen allows us to display two laps simultaneously—normally a target lap set by an instructor and a lap by the driver being coached. It paints a pretty clear picture of what the driver is doing in the car and how the driver's technique results in gains and losses of lap time.

FROM WARM-UP TO FAST LAPS

"Do a *warm-up* lap or two": a simple statement and one which most of us understand, subjectively. The degree to which a warm-up lap is slower than a race pace depends upon the driver, of course, but let's look at the difference between what an experienced driver

does warming up and what he does on the fastest lap of the day.

The fastest flying lap on this particular day in car No. 22 will be a 1: 23.85 lap. The warm-up is a 1:29.4, over 5.5 seconds per lap slower—a huge difference in racing terms, but on a percentage basis, only 6% slower. Let's take a look at the accompanying breakdown of each lap to see where this time comes from.

Note Speed Differences
First, peruse the differences in speed between the warm-up and fast lap at key points around the racetrack (Fig. 8-1). The first thing that pops out is that the corner exit speeds in the slow corners are not very different in the two laps. This is a key fact to remember: when you're trying to lower lap time, you're usually not looking for a 10 m.p.h. improvement, especially in the corners taken below third gear (3, 6, 7, 9, 10). The difference in corner exit speeds for laps that vary by 5.5 sec per lap is, *at most*, 3 m.p.h.

All of these corners are first or second gear corners, and the fact that the exit speeds are close has a lot to do with the comfort level of accelerating and turning in the lower gears. You're in control, pushing on the accelerator, and if the path seems wrong, a little breathe out of the throttle fixes things. Also, when you're driving under 70 m.p.h., there's nothing intimidating about using aggressive power coming off of a slow corner. As you work your way to faster laps,

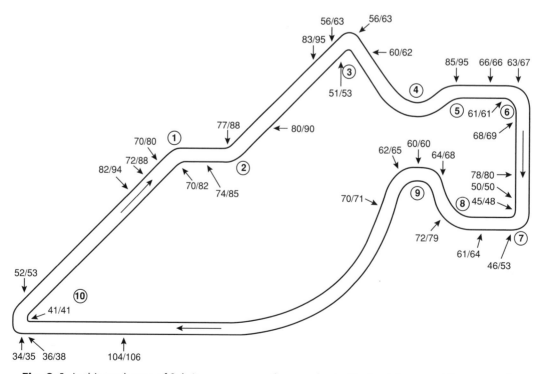

Fig. 8-1. In this track map of Sebring, we can see the speeds at critical points around the racetrack on a warm-up lap (the first number in each set) versus a hot lap (the second number).

don't expect that your exit speed out of slow turns has to increase by a huge amount in order to make up significant time.

Another factor at play here is experience level. Although this is a warm-up, our driver has vast experience at this racetrack—the line through the corners is practically instinctive and, consequently, very accurate. You couldn't say the same if it were a driver's first-ever lap.

Identify the Most Important Corners
This small speed difference coming out of slow corners puts a new wrinkle on the theory of identifying the most important corners on a racetrack. In "The Real-World Line" we pointed out that the more important corners were those which led onto long periods of full throttle acceleration. In practical terms, however, drivers of widely differing skill levels seem to be able to closely match speeds coming out of slow corners; getting a significant advantage over others in the field in these slow corners is rare. A fast corner leading onto a long straight is another matter.

In Turns 1 and 2 the speeds between the warm-up and the fast lap differ by over 10 m.p.h. Partly it's a matter of relative comfort: the high speed stuff is going to be more difficult than a second gear turn. Also, in the specific case of Sebring there is the problem of a scarcity of obvious turn-in reference points for Turns 1 and 2. For the first few laps in a racecar you're still looking for points which will work to guide you to the best line.

This cautiousness in the fast corners costs plenty. In Turns 1 and 2, the segment time for the warm-up is .95 seconds slower. This doesn't count the corner entries, just the time from the apex of 1 to the entry of 3. Almost a full second of our 5.5 second deficit is going to come from driving through 1 and 2 faster.

Faster corners are longer, and the difference in speed between a driver who's right on the limit and one who is just shy lasts for a longer time, producing a bigger difference in lap time. Couple a fast corner with a long straight, and the difference gets magnified even further.

Compare Segment Times
Now, let's figure out how much of the rest of the 5.5 second shortfall is coming out of the corners and driving down the following straights, and how much is in the braking zones.

In the track map in Fig. 8-2 the course is divided into corner exit zones (from the apex to the next corner entry) and corner entry zones (from the braking point to the apex). As you can see from the table in Fig. 8-3, there is a 3.2 second difference in lap time in the corner exit segments and a 2.35 second difference in the corner entry splits. This really shouldn't come as a surprise, since there is a lot more distance covered and time spent on the corner exit portion of the course. What is important to remember is that corner exit speed is easier to get than corner entry speed.

You can see why we stress using a progression of 1) concentrating on line, 2) working on getting greater

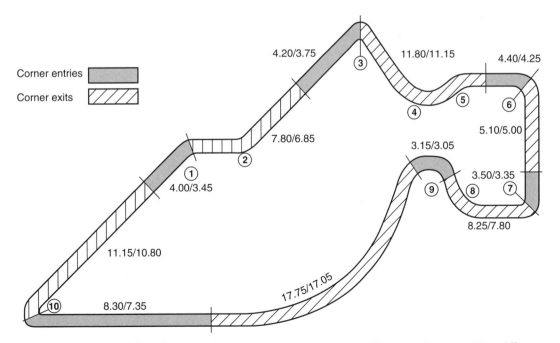

Fig. 8-2. In this map of the Sebring course, compare the corner entry and corner exit segment time differences in a warm-up vs. a fast lap (first number in set is warm-up time, second number is hot lap time). There is significant time to be gained by concentrating on corner exits before approaching the limits on corner entry.

Corner Exits	Warm-up Lap	Fast Lap	Time Shortfall
Exiting Turn 10 to Turn 1	11.15	10.80	.35
Exiting Turn 1 to Turn 3	7.80	6.85	.95
Exiting Turn 3 to Turn 6	11.80	11.15	.65
Exiting Turn 6 to Turn 7	5.10	5.00	.10
Exiting Turn 7 to Turn 9	8.25	7.80	.45
Exiting Turn 9 to Turn 10	17.75	17.05	.70
Total (sec.)	61.85	58.65	3.20

Corner Entries	Warm-up Lap	Fast Lap	Time Shortfall
Entering Turn 1	4.00	3.45	.55
Entering Turn 3	4.20	3.75	.45
Entering Turn 6	4.40	4.25	.15
Entering Turn 7	3.50	3.35	.15
Entering Turn 9	3.15	3.05	.10
Entering Turn 10	8.30	7.35	.95
Total (sec.)	27.55	25.20	2.35

Fig. 8-3. These tables reveal the important corner exits and entries at Sebring for gaining lap time (warm-up lap vs. fast lap). Taken separately, the time losses may look like small potatoes, but they can really add up.

cornering speed and exit speed, and 3) finally working on optimizing corner entries. In this Sebring example you wouldn't worry about using the car very hard until you came close to consistently putting the car in the right place. If you did just this, you could get within 5.55 seconds of the fastest time. Increase exit speed in the slow corners and use full acceleration and crisp upshifting, and you can knock off 1.35 seconds just on the two longest straights (3 to 6 and 9 to 10). Add in all the other acceleration zones, and there is another .90 seconds available. Pick up the pace in 1 and 2, and you get almost another full second.

Without concentrating on braking and entry speed you could do a 1:26.2 versus a fastest of the day at 1:23.85. That's not very far off, considering that you've paid no attention to trying to brake late or carry speed into the corners.

Corner Exit: First Place to Make Up Lap Time

Once warm-ups are over, you can make up this time in two ways. The first is running closer to the car's limit coming away from the two important corners which lead onto the longest straights. It's interesting to see just how little exit speed improvement is needed. The second chunk of the 2.25 seconds available in the acceleration zones comes from using full power and minimizing the time between gears. In the warm-up, upshifts took close to a half second. In the fast lap, the throttle pedal went from full on before the shift, to off between gears, and back to full on in just under two tenths of a second. The three tenths difference at each shift adds up to straightaway speed and lap time.

The catch to faster shifting is that the more you rush it, the greater the chance of missing a gear and over-revving the motor. You can be conservative and take a bit more time with your upshifts, but it will cost you lap time. You have to develop the ability to coordinate your feet and your right hand to change up quickly and accurately.

The .95 second difference in 1 and 2 is going to be harder because of the difficulties we noted earlier, but the 10 m.p.h. speed deficit can be closed by taking ten 1-m.p.h. nibbles, working the comfort level up, without doing anything dramatic at the corner entry. Ten 1-m.p.h. nibbles get you into contention: two 5-m.p.h. bites get you in big trouble.

Corner Entries: Last Bit of Time

Using the map in Fig. 8-2 and the table in Fig. 8-3, let's look at the shortfall on corner entries. Starting with Turn 1, the time is off .55 seconds from the lap record—not surprising since the turn-in speed is 10 m.p.h. slower than the fast lap. The braking in the warm-up is long and light and just picking up the pace, even with light braking, will make up tenths easily.

At the approach to Turn 3 there is another .45 seconds: a 12 m.p.h. difference in approach speed and 7 m.p.h. at the turn-in. Pick up the pace out of Turn 2 and, without braking any harder, carrying some more speed up to the turn in will make up half the deficit.

The corner entries of Turns 6, 7, and 9 together amount to just .4 seconds, so you won't expect to have to change the approach to these very much.

The big corner entry difference is the approach to The Hairpin, Turn 10, with a .95 second difference. There is just as much lap time available here as in picking up the pace in the esses.

In the fast lap, the brakes come on just 280 feet short of the turn-in point while in the warm-up, the braking uses less than half the pedal pressure and starts almost 200 feet earlier. The message here is that the high speed-loss corners are going to be the ones where approaching the braking limits will have the biggest effect on lap time. Keep in mind, however, that part of this lap time difference comes from the speed to which you slow the car at the turn-in point. In the fast lap, the car is 2 m.p.h. faster at the turn-in point.

Consider that on the warm-up, you're giving away a total of 1.5 seconds on the corner entry of 5 other corners and almost a full second approaching The Hairpin. This information should lead you to another conclusion about the order of efforts to reduce lap time: not only should you leave limit braking for last, but once you concentrate on braking, there is much more to be gained by starting with the high speed-loss braking zones.

CHASING A FASTER PACE

In the warm-up comparison, one driver is choosing between one pace and another. The more important comparison is between a driver who is at the lap record pace and one who can't get there, even though he or she is trying hard. Let's use the data collection system to see if we can identify common sources of problems with drivers who have the basics covered but find themselves off the pace.

Computer Coaching
We'll use the same techniques we use in our "Computer Lapping" program at Skip Barber Racing School. An instructor shakes down the car first thing in the morning to set a target lap for comparison pur-

poses. It's important that this target lap be done in the same car on the same day as the driver who's being coached. As we said before, conditions change day to day, and we want to be certain that we're making apples to apples comparisons. On the day we'll be looking at, our data collection instructor, Bruce McQuiston, puts in a real flyer—a 1:23.60—the fastest lap yet.

Within the hour, the driver we'll be coaching does 20 minutes of warm-up (he'd done 80 miles of testing the day before), then a six-lap collection of data. The fastest lap of his collection is a 1:25.55, within two seconds of the target. At first, two seconds sounds like a huge difference, but as you work your way around the lap (see Fig. 8-4) you can see that there aren't any glaring exit speed or straightaway speed differences. There is a mile per hour here or there but you wouldn't think that there is two seconds worth.

You can see, however, that the largest speed differences seem to come at the corner entries, especially at the minimum speed points, which are found between the turn-in and the apex. While these speed comparisons are interesting, what really helps the pursuit of lower lap time is to look at the segment times.

The first step in the analysis is to compare the segment times of each collection. The data collection software allows us to lay one lap over another and scroll through each segment of the track to see the segment time differences in each section (Fig. 8-5).

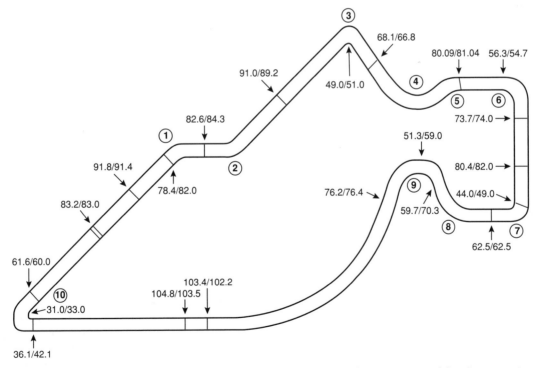

Fig. 8-4. This track map compares the speeds of the two drivers—the instructor and the client—at significant points around the course (first number in each set is client speed in m.p.h., second is target speed). The largest differences in speed seem to come at the corner entries.

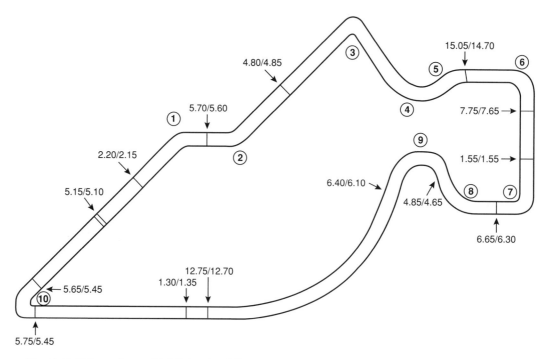

Fig. 8-5. This track map highlights the differences in segment times between the two laps (measured in seconds; first number in each set is client time, second is instructor time). Concentrating on the corners with the largest segment time differences allows you to focus on problem areas.

Looking for the Biggest Shortfall

Beginning at Start/Finish and going right through the exit of Turn 2, there is only a tenth of a second difference between the two runs—no big problem in the fast stuff.

The next big segment, from the approach to Turn 3 up to the entry of Turn 6, is a different story. The slower lap shows a loss of .35 seconds here, definitely worth looking at.

Moving along, the spread in the turn six segment and up to turn seven is another wash—a tenth of a second over a nine second segment.

Big differences begin to show up between the entry of turn seven and the exit of turn nine. The slower lap is off .35 seconds just in Turn 7, loses another two tenths up to Turn 9 and another three tenths in 9 itself. This relatively small section of the racetrack accounts for .85 seconds of the lap time deficit. You have to dig a little deeper to find out why.

The main straight is even, both segment times are identical, but there is a real difference, three tenths, in the deceleration zone for the hairpin. Another two tenths is available in the hairpin itself, so you're looking for a half-second on the approach to, and the run through, The Hairpin.

WHERE THE TIME GOES

Let's go after the biggest chunk of lap time first, the entry to Turn 7 to the exit of Turn 9, looking at the speed differences through the segment, then the cause of the speed deficit.

You can get the details of the lap by graphing any of the channels of information which are recorded. We usually start with speed, pinpointing where in any segment, the car is slower than the target.

How to Read the Computer Graphs

To make the following graphs more clear, let's go over the main features of the performance monitor primary screen first.

Looking at Fig. 8-6, on the lower left (A) are the particular runs—in this case, the target, NSMQ600, and the session by the driver being coached, NSHW52. To the immediate right are the individual laps we are comparing (B)— the number of the lap in the run and the lap time.

The far right column (C) lists the recorded data. We can choose to graph speed, brake effort, steering angle, lateral G, and longitudinal G (in this series of collections the longitudinal G accelerometer was frozen at a bogus setting, so throughout the following graphs disregard LONGG).

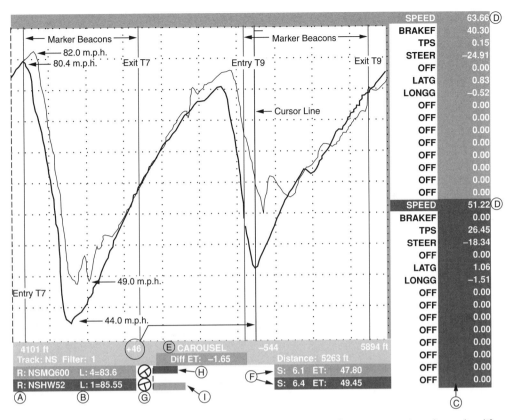

Fig. 8-6. This printout of the primary analysis screen on the performance monitor shows the different aspects of the Turn 7 through Turn 9 segment that can be measured—in this case, speed.

By using the mouse, you can highlight which channel to graph. Here, we have selected just speed (D) for each run. On the graph itself there are a series of vertical lines. The lighter lines represent the infrared markers defining the beginning and end of a segment of the racetrack. The darker vertical line is a movable cursor line that moves right and left. In this graph this line is placed 46 feet into the "carousel" segment. The tables to the right display the values for each channel of information for wherever the cursor line is placed. In this graph we placed the cursor line at the minimum speed point in the carousel for the slower lap and you can see that the speed table at this point of the lap reads 63.66 m.p.h. for the faster segment vs. 51.22 m.p.h. for the slower pass. As you move the cursor line, the segment it's on is identified (E) and the segment time for the laps being compared is displayed (F). You have the ability to zoom in and out to look at an entire lap or a small segment of the lap.

You can also see how much the steering wheel is turned (G) at the location of the cursor line as well as the relative level of braking force (H) and the level of throttle application (I).

Speed Differences

By just graphing the speeds from the entry of Turn 7 to the exit of Turn 9 (as we have in Fig. 8-6), you can figure out that the problem is not the speed at the approach to the corner, nor is it, for that matter, the corner exit speeds. The main difficulty is that the slower driver is giving away too much speed in the first half of the corner by over-slowing the car.

The first third of the speed graph is the entry through the exit of Turn 7. The slowest speed in the corner on the fast lap is 49 m.p.h., compared to 44 m.p.h. for the slower lap—a 5 m.p.h. spread. This might be caused by braking too soon or too long.

Braking Variations

If you graph brake pedal effort in the two runs (see Fig. 8-7), you can see that the brake point for the slower run was 48 feet earlier than in the target lap. In addition, while the initial level of braking was good, over seventy pounds of brake pressure was released to accommodate the blip for the downshift. It's not a big surprise that using between 40% to 60% braking over a distance of close to 100 feet on the approach to Turn 7 requires that the process start sooner.

We suspected in our first look at the racetrack that this corner, because it is so short, would require rela-

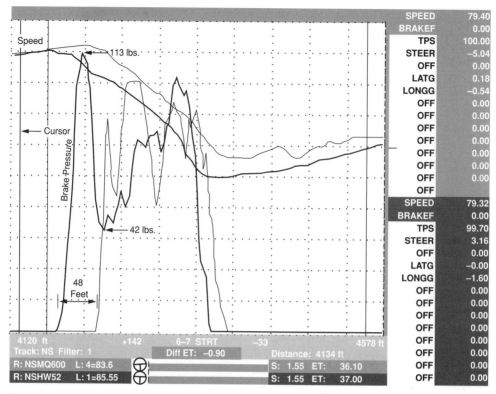

Fig. 8-7. In this graph of both speed and brake pressure for the two runs, in the slower run (darker trace) the brakes come on early, making the speed lower throughout the braking zone. Also, brake pressure is drastically reduced from threshold when the driver blips the throttle for the downshift.

tively little trail-braking, and you can see that this is supported by the data. The faster driver trail-braked just 35 feet past the turn-in and gave a quick application of lots of throttle. The slower driver released the brakes sooner and went back to partial throttle earlier. In the target lap, the throttle application started later, but got to full sooner. However, a breathe off the throttle was necessary in the fast lap to control oversteer. Both drivers were at the same speed, 62.5 m.p.h., at the corner exit beacon.

Not surprisingly, you can see the same overslowing problem at the entry to Turn 9. Since both drivers exited Turn 7 at the same speed, the two tenths segment time difference again comes at the corner entry.

In Fig. 8-8, we've graphed the braking effort and the speed trace for each run from the exit of 7 through the exit of the carousel. The difference in speed is very graphic, a minimum speed of 59 m.p.h. for the target, and 51.3 for the slower lap. You can see that the brake point for the slower run is 40 feet earlier than the target. The loss in entry speed actually started in Turn 8, the right hand sweep up to the turn-in for 9. The slower run shifted to third gear earlier and the acceleration rate in the lower RPM range in third starts to fall off relative to the faster run, which stretches second gear to the redline, then ends up at higher RPM in third gear after the later shift.

The Carousel
Taking a closer look at the braking for the carousel (Fig. 8-9), you can see some significant differences which account for the segment time difference. Again, the slower run starts the braking earlier—40 feet—and there is a significant drop in brake pressure when downshifting. Note also the long gradual trail off braking effort as the car turns in to Turn 9.

In the faster run, the driver starts at threshold on the approach, then trails back to a lower, but constant, level of braking up to the brake-throttle transition. We suspected that this would be a workable approach; since there is a long distance between the turn-in and the throttle application point, you can use the early portion of the corner to slow the car while it's turning.

You will notice in Fig. 8-9 that at the cursor line the speed differential is 5 m.p.h. Yet, looking at the throttle position bar, the slower run is at full throttle while the faster driver is at about 80% throttle. This is possible because at the lower speed there is excess traction available, and the driver can use full throttle without overtaxing the tires' grip, making up some of the deficit at the exit of the corner. It's a trade-off. The slower car can accelerate faster from the lower speed (the speed trace catches up with the faster run at the corner exit).

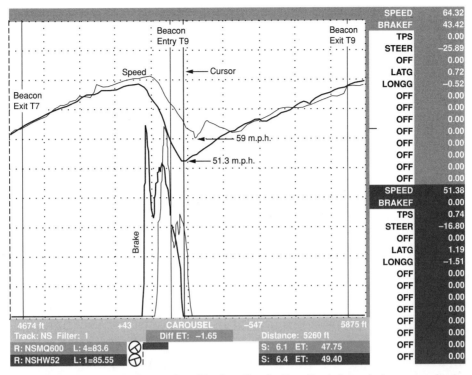

Fig. 8-8. Graphing both speed and brake effort for Turn 7 exit through the carousel exit, you can see that a half-second of lap time is lost, again, on overslowing the car. Note that the speed trace at the exit of both Turn 7 and the carousel are nearly identical.

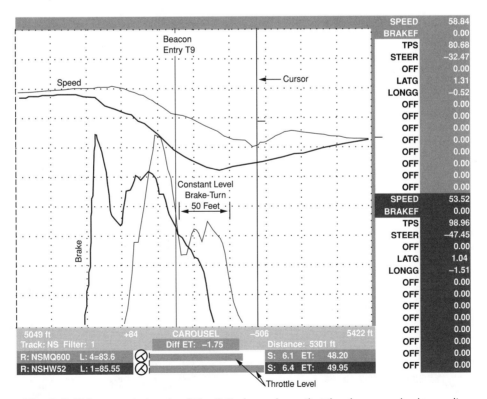

Fig. 8-9. This expanded scale of Fig. 8-8 above shows that the slower run brakes earlier and is 6 m.p.h. slower at the minimum speed point of the corner. The driver was able to use more throttle earlier than the target run, but the superior acceleration didn't make up for the time lost at the corner entry.

In the faster run, since the tires are closer to their traction limits the driver has to be more sensitive to mixing throttle and cornering. Still, acceleration off the corner starts at a higher speed, and as long as exit speed isn't compromised, and a longer segment time down the straight results, the time made up on the corner entry is time in the bank. In this run, no exit speed is lost; and the segment time down the following straight is identical to the car that got the power on sooner, harder, but started 6 m.p.h. slower.

The Hairpin

The next largest chunk of time during the lap, a half-second, comes from the approach through the exit of The Hairpin. Three tenths is lost in the last 700 feet of the straight, up to the turn-in point. If we look at a speed comparison between the two runs (see Fig. 8-10), you can see that the approach speed in the slower run is actually higher but, again, the minimum speed in The Hairpin is 2 m.p.h. lower than the target lap.

The biggest difference, however, lies in how long each driver took to lose the speed. In the faster run the braking starts 281 feet from the turn-in, versus 416 feet for the slower run. The three tenths in this segment comes from driving 135 feet closer to the corner before going to the brakes. Without a doubt, the slower driver wouldn't believe he could go 135 feet deeper,

and in fact he couldn't unless he reached a braking level that would allow him to lose the same amount of speed over a shorter distance.

This graph also reveals that there is a big pressure release when the slower driver blips the throttle for the fourth to first downshift, and a long gradual trail out of the braking level on the approach to the corner—not great footwork.

By contrast, the faster driver goes through each gear, three separate blips, and the brake pedal pressure varies by, at most, 20 lbs. The slower driver uses a peak pressure of 84 lbs and a low of 26 lbs, as opposed to the target threshold pressure that varies between 109 and 90 lbs for the bulk of the deceleration.

This is one of those instances when late threshold braking is worth significant lap time. As we said earlier in the chapter on braking, corner approaches where significant speed loss takes place put a premium on threshold braking. Here the premium is a potential three tenths of a second. The underlying lesson here is that just going deeper won't do it—you have to reach closer to the threshold level of pressure *and stay there* despite the blips for the downshifts.

Losing Too Much Speed

If you look again at the speed comparisons at significant parts of the hairpin, you can pick out where the

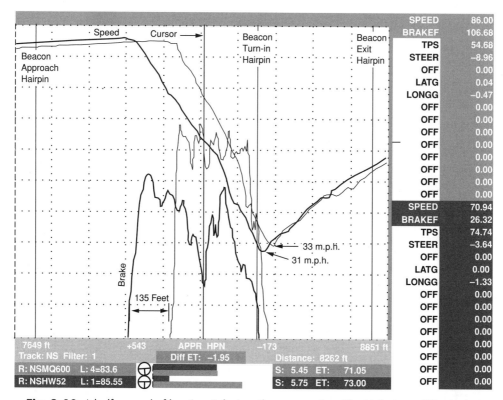

Fig. 8-10. A half-second of lap time is lost on the approach to The Hairpin and The Hairpin itself. You can see on the approach that the problem is light, early braking. In the corner, over-slowing the entry cost .2 seconds even though the exit speed is 1.6 m.p.h. higher.

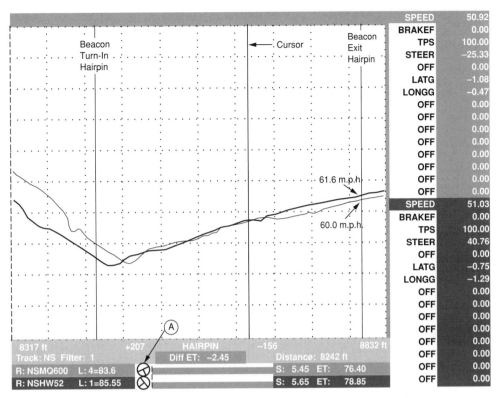

Fig. 8-11. One determinant of corner exit speed can be the amount of tire scrub or drag against the road surface, which is created by large yaw angles. The steering wheel in the right-hand Hairpin is turned 40 degrees left, indicating considerable yaw. The throttle, in this case, was never modulated, yet the exit speed is lower than the car with less yaw.

other two tenths of a second comes from. Just as you saw in Turns 7 and 9, the slower driver loses more speed than necessary: he's 7 m.p.h. down at the turn-in, 2 m.p.h. down at the minimum speed point and 1 m.p.h. off at the apex. Toward the exit of the corner, however, the slower pass makes up some of the time (.05 seconds) lost.

As you saw in Turn 9, however, overslowing the entry does allow for more aggressive acceleration; and, if you look at the speed trace, the slower driver does gain an advantage in the second part of the hairpin. At the lower entry speed, the slower driver was able to begin the acceleration through the apex of the hairpin some 30 feet earlier than the target lap, and the result was an exit speed of 61.6 m.p.h. vs. 60 m.p.h. for the target lap.

The acceleration rate is higher for a car under the absolute limit of cornering grip, but the ability to use more throttle is only part of the story. The drag from tire scrub must also be taken into account. At the yaw angle in the range of limit cornering, since the tires are sliding at an angle to the true direction of travel, they create more drag from scrubbing across the surface of the road. In a car with limited horsepower, this drag also slows the acceleration rate. Still, if the accelera-

tion starts at a higher speed, there is usually a gain, not a loss.

In Fig. 8-11, you can see one of the reasons that the target lap speed trace falls off at the exit of the hairpin: the steering wheel for the target lap (A) is turned about 40 Degrees left in this right-hand turn— an indication of substantial oversteer. Although the driver didn't have to surrender throttle position in this instance, the additional tire scrub flattens out the speed trace, resulting in slower exit speed. Everybody, even test drivers, makes mistakes that cost lap time. On subsequent runs, McQuiston's exit speed out of The Hairpin was consistently 1.5 to 2 m.p.h. quicker.

Closing the Gap
Correcting the problems in Turns 7 through 9 and improving The Hairpin has the potential of gaining 1.35 seconds, a lap time improvement sure to bring a grin to any driver's face. The next biggest chunk, .35 seconds, could come from the Turn 3 to Turn 6 segment. Without even looking at the graphs, it would be a good bet that the lap time comes from the same faults you saw at the other corners—inefficient threshold braking and overslowing the car between the turn-in point and the minimum speed point of the corner.

If you look at the braking graph for the Turn 3 segment (see Fig. 8-12), you can see that the slower driver braked 60 feet earlier and went to a significant level of braking, 115 lbs of pedal force, initially. He modulated out to 25 lbs. again, however, to accommodate the downshift, and did most of the deceleration for the corner in the 50 lb. range. The faster pass wasn't as picture perfect as the braking for The Hairpin, but stayed in the range of 125 lbs to 90 lbs for the duration.

The throttle application in the two runs is similar. In the target lap, the throttle application begins at the same point, but it is done more aggressively. You can see by the speed trace for the target lap that there was wheelspin generated. Once the tires bit, the target lap exit speed was slightly below the slower lap but, interestingly, further along the run toward Turn 6, the target lap speed jumps ahead of the slower lap. Let's graph throttle position and see if one upshift was faster than the other, causing the target lap to pull ahead.

As you can see in Fig. 8-13, the target lap upshift takes .2 seconds from off the throttle until the throttle is at 100% again. In the slower lap, the shift takes .4 seconds and the speed advantage of 1.3 m.p.h. out of Turn 3 turns into a speed deficit of 1 m.p.h.

IMPLICATIONS OF THE DATA

The driver who participated in this computer coaching session obviously can take this information and work on the techniques that will make up the lost time. For those of you with a more general interest, you can take away some overall lessons by looking at where the lap time was in this case.

Exit Speed vs. Entry Speed

We encourage drivers to make a routine of looking at the tachometer at the exit of every corner to get an idea of whether their performance through the corner is improving or not. But if you check the exit speed numbers in these two laps, all but one corner are within a mile per hour of each other and, in some cases, the exit speed for the slower lap is even higher than for the target. So once you're close to the fastest pace, it is difficult to work on improving by checking exit speed RPM. The peek at the tach will be a tool that's most useful in the early stages of lapping a course, when you're ten seconds off the pace and working it down. When you're close, corner exit speed is often right near the maximum. You can still use the tach as a reference, but don't be surprised if you don't see much variation.

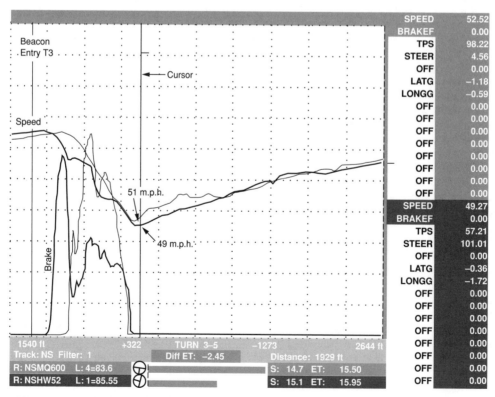

Fig. 8-12. The problem with Turn 3 is the same: poor brake level control, especially when downshifting. On the positive side, the minimum cornering speed is within 2 m.p.h. of the target run.

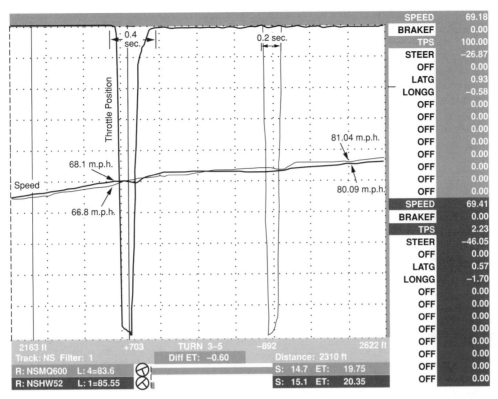

Fig. 8-13. This is a graph of throttle position and speed for the exit of Turn 3 toward the approach to Turn 6. We can see that the upshift for the target lap takes less time and, as a result, the speed trace, which was lagging slightly, bumps ahead of the slower lap.

In these comparisons, most of the time was at the corner entry. These results are typical of what we find when drivers are looking for the last percentages of improvement. Just screwing up the courage to go deeper, without developing the ability to threshold brake, will be a waste of time, but if you work on heel-and-toe technique so that you can brake effectively and do the blip at the same time without affecting the brake level, you stand a good chance of finding that lap time.

It Takes Time to Find Time

We've covered over and over again the idea of developing some perspective while behind the wheel. In these computer collections, you were looking at two drivers working within two seconds of as fast as the car will go around this racetrack. Neither driver got this good without investing the time it takes to get this close—time spent developing accuracy of line and car control skills. The driver receiving the coaching did over 50 laps on this day—laps where he was trying hard to go faster, yet he didn't have one spin or significant departure from the line. If you're spinning or missing apexes or driving sloppily, there's just no way to work on shaving the tenths of seconds here and there which eventually add up to substantial improvements of your lap time.

Beware the Red Mist

When you get frustrated with your lap time, which you will inevitably do, you have to avoid the temptation to get lathered up and just increase your aggressiveness and risk-taking everywhere around the course. In these collections, you can see that although the slower driver was almost two seconds off the fastest pace, he did quite well in numerous parts of the racetrack. Trying to go faster in the fast esses, for example, would have been a waste of time and effort—trying harder there probably would have *lost* lap time.

> "I've often found that if I'm having trouble in a racecar, it helps to stop, get out of the car, and go away and relax for a while. I don't necessarily think about it directly—I just get away for a bit and give it a chance to slow down in [my] mind."
>
> —Danny Sullivan

The reality is that significant pieces of lap time come from being just a few m.p.h. slower than the fastest driver in a few significant places. The trick is identifying those places and putting the effort there, not on parts of the circuit where you're doing fine.

Going to School

As you've seen, with a data collection system and a target time to chase, you can clearly identify where the gaps lie. But, with or without these high tech aids, self-criticism is at the core of finding lap time. Are your downshifts as good as they can be? Are you always on line? Are you at threshold braking for the high speed loss corners? Are you suiting your braking to the speed loss required by each corner? Are you working at moving throttle application points earlier? Losing less speed on the way to the apex? If you're not thinking about the specifics, finding a trick that results in a lower lap time is a crap shoot.

Short of a session with a data collection system, you can make comparisons of where on the racetrack your problems may lie by following a more skilled driver. In order to get any advantage from this, you have to get close enough so that you can see where gaps emerge and this can be tough when the better driver is pulling away at two seconds per lap. More often than not, you'll learn what you can from more than one driver as practice sessions go on.

Assuming that you can stay on line and that there are no obvious problems with braking or shifting, the likely problem areas will be what you've seen in the above data collection. In all the computer coaching we have done at the Racing School, the trend is the same. In high speed-loss situations, the ability to threshold brake is important, but more important is the speed to which you slow the car—the minimum speed point in the corner. In all corners, the speed from the turn-in to the apex is where significant time can be found.

The oddity in our example was that the slower driver had no problem with the fast stuff. That's unusual. Fast corners are more intimidating and drivers with less experience have a harder time feeling comfortable with 85 m.p.h. slides than 35 m.p.h. slides. If you can get close enough to a faster driver, you can begin to get an appreciation of what is possible—with two caveats that you must keep in mind.

1) Are you driving comparable equipment? If the faster driver has a car with more downforce or fresher tires, it might be impossible for anybody else to be as fast through the corner.

2) You might not be able to match the faster driver's talent. Let's face it: some drivers have developed the finesse and car control to master high speed slides, while others aren't there yet.

Personal Limits

Don't get caught by the "If he can do it I can do it" attitude. Get there in small bites, and if it feels too fast, maybe you've reached your personal limit.

Personal limits: it's an important idea to keep in mind. We approach driving as if everybody who gets into a racecar wants to be the fastest driver on the course. Everyone, in reality, chooses how fast they really want to go, and what combination of risks versus rewards they want to pursue.

> *"You've got to be careful making comparisons from driver to driver. Somebody says they're going to the 200 marker before braking—how fast will that car slow down compared to yours? Is he braking when he sees the 200 marker or braking at the 200 marker, or is he just not telling the truth? ...I would take any information I got from a competitor with a big pinch of salt. I'm not saying, don't talk to other drivers, but you have to be careful."*
>
> —Danny Sullivan

CHAPTER 9

PASSING

Passing on the racetrack requires an understanding of the conventions in play and the techniques required to improve your position or to fairly defend it.

PASSING MAY SEEM LIKE nothing more than just putting your foot down and steering around the car ahead of you, but it's not that simple. The uninformed observer misses the point that on the racetrack, *everyone* has their foot on the floor. You even hear shades of this misconception from television race commentators. One driver will be methodically catching another and the announcer says something like, "Wow, Bobby, Stroker Ace is really putting the hammer down now," as if he were driving around on half throttle for three quarters of the race and only just now decided to go full out.

The pass of choice for anybody that ever put on a helmet is the "Big Horsepower Blow-By." As Walt Bohren, Skip Barber instructor and two-time IMSA GTU Champion, says, "You *can't* have too much horsepower." The people who make the rules, however, spend a lot of time designing regulations that make it difficult for any one competitor to get this kind of advantage. By restricting the weight, engine size, and shape of racecars, the sanctioning bodies try to limit the possibility that any one team can get a huge technical advantage over the others.

The result is that in any well-contested class of racing, racers in the top 25% of the field have little or no performance advantage over each other. Passing then becomes a matter of being able to wring more performance out of the car than your competitor: a contest of driving skill.

THE RULES

Although the racetrack can seem like a wild place where chaos reigns and the competition between strong egos knows no bounds, there are some conventions that are observed to prevent total anarchy. For example, it is the overtaking driver who has the primary responsibility to do the overtaking without making contact with the car being passed. The major sanctioning bodies for road racing in the U.S. agree that the overtaken driver also has the responsibility

to help make the pass a contact-free affair.

The primary problem occurs not on the straightaway, where driving on any one part of the straight holds no advantage over another part, but in corners, where everyone wants to be on-line. The most important question in passing situations is who's got rights to the line and who will yield.

Rights to the Line

Our standard for rights to the line hinges on the relative positions of the cars at the approach to the corner. The SCCA rulebook says, "The responsibility for the decision to pass another car rests with the overtaking driver." If, at the brake point, your car is dead alongside the car you're trying to pass, the overtaken car is obliged to leave room for you and not simply turn into you at the turn-in point. If, however, you're trying to pass but you're not quite alongside, as in having the front wheels up to the middle of the other car at the brake point, you haven't made the pass; it's your responsibility to get out of the way of the other car and yield the line in order to avoid a collision. The other driver might yield and give you room at the apex, but you can't count on it. He may not even have seen you

Fig. 9-1. If the car attempting the pass is alongside at the approach to the corner, the car being overtaken is obliged to yield.

Fig. 9-2. If the overtaking car is only partway alongside on the approach to the corner, the convention is that the car in the lead has the right to the line and the burden is on the overtaking car to avoid contact.

if he hasn't been looking in his mirrors. If you're not alongside, you've got to expect to be "chopped," which is the racing term for another driver pulling across the nose of your car going to the apex.

> *"I go with the conventional way of looking at rights to a corner. I agree 100% that the guy getting into the corner first has the corner. Some people don't see it that way. If you're trying to pass me, and at the point of turn-in I've got you by half a car length, then I've got the lead going into the corner and I'm going to go for the apex."*
>
> —*Dorsey Schroeder*

Pushing the Envelope

If you watch races on television, you can see plenty of examples of passes attempted by top-level professionals that lead to crashes rather than changes of position. Invariably, they are caused by the driver behind forcing the issue, trying to complete a pass by putting the burden of accident avoidance on the overtaken driver. If the overtaken driver isn't in the mood to be bullied out of his position, the two cars crash. We don't have to name names, but if we did, it would include some of the top names in the sport.

Before the cars and racetracks became as safe as they are today, cars making contact, especially open

wheel cars, often led to fatalities. The drivers raced hard but they passed because they drove faster, not because they were willing to run into other cars. Perhaps the relative safety of the cars and circuits today has made drivers less protective of each other's lives, since most of the time a crash only tears up equipment rather than killing a fellow competitor.

Different Rules for Different Arenas

We put on over 200 individual Formula Dodge races a year, and in these races, we have made a clear distinction between a driver who causes an accident in a passing situation (and pays for the damage to both cars) and the victim. If the overtaking driver is not at least alongside at the turn-in point (at the latest) and there is contact between the cars as a result of the pass attempt, the overtaking driver is at fault. If the overtaking driver is alongside and the overtaken driver turns into him, the blame is on the overtaken driver.

Our rules work pretty well with cars that have comparable corner entry speeds, but the situation is different if one car approaches and enters the corner 20 m.p.h. slower than another. Sometimes, especially in a long corner, the faster car can be significantly behind the slower one at the braking point, yet because of the high closing rate, get safely by before the apex. You'll run into this situation at races in which multiple classes compete. Because of the varying speed potential within the same race, the pro rulebook puts responsibility on both drivers to assure safe passing.

The rulebook reads, "It is the responsibility of both the overtaking and the overtaken drivers to assure safe passing at racing speeds....However, if it [the overtaken car] is overtaken by a faster car, the driver must give way to the overtaking car."

It can be confusing for novice drivers to sort out their rights and responsibilities in passing. In many forms of racing, a good pass is one you get away with. Still, there are guidelines and conventions that help sort out the conflicts. We think you can break down most situations into the following three categories:

I. Equal Cars Racing for Position.

1) If you are attempting a pass and are alongside at the braking point, you have rights to the line from the turn-in to the apex. The overtaken car should yield.

2) If you're not quite alongside at the brake point but draw alongside before the turn-in point, you technically have rights to the line, but if contact happens, you're really to blame. You are taking the chance in this situation that your guesstimate of the closing speed is correct—that you'll make up the distance of a quarter car or half car between the brake point and the turn-in. If you guessed wrong and the other car is still half a car-length ahead at the turn-in, expect that the other driver will take the line and go for the apex. You didn't do the pass—you got in the way.

3) If you're behind the other car and attempt to make up a car-length or more between the brake point and the turn-in, you're either a wild optimist or a lot better braker than the other driver. Either way, if you blow it, it's your fault.

II. Equal Cars where One is Being Lapped or is Uncompetitive.

1) If you're driving the slower car and the faster one is alongside you in the braking zone, you should yield the line.

2) If the faster car is not quite alongside you, you should still yield the line.

3) If the faster car is behind you at the turn-in point, you should, as a courtesy, leave one and a half car-widths between your car and the apex, letting the other driver decide whether to do the pass in the corner or on the following straight.

III. Races with Multiple Classes of Car.

The big difference in this type of race is that you may be racing for the lead in your class when another car, or group of cars, appears in your mirror, about to lap you. Typically, they are racing for the lead in *their* class, going 5 seconds per lap faster than you. You don't want to hold them up by getting in the way, but you sure don't want to slow up and lose time to the competitors in your own class.

In professional sportscar racing, where this happens frequently, the rulebook states that you should give way to the faster class of car. This doesn't necessarily mean that you pull off the racetrack, you just make it easier for the faster cars to get by without overly handicapping yourself. The faster cars should have no trouble getting by on the straights even if you stay on the normal line. Ideally, they would like to pass you and get back on-line before the next corner, and when the timing works out this way, passing is no problem. Just as often, the faster cars don't get by you on the straight but are closing ferociously in the braking zone and corner. If you see this developing and you're racing hard for position in your class, give them the car-width and a half at the apex. You won't have to slow down too much to make this happen without spoiling the race in either class.

If you are uncompetitive in your class or running a minute behind the car ahead and a minute ahead of the car behind, you can spare more road—and more lap time—to help faster cars through.

On some circuits, the race organizers may ask the drivers of slower classes of cars to keep to a certain lane on the high-speed straights or on the banking. You'd be expected to finish the corner leading onto the straight by tracking out to the edge, then working your way carefully to your lane. At the end of the straight you can work your way back out to the turn-in point if there is no traffic. If a faster car is going to get there at the same time, you'll have to stay where you are and enter the corner off the optimum line, which is going to require an adjustment to your braking and turn-in points.

When you are yielding to faster cars, unless specifically instructed by the race organizers, drive the normal line down the straights. Be sure to check your mirrors at the beginning and end of every straight. If you get caught at the corner, give the faster cars a car-width and a half from the turn-in through the apex to allow them to choose to go by in the corner. If, on checking your mirrors, you judge that they won't catch you until the following straight, stay on-line through the corner so as not to lose any time to your competitors.

COOPERATING

In all of these iffy passing situations, it takes a lot of the anxiety away from the overtaking driver if it's obvious that the slower car ahead is going to yield the line. Wondering whether the driver alongside is going to yield or turn into you is uncomfortable.

The Point-By

One way to alert the faster driver that you're yielding is to point to the side where you're going to leave room. This move is known as the "point-by," and it isn't a command for the overtaking driver—it's merely a suggestion. The overtaking driver may have already made the decision to pass on the other side, so don't be surprised if you point one way and are passed on the opposite side. For the passing driver, the value of

Fig. 9-3. The point-by takes the worry out of passing situations and is an indicator of a heads-up driver displaying sportsmanship.

the point-by is not so much the suggested direction but the fact that you know he or she is around.

Don't point if you don't mean it. If you're at the turn-in point and you point inside to signify that you're prepared to leave room at the apex, don't then go for the apex and shut the door. The overtaking driver may not have gone for the pass in the corner except that you encouraged it by pointing. Going for the normal line has the effect of suckering in, then taking out your competitor. We've seen it many times: in fact, we've named it the "Point-Bomb."

> "In my type of racing it's amazing that the guys generally do a really good job of point-bys. You try to help that by showing your appreciation. Every car I ever passed I've stuck a hand out the window and waved back if I could. It establishes a communication between drivers, and a respect—and that works real well, especially in endurance racing where you're going to see each other again and again."
>
> —Terry Earwood

Driving Off-Line

You can also help faster drivers get around by leaving the normal racing line so that they can get by on-line. However, slower drivers, especially novices, can overdo it in an effort to be cooperative. As a faster driver approaches a slower car he or she is watching to see where the slower car drives. The faster driver plans a pass for a part of the racetrack where it's possible to get by while losing as little lap time as possible. The faster driver is planning on your car being in a particular spot, and if you drastically alter your line

in an effort to cooperate, you may end up right in the spot the faster car had committed to go, causing more problems than you solve.

The best procedure for a slower driver is to drive the same line lap after lap, allowing the drivers behind to plan their passing moves. If you do make a departure from the line, make it a subtle one: one and a half car-widths off the apex, for example. Don't try to help by braking 100 yards sooner than you did in the last lap. The driver behind would never expect that drastic a change in braking point, and you'd surely get punted from behind. It pays to be consistent.

PASSING EQUAL CARS

Two cars that have the same speed potential make passing difficult. The easy pass—one car going a lot faster than the other on the straight—isn't going to happen. With the same acceleration potential, both cars' top speed should end up the same, provided they start at the same speed. If one driver does a better job than the other through the corner leading onto the straight and starts the straight at a higher speed, that car will gain ground on the other.

The Exit-Speed Pass

One of the basic laws of passing is that in order to pass another car, you need to be going faster than it. That concept doesn't sound too complicated, yet frequently we see drivers pull out from behind another car going exactly the same speed, expecting to pass it. The only thing accomplished is two cars driving down the straight in formation, doing a fly-by of start/finish.

In order to come onto the straight faster than the driver ahead, you can't put yourself in a position where the car ahead can determine your cornering speed. The most common mistake we see in passing technique is a driver that follows the car ahead so closely that he or she can't go any faster without hitting it. The driver then bitterly complains that the driver ahead was blocking, slowing up the run

Fig. 9-4. Setting up an exit-speed pass requires leaving room ahead to accelerate as the cars come to the corner exit.

Fig. 9-5. Staying right on the gearbox of the car ahead allows that driver to dictate cornering speed.

Fig. 9-6. The properly executed draft-by pass starts by leaving room ahead to accelerate into (top), then smoothly transitioning out from behind the car ahead (middle) and using the speed advantage to pull alongside in the braking zone (bottom).

through the corner. The fault, of course, is on the driver that allowed the block by not leaving enough room so that he or she could take the corner faster.

In order to pass using an exit-speed advantage, you need room to accelerate, not allowing the slower car ahead to impede your progress. You would like to time it so that you don't catch the car ahead until you're on the straight. At that point, for example, a 2-m.p.h. advantage gained from doing the corner better would convert to 3 feet per second. Exiting the corner at that faster rate, you'd be alongside a 12-foot long car in 4 seconds, and a car-length ahead in 8 seconds.

How Drafting Increases Speed

A lot of your engine's horsepower is used to push the air out of the way of the car: in a Formula Dodge, for example, over 80% of the car's total horsepower is being used to overcome the aerodynamic drag of the car at speeds in the 100-m.p.h. range. Most of the rest of the engine's horsepower is used up by overcoming transmission frictional losses, the rotational inertia of all the moving components, and the tires' rolling resistance. Eighty percent of the resistance to going faster at the end of the straight is aerodynamic and, therefore, if this drag is reduced, more of the horsepower is available to accelerate the car; as a result, it goes faster.

Two cars in line, regardless of their shape, present a more streamlined shape to the air and as a result, both have lower form drag. The longer the line of cars, the greater the form-drag reduction and the faster the whole train will go.

With equal racecars, the car ahead is at a disadvantage—even though it is getting some benefit from the draft—because it is the one punching the hole in the air, while the one following behind gets a speed advantage. The draft-by pass involves the driver behind using this speed advantage to close on and pass the car ahead.

Phases of a Draft-By Pass

In using the draft to pass a single car, you should think about each aspect of the pass. The first step is to leave some room ahead. You'll probably want to draft by on the fastest parts of the course where the draft is greater, so you'll pick a corner leading onto one of the high-speed straights as a place to set up the pass.

If you're right on the gearbox of the car ahead, you'll need to leave some room—one, two, or three car-lengths—so that you can use the draft to close on the car ahead coming onto the straight. You'll try to time it so that you come off the corner faster and get a run down the first third or half of the straight, never having to lift off the throttle, building the speed differential that will carry you by. As you can see in Fig. 9-7, the relative vacuum behind the car ahead allows you to go faster.

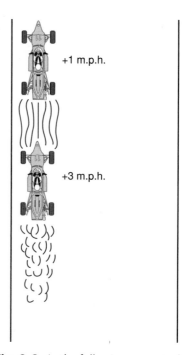

Fig. 9-8. As the following car gets closer, it smooths out the turbulence behind the lead car. Both gain speed, although the following car maintains its previous speed advantage.

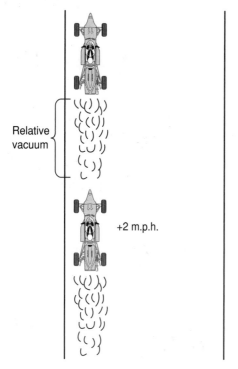

Fig. 9-7. The following car gains speed because its aerodynamic drag is reduced in the relative vacuum behind the lead car.

As you get closer (see Fig. 9-8), your car smooths out the turbulent wake behind the lead car and it also sees a reduction in drag and gains speed, although, since you are closing on the car, your advantage is greater.

When you're one to one-half car-lengths back, you steer to the inside to drive around. When you leave the spot directly behind the car ahead you no longer smooth out the airflow for the leading car. As you can see in Fig. 9-9, the turbulence reappears behind the lead car, making the drag higher and slowing its acceleration. This can be a big problem for both cars if the passing driver doesn't anticipate the change in closing speed.

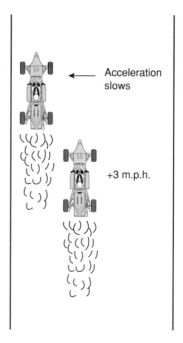

Fig. 9-9. When the following car pulls out from behind, the turbulence reappears behind the lead car, slowing its acceleration.

> *"At the Glen, running by myself, I'd see 125 to 126 m.p.h. at the six hundred marker at the end of the straight. When Scott Gaylord came out in another of our cars, I tagged on to him and I saw 131 on the speedometer. 5 m.p.h.! Free horsepower! The tow was so good that if you didn't pull out to pass, you had to run two-thirds throttle all the way down just to keep from hitting him from behind."*
>
> —Terry Earwood

Watch the Changing Closing Rate. As you approach the rear end of the car ahead, getting a run on it, you watch the closing rate between the two cars and time the pullout so that you miss the lead car's rear corner with your front corner as you go by. Because the drag reappears for the front car when you pull out from behind, the closing rate between you accelerates—the car ahead seems to dart back at you. To avoid tapping the car ahead as you pull out of the draft, a smooth pullout of the relative vacuum behind the car ahead works best. Remember too that you want to turn the steering wheel as little as you can get away with. Big jerks of the wheel will only scrub speed away—the more you turn the wheel, the more drag the tire creates against the road.

Another reason to avoid jerking the car out of the draft is that the hole in the air made by the front car doesn't only extend directly behind the car. A car pushes the air aside much like a boat pushes water aside, creating a bow wave and a wake. There is still draft advantage to be had alongside the rear quarter of the car (see Fig. 9-10).

Close, Pull Out, Pull Back. Once you've pulled out of the wake of the car ahead, it would be ideal if you had gained enough speed that momentum would carry you completely around. This isn't always the case since, once you're back alongside the other car, all the drag that you would have had running alone reappears. Your car doesn't instantly slow to its original one-car top speed: the speed advantage you gained from the draft deteriorates as you pull alongside. If you had your choice, it wouldn't fall to zero before you got completely past and pulled back in line, but it doesn't always happen this way.

Sometimes your car runs out of steam when you're 7/8ths past. You can't pull back in line until you've checked in your mirror that the car you just drafted is indeed behind you. Just because you saw his nose at your shoulder three seconds ago does not mean that you're completely past. Your speeds may have equalized since then and you still need a few feet to get completely ahead. Move over without looking, and you risk contact—on the fastest part of the circuit.

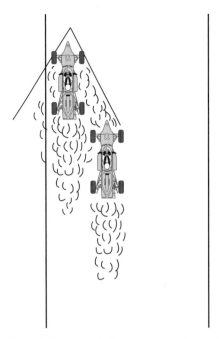

Fig. 9-10. A relative vacuum also exists alongside the rear quarter of the lead car.

If you're in the car that just got drafted, you have to realize that the driver of the other car is susceptible to this kind of mistake and be prepared for the worst. You might even help him along by breathing out of the throttle and letting him tuck back in front. Remember that both of you will have less drag in-line than running side by side. If there are others in the race, as is most often the case, the two of you can go faster than any other single car if you work together.

> *"A successful draft-by pass starts before the corner leading onto the straight. You have to slow down the entry and time it so you do the corner as fast as you can, but never get held up by the driver ahead—you know, leave one, two, or three car-lengths ahead of you. It's hard, especially for new drivers to have the confidence to drop back a bit. Getting the run is what makes it happen."*
>
> —David Loring

In this case you've been drafted and almost passed by the other guy—there's no possible advantage in sticking to his rear quarter. When you get to the corner, he'll have to drive off-line because you're in the way at the turn-in. You'll have to drive off-line because he's in the way at the apex. By surrendering three feet of room and letting the car back in front, you lower each other's drag *and* you're able to run through the next corner on-line—the fastest way. By being difficult, you slow both cars up and give an advantage to the drivers behind who are chasing you.

Planning on the Draft-By

There are too many variables involved in passing to be able to predict whether you'll be able to do a clean, unimpeded draft-by pass on the straight. For certain, it's one of the easiest passes—almost as good as the Big Horsepower Blow-By. It doesn't compromise your line through the corners and, if anything, should make you faster down the straights. Whether you can do it depends upon a lot of things. For example, the racetrack has an effect on your passing technique: if the track has short, slow straights, it isn't going to be good for drafting and it won't play a big part in passing strategy.

Horsepower also plays a part in strategy. A high-horsepower class of cars, where the acceleration is still strong at the end of the straight and the aerodynamic drag absorbs a smaller percentage of the overall horsepower, won't show as dramatic a draft effect as lower-horsepower cars.

In terms of car design, some racecars are extremely slippery, making a smaller, less disturbed hole in the air and consequently reducing the advantage to cars behind. You can try to draft off these cars, but nothing will happen, since the reduction in drag is so slight that your car can't gain a usable amount of speed.

But sometimes the car and racetrack combine to create a killer tow, and driving by your competitor on the straight every other lap is a cinch, as long as you can stay within six or seven car lengths on other parts of the course. Of course, if you can do it to others, they can do it to you; often, you'll see cars swap positions on successive laps all race long, each using the draft advantage to get by the other. If neither driver can pull away on other parts of the circuit, the race comes down to the position of the cars at start/finish on the last lap and strategy plays a big part in who wins.

PASSING IN THE BRAKING ZONE

If neither the draft nor better exit speed provides you with enough speed advantage to actually pass the car ahead on the straightaway, you'll have to complete the pass under braking. Being able to threshold brake at the last possible moment when you want to or need to is possibly one of the most important skills for racing. It's the way you end up doing a lot of your passing, and it's another vital weapon in your arsenal.

Don't Pull Over

The idea of a corner entry pass is to change the relative position of the cars. At the turn-in point of the corner, you are going to be off the normal line by at least a car width. In order to avoid early apexing the

corner, you'll have to make an adjustment to your turn-in point.

Since you're going to be forced to drive off-line, the lap time for the lap on which you do the pass is going to be slower than normal. Giving up a car width of radius in the first part of the corner is going to limit your cornering speed in comparison to the normal, bigger radius line. This is okay, since here, you're interested in changing position, not lowering lap time. At the same time you want to minimize the sacrifice you make, surrendering as little lap time as possible. To do so you want to get back to the normal racing line and up to your normal corner exit speed as quickly as possible.

Your goal is to be back on-line and on power by, at the latest, the apex. If you don't manage this, you'll lead going into the corner but get passed by your competitor going out.

> *"I brake as late and hard as I feel comfortable doing, all the time, but there are times when I end up going beyond that. That's the difference—you can extend yourself beyond what your comfort level is, but for a reason."*
> —Bryan Herta

The Perfect Corner-Entry Pass

Let's follow the progression of a corner-entry pass that works. At the normal brake point the cars are side by side. Both drivers lift off the throttle and go to the brakes. The driver on the inside has gotten alongside and established the right to the line at the apex according to the generally accepted rules of the road.

The Driver on the Outside. In most cases it is in the best interests of the driver on the outside to yield to the overtaking driver for the following reasons. First, as you learned earlier, the car on the inside has the advantage of the laws of physics. That is, the outside car has a longer way to drive around the outside and, given cars with equal cornering power, the car on the outside will lose ground to the inside car as they drive through the corner. Second, the driver outside is off the normal racing line and the asphalt is likely to be more slippery out there, making the car corner worse than the car on the inside. Third, if the inside car should slide wider than intended at the exit of the corner, the outside car will be the first to end up on the dirt—or whatever lurks outside the track-out point.

The decision to yield does have something to do with where in the race the pass is taking place. If it's the fourth lap of a four-hour race and the driver on the inside is one with whom you expect a long seesaw race, yielding is no big deal, since you'll probably get ahead on the next lap or the lap after that.

If it's the last lap and the finish line is 50 feet past the exit of the corner—well, that's something else. In a mid-race situation you concede the corner if the other driver is alongside in the braking zone. If anything, you brake a little bit early and plan to get in line behind the other car. As you'll soon see, there are mistakes the overtaking driver can make that may put you back in front in short order. In order to be prepared to take advantage of any mistakes on the other driver's part, you want to nail the turn-in point and be perfectly on line. Next, you want to be set to attempt to get the throttle open a little earlier than normal if the opportunity presents itself. If the overtaking driver does the pass well, you can expect that you won't be able to apply throttle until the car ahead does, but if the other driver makes a mistake and is not directly in front of you as you approach the apex, you may be

> *"Going in deeper on the brakes in a passing situation is probably the most difficult thing to judge in a race car. You get a draft on a guy and you are coming into the braking zone with more speed—where do you put on the brakes? You want to go deeper than the other guy but you're also on a piece of road you're not normally on. It's the toughest thing to judge."*
>
> —Jeremy Dale

able to get an exit speed advantage by beating the other car to the acceleration away from the corner.

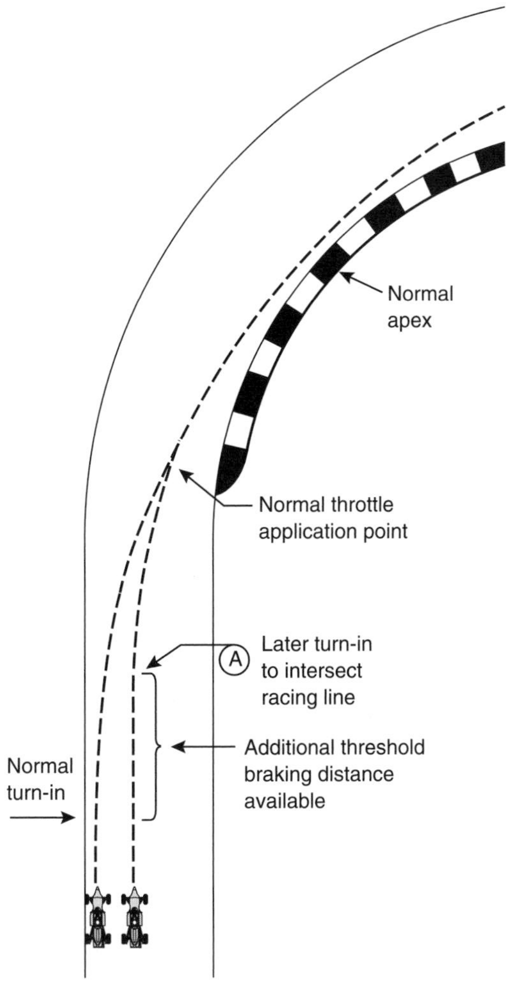

The Overtaking Driver. The overtaking driver, in order to give away as little radius at the corner entry as possible, does not want to give the car being passed any more room than necessary. A common mistake is for drivers to be very gun shy of the car next to them and to leave two or three car widths of room between them in the braking zone. All you need is two feet in open wheel cars, less in cars with fenders.

You also want to brake parallel to the edge of the racetrack. Many drivers, feeling edgy about the car next to them, head diagonally toward the apex, opening up the possibility of early apexing, which is going to cause trouble at the corner exit.

Sketching out the approach to the corner, the two cars are side by side (see Fig. 9-11). The car on the inside should intersect the normal racing line by the throttle application point or, at the latest, the apex. To do this, the turn-in point moves down closer to the corner to point A. The distance between the normal turn-in point and the new, later turn-in is distance that can be added to the threshold braking portion of the corner entry. Even though the radius going into the corner is tighter than normal and requires a slightly lower turn-in speed, this longer threshold braking zone can allow you to wait just a tiny bit longer before going to the brakes.

Going a little bit deeper assures the pass. If the driver on the outside had any lingering thoughts about contesting the corner, watching you dart ahead a half car length as the brakes go on should settle the argument.

Keeping the Position. Now you need to make sure the other driver doesn't get an advantage coming out of the corner. If you early apex the corner and have to be off the power, struggling to get the car to change direction at the corner exit, the cagey competitor will try to give you the corner entry and plan to get on the power earlier than normal, on the perfect line, and get you coming out.

By making the apex, you don't have to worry about hitting your normal throttle application point. The

Normal apex

Normal throttle application point

Later turn-in to intersect racing line

Additional threshold braking distance available

Normal turn-in

Fig. 9-11. Off-line on the inside, the job of the overtaking car is to get back on line as soon as possible. This will require a later turn-in than a normal lap would call for.

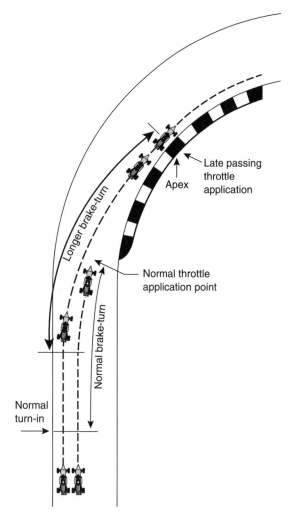

Fig. 9-12. By getting the car back on-line by the apex, the passing car not only changes position, it also determines the throttle application point of the car behind.

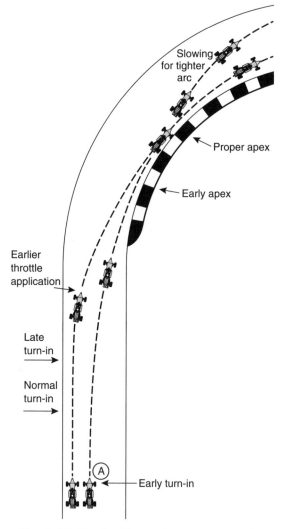

Fig. 9-13. The double pass is very common. It results from the passing car taking an early apex and needing to slow at the exit of the corner to keep the car on the racing surface.

driver behind can't accelerate until you do unless he or she wants to drive around the outside of your car. To make the pass and keep it, the key is to determine your opponent's throttle application point which, simply by virtue of human reaction time, is going to be slightly later than yours (see Fig. 9-12).

Passing Briefly: The Double Pass
Look at what happens when you get nervous and turn in early (see Fig. 9-13). Turning at point A, you can run a faster, broad-radius arc down into the corner, easily getting past your competitor on the way in. Once past the apex, though, the path you're on carries you away from the normal racing line, opening up a path for the driver you just passed.

In addition, you'll probably have to still be braking and turning at this point, slowing the car down for the tighter arc you'll have to negotiate late in the corner. Your opponent can see you headed for an early apex and, if anything, turn a little later than normal, concentrating on throttle application. While you're scrambling around on the outside of the road trying to keep your car from going off, he's on the throttle, passing you coming off the corner.

The early apex really kills you going down the next straight. Since the exit arc is tighter and your throttle application point is later, your corner exit speed will be much lower than normal and you'll lose ground all the way to the next corner.

The Early Turn-In Pass
Watch enough races, and you'll see drivers successfully pass by taking a broad arc into the corner inside

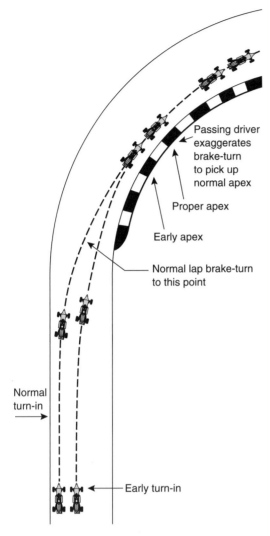

Passing driver
exaggerates
brake-turn
to pick up
normal apex

Proper apex

Early apex

Normal lap brake-turn
to this point

Normal
turn-in

Early turn-in

Fig. 9-14. An early turn-in can work if the passing driver is adept at braking and turning *and* is able to be back on line for the second part of the corner.

their competitor. It looks like an early apex coming, but if the driver can brake and turn all the way to the apex and get back on-line for the exit, it works out (see Fig. 9-14).

The key is being on-line coming out, maintaining your exit speed potential and thereby dictating your competitor's throttle application point. Do this and the pass is made and kept.

THE OUT-BRAKING GAME

If the pass for position comes long before the end of the race, the driver you pass will probably not fight tooth and nail to keep you behind. When it gets toward the end of the race, however, you can't necessarily count on getting cooperation.

> "If someone's pressuring you and trying to pass you, you can always brake at a point where you feel it's conservative, then release some brake pressure and coast up alongside him. You're safely, effectively doing the same thing as late braking, while still leaving a margin for error. You're matching his speed at the corner entry."
>
> —Dorsey Schroeder

Waiting Each Other Out

When you're fighting for position, the contest may boil down to who brakes last and who gets to the apex first. When you're side by side on the approach to the corner, the driver on the outside has a tough job defending the position, but it's possible. If the outside driver brakes later than the driver on the inside and, at the turn-in point, is a car-length ahead, the outside driver can go ahead and turn in, successfully turning back the passing attempt. Although the car making the passing attempt established rights to the line by getting alongside in the braking zone, you can't expect the other driver to just roll over. You have to go at least as late on the brakes as the driver you're attempting to pass. You can count on the fact that the other driver will try to brake later than normal if he or she is a tough competitor.

In a way, outbraking passes are like a game of chicken—who's going to lift first. You can't, however, just decide to key off the other driver, not braking until you see the other car start to slow. The other driver may have decided to do the same thing and be waiting for you to brake. The result could be that both of you go hopelessly late: too late to make the corner.

Point of No Return

Either driver, inside or outside, can try to wait for the other to brake, but if you're going to play this game, you should have a point beyond which you won't go.

> "Racing somebody down into the braking zone, you think, 'I'm not going to brake 'til he does.' But you do that a couple of times and go sailing down the escape road and lose a ton of time and you realize that you have to draw the line for yourself. I'll go deeper than normal, sometimes a lot deeper, but there's a deepest point I'll go regardless of what the other guy does. Just because he does it doesn't mean you can. The other car can be lighter, have better brakes, better tires. Sometimes you run out of talent before he does."
>
> —David Loring

If the driver on the outside, for example, goes just 10 feet past the point where it becomes impossible to make the corner—the driver on the inside wins. It's an error you're bound to make if you're on the outside and you just blindly try to brake after the driver on the inside does: you leave yourself wide open.

If, on the other hand, you want to hold off the inside pass attempt and through better skill or more experience you go to a last ditch point which is later than that of the driver on the inside, picking up a car length, you'll beat the driver on the inside to the apex. Since the driver on the inside had a "latest point" that was earlier than yours, he or she lost the opportunity to pass but didn't get pressured into going impossibly late and crashing as a result.

Vulnerability

If you're on the outside, you're in more of a position to be a victim of a late-braking mistake. If you go too deep and can't make the corner, at least you don't get in the way of the car on the inside. If you're on the inside and you decide to go deeper, there's a chance that you'll brake too hard, lock up the front tires, and be unable to turn when you both get to the turn-in point. If the outside driver turns in without looking—bang.

If you're the outside driver in this situation, even if you don't turn in, your options are limited to following along on the outside until you *can* turn in behind the other car. Sometimes you can't, and the car on the inside just escorts you down the escape road, if there is one. Without an escape road, you get escorted into the boonies.

How Deep is Deep?

As two Formula Dodges approach a corner like the Sebring Hairpin, they are decelerating from around 110 m.p.h. down to the neighborhood of 40 m.p.h. at the turn-in. Either driver, outside or inside, would like to gain one car length over the other between the brake point and the turn-in. The cars are only 12 feet long, so the battle is to gain 12 feet over the distance of the braking zone.

A Formula Dodge in Race Series trim decelerates at slightly under 1.2 G and, at this rate, it's going to take 2.6 seconds and 290 feet to get slowed from 110 m.p.h. to 40 m.p.h. Since either car needs a 5 foot-per-second advantage to gain 12 feet in 2.6 seconds, you can pull this off by braking .125 seconds (1/8 second) later than the other car. At the approach speed of 110 m.p.h., that means about 20 feet later.

By going 20 feet later on the brakes, the overtaking driver covers the braking zone at an average speed about 3 m.p.h. faster than the other car. This extra 3 m.p.h. can be problematic at the turn-in point. The only way to make the turn-in is to extend the straight line braking zone, knocking off some of the extra speed, and exaggerating the brake-turning effort at the corner entry.

In order to slow the car down to the normal corner entry speed, you would have to come up with an increase in braking ability of almost 5%—not likely if you're already running close to the limit. Going 20 feet deeper is going to take a lot of work and skill.

Standing by the side of the racetrack, 20 feet doesn't look like a lot of distance but, given drivers of equal threshold braking skill, the 20-foot difference in the brake point can mean the difference between winning and finishing second. Few drivers can make up a car-length in the braking zone alone and this is a reflection of the level of parity that you find at the top of each field. When running with the fastest drivers, a 20-foot change in the braking point isn't going to be easy to find, since everyone is bumping up against the edge of the latest possible brake point on normal laps.

DEFENDING YOUR POSITION

In an outbraking situation, you can challenge the other driver to match your brake point. You can test the commitment to the pass by trying to hang alongside on the outside line. Another tactic is not to give the other driver the inside line in the first place. You could drive down the side of the straight that leads to the inside edge of the corner, forcing the overtaking driver to draw alongside on the outside edge of the racetrack, as in Fig. 9-15. At the corner, the outside car ends up being at a disadvantage.

> "Recently in the Pro Series...we had one driver who could really go around pretty well all by himself—when he would get into the defensive driving mode, he'd manage to hold somebody behind him, but seven other guys would catch them both. He'd end up much worse off than if he'd just let one guy by. Instead of going second place to third place, he'd go second to ninth."
>
> —Skip Barber

Sometimes, however, this can backfire. When you're on the inside, you have to slow enough to keep the car on the tight radius around the first half of the corner. If you're on the outside, you could brake slightly earlier than normal, drive on the right line for the corner and time it so that you're closing on the car on the inside past the apex, where an open passing lane would open up for the pass on the corner exit.

Surprisingly, this doesn't happen very much. Seeing a car drive defensively up the inside tends to befuddle the driver on the outside and more often than not, they give up the passing attempt. It can be done, but most drivers don't like to take the chance of being hung out to dry on the outside.

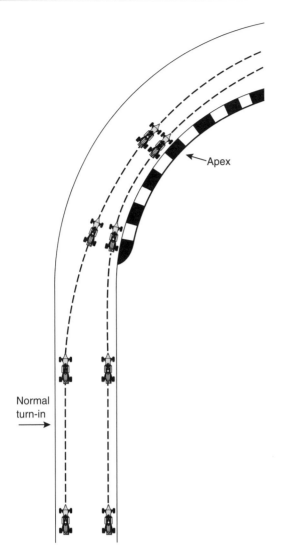

Apex

Normal
turn-in →

Fig. 9-15. Driving defensively is different than blocking. You can choose to drive up to the corner on the inside edge of the road and challenge the other driver to make an outside pass.

As for the ethics of this technique, it's not really considered blocking, so it's not a dirty move. Any driver has the right to decide on the path they'll take around the racetrack. Driving down the inside of the straight in order to make a pass more difficult for your

competitor—as long as you make the decision to go for the inside *before* the overtaking driver starts to pass on that side—is okay. But if the following car has to get out of the throttle to avoid running into you or has to run off the road because you moved in reaction to a pass attempt, then it's a block.

> *"There's a time when you want to drive defensively, but I don't believe in this weaving that you see. You can...hurt the momentum of another driver, just occupying a space he wants, and this is especially true on ovals. They have a rule now in Indy Car that you get to move one time. You move a second time and you get black-flagged, and I think that's right. You don't go messing around too much because, especially with open wheelers, they're so easy to get up in the air. People can get killed, and have, and it doesn't take much."*
> —Danny Sullivan

Blocking

Blocking—weaving down the straight with your eyes on the mirrors, trying to cut off the driver behind—qualifies you as a lower form of life. Like any other sport, racing requires sportsmanship, and if the only way some racers can win is by weaving in front of faster drivers, perhaps they ought to get out of racing and do something more in keeping with their personalities—we hear professional wrestling pays well.

> *"As professional drivers, I feel that we're all supposed to maintain a certain integrity, a certain honor. I feel like I'm going to race with you just as hard as I possibly can, but if you're driving a better car or you're driving better on that particular day, then you deserve to be in front of me. That doesn't mean I'm going to let you go by easy, but it means if you outdo me, then you're going to get the line. All that I can do is kick myself in the butt and figure out how you did it and get you back."*
> —Brian Till

CHAPTER 10

THE REALITY OF RACING

> **Wheel-to-wheel competition creates additional mental and emotional demands on top of your existing set of skills and knowledge.**

Your APPROACH TO A race should always be to do your best behind the wheel, but the level of excellence required and the risks you take to succeed change as you climb the racing ladder.

You approach the limit of your own abilities and the car's potential as closely as you can, but the closer you get, the finer the line is between a little mistake and a loss of control. Goal number one in your early races is to finish—it doesn't matter where—just finish and get car time in race conditions under your belt.

There will be races where you have to be right on the edge from start to finish in order to compete. There will be those where the level of intensity will be lower. It's easy to get carried away, so you should allow for at least one moment during a race weekend to remind yourself that this is most likely *not* the only thing that matters in your life.

QUALIFYING

Almost all types of racing establish the starting order of the race based on qualifying times. The fastest car sits in the pole and the cars are laid out two by two (or at some places, three by three), in descending order of their fastest lap times. Obviously, there are clear advantages to starting in the front. It's handy to not have to pass anyone—just hold your position from start to finish—but putting the car on the pole, or close to the front of the grid, takes on a different level of importance in different races.

Decisions, Decisions

A key factor in the importance of a good grid position is whether the racetrack is one with numerous good passing zones or one like a tight street circuit without any long straights, where it's going to be difficult to get by a lapped car, let alone a close competitor.

Another fact to remember is that in qualifying, in most cases, the grid position is based on one lap. Unlike the race, where a good average lap time can beat another driver who does an occasional faster lap but can't sustain it, doing well in qualifying only takes one good one.

The first consideration when approaching qualifying is to make an honest judgement about the importance of qualifying well in *this* race, at *this* racetrack. If it's one of your first few races, and you've got a lot to learn, it's not very important to do an all-out qualifying attempt. What you need at this point in your career is time behind the wheel of a racecar and you won't get that if you ball up the car in a banzai qualifying run. You may rightly decide to run qualifying somewhat conservatively, doing as well as you reasonably can, but not pulling out all the stops and risking your opportunity to get valuable race experience.

At the other extreme, if you're in a season-long chase for a championship and the pole earns points toward the title—and gets you the advantage of starting ahead of the rest— you and your team have to do everything you can to put in one blistering lap.

> *"In practice and qualifying you drive 100% the whole time, no— in qualifying you pick it up a little. In practice and qualifying at Long Beach this year I think I hit the wall six times, only doing damage once. Lots of times you brush the wall on the way out but that hasn't caught me out yet. You're just using all the road—if you've got a big power oversteer when you do it, obviously you're going to snap something. But at that level of racing and the seriousness of the competition, if you're not doing that stuff, you're not going to be on the front row. If you're leaving four inches from the edges during qualifying, you're not going to do it."*
>
> —Robbie Buhl

Car Set-Up

Car set-up for qualifying is necessarily different. For the race, the car has to be prepared to run for at least a half-hour, and in some cases up to 24 hours. In qualifying it has to go fast for a short period of time and this can mean that you change some systems on the car to give it a short-lived burst. To start, brand new tires are a must in qualifying because race tires have their ultimate grip in the first few laps of their life, then the grip stabilizes at a slightly lower level.There are all kinds of other tricks, from blocking off radiator and brake ducting, bypassing oil coolers, running thinner gear lube, and lowering fuel weight, all the way to installing a five-lap motor. The effort you put into tweaking the car for qualifying depends upon how important it is. It is often more important to spend practice time getting the race set-up right rather than playing with the ultimate one-lap set-up.

Your Driving Plan

From the driving standpoint, doing well in qualifying depends upon your ability to raise your driving to a higher level for a short burst. This takes intense concentration and a plan.

Frequently, using the draft of a teammate or a fast competitor can result in substantial lap-time gains.

> "What I change for qualifying is that I'm more aggressive for a short-term period. I think that concentration is a big factor. I'll get tuned up to do three laps hard where I don't leave any cards on the table—I'll use the track up. I'll get really close to apexes.
>
> "I consciously try to brake later in qualifying—really get the car in deep under braking. When you're talking six inches from the edges in measurements, that last six inches that you've left for a margin of error before nets you a qualifying time that picks up—whatever—two or three tenths, which you need in qualifying.
>
> "Yet you couldn't race that way for a long time, leaving yourself no margin. If you take the margin for error out and you give it all you've got, I guarantee you're used up in three laps. You couldn't do any more because you've thrown all the cards on the table and cheated death. I don't even need to be told. I'll tell my guys before I even get to the start finish line, 'Get this lap, this is good,' and I'll get past start finish and get out of the throttle 'cause I'll know I can't do any more."
>
> —Dorsey Schroeder

The draft has to be timed well. Two cars running in close company can both get a lap-time advantage since the two cars together will have less drag per car than each running alone, but sometimes this gain can be nullified for the following car if aerodynamic download on wings or ground effects is disturbed. The following car will get a straightaway drag advantage, but may suffer in the corners if the downforce is disturbed in the wake of the leading car. Using the draft, however, has the greatest advantage if the following car is not held up in corners by the car ahead, but can draft past the lead car on a long straight, getting to start/finish with a two- or three-car-length advantage relative to a normal lap. That three-car-length pop is worth .2 seconds at 120 m.p.h.

You have to weigh the draft advantage of following another car against the possibility of getting held up by the lead car. In some cases, it's better to find an open portion of the track to do a number of fast laps without the possibility of getting balked. This decision to tow or not to tow often depends upon the car: a car with relatively low horsepower relative to the amount of drag it creates will get greater benefit from drafting than a high horsepower car, slippery car, or one where aerodynamics are responsible for a good deal of their cornering grip.

REHEARSAL'S OVER

There are two fundamental problems drivers need to deal with when moving from practice sessions into an actual race. The first is the presence of other cars and their reluctance to allow you to pass, and the second is the mental pressure of the competition.

Traffic

In practice sessions, and even in qualifying, you always have the option to avoid traffic and find your own portion of the racetrack where you can operate freely, away from the influence of other cars. The fundamental problem in a race is that other cars may be where you want to be. Other cars will cause you to drive off-line in the corners, will affect your braking points, and will often determine when you can begin accelerating through and away from the corner. If you have set up reference points around the circuit to keep you on the optimum line and trigger your operation of the brake and throttle, a race situation is going to force you to adapt.

"Time trial" events, where only one car at a time is on the course, eliminate the traffic problem; but knowing you're on the clock cranks up the pressure just like a wheel-to-wheel race. It can be difficult to adapt to the conversion from the relatively low-pressure practice environment into the center stage of competition, where your performance is judged and rated by your finishing position.

Pressure

The tension is undeniable. You may have done hundreds of laps of a circuit, feeling perfectly comfortable and relaxed in the car, yet once you're in the middle of a field of other cars, you'd have to be on Thorazine not to feel pumped, especially in your first few races. The truth is that you'll never be able to totally control this heightened level of excitement, nor would you want to. Take the adrenaline out of racing and no one would do it. The trick is to not let it negatively affect your performance behind the wheel and your chances of beating as many of your competitors as you can.

Dealing with the pressure starts well before you get in the car and you can try a number of techniques to assure that the butterflies don't interfere with your hard-earned skills.

> "My first professional race was a Barber Saab race at St. Louis and I remember I was extremely nervous. We went out on the pace lap and I forgot where I was on the grid. I was 10th or 12th—way back. When the pace lap started, my right leg started seizing up—I couldn't even push the throttle pedal, it was so bad. And the more I thought about it the worse it got—I mean, it was completely cramped up and frozen. I'm thinking, 'Oh no, we're going to come around to the green flag and I'm not going to be able to go 'cause I just can't push on the throttle!' I was just barely keeping up with the pace car and I'm thinking, 'Oh my God, I can't do this!'
>
> "Luckily, the guys at the front were so screwed up that the start was waved off and we didn't get the green flag. That was such a relief that suddenly my leg started to come back. By the time we got back around again my leg was back to normal again and I was able to go. That was kind of the last time I was ever nervous at the start."
>
> —Jeremy Dale

Organize Your Time. The first step is to try to organize your time leading up to the race in order to avoid any last minute panic. Start by knowing the schedule of events and any specific rules and procedures which apply to the particular race event you've entered. For example, you may have a mandatory drivers' meeting preceding your race. Miss it and you may miss some important information from the officials—details like a changed start time for your race, or information about the track surface breaking up in a particular corner. You want to scrupulously avoid being late for any schedule deadline during the course of the event.

As the driver, it's your job to make sure that all your driving gear is available and ready to go. There's nothing more disconcerting than scrambling around at the last minute looking for a missing driving glove or having the visor of the helmet come off in your hand. Check over your stuff well in advance of start time and make sure nothing is missing or about to break. You wouldn't think that a broken shoe lace is any drama—until, that is, it happens three minutes before the start.

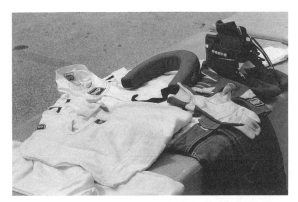

Fig. 10-1. Keeping all your driving gear in one spot and checking to see that it's all there, well before you have to get dressed, avoids the potential last-minute anxiety of searching for a lost glove.

Be certain of the time the car needs to be in the false grid area. Most road course events are run with multiple groups of races and as one race is underway, the officials will assemble the next group of cars in an area close to the pit lane called the false grid. They do this in order to get the next race underway without delay. In many events, you can lose your qualifying position and be moved to the back of the grid by arriving late at the false grid—an experience that isn't going to help your ability to stay calm.

Take Care of Yourself. You've got to remember to take care of your body too. Caffeine won't help the nervousness, so you might lay off the four cups of coffee you normally use to jump-start yourself in the morning. It also goes without saying that the dangers of alcohol and other mind-altering substances far outweigh any calming benefits they might provide.

If it's hot out, you'll need to keep plenty of liquids in your system as the race approaches. It's a guarantee that you'll sweat buckets anyway in the car, so water is crucial before you start. Consequently, you'll want to visit the bathroom shortly before you get in the car.

Confidence in the Car. You want to begin your race without any worries about the car's ability to perform. This is certainly more of a factor if you're transporting and prepping your own race car. Your race prep checklist should include all the last-minute details that need to be attended to: most importantly, the simple things like tire pressure, fuel, oil, coolant, wheel torques, etc.

If a professional crew is prepping the car, it's worth asking the crew chief about their pre-race check procedure, just to give yourself the peace of mind that comes from knowing that the car is as ready to go as is humanly possible. Give the car a visual once-over yourself, looking at the suspension on each corner for loose jam nuts, disconnected sway bar links, missing safety wire—all of the little things that can go awry. Try to do this early, before the car is rolled to the false grid, so that in the one-in-a-thousand event that something is suspect, the crew can deal with it before it's crunch time.

Put Yourself in Neutral. Each driver has a slightly different approach to calming the butterflies. Jackie Stewart, one of the greatest Grand Prix drivers of all time, described the build-up of pre-race tension as akin to an inflating emotional balloon and his pre-race mental exercise was an effort to deflate the balloon—to try to become emotionally neutral so that his in-car decisions would be rational, not emotional. Remember that, after the first few corners, you'll be

> *"I don't know how to tell you to deal with race-day butterflies. I think everybody has them. I don't think your body or your mind can fathom going into a race, whether it's in a 230 m.p.h. Indy Car or a 110 m.p.h. Formula Ford, and not be nervous to some degree. Yes, there are people who are very confident in their ability, but still, racing is full of unknowns. It doesn't have to be your fault. There are 18 or 20 other racers out there that can take you along in their little deal.*
>
> *"I think the best thing to do is not lock yourself away from everybody in the morning. If I leave myself alone for too long, then I get to think about it more, and the more you think about it the more nervous you become.*
>
> *"I like to spend time with the guys and talk about what we're going to do and the strategy and all that's planned. Concentrate on the race, but from more of a technical standpoint than anything else. And then, 30 or 45 minutes before the race, I'll go spend some time by myself and run some scenarios in my mind—what I want to do and who's around me, what I can look for and what to gain, how to protect myself, and that kind of stuff. I think everybody has their own preferred method."*
>
> —Brian Till

back in an environment where you'll be too busy to consider the tension and it will vanish as you concentrate totally on the driving.

> *"I don't think anybody handles the butterflies the same....[B]efore I got into the higher levels with sponsors and everyone, I slept. I'd get nervous enough that I'd start to yawn—people thought I was bored—but the nervousness made me sleepy. I'd lay down and take a cat nap—doze away for 15 or 20 minutes."*
>
> —Danny Sullivan

STARTS

The most common type of start in U.S. road racing is the rolling start. Although each organizing group has slightly different procedures, typically you'll be given notice of the time until the start, three to five minutes before the officials signal you out behind the pace car. You stay in grid order around the pace lap as you perform your pace lap warm-up duties. As you complete the corner leading onto the start/finish straight, the pace car pulls off, leaving the pole sitter the responsibility of determining the pace of the start. The starter surveys the field and if the field looks orderly—that is, if everyone is in line and going approximately the same speed—the starter will wave the green flag and the race is underway.

If drivers are out of line or if the last rows are gaining on the front rows (or are past them) the starter will typically shake his head, "no," and continue holding the flag furled out of sight. A "No Start" can be hairy if some of the drivers don't get the message and go racing into Turn 1 as everyone else is slowing down. When it's an obvious "No Start," all drivers should get an arm in the air signaling to the cars behind that they're slowing down. When everything settles down, each car falls back into its original grid position and the pole sitter now controls the pace of the second pace lap.

Your Starting Plan

Be sure to check with the particular sanctioning body's rulebook and the supplementary regulations for the weekend so that you fully understand the start and re-start procedures being used, as well as the potential penalties for starting infractions like jumping the start. Conventions differ, and it's your responsibility to know the rules.

Be Flexible. When it comes to starting, preparation is everything. There is an important distinction between a starting plan that helps organize your thoughts and one that absolutely locks you into a single course of

Fig. 10-2. Gridded up and ready to go, the pace lap is about to begin.

> *"I think that at the start, you have to have a plan. Sure, when the flag drops and the race starts, everything is going to go out the window anyway, but at least you've put your mind in gear and made it start thinking about what you're going to do. You can't have an ironclad plan—you've got to adapt to what you get, but thinking ahead is worth the effort."*
>
> —*Danny Sullivan*

action. You can only go so far in planning specific moves to try to improve your position at the start, since it's likely that your vision of the start will be different from the reality. Deciding beforehand that you're definitely going to try to go outside to pick off the driver ahead of you might lead you to try it even when reality dictates that the opening isn't there. You need to be flexible enough to revise your starting tactics as the situation unfolds. Your plan should incorporate not only the routine aspects of all starts but should also take into account any factors unique to the particular race you're about to run.

Routine Factors. The routine aspects involve solving the standard problems which crop up when the green flag comes out. One is trying to race a cold car.

Taking a cold engine to its rev limit can be disastrous, so part of your plan should involve warming the engine on the false grid while you're waiting to go. Since many racecars have cooling systems that don't work very well when the car is sitting still, you have to be careful about not overdoing it—160 degrees of water temp will usually do. The pace lap will warm it up the rest of the way.

Once you're rolling, the next step is to try to get some temperature into the brakes, tires, transmission and differential. For the brakes, the most effective way is to get your left foot over onto the brake pedal and run the brakes against the motor, gently at first, then harder, to build the temperature in the pads and brake rotors. Since the tires are cold and the braking is biased toward the front when running the brakes against the motor, you have to be careful to avoid locking the front tires and flatspotting them.

The braking action can start to build heat in the tires and if you have a powerful enough engine, you can try to spin the rear tires to elevate their temperature. Most often you'll see drivers swerving right and left, scrubbing the tires with cornering force in an effort to get them warm. If you can do it, a long scrub is better than a lot of short ones, but traffic and the length of the racetrack will determine which method you can use. In any event, you'll never get them up to operating temperature this way, but it will improve the traction from what it was when the tires were stone cold.

You can count on the fact that, depending on the type of car, it will take one to three laps at racing speed to get the tires to their optimum temperature; and you just have to deal with the limited grip until they get there. Most street tires don't need a significant warm-up to deliver their peak traction so there isn't much need to scrub them in on the pace lap, short of scrubbing the dirt off them.

You *do* have to be careful about all this braking and swerving on the pace lap, since many other drivers will be trying the same thing. If you get out of sync—for example, braking while the driver behind is accelerating—you can manage to crash out of the race before it starts.

> "On the pace lap, I always left-foot-brake the car, and I'm surprised more guys don't do this. I don't keep it nailed down, but my left foot is always covering the brake pedal. I find that when you're scrubbing tires back and forth, the car is more stable with a little bit of brake pedal in it. It serves two functions—it stabilizes the car and it warms the brakes. That's about all I do on the pace lap, except maybe on cars that tend to load up a bit, I'll be sure to rev the motor to keep it cleaned out."
>
> —Jeremy Dale

Be Observant. The pace lap gives you a chance to check out the track environment since it may be different than the last time you were on course. If it's a day of changing weather, be aware of cloud buildups, shaded areas of the course and the wind conditions. A 20-m.p.h. tailwind which wasn't there in qualifying can entirely change the nature of the braking zone at the end of the straight.

The pace lap will also be your first look in a while at the track conditions. Look closely, because you may encounter oil laid down in a particular corner or a huge collection of marbles (bits of rubber debris and dirt) off-line, built up from previous races.

Also get back into the routine of checking the critical gauges on your car, and expand your vision of the scene to include the peripherals, like corner stations and multiple rows of cars, not just the tail lights of the car directly in front.

Watch Corner Stations. We spoke earlier of trying to get a broader view—of avoiding the tunnel vision that occurs when you focus on the car or the road immediately ahead. This is especially critical when it comes to communication from the flag stations around the course. Seldom are they located directly in the line of sight of the drivers, and it takes some effort at first to pick up flags in your peripheral vision. There is truly *nothing* more embarrassing—and no greater proof of tunnel vision—than missing the checkered flag which ends a practice session or race.

> "You really have to watch the corner marshals. When they wave a flag, you have to appreciate that the flag is there for a reason. One of the first times I was in Mosport Park in Canada, a driver was killed in a Formula Ford because he came into a corner, racing, and ignored a yellow flag and ran under an ambulance that was parked around the corner for another accident. You can sometimes lose ground over it, but the flags are there for you and you have to pay attention."
>
> —Danny Sullivan

Know Thine Enemy. Another important part of your pre-race plan is to know who you're racing against. Especially when you're new at it, you have to work at finding out who you can trust to run close with and which drivers are accidents waiting to happen. A standard part of your pre-race routine is to study the grid and identify the driver/car combinations that may present a problem. For example, if the driver starting next to you is fast but has spun out of the last six races, you might not worry so much if he gets by you early on, knowing that he's not likely to be there at the end of the race. If a certain driver has a history of dive-bomb passes, you'll know to take a second look in the mirror at corner entries when he's right behind you and to plan to set him up for the double pass coming out of the corner.

Studying the grid is especially important if you're racing in a field consisting of multiple classes. If a car in a faster class had mechanical problems in qualifying, problems which have been fixed for the race, that driver may be gridded behind you. After the start, you can expect that the car will be passing you based purely on car performance and that you don't have to waste time and energy defending your position against him. In fact, you may be able to tuck behind this car and make use of its draft to pull clear of competitors in your class.

Accordion Effect. One phenomenon you often encounter in starts is the accordion effect. You see it in street traffic every day. When the first car in a line accelerates, there is a bit of a time delay before the second car does, and on and on down the line, so that the field will tend to spread under acceleration.

The opposite happens under braking: the spacing between cars shrinks under deceleration. Depending upon your position in the field, you need to consider how the accordion effect will influence your approach to the first few corners.

If you're back in the field, as you're likely to be in your early races, the most profound effect of this positioning on your driving will be the stack-up under braking for the first corner. If you're 8 or 10 cars back from the leader, you'll need to brake at least 8 to 10 cars earlier than you might have if you were running alone, just in order to keep from hitting the car immediately ahead.

> "The biggest scare I ever had in a racecar was at the kink at Road America in a Formula 5000 car. I was on the pole and got beaten on the drag race at the start, and on the first lap I was a car-length behind the car ahead heading into the kink and he put the brakes on big time—a lot earlier than I was—and I nearly ran into the back of him. Could have been a 140-m.p.h. crash. AAAUUUGH—right up under his rear wing."
>
> —Skip Barber

This is likely to feel really slow—and it is. The first lap of a race is often significantly slower than the later laps when the field spreads out—that's simply the way it happens. When you're new at it and focused on using distinct reference points for braking, the start will be the area where you need to go back to using your depth perception and judgment in traffic, just like you do on the street, but faster.

Elements of the Basic Plan

All of these aspects of your standard start plan aren't oriented toward taking any special advantage of your competitors. They're just your insurance that you have a car and driver combination which works reasonably well when the green comes out. To increase the odds of a good start, you can use this short list to prepare for every race start.

1) Assure that the car is completely ready, early.
2) Know your competition.
3) Get to the false grid on time.
4) Driver equipment accounted for and ready.
5) Warm motor.
6) Warm-up brakes and tires on pace lap.
7) Be observant.
8) Anticipate stack-up under braking for Turn 1.

Start Tactics

Now that you know the standard race problems are under control, the next step is to find a way to give yourself an advantage that can result in picking up positions early in the race.

When you're plotting a strategy for gaining positions at the start, you have to temper your plans with one irrefutable fact: *Few races are won in the first corner of the first lap but many are lost there.* If there are advantages to be gained without undue risk, by all means, take them. Just remember that the start represents a very small part of the race but one where there are a disproportionate number of car-to-car incidents.

The Green Flag Run. Much of the jockeying on the last part of the pace lap is an attempt to leave acceleration room ahead of you while at the same time trying to not let the driver ahead beat you to the accelerator

Fig. 10-3. In the early laps when cars are nose to tail, the brake point for heavy-braking corners like the Hairpin will be earlier than normal since you need to brake *when* the first car in line brakes, not *where* they brake.

Fig. 10-4. When the green flag comes out, try to take advantages where they exist, but remember that many more races are lost on the first corner than are won there.

when the green comes out. Meanwhile, everyone is trying to second-guess when the cars on the front row are going to floor the throttle and go. If it weren't so nerve-wracking, it would be comical. More often than not, you try to leave some room ahead and, as you back off the throttle to fade back, the field takes off and leaves you in the dust.

Your goal at the start is to pick off a car or two, if you can, and keep from being picked off yourself. In a class of relatively equal cars, if everyone begins accelerating at the same time, they should end up at the end of the straight in the same relative order in which they began. If you're anywhere behind the front row, you would like to time the start so that you leave enough room ahead to accelerate to a higher speed than the car in front of you. That way, you'll be gaining on the other driver at a closing speed of 50 m.p.h., still perfectly in line, just as the green flag comes out. That's your fantasy plan. In reality, a closing speed of two or three miles an hour would be sufficient. Then it's a matter of finding an empty piece of road to use to drive past the car ahead.

If you are able to get an advantage by getting a run on the car ahead, you now have to make a quick decision about which side to pass on. The mirrors are indispensable here, since someone may be gaining on you and an impulsive move with your eyes trained straight forward can cause big trouble. Sneak a quick peek before you pull out of line. Given the choice, you'd rather go inside—that is, on the apex side of the corner you're approaching. You can go outside, but you have to weigh the possibility of ending up being the only car outside the train that forms going toward the apex of the first turn. If the entire field ends up

nose to tail, you'll never get back into line and you'll lose many more positions than the one you've gained. Going toward the outside can work if there's a way to get back into the train, but it's risky.

Mind the Tach. The standard pace for the start of the race should be whatever speed results from being in second gear at an RPM in the middle of the engine's power band. In reality, it could be at any speed from a clutch-slipping crawl in first gear to as fast as you can go in fourth. Once the pace car leaves the field, it's up to the pole sitter, and he can choose whatever starting speed he thinks is to his best advantage. With cars that have relatively equal power, and especially with those that draft well, it may be an advantage for the leader to start the race very slowly in order to deny a significant draft advantage to the cars behind. Some drivers will choose to try to take advantage of the accordion effect and start full acceleration toward the flag as soon as the pace car clears the way, hoping that the field will string out before Turn 1. Although certain drivers fall into patterns, you can never be sure how the pole sitter is going to do it each time.

This makes it all that much harder to pick the right gear/rev-range combination that will give you the best acceleration run. In addition to sizing up the traffic and spacing yourself out correctly as you approach the start, you have to keep switching gears so that, if the flag comes out in the next instant, the engine is working in an RPM range where it's making some power. Once the race starts, you put your foot to the floor and go, but in all the jockeying and looking for holes, it's easy to forget that you have to shift it up to the next gear to keep from scattering the engine. You soon realize that in normal laps, you very seldom look at the tach and follow the needle's progress toward the redline. Most often, you shift by the point of the track you're on or by the sound of the engine. At the start, however, you're at a unique portion of the track in an unusual gear; and you usually can't hear your own motor over the roar of the others. You have to keep sneaking looks at the tach as you approach the start and shift up when it hits the redline. Many an engine has been blown by this simple oversight.

Watch the Early Apex. The advantages of being on the inside of the first corner tend to make drivers rush to get there and, as we all know, if you're in early, the car will go wide at the exit of the corner and be slower than another car on the right line because of the tighter arc required late in the corner. Going in early could lead to making a pass on the way in, but losing it on the way out. It's even worse if you go in early and get alongside another competitor, but can't hold the car down to the inside because of your excess speed. As you drift up, the driver on the outside either gets pushed off the road at the exit or you hit—neither is a very attractive alternative.

Going into the corner early is, however, an acceptable strategy *if* you do it right. The value of beginning Turn 1 near the inside of the road rather than out at the turn-in point is both offensive and defensive. On the offensive end, you're better off being on the inside in tight traffic. As you saw earlier in our discussion of the line, when two equal cars corner side by side, the elapsed time of the inside car always beats the time of the outside car. In addition, if there is any leaning on one another (which we certainly don't condone, but it happens), the outside car usually gets the worst of it.

> "In starts, there's a difference between being optimistic and being opportunistic. The biggest problem for the optimist is when Turn 1 is a wide corner, like Turn 1 at Sebring. You look up and there's all this virgin territory wide open around the apex, and you're tempted to take a straight short cut to the apex. You get there and realize that there are nine people headed toward that apex from the real turn-in point. You have to avoid that temptation.
>
> "The opportunist is ready to take advantage of somebody else's mistake."
>
> —Terry Earwood

On the defensive side, beginning the corner 7/8ths of a car width off the inside edge of the road effectively denies drivers behind you the opportunity to sneak inside on the way to the apex.

The key to making the early entry into Turn 1 work is to make sure to slow the car enough so that you can get back on line by the apex and have the car pointed in the same direction it would be on a normal lap.

Surviving Off-Line. Much of the overtaking going into the first corner is going to happen off the normal racing line. On some racetracks, the traction is comparable on-line and off, but in many situations, the grip will vary widely. It is very useful to devote some practice time to trying out different parts of the racetrack, especially the braking area on the inside of the road approaching Turn 1. It's possible that you may end up being forced to the outside of Turn 1 at the start, so it's a good idea to try running through the corner at progressively wider distances from the apex to see what

Fig. 10-5. At the start, remember that drivers who are able to stay on-line, single file, will have an advantage over those driving side by side through the corners.

it's like out there. Often you'll find that the grip is reasonable up to the point where the marbles make the track surface practically undriveable. Knowing acceptable off-line options will have a significant effect on your choices going into Turn 1.

Passing Positions. As you approach the braking zone for the corner, you have to make some quick decisions about your positioning. Can you get alongside one more car before the turn-in, or do you consolidate your gains and tuck into line? Will the driver coming up the inside yield when you go to the apex, or should you be the one to yield?

The conventions of passing hold sway as you approach the first corner. If you're inside and dead alongside or slightly ahead of another car at the turn-in point, they are obliged to yield. If you're halfway up, it's not good enough, and you should yield and pull in behind. If everyone in the field scrupulously followed these guidelines, the field would sort out quickly, but sometimes the driver on the outside will still try to beat you to the corner exit by staying outside. Sometimes a competitor gets a front wheel even with your rear and refuses to give up the two feet of road it would take for both of you to get back onto the racing line.

You want to keep in mind in during all this jockeying for position in the first lap that the drivers that are able to stay on-line are going to have a speed advantage over cars driving side by side through the corners. If you're stuck in a side by side duel, fighting for fifth and sixth place, there's a good chance that the first four cars may get away for good by staying on the racing line. Knowing when not to race—having the discipline to give up the chase of the moment for a chance of a higher finishing position later in the race—is the mark of a smart, seasoned racer.

THE BODY OF THE RACE

Once the drama of the start settles down, you can take stock of the situation. After a lap or two, you should have a good idea of any car or racetrack problems you'll need to contend with and plan how you'll adapt to the new situation. One or more corners may be more slippery than you anticipated and will take an adjustment in corner entry reference points or an adaptation of line. In cars with adjustable brake bias or sway bars, you may have to make a change in trim to improve the car.

You'll also get a good idea of how the field is shaking out so you can narrow down the number of competitors you'll have to deal with. The qualifying system, if it works correctly, should lump together drivers and cars that have been turning laps in the same range of lap times. Whether you're gridded 3rd or 23rd, you can expect to compete with the drivers who qualified a little faster and a little slower than you: this group can consist of 2 cars or 8 cars.

For drivers of all skill levels and experience, the gratifying fact is that racing with three cars for the lead of a race is just like racing with three cars for 10th. Your approach will vary in races with different types of cars and different durations, but many considerations apply to all races, whether they be 24-hour endurance events or 20-minute sprints.

> *"If you ask most racecar drivers about what was their best race, often it's not the one that was the best result. Some of the most heated battles I've had were for 7th or 8th place. I remember the South African Grand Prix in 1983 where I had to start the Tyrell from pit lane because we had some last-minute car problems. In the end, I finished 7th, and for me, it was really satisfying."*
>
> —Danny Sullivan

Seeing Independently

As you saw at the start, your well-drilled reference points around the racetrack have sometimes got to be abandoned and replaced by your best guess and estimate of the path and speed that will work. Once traffic thins out, it gets easier to pick up the routine, but even if there is only one car in front of you, you can't see ahead as well as you did in practice when, for the most part, you were running alone.

> *"You've got to be careful not to just copy what the car ahead is doing, especially if you're coming up on a slower car. There are two possibilities. He's either watching you too closely or not watching you at all. If he's not watching you, he'll drive you off the racetrack if you give him the chance. If he's watching you carefully, more often than not, he'll miss the turn-in and end up wide of the apex. If you're following him too closely, it's easy to do the same thing. I really try to look through the car and get an overall feel for where I am, and get by on the path I choose."*
>
> —Jeremy Dale

During a race you have to work hard at looking past the car ahead to pick up your braking and turn-in points. It's very easy to follow the driver ahead and get caught up in doing just what he or she does. You have to remember that your goal is to do a better job than the driver ahead and you certainly don't want to end up repeating anyone else's mistakes.

Fig. 10-6. Finding your reference points is more difficult when nose-to-tail with other cars. You have to look past the car ahead, rather than just mimic what they do.

To Pass or Not to Pass

As a general rule, when the opportunity to pass the car ahead presents itself, take it. There are a few things to keep in mind, however. If the pass puts the two of you side by side through a corner or two, you'll both have to go slower than you could have by staying on line through the turns. Driving side by side, lap after lap, will let drivers ahead get away, and let drivers behind catch up.

If possible, you would like to complete the pass and get back in line for the corner. Ideally, you would then pull away from the driver you just passed and set off after your next victim. In many classes of car, however, the draft effect is so significant that the car you just passed can stay with you, using your draft, even if you are slightly faster through most of the corners. If the other driver stays with you but can't seem to muster a draft-by, it's unlikely that there's much chance of

Fig. 10-7. Mistakes create opportunities. Here, car No. 38 has gone hopelessly wide and will be gobbled up on the way to the next corner.

being overtaken unless the driver behind tries some kind of desperate move. Keep checking the mirrors as you approach the most likely out-braking sections of the course so that if the other driver tries the dive-bomb, you won't get taken out. In a lap or two it will become apparent whether the other driver is much of a threat or just a drafting aid that will help you claw closer to the front.

The car behind is hoping for you to make a mistake—overreaching on your brake point, getting wide of the apex, or early-apexing a corner—and will take advantage of any bobble. Your job is to concentrate on driving as well as you can and to try to improve your lap time using the old Line, Exit Speed, Braking progression.

> "Anytime, whether it's the third lap or the third to last lap, if there's a car in front of me, I want to catch that guy and get by him as quickly as possible. The fact that it's close to the end of the race doesn't add any sense of urgency to me....[although] I suppose it depends on the situation a little bit. If it's the last lap of the Indy 500 and you've got a shot, you're going to take it, almost regardless of what the risk is."
>
> —Bryan Herta

Meeting Your Match

There are occasions when you'll be so evenly matched with another competitor that you'll be able to draft by each other on the long straight, every lap. You'll lead a lap, then get passed in the braking zone. He or she will then do the same. If this sort of scenario is developing, you can make the choice to keep swapping positions, to work together to get better lap times for both of you (either to catch the drivers ahead or leave the rest behind), or to settle back and follow, plotting a strategy of how to wind up in the lead on the most important lap—the last one.

Working together requires the active participation of both drivers. Once you've felt each other out and it becomes obvious that neither one of you has the capability of pulling away from the other, you can try to communicate with the other driver your willingness to work as a team. As the other driver drafts by, you can signal by first trying to make eye contact with the other driver, then pointing straight ahead, essentially saying, "Let's go." Using your full hand, karate-chop style, also conveys the meaning, "Let's stay in line." You're trying to arrange it so that both of you can take advantage, on successive laps, of the extra straight-away speed you get from the draft without losing the lap time advantage. You don't want to arrive at the entry of the turn at the end of the straight side by side, forcing both of you off-line in the first part of the corner. The driver who's getting passed may need to breathe off the throttle toward the end of the straight to allow the other to get completely by so that both of you can run through the turn on-line. At some point, four or five laps from the end of the race, the cooperation will end as each of you try to maneuver your way into finishing ahead of the other on the final lap, but the pair of you can end up closer to the front by calling a temporary truce.

If you can't get the cooperation going or if you're in a race of your own by being far ahead of any others and pulling away (or steadily losing ground to cars at the head of the field), you may choose not to pass the other driver, even though you could. Following can do two things: it tends to put more pressure on the driver ahead, making him or her more prone to mistakes, and it allows you to survey the other driver's relative weaknesses and strengths.

Watch and Learn

You're hoping to find a corner or two where you are clearly faster, not enough to pull alongside or pass, but a speed at which you would pull out a few car lengths if you were ahead. This knowledge can be useful later in the race when you come upon other traffic. If the two of you are approaching a lapped car, you could try to maneuver yourself into a position where you're leading your adversary as you approach traffic. Try to adjust your pace so that you can pass the lapped traffic following your fast corner, on the chance that your adversary might not get up enough steam to get by the lapped car before the next corner. You'll pull out some distance in your good corner and more distance if your competitor is balked by the lapped car in his better corner.

Another advantage of following is that you can go to school, learning how your foe manages to go quickly in corners where your speed is lacking. If you adapt your technique to mirror his, and over the course of a few laps manage to match his pace in the corners where you were lacking, you might combine your new-found speed with your advantage in other corners to be able to pass and pull away. Once you feel that you know some new tricks, go ahead and take the lead and you'll have one lap, two at most, to try to put the lessons to use and pull away enough to break the draft (and sometimes your rival's spirits). If you make mistakes on your killer lap, the other driver will be able to keep up and then go to school on you; so, to make this work, you've got to do the best lap you can manage, or you're back to square one.

THE FINAL STAGES

When it comes down to the final few laps, the game becomes one of maneuvering yourself into a position to arrive at the finish line before your competitor on the last lap.

The order on the previous lap doesn't matter, and in many cases, it's better to be behind your competitor on the next to last lap than ahead. If the draft is a big factor, you may be the victim if you're leading on the run to the finish line. There's really nothing you can do to break the draft, other than be far enough ahead so that it's not a factor. You should know by the end of the race whether the draft effect is enough to allow you to pass the car ahead by the finish line.

> *"The final laps of a close race? You need just incredible focus and concentration, not trying to force the car into something it doesn't want to do. Not overdriving the car, but you have to be perfect, running it as hard as you can. For me that means getting super focused and shutting everything else out completely. You have to think about how you're going to drive the car and not how great you're going to look on the podium. The 'how' carries the win along with it. You can't waste your energy wishing for it to happen."*
>
> —Jeremy Dale

During the course of a close race you should try a number of draft-bys and see where it puts your car relative to the other as you cross start/finish. You'll also get an appreciation for whether your opponent has a draft or horsepower advantage on you. Swapping places early in the race can let you see if your rival's passes get completed before or after yours do.

Knowing the acceleration potential of your car helps form your last lap strategy. If your car is a little stronger, but on a normal run off the last corner the other driver is still able to squeak by at start/finish, you may be able to use your acceleration advantage to thwart his last lap attempt. A good draft-by pass starts with the second car in line having room ahead to accelerate into. With slightly more horsepower, you could lead into the last corner but take it a little slower than normal and close up the distance between you and the car behind. You have to do this in the corner, where the other driver is forced to stay on-line behind you. Once he's tight behind, the other driver can't accelerate away from the corner until you do; and if you have a slight acceleration advantage, your rival won't be able to get by at the flag.

If you're following, you may find yourself breathing out of the throttle on the approach to the last corner to keep sufficient spacing between you and the driver ahead. It can turn into a real game of cat and mouse with the lead driver slowing to impede the driver behind and the following driver slowing further to leave space ahead. At some point, the leading driver may slow so much that the driver behind will switch tactics and accelerate hard, trying to pass on the way into the corner. Sometimes the third driver in line is the true beneficiary of all this slowing down.

If the draft isn't the issue, the relative placement of two closely-matched cars often comes down to who's ahead at the end of the last of the two or three best passing places on the racetrack—corners which require a significant speed loss. If the braking zone is relatively long, there is a chance that, even without a significant draft advantage, one driver can outperform the other in braking to an extent that he or she can pull alongside by the turn-in point. On the last lap, the lap time doesn't matter nearly so much as the relative positions of the cars, and a late-braking maneuver, although it might make both cars slower overall, can accomplish the goal of changing positions.

Defense
If out-braking is the issue, the lead car can defend by making it tougher for the opponent to pull it off. It's much harder to brake late and beat the car ahead to the apex if the lead car is on the inside of the road at the approach to the corner.

On the inside, it's a shorter route to the apex and easier to get there first, consequently taking the preferred line away from the car on the outside. It's possible to make the outside out-braking maneuver, but it's so uncommon that just your presence on the inside may dissuade the other driver from trying it.

There's nothing dirty about driving up to a corner on the inside of the road and denying your pursuer the preferred out-braking path, but you have to choose this path before the car behind makes a move toward it. If you drive in your mirrors, intentionally driving to get in the way of the path the driver behind has chosen, you're stealing your position in the race, not earning it, and you deserve the contempt you will no doubt get from your competitors.

CARING FOR THE CAR

The driving, especially in tight traffic, will use up a great deal of your conscious attention, but you also have to make certain that your engine is not going to fail you. At least once a lap, you need to look at the water temperature and the oil pressure gauges to see if the motor is staying within its parameters. It takes less than a second to peek at the gauges—time you can afford to spend, especially considering the cost to repair a blown motor caused by running it too hot or low on oil pressure. The easiest place to do this is on a long straight after you have shifted to top gear. Work your way from the left mirror to the gauge furthest on the left and continue on from left to right surveying the gauges until you finish off the drill by looking in the right hand mirror. Make a routine of checking gauges by doing it on the upshift to top gear once a lap, and eventually it becomes automatic, leaving more time for conscious decisions.

Sterling Moss claimed to have developed the ability to read the gauges with his peripheral vision, never having to glance down from the road ahead to study their readings. So that there is no need to consciously try to read a numerical value off the gauge, it's helpful to paint a line on the surface of the gauge at its critical value: a minimum value for oil pressure, a maximum value for water temperature. If you see the needle on the gauge on the wrong side of the painted line, you can then decide to take a closer look to see specifically what value you're at.

Traffic and Cooling
If the race is a tight one and you end up running close behind another car or cars for many laps, the lack of clean air may affect your car's cooling ability. This goes for both engine coolant temperature and the temperature of the brakes. Without a straight shot of undisturbed air into the radiators, the engine temperature often rises. You may have to move out of line on

> "I'll never pull over on a guy if he's already committed. I'll run down the middle of the racetrack or on the inside approach to a corner, but as far as forcing the other driver to make a reactive move—I just don't do it. I grew up thinking "I'm going to give you a certain amount of pavement, you've got to give me a certain amount of pavement." You don't have to be a jerk. I pride myself on bringing the car in after a six- or twelve-hour race without a scratch on the car, and maybe coming in with a checkered flag.
>
> "It's okay to drive a different line. If you can alter or confuse the other driver's game plan, that's all fair. But the bobbing and weaving stuff just doesn't belong."
>
> —Terry Earwood

> "At races where the ambient temperatures are high and you don't have long straights to get a lot of air to the brakes—even on something like an Indy Car, which generally has great brakes—they can overheat. What you do is brake a little longer and lighter, carrying the same entry speed to the corner, but taking a longer period of time to do it. You can't race someone like that because they'll eat you alive in the braking zone, but you can't just retire. Once you're aware of the problem, you reach over with your left foot and tap the brake pedal as you're driving down the straight to make sure it's up. Hello? Anybody there?"
>
> —Brian Till

the straights in order to get a fresh charge of air into the radiator to keep your car from overheating. This influences your decision to lead or follow in your individual duel with another competitor. If your particular car has excess cooling capacity, traffic probably won't be an issue; but it always seems that racecars following too closely for too long will push the engine temperature over the edge.

The same goes for brakes. They need an ample flow of air over the rotors and calipers to keep the brake fluid under its boiling point. Reduce the air flow by following in the draft, and the fluid may begin to vaporize, making the pedal feel progressively spongy and limiting the squeezing capability of the caliper.

If the brakes are overheating, it's usually a progressive thing. Normally, the caliper with the worst air flow to it will go first. If it's a rear caliper, you'll feel more travel and sponginess in the brake pedal, followed by front-tire lock-up. Since you have a nonfunctioning rear brake, the fronts pick up the extra braking load lost by the rear, and this overload exhibits the same symptom as too much front brake bias. If a front caliper boils first, you'll feel sponginess in the pedal and a rear brake bias—much tougher to handle, since the rear end of the car will want to step out in either direction at the slightest provocation.

If the brake pad material goes beyond its optimum temperature before the brake fluid boils, you'll feel a loss in stopping power but the pedal won't feel spongy. If the brake pedal is rock hard but the car doesn't seem to slow like it used to, you're probably overheating the pad. They seldom go all at once, so you're likely to feel a change in brake bias too.

You can try to nurse the brakes back to health by getting into some clean air on the straights. You also have the option to take some strain off of the brakes

by braking earlier and more lightly and using downshifting to help the deceleration process. If the fluid has boiled, the pedal will never come back to being as hard as it was at the start. You can help make it better by pumping the brake pedal as you approach the braking zones. This compresses the vapor in the lines and calipers so that when you finally do go to the brakes in earnest, the fluid has a smaller pocket of vapor to compress before it applies pressure to the pucks and pads.

If the problem is overheated pad material, cooling the brakes down will restore the original braking ability of the car; but as they cool, the fronts and rears are likely to come back at different rates and the brake bias is likely to change as the process goes on.

POST-RACE CRITIQUE

The process of self-critique is one which goes on continuously as you drive the car. To develop as a driver, it is very useful to evaluate your performance immediately following a race.

We all fall into the trap of judging our progress purely by finishing position. The reality is that, in certain fields, you can finish high up but still have done a less-than-stellar job as a racer. To progress, you should take stock of the aspects of your racing technique which only you know about—be perfectly honest with yourself about your performance. Whether you use a written or mental checklist, evaluate your performance in each of the following areas and you can review your shortcomings before the next event in order to work on improving them.

1) Pre-pace prep: car and driver
2) Pace lap
3) Start
4) Line
5) Corner exit and car control
6) Braking
7) Shifting: up and down
8) Reading car changes
9) Routine for gauge-checking
10) Use of mirrors
11) The broad view
12) Concentration lapses
13) Approach to going faster
14) Passing technique

It's seldom that any of us, even after winning a race, can give ourselves high ratings in all categories. If you have a measure of success, however, you're likely to take on the next level of competition; and it gets tougher and tougher as you get closer to the top. This kind of post-race self-analysis helps keep you honest and gives you a chance to recognize mistakes so that you can meet the challenge of faster drivers.

Fig. 10-8. Nothing beats winning, but avoid the trap of grading your performance simply by your finishing position, especially when you're just starting out.

CHAPTER 11

ACCIDENTS

DRIVERS WITH GOOD CAR control seldom spin; and if you want to be considered a good racedriver, part of the bargain is to bring the car back to the pit lane with the same number of wheels it had on it when it left. Still, no matter how good you are, accidents happen.

To be fully prepared for the possibility of accidents, you need to have solutions up your sleeve to minimize the effects of classic racing mistakes.

Early in your career, it's likely that you'll go off the road at some point, primarily because you'll be faced with the unexpected without the experience to use the solution that worked "last time." But you try as hard as you can to keep it from happening. Too many new drivers are willing to accept complete losses of control as an acceptable part of driving a racecar, but it is a failure at the most fundamental level.

"Nothing good happens to a racecar when you take it off the track. The faster the car, the worse it is. Keeping the car on the racetrack is part of being a professional.

"Let's put it this way—I've never pushed to the point of the car spinning to find the limit. Guys who think you have to spin to go fast—I guess a lot of those folks have never been to Indy. You wouldn't do it there."

—Bryan Herta

RISK IS INEVITABLE

Fortunately, auto racing today is a much safer sport than it was forty years ago. Today, the cars are generally much stronger, they have real rollover protection, functional driver restraint systems, and, most important of all, fuel containment systems which greatly reduce the risk of fire. Drivers themselves are better protected by helmets, suits, gloves and shoes; and today, racetracks are designed and constructed to reduce the chance of injury.

Still, you can get hurt or killed driving a racecar—any racecar. Even the slowest, most substantially-built car cannot withstand a 90-m.p.h. impact by another car to the driver's side without injuring the occupant. If you're going to go racing, you have to admit that there are risks. To think that racing has become perfectly safe is a mistake.

Dr. Harlen C. Hunter and Rick Stoff, in their book entitled *Motorsports Medicine*, have done the best research currently available on the risks inherent in racing, and they report the following, based on their most recent research: "It should be safe to assume that the annual incidence of driver fatalities falls between 7 and 14. According to participation and fatality data from the National Safety Council, those rates would put driving race cars in the same hazard range as swimming, alpine ski racing and boating. Race driving would be slightly less risky than scuba diving and mountain hiking and far less dangerous than parachuting and hang-gliding."

"No matter how great I think I was at the height of my career, shit, you still make mistakes. If you're trying, things can [still] go wrong. As much as I or Skip try to tell people everything we know about racing, you ultimately have to learn it for yourself, and part of learning is making mistakes."

—Danny Sullivan

THE SPIN

If your car isn't sliding through the corner, you're not going fast enough. The slide, with a yaw angle that gets the tires to a range of slip angle that maximizes the grip, is your goal. If, however, you over-rotate the car to a point where the momentum of the rear end of

> *"This is a dangerous business. You know, we put that in the back of our minds and forget it and there's probably not a person in the garage area right now that is saying, 'Oh, this is really dangerous.' It's a business where you know you can get hurt, but you always put that out of your mind. When something bad happens, it's a cold slap in the face and it wakes you up to the fact that it really can be an evil sport and it will bite you. It will bite you in a hurry if you don't treat it with respect."*
>
> —Brian Till

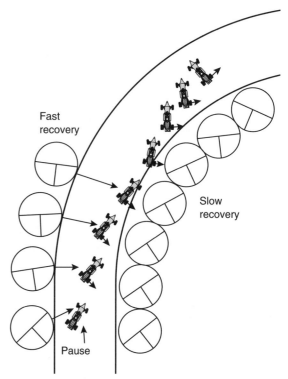

Fig. 11-1. Fast recovery is the key to avoiding second-reaction spins. Once the momentum of the car starts counterclockwise at the pause, the steering wheel has to come back to straight quickly, as on the left. In the steering wheel positions on the right, the steering wheel doesn't come past straight ahead until the spin to the left is beyond saving.

the car can't be stopped, and it goes past 90 degrees of yaw, you've spun.

Many new drivers give up too soon and abandon hope on a car that might have been saved. Once a car goes past the point of yaw you wanted for good grip, you have to make a quick mental switch from speed mode to survival mode. When you're in speed mode, you're concentrating on being subtle with yaw angle and control input, trying to balance the car on a fine line that shaves a tenth of a second here and a tenth of a second there from your lap time. When the rear end suddenly pops out 45 degrees more than you intended, style and subtlety be damned—you want gobs of correction *right now*. If one turn of the steering wheel isn't enough, grab another handful and dial in more correction until you've corrected the extreme yaw.

Recovery Is Critical
If you do finally catch it and the velocity of the rotation slows, then stops, at whatever angle, you have to recognize the pause. The pause is your trigger to begin unwinding the opposite lock toward straight, recovering the car. Innumerable spins are caught on the first rotation, but lost again as the car rotates back in the opposite direction with a vengeance, and the steering isn't brought back the other way fast enough.

The recovery has to be slightly ahead of the motion of the car. Slightly behind causes the car to oscillate, the rear sliding out to the right, then left, then right again, then left again—the driver just a little behind each slide. With typical macabre humor, our instructors have developed terms describing these oscillations. The type with big rotations, both right and left, with exhausting corrections by the driver, is called a "tankslapper," a term derived from motorcycle racing, where this type of oscillation literally slaps the tank with the handlebar at the extreme of each rotation. The more subtle, but no less scary version of this problem involves smaller oscillations with higher frequencies and is called the "death wiggle."

In either case, the problem is that the driver is not getting the steering wheel straight fast enough to dis-

sipate the energy of the car sliding back from its extreme of yaw. This is commonly called over-correction, but *over*-correction is not the problem: any correction that stops the rear from passing the front is *just the right correction*. It's *slow recovery* that causes the problem (see Fig. 11-1).

We've seen tankslappers or death wiggles go on for seven or eight oscillations. The best cure is to just freeze the steering wheel, dead ahead if you can manage it. You won't be correcting for any swerves, but at least you won't be causing any. The car will quickly settle down, perhaps not pointed perfectly down the straightaway, but you can carefully steer it where you want it to go once it settles (see Fig. 11-2).

Spinning's Golden Rule
When it comes to spins, the proven best advice is "If you spin, both feet in."

In any one of these rotations, the first or the sixteenth, if the rotation gets past 90 degrees, the show is over—you've spun, and any further attempt to use throttle or steering will probably make the situation worse. Once it's spun, lock up the brakes and put in

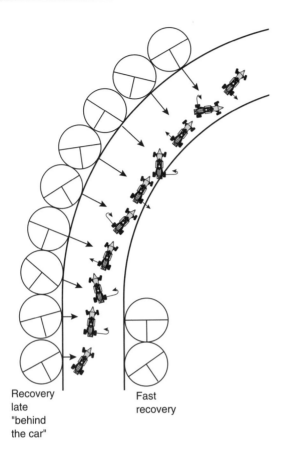

Recovery
late
"behind
the car"

Fast
recovery

Fig. 11-2. Here there are lots of big corrections, but the recovery has to be quicker to stop the oscillations. Getting the steering wheel straight, quickly, then allowing the car to settle, is the cure for the "tankslapper."

> "Not that I've had a lot of experience along these lines, but locking [the brakes] up is the best thing to do. There is that one in ten where you can release the brakes to keep from hitting something, but that's not something I'd ever teach in a school. Still, if Danny Sullivan hadn't released the brakes at the right point, he wouldn't have won Indy."
>
> —Jeremy Dale

> "When I spun at Indy in the 500 that I won, my first thought was, 'Oh shit, I just got into the lead of the Indianapolis 500 and now I'm going to blow it and hit the wall.' I locked up the brakes and dipped the clutch. You're engulfed in smoke, but when it came around the wind was blowing it away from me and it was clear ahead. I had the presence of mind (and it was the only thing I did that was presence of mind) that I took my foot off the brake and gathered it up. The engine was dead from the spin so I had to jump start it and it did another wiggle when I got the clutch out. I was pretty lucky."
>
> —Danny Sullivan

the clutch. If you lock up all four tires they'll lose all their cornering ability and the car will continue on in a straight line tangent to the last arc you were on. This is a real help to others on the racetrack who are trying to avoid hitting your spinning car. If you don't lock the brakes, the car could do one and a half rotations, catch cornering traction, and dart back across the racetrack into the path of other cars—a much more dangerous impact than hitting a tire wall. The only exception to this rule is if, under lock-up, you're heading for a truly substantial stationary object (like a bridge abutment). Here, unlock the brakes and hope that the car changes course toward something softer.

Keeping the brakes locked is also very effective for losing speed, making any subsequent meeting with stationary objects less damaging. With big, sticky slicks on a light car, it's remarkable how quickly they'll stop.

It's key to keep the tires locked up until the car has really stopped. Often, a single car spin is almost over, the car spinning down the middle of the track and all

the traffic finds a clear way by, and suddenly the driver in the spinning car releases the brake at 5 m.p.h. and rolls in front of a following car that would have made it by if the hole didn't close. In a spin, lock them up and keep them locked until the car *absolutely stops*.

If you successfully push in the clutch when the spin starts and heel and toe to keep the engine running, you can go back to first gear (even in mid-spin) and be ready to get out of the way of following cars. If you can't see oncoming traffic clearly, stay put. Look to the nearest corner station and they'll help you re-enter safely. The accepted method is for a worker to point repeatedly at the car they want you to re-enter behind, then wave you on as it goes by. Try not to be so impatient and frustrated with the spin that you spin the tires on re-entry and spin again, unless, of course, you like to provide extra amusement for the fans.

Sometimes the spin doesn't have a happy ending. If you get off the racetrack and make it to a barrier, your race is over. If the car has hit and stopped, you'll be surprised to find that your first instinct is often to try to back it out of the barrier and get back on the track. Your competitive blood is still up and you find yourself thinking, "It can't be *that* much slower with three wheels." When you're tempted, just give a moment's thought to the additional damage you can do to the car and yourself by trying to drive a twisted car back to the pits. Then again, in 1990, Barber Saab champion-to-be Rob Wilson drove the final 3 laps of the Tampa round on three wheels to finish 9th out of a field of 18 cars. Some guys just never give up.

HITTING HARD

If you hit hard and it's obvious that you're not going anywhere, the first thing you should do is to shut off the master electrical switch, reducing the chance that an errant spark could set off an oil or gasoline fire.

There are actually things you can do to help protect yourself between the time you lose it and the time you hit. Your first instinct, especially in a Formula car, is to scrunch down and hide in the cockpit, squeezing the stuffing out of the steering wheel. You can reduce the chance of injury by doing the exact opposite: if you hold onto the wheel tightly and the impact involves the front wheels, the steering wheel may spin violently, damaging your hands or wrists. It's against your nature to let go of the wheel, but if impact is inevitable, it's the best thing to do. If it's going to be a frontal impact, you might want to lean forward and put your chin on your chest. It probably won't help to take your feet back from the pedals since the Gs of impact will be stronger than your efforts to keep them back. In a rear impact, you want to push your back against the seat back and your helmet against the headrest to lessen the chance of whiplash.

If it's never happened to you, it's hard to believe that you have time to think about these things, but as a rule, most drivers feel like time passes very slowly between the time they lose control and the time they hit something.

Stay in the Car

If you hit really hard, once you've turned off the master switch, resist the temptation to undo the belts and jump right out. The only reason to hustle out of the car is if it is burning, and believe me, you won't need our advice to get out if it is. If it's not burning, take some time to assess the situation. If you crashed because of a sudden downpour or oil on the course, more cars may be along in a moment and you certainly don't want to be half in and half out of the car when another one runs into it. You're safest securely belted inside a substantial roll cage in these situations.

Even if there's little chance of another car coming along and joining in on your accident, stay put for a minute and assess whether you're okay. If you're dizzy, have back pain, neck pain or numbness anywhere, don't move or thrash about. You may have an injury that you can aggravate by moving. Don't take your helmet off. Sit still and wait for the emergency workers to arrive. They are trained in emergency procedures, extrication techniques, and fire fighting, and they are your best chance of getting through in the best shape possible.

If your self-assessment reveals that you're physically okay (you'll certainly be mentally depressed), look back and make sure that traffic isn't coming your way before you undo the belts and get out. The corner workers will direct you to the safest place.

COMMON ERRORS

Once you're physically okay, the first thing you should do while the memory is fresh, and before you have time to make up rationalizations, is to try to figure out why the accident happened. Spins and crashes are most often caused by mistakes and not equipment failures. Unless you'd like to make the same mistake again in the future, with the same result, you'll want to identify the error and cure it. In order to help define what you did wrong, you can use the following shopping list of common errors, some of which we have covered earlier.

Early Apex

If the spin came in the second part of the corner, especially from dropping wheels off at the corner exit, this classic line mistake can be at fault. Sometime when you're on the track, take a look at the skid marks coming off of corners (see Fig. 11-3). They tell the sad story of how common this type of spin is.

Sensing that the car is running out of road can lead you to turning the steering wheel more, pinching off the cornering radius late in the turn. If the car isn't already at the limit, it will get closer to it or over it if you tighten the arc. If the car is already sliding and drops wheels into the loose stuff at the exit, it will rotate fast.

Fig. 11-3. Notice the path of the skidmarks here at the exit of Turn 7 at Sebring, all caused by early apexes.

Jerking the Car Back On

Sometimes the car drops the two outside wheels off the track coming off the corner, most frequently as a result of an early apex; and the inexperienced driver tends to act too suddenly, jerking the car back onto the racetrack. If you use a lot of steering lock very suddenly, the outside front tire which starts out in the dirt doesn't provide much direction change—at first. When it makes it from the dirt back to the asphalt, it takes a big bite and hurls the front of the car violently toward the inside of the course. The back end of the car, of course, comes around too quickly for you to save. The accident looks like it's going to happen on the outside, but the car ends up on the opposite side of the track, often unnecessarily (see Fig. 11-4).

You can ride out this mistake by straightening the steering wheel and reducing the cornering demands on the car to zero. With the wheel straight, the car can bump along in a straight line, two wheels on and two wheels off, more or less under control. Next, you gently coax the car back onto the racetrack with tiny steering wheel inputs over 100 to 150 yards or so.

TTO

Trailing throttle oversteer (TTO) will sometimes get the tail out so suddenly that it can't be saved, especially if the throttle is snapped off, not relaxed. It can happen anywhere in the corner, from turn-in to track-out. To identify it, you have to think clearly about what your right foot is doing on the throttle throughout the course of the corner.

Often TTO is combined with other mistakes, like the early apex, to cause the spin.

Mismatched Downshift

In most cases, you'll choose to do a downshift on the straight approaching the corner, but there are plenty of situations where you're forced to do it while turning. Going down a gear while cornering and doing it badly without matching the engine speed to wheel speed can spin a car instantly, almost as fast as yanking up on the handbrake.

Going Too Deep

It's easy, especially when you're running at a familiar racetrack, to get overly optimistic about your brake points and wait too long before going to the brake pedal, arriving at the turn-in point too fast. If the corner has an escape road, you can just go straight on and give up the corner. Without runoff, you try to turn down into the corner, but remember that the radius of the arc is a direct function of the speed. With decent car control, you won't necessarily spin as long as the car stays on the asphalt. The only way to make the apex is to be close to the speed that coincides with an arc that reaches the apex. Too fast, and you're likely to

Fig. 11-4. Here at the trackout of Turn 2 at Sebring, the driver dropped two wheels off at the exit, then hurriedly tried to force the car back onto the racetrack. When the outside front wheel came off the sand, back onto the asphalt, the car turned sharply left.

miss the apex because the arc you're committed to is too broad to make it down to the inside of the corner. How far off you are from the apex is a function of how overly fast you're going. Slightly too fast, and you miss it by a couple of feet. Way too fast, and you might miss it by the width of a racetrack. Once you're on the grass, the party's over.

If you routinely use the braking and turning ability of the car, getting in too fast can be saved by continuing to slow down while bending the car into the corner. Trail the brakes as deep into the corner as it takes to slow it down to a speed that keeps it off the grass. If your habit is to do only straight-line braking, the possible fixes to arriving at the turn-in point too fast are limited to continuing to brake straight until you run out of road. Braking and turning makes a lot more of the road and many more options available to you.

> "To me, one of the most valuable things about braking and turning is saving your butt when you take too big a bite in braking. Most corners, you don't brake and turn way down to the apex—it's more often a trail brake—so if you do get to the turn-in point going too fast, you just extend that zone down deep into the corner, bowing the car toward the apex. It's a valuable asset."
>
> —Terry Earwood

Failing to Warm Up

A similar situation occurs when you fail to get the brakes or tires up to operating temperature and try to go to the normal brake point with a car that isn't prepared to perform at its usual level of braking. If the brake pads and rotors are cold, they don't create the same braking friction that they do when hot. If you step on the brake pedal with the usual force at the usual place and the brakes are working at only half of their capability, the result is that you arrive at the corner entry going way too fast.

Even if the braking system is up to temperature, a fresh, cold set of tires don't generate their grip until they warm up. Slicks, for example, operate best at temperatures over 200 degrees Fahrenheit. Roar out of the pits with 65-degree tire temperatures and the tires will lock up if you push on the brake pedal with your accustomed level of pressure. Push more lightly to avoid lock-up, and it takes longer to slow down. To fix this problem, warm up the brakes and tires before flirting with your normal brake points.

If you haven't been in a racecar for a while, you can lose the sensitivity to just how hard you can push on the brake pedal in a racing situation as compared to the street-driving world. Often, cars get into a corner

too fast not because the driver went too deep but because he or she went to a brake point that would have worked if all of the car's braking potential was being used. Every time out, you have to re-establish the level of brake pedal force for that day. You do so by intentionally braking earlier that the traditional brake point and pushing harder and harder, searching for a trace of lock-up. Once you find the threshold, you can then work the brake points closer to the corners.

Stackup

Corner entry can be tricky enough when running alone, but stirring other drivers and cars into the mix can bring on additional complications. One common cause of problems is not anticipating the brake application of the car ahead and, as a result, either drilling the lead car from behind or losing control in the swerve to avoid it. You have to make a braking adjustment when following another car closely. You can't afford to focus on your traditional brake point and be blindly determined to go to that spot before you go to the brake. This holds especially true if you're gaining on a slower driver. If you're catching the car ahead, it's likely that the other driver is losing some time to you in the braking zone, for one reason or another, braking early. You've got to anticipate this and adjust your brake point based on what you've seen the other driver do in the last few laps.

Multiple car trains are another prime opportunity for a stackup. If six or seven cars are in line, even though they are turning exactly the same lap times, the last car in line has to brake when the first one does. If each car is 15 feet long, the last car in a seven-car train has to put the brakes on 105 feet sooner than the first car in order to avoid running into the car immediately ahead (see Fig. 11-5). This situation arises most often at the start of a race when the cars are the most closely bunched, and it's a key problem to remember before each race start.

Fig. 11-5. The driver of car No. 19 didn't anticipate that coming into the Hairpin sixth in line required a much earlier brake point than normal. Luckily, the car contact with the rear of car No. 24 resulted in minimal damage to both cars.

Passing

Many car-to-car incidents take place in passing situations, as you saw in the earlier chapter on passing. For example, waiting until the last possible instant to pass, then jerking the car suddenly out of the wake of the car ahead, is the cause of many an accident. The violence of the swerve can upset the car so badly, it can spin on the straight. Another dangerous move is get the pass wrong and clip the other car as you go by: this move leads to air time in open-wheel cars. Pulling back in line too soon is another common boner, easily solved by taking a quick glance in the mirror.

Sometimes the driver of the passing car figures that two objects should be able to occupy the same space at the same time, forgetting that it is the responsibility of the overtaking car to pull off the pass without contact. The net result is most often two cars eliminated from the race. The sad thing in this type of situation is that someone else's error can take you out: sometimes, you're the victim.

BEING THE VICTIM

All of the previous categories have been incidents that resulted from mistakes. But the mere act of putting yourself in a racecar exposes you to the possibility of accident through no fault of your own. To quote the classic line in motorsports, "That's Racing."

Sudden Oil

If you're the first to arrive at a corner at which the previous driver coated the line with oil from an exploded motor, you're probably going to spin and the severity of the accident will be a matter of luck. The same is true for other common racetrack lubricants like engine coolant, sudden rain or sand kicked up on the track from a previous spin. The corner workers will try to warn you with the appropriate flag, but if you're the first one along, they might not be in time.

Oil and coolant leave a trail on the racetrack if the motor failure is the slow, agonizing type rather than the sudden *boom* type. With both oil and coolant, you can see the sheen they give to the racetrack, especially if the sun is low in the sky. If the track suddenly looks shiny, try braking early to see what you've got, reserving the option to head off-line to get some braking grip back if your suspicions are confirmed. Heading off-line, or at least off the oil path, is the best option in these situations, since an oiled racetrack is sometimes difficult to stand up on, let alone drive on.

Breakages

Sometimes the stupid cretin that's oiling down the racetrack is you. If the motor is going away and oil and coolant are spraying out the back, this glop can get directly on your tires and spin you—an event all the other drivers will applaud. If it happens suddenly, as in the motor going off like a grenade, it's not your

> "I've been surprised by an oiled-down corner more times than I can count. It's easy to think, 'Oh well, I'm going to crash,' but if you keep your wits and don't give up, you can save it. You just have to switch over to survival mode and forget about speed, forget about line and scrape through the corner, even if you have to nearly stop. The oil's not everywhere, so once you spot it, you get off onto a part of the racetrack that's dry. You learn not to correct the steering wheel too much or to do anything sudden or violent while you're in the oil—let the car slide. If you do a big correction, then hit the good part of the track again, the car will hook and off you go. Just stick with it and don't quit. Like pilots say, 'Fly it all the way to the ground.'
>
> —David Loring

> "As a group, we racers are so optimistic about how well things are going to turn out each day that we turn our backs on all the things that could go wrong....There's a certain amount of denial at work. A piece on the car could fail at the kink at Road America or any of a dozen places that wouldn't be good. A car's a machine and machines sometimes break. Happens to the best of them. Rick Mears, driving for one of the best teams in the world—a radiator hose blows at Indy and puts him in the wall.
>
> "You have to be concerned before you get in the car. Is the car I'm getting in safe? Are the guys who are preparing the car top notch? Is the car owner supplying the proper parts or are we pushing it? I remember it was a big day when I had the opportunity to drive a car and I said no. Thank you, but no thank you. You don't have to drive every one that you can."
>
> —Jim Pace

fault (whatever consolation that may be), but if the water temperature is rising and the oil pressure is falling, you can't see the cars behind you through the smoke, and yet you continue on, you're being a fool. A totally exploded motor is much more expensive to repair or replace than one that still has most of its parts bolted together, no matter how worn or hot those parts may be. If the motor is on its way out, get off-line—make the effort to avoid ruining the race for everyone else.

Any component—a motor, a tire, some key part of the braking system, a rod end, an upright, a wheel—

can fail unpredictably, with disastrous results. No amount of money or engineering expertise can overcome this possibility. As a driver, you have to accept this fact as part of the game—that through no fault of your own, the car can betray you and hurt you. You don't dwell on it and you certainly don't let it affect your desire to take the car to its limits—it's just part of the deal. The best defense is to make sure that you drive well-prepared racecars and that you own and use good safety equipment.

PREPARE FOR THE WORST

The best advice in preparing for the possibility of an accident is to outfit yourself and your racecar with the best safety equipment you can acquire.

Fig. 11-6. Buy the best helmet you can afford, with the current Snell test standard.

The Car
The car has to have a six-point belt with a submarine strap, attached to failure-proof mounts. The rollover bar or roll cage should be stout and plenty high enough to keep your head off the racetrack in case of a rollover. The major race-sanctioning bodies have stringent and well-proven guidelines on the level of car preparation required to run.

You need to be careful and consider the risk involved in competing in club events in street cars unequipped with roll cages or fuel cells, and with no more than a stock seatbelt anchor. These cars, even driven singly against a clock, can get upside down. We won't try to dissuade drivers from competing in this branch of the sport, but they should be aware that in many ways, these cars are more dangerous than a fully-prepared racecar.

Driving Gear
Your driving gear should include the best full-face helmet you can afford (the old adage is that you should get a $50 helmet if you have a $50 head). Open-face helmets are common in full-bodied racecars, but the full-face helmet is no more uncomfortable than an open-face and offers more protection to the side of your head people see most (see Fig. 11-6).

Your fire resistant suit should be at least two layers thick; and gloves, socks, racing shoes, and a hood (if you have facial hair) should be worn whenever you're in a racecar (see Fig. 11-7).

Neck collars are becoming increasingly popular and it would be valuable to try one out (see Fig. 11-8). Some drivers find them restrictive, while others find the support they give to the neck and helmet valuable.

In open cars, arm restraints (see Fig. 11-9), which give you freedom of movement but keep your arms from flying out of the cockpit in an upset, are required in some forms of racing but not others. It's hard to come up with an argument for not using all the safety gear you can find—it's normally not a hard sell.

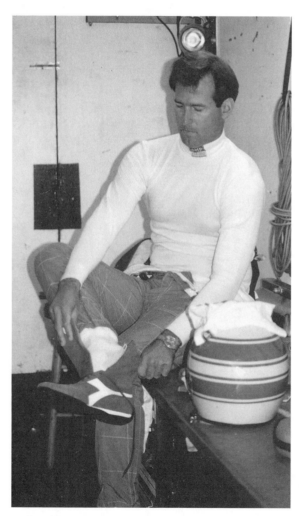

Fig. 11-7. Fire-resistant apparel and proper racing attire are crucial to safety.

Fig. 11-8. Neck collars that restrict helmet motion under deceleration are increasingly popular.

Fig. 11-9. Some sanctioning groups require arm restraints in open cars to limit the travel of your arms outside the cockpit.

Fig. 11-10. Tightening the belts, really tight, starts with the lap belts first. Use a helper if need be.

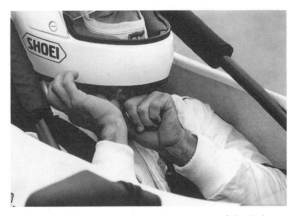

Fig. 11-11. Always check the security of the helmet chin strap, then check again before leaving the pit lane.

Sometimes safety gear is not used properly, reducing its effectiveness. The most common safety mistake is to not do up your belts tightly enough. You should start with getting the lap belt tight—really tight—low down across your hips, not up high on the soft part of your abdomen (see Fig. 11-10).

Next, the shoulder belts can be tightened. It's important not to do it the other way around—shoulders first, lap second—because the lap belt rides up too high into your belly area. The submarine belts are the only ones that don't need to be ultra-tight, for comfort's sake and because their major job is to keep you from sliding out from under the other belts.

As you or a helper tighten the belts, wiggle around, trying to take as much slack out of the belt system as you can. Once you get out on the racetrack, the cornering and braking loads will push you around in the seat, loosening the belts. They're hard to adjust underway, so you really have to get them right before you leave the pit lane, perhaps having them uncomfort-

ably tight in anticipation that a few laps will loosen them. There's a performance advantage in being securely belted into the car. If there is no need to brace yourself to keep from sliding around the cockpit, you'll find that your muscle tension will be lower and you'll be able to make more accurate motions on the controls. Any extraneous motion side to side and fore and aft has to make it more difficult for your central nervous system to sense the subtle accelerations involved with car control. So belt up tight.

Silly as it sounds, drivers sometimes forget to do up the chinstraps on their helmets. The helmet won't do you any good if it doesn't stay on your head. Check the chin strap every time (see Fig. 11-11). It's a good habit when leaving the pit lane to tug on the shoulder belts one more time and to check the helmet strap.

LAUGH AND THE WORLD LAUGHS WITH YOU

Drivers have developed a version of gallows humor about accidents—partly from sheer amazement that they got through it, partly to deflect the dead seriousness of the subject. Here are just a few examples.

Soon after a huge accident that he had in Florida, Mike Rand, former Formula C National Champion, was recounting to Price Cobb how it all happened. "I got down to the end of the straight and Shelton, who had just drafted me, pulled back too soon and hit my left front and the car went *bang!* straight up in the air. I closed my eyes—"

"Closed your eyes?," interrupted Price, "You missed the best part."

Former World Champion Jody Scheckter describes a big crash: "I slid down in the seat as far as I could, closed my eyes and waited for all the banging to stop. Then it gets quiet, and that's the tricky bit. You don't want to undo the belts quite yet because the quiet part means either it's over or you're flying through the air and the banging may start up again."

Dorsey Schroeder had the opportunity to compete in the International Race of Champions and got a rare chance to race at Talladega, one of the fastest tri-ovals in the world: "We were running constantly flat out, never even thought about lifting, and I was doing well, running 6th when I got tapped. I must have been going 185 m.p.h. and it came around and there was nothing I could do about it. I had never spun at that speed before and I thought, well, this is a new experience. I had seen Rusty and Dale and other people go on big rides and I thought, 'so this is what it's like.'

"I didn't like it. Then the car takes off into the air, still going a zillion miles per hour and I'm thinking 'Oh, no.' It got down on the infield grass, which was soaking wet, upside down, and it's just scooping mud and water and I don't know what else, all inside the car into my helmet, in my eyes. It was terrible.

"The car finally stopped and I thought, 'Now that I know what it's like, I definitely don't want to do that ever again.' I undid the belts and crawled out of the window, absolutely covered from head to toe with mud, dripping wet. The ambulance got there a minute later and roared up to me. The back doors to the ambulance flew open and the girl EMT inside took one look at me and said, 'You're not getting in *my* ambulance looking like *that*.'"

There's a million of 'em.

CHAPTER 12

RACING IN THE RAIN

U_{NLESS YOU'RE WILLING} to withdraw from a racing event when it rains—an act which carries with it a certain stigma of dishonor—sooner or later you'll have to come to terms with how rain affects your racing performance. Other than moving to Arizona, there are numerous adaptations that can be made to increase the chance of racing success when it turns crummy. It's worth spending some time planning how you're going to deal with rain before you're actually confronted with it on the track.

> There are three major areas where you can gain the advantage by altering your dry-weather approach to racing:
> 1) maintaining the ability to see,
> 2) altering the racecar, and
> 3) rethinking driving technique.

Car Control

There are two fundamental problems with racing in the rain: restricted visibility and loss of traction. Both problems have to be dealt with in order to retain control of your car in wet weather.

Obviously, first and foremost, you can't control your car if you can't see where you're going. Maintaining the ability to see comes even before car changes as a priority in wet driving.

Second, it's possible for your tires to lose all contact with the racetrack; and when they do, all your ability to control the car's speed and direction goes out the window. This happens when the water sitting on top of the asphalt is allowed to pack up between the tire and the road—you're literally driving on water, not asphalt. The phenomenon is called "hydroplaning," and it can happen in your street car, in an airplane on the runway, in anything where a tire is rolling over a wet surface.

If you can handle those two problems, then you can go on to make the changes in driving technique that will be required to lower lap time in the wet.

MAINTAINING VISIBILITY

There are a few problems in maintaining visibility: some which you can solve and some you're stuck with. In the "stuck with" category, you have the spray off the wheels of the other cars in the field. In open-wheel cars, it's the worst, since every car is sending up a roostertail of water from each tire and the spray just hangs in the air. Other than being on the front row, there is not much you can do to improve the view, especially in the early laps when the field is bunched.

Fig. 12-1. Spray, especially off the wheels of an open-wheel racecar, makes visibility difficult for following cars.

"I think driving at the limit in the rain takes more thought than driving at the limit in the dry where conditions don't change drastically. In the dry, pretty much, the track is a constant. Sure, it changes, but it doesn't change every second. In the rain, what you can see changes constantly. The spray changes, it rains harder on one end of the track than the other—I think it's much more a thinking game.

There were times racing at Mosport in Canada where you would get wheelspin ten times a lap going down the straightaway. It's not like the dry where the drama is in the turns, then you're waiting for the next corner. You're driving it on the limit all the time."

—Skip Barber

Fig. 12-2. To encourage air flow over the inside surface of your visor, prop the bottom edge of the visor open with a small cylinder of racer's tape.

A problem you *can* work on is to try to keep your visor (or goggles if you wear an open faced helmet) from fogging over. A full-face helmet on a rainy day is the ideal environment for mist to collect on the inside of the visor: the relative humidity is high, the temperature of the visor is colder than the air inside the helmet, and your heavy breathing is supplying an ample source of warm, humid air.

There are a number of potential fixes for the problem. One is to get outside air flowing over the inside of the visor. On most helmets you can ratchet the visor up a quarter inch or so, leaving a slot at the bottom wide enough for air to get through but narrow enough to keep water out. To keep the slot from closing down from wind pressure, you can roll up a quarter-inch cylinder of racer's tape and tape it between the helmet and visor so that the face shield can't close.

The ventilation normally helps, but you still have to deal with the warm, moist air you're breathing out. You can easily solve this problem by creating a cone of racer's tape, taped to your nose, that directs your breath away from the visor and down out the bottom of the helmet. Some drivers have gone as far as using a flexible snorkel or modified aircraft oxygen mask to get the job done. Whatever works!

Coating the Visor

There are preparations you can apply to the inside of the shield to cut down on fogging. "Fog Free" is a product you can buy at most racing or motorcycle shops and it works pretty well most of the time. Many drivers have had success coating the inside of the visor with liquid dishwashing detergent. Applied in a thin film of liquid, it doesn't distort the view and any condensation that forms turns instantly to a liquid you can see through. Lemony-fresh Joy is a special favorite since it also functions as an air freshener.

For the outside of the visor, some drivers use "Rain-X," a formulation which beads water, but others don't like the idea of a bead forming directly in front of an eyeball. In open cars, the air rushing by normally blows the visor clear, and a good clean visor stays transparent without any special coating. Avoid using "tear-offs," thin transparent sheets attached to the visor that can be torn off as the race progresses. In the rain, water gets between the sheets and distorts the view.

"Believe it or not, somebody once told me to try tobacco on the inside of the visor to keep the fog down—and it works! You tear apart a cigarette and wipe the tobacco on the inside of the visor with your hand, then lightly wipe off the pieces with a cloth. I was amazed."

—David Loring

There has been a lot of experimentation with visor color in rain conditions. Obviously, you want to avoid using darkly-tinted visors in low-light conditions. A brand new, unscratched, clear visor gives you a real-world view. Yellow visors heighten contrast and many drivers like them. You do, however, have to check with the race-organizing body to see if they are allowable, as some groups feel that they make it difficult to distinguish the color of flags.

Mud and oily spray can be a problem and once the visor gets splattered, you can often do more harm than good in trying to clean the mess up. A useful trick is take a small towel, sponge or chamois along with you in the car and stow it under a shoulder belt or alongside your hip.

In closed cars, you need wipers in hard rain; and the inside of the windshield, as well as your visor, can get foggy. Dorsey Schroeder and Walt Bohren, both IMSA GTO veterans, carry squeegees with them in rain races to wipe away the fog. If the squeegee has a long enough handle, you can use it to clean the inside of the windshield between gear shifts. You can use the same anti-fog preparations on the windshield as you do on your visor. Windshield ventilation also helps, so think twice before discarding the defroster from a sedan racecar. You will someday wish you had it back.

> "It's amazing. The most important thing is the visibility through the windshield, and so few [GTS] cars have proper wipers or defoggers on them. Big budgets, but nobody's getting it right, you know? When was the last time you heard a guy get out of the car after a rain race and say 'The wiper worked flawlessly—the visibility was great!'?"
>
> —Jeremy Dale

OPTIMIZING TRACTION

Once you're sure that you'll be able to see where you're going, you can concentrate on optimizing the car for slippery conditions.

If you normally run slicks in your form of racing, the first hard rain-related decision will be whether to run rain tires or not. If the track is merely damp and the weather looks like it's improving, you may choose to start the race on slicks in the expectation that the track will dry and you'll only suffer in the early laps. Of course, it might rain harder and you'll have to stop in the pits once the race is underway to change to rains. It's a guessing game, and if you race for a while, you'll guess wrong as often as you'll guess right.

If you're undecided up until the last minute, it's a good idea to roll the car to the grid with two rain tires and two slicks mounted to the car, so that when you make your final, last-minute decision, you'll only have to change two tires, not four.

Rain Tires

Racing rain tires are designed to accomplish two goals: 1) to evacuate water from under the contact patch and 2) to allow the rubber compound to reach a temperature where it can provide maximum grip given the cooling effects of the water.

Here's a good model for how the rain tire works: the first third of the contact patch evacuates the water toward the side of the tire, the second third squeegees the road surface dry, and the final third provides grip, using the same bonding and shearing mechanisms that the dry tire uses.

To take into account the cooling effects of running in water, the rubber compound of a rain tire is soft enough that it will reach the low 200-degree range in racing conditions. If the tire is run in the dry, the added friction and the lack of cooling water will quickly overheat it, changing the molecular structure of the rubber as well as blistering and chunking the tire.

If you start a race on rains and the track dries, you'll be forced to change back to slicks. In a race where the final four to five laps are run in drying conditions, you'll see drivers driving off-line through the puddles in an effort to cool the tires enough to keep them from coming apart so that they can make it to the finish without having to pit.

If you race in an area where it rains infrequently, you have to be careful about using old rain tires that have been sitting in the trailer for two seasons. Time slowly deteriorates the rubber compound, and you could find yourself at a distinct disadvantage running against other drivers with freshly-purchased rains.

> "If we have different types of rain tires available, we'll test tires in the rain. It depends. If we have something specific we want to try in a rain situation, we'll go out, but not just to run around."
>
> —Bryan Herta

Shaved Street Tires

In classes such as showroom stock where you normally run on shaved street tires, your rain choice should be the same type of tire with more tread thickness. How much more depends upon the depth of water involved. In a deluge, you'd opt for full tread depth, but with less and less water on the track, you can go progressively thinner on the tread. With our Formula Dodges, 5/32 inches of tread depth is about as deep as you can go without affecting dry track lap time. In light rain or in drying conditions, tires with 5/32 inches of tread will evacuate water well and not give away anything if the track dries. In order to know for sure what suits your racecar, you have to test different combinations.

One useful experiment for showroom stock would be to try to run a treaded tire with a higher aspect ratio: for example, a 70-series vs. a 60-series tire. The narrower contact patch would enhance braking and acceleration grip and sacrifice some cornering potential. Since cornering potential tends to suffer in the wet in greater proportion than accelerating and braking, boosting the car's existing strengths may be to your advantage.

We also recommend boosting inflation pressures as a potential fix for hydroplaning. Airline pilots have known for years that the hydroplaning speed of a tire increases as the square root (multiplied by a constant) of the inflation pressure, and this remedy might be worth trying on your racecar.

CHANGING YOUR SET-UP

When it comes to modifying the mechanical set-up of the car for the rain, we can offer some suggestions but, from decades of experience, we've found that what works for some cars doesn't necessarily work for others. The only definitive way to find advantages for your car is to continually experiment and test every change you make.

> *"Most teams don't come up with a strictly wet set-up. The reason is that when it rains, changes in the weather are unpredictable; and if you go to a set-up that's good in the rain, generally it's absolutely horrible in the dry. With Indy Cars, they can dry the track so quickly that if it starts to lighten up and you get any dry at all, you're out to lunch with a wet-weather set-up. Conversely, a good dry set-up is not bad in the rain. You'll make some adjustments to the dry set-up, primarily to change the balance of the downforce. You can take front downforce out of the car to help secure the back. That's the only change you'd make because it doesn't totally ruin the car if the track dries."*
>
> *—Bryan Herta*

Testing in the wet is unpopular. You tow your perfectly clean and tidy racecar, fresh from its winter rebuild, to the track for testing and if it rains, it's the rare team who doesn't just turn around and go home. As distasteful as it might be to run in the slop, finding improvements in your wet-weather set-up will turn out to be a big asset by the end of the season, especially if your competition hasn't bothered to test in the wet.

Brake Bias Adjustments

It's almost impossible to say categorically that such and such a change will work for all cars. The one wet-weather tweak that comes close to being universal is changing the brake bias of the car: we've seen many a car do well in the rain without changing a thing, other than brake bias. With less grip in slippery conditions, there will be less deceleration and therefore less load transfer onto the front tires. If the brake bias was set in dry conditions, it will be proportioned too much to the front for the wet and will need to be adjusted toward the rear. To find out how much to adjust, you'll have to test as you go along.

> *"Testing in the wet is very important. Penske was one of the only ones to test in the rain, but even there, they were reluctant. The problem with testing in the wet was that there's a big risk. You're worried that you could stick it in the fence or get hurt.*
>
> *"We sat out at Portland one time for a couple of days—we were supposed to test for three days and it rained all three days. We sat around a lot until finally, on the third day, I said, 'You know what? It's wet. Let's go run.' We did because it wasn't puddling. If you've got puddles, you can really aquaplane and if you crash a car, you've just set yourself back so far. Even with a team like Penske. It takes about 800 hours, roughly, to build a car.*
>
> *"The big thing to me was that we did it and developed a rain set-up that stayed with us for two years. Unless you're in a series that doesn't run in the wet, sometime you're going to have to do it."*
>
> *—Danny Sullivan*

Suspension Changes

Generally, we have seen success in going softer with shocks, springs and anti-roll bars in wet conditions. There are two reasons for this theory. First, when traction is limited, the driver can more easily deal with finding the limit when loads transfer gradually rather than suddenly. If the car has more motion in roll and pitch, which it would with softer suspension settings, individual tire loadings change more gradually, giving the driver a better chance at tiptoeing up toward the limit without overstepping.

Second, with limited traction, the car will have lower forces acting on it in pitch and roll. A softer setting will allow the car to move the same amount that it does in the dry with higher forces and stiffer settings. The alignment settings, especially camber, are designed to be optimum when the car rolls due to cornering forces; and the softer set-up allows the car to get to this range with lower lateral forces working on it. How much to soften your particular racecar is, again, something you have to find out by testing.

Pedal Changes

Take a close look at the pedals in your car. If the faces of the pedals, as they are in many racecars, are made of a smooth metal surface, they will be very slippery when wet. It's worth the effort to have rain pedals made, especially a custom brake pedal, with a face made of a rough surface such as expanded metal screen. Non-skid tape works in a pinch. Also, your racing shoes, with their thin leather soles, can get incredibly slippery when they get wet. To prevent your

Fig. 12-3. In wet conditions, drying the soles of your driving shoes makes them less likely to slip off the pedals.

feet from slipping off the pedals in the rain, dry your soles or try wearing deck shoes for better traction.

Take a look at the pedal heights as well. Normally, the relationship between brake pedal and throttle pedal height is set so that under hard braking, the throttle can be easily reached with the right side of your right foot in order to blip the throttle on the downshifts. When it's wet, you won't be pushing on the brake pedal as hard and you might find the throttle too low to do good blips. Always remember to re-adjust the brake-throttle relationship before racing in the wet. It will be much easier to spin on a mismatched downshift in the wet, so give yourself some help by getting the pedal relationship right.

Engine
Motors, especially their electrics, don't like water, so find out in testing whether you have a problem with too much water entering the engine compartment. Pay special attention to air intakes for the induction system. A ram air set-up which is terrific in the dry can drown a motor in the rain. An alternate air source that is clear of direct spray usually does the trick.

If you race a car with big horsepower, your biggest problem in the wet will be trying to keep the driving wheels from spinning. Take a close look at how much throttle pedal travel you normally have. If one inch of travel covers the range from minimum to 600 hp, it's going to be very difficult to modulate out of wheelspin. By making up a special bellcrank or throttle pedal, you can greatly increase the amount of total pedal travel so that it's easier to make subtle changes in throttle position.

> "When we built the Eagle Formula Ford, we had five or six positions on the throttle pedal where we could afix the throttle cable, so we could have the choice of a quick throttle for some racetracks and we'd be able to give it a long throttle arm for the wet so you could modulate it better. Gurney fit the same type of set-up to the Indy Cars so that when you went to road races you could have a longer throttle throw than you would on an oval."
>
> —David Loring

Gearing
Some drivers feel that using a higher-than-normal gear makes it easier to avoid wheelspin in the wet. Another school of thought maintains that using a lower gear allows better throttle control and better straight-line acceleration. Ultimately, it's up to the individual driver—and the stopwatch—to decide which is the better course. We vote for using an RPM range that produces the most horsepower, as well as for controlling the wheelspin with your right foot.

Always Test First
In 1980, John Fergus, 1990 IMSA GTU Champion and former Pro S 2000 Champ, ran a Crossle S-2000 car, the first of its kind in the U.S. Its inaugural race was an SCCA National at Moroso Motorsports Park in Florida and, as is common with new cars, it arrived

> *"I've gone to using a higher gear in cornering in the wet to try and tame down the torque available and the wheelspin capability. I've done that and sometimes gone down a gear once I'm through the corner where you can get a little more grip and use the extra torque to shoot you down the straight."*
>
> —Terry Earwood

at the last minute with only one test day available to see what we had.

It rained on the test day, of course, and we were tempted to call it off but thought better of it. We went ahead and mounted the rain tires and rolled this absolutely new car out into the muddy paddock. John roared off onto the circuit and one lap later was back in. The car was undriveable in the wet, not because of a handling problem, but because of its aerodynamics. The shape of the nose bodywork was such that, at speed, it concentrated the spray of water off the nose directly into John's face. "Just like looking into a fire hose," was John's comment.

We fixed it with a jury-rigged spoiler and a windshield extension. Did I mention that you should test in the wet?

RAIN-DRIVING TECHNIQUES

Once you solve the vision problem and have got the car sorted out, the final adaptation to the rain is how and where you drive the car.

Find a New Line

In the dry, all our efforts in terms of line are geared toward finding the biggest radius possible for each corner in order to maximize cornering speed. In the rain, this changes. It's possible, especially if there's a deep puddle at the normal apex, that the cornering force of the car can go to zero. With zero cornering force, it doesn't matter how big you try to make the radius of the corner: the car is going straight.

In rain driving, the classic dry line becomes secondary to the effort to find cornering grip. Often the

> *"In the rain, there's no rules. There are some cases where you drive the 'traditional rain line,' some where the dry line works and others where you drive something in between. You just go out and look for traction. The guy who is comfortable in the car in the wet, has good car control, and goes and finds the traction is going to go the quickest."*
>
> —Jeremy Dale

Fig. 12-4. In the dry, the concentration is on carving the biggest radius through corners, while in the wet, the focus is on maintaining traction by avoiding areas, like this deep puddle at the apex, where the traction could go to zero.

dry line is the last place you want to be when it's pouring out. Since the line carries most of the racing traffic, the track is often polished smooth from rubber being laid down, filling the tiny irregularities in the track surface. Water just sits on this polished surface and easily forms a sheet between your tires and the road. To make matters worse, all of the spilled oil and antifreeze from previous races lies on the conventional line. Put the two together and the dry line can be practically undriveable.

Go off-line, however, and there is less spilled lubricant and the track surface is much more porous, giving the tires much better bite.

Another advantage of driving outside the dry line is that any banking in the corner is going to allow the water to run away from the outside of the turn down toward the inside. The outside edge of the corner will simply be drier than the inside and, given the choice, you want to drive on the driest pavement.

We did an experiment at Lime Rock, using our data-collection Formula Dodge, where we did back-to-back rain sessions on the dry line vs. driving around the outside rim of every corner. The average lap time around the outside was eight seconds per lap faster. Eight seconds!

The rim-shot method (see Fig. 12-6) worked in our test, but since wet weather is so unpredictable, there is no one right way to modify your line. The key is to continually experiment, trying to find a faster method. An indispensable tool for this experimentation is the tachometer. Just as you should in the dry, you check the tach reading at a consistent point at the corner exit to see if a change in approach yielded better corner-exit speed. As conditions change, as it rains harder, more lightly, or begins to dry, you continue to try different approaches and use the one that gives the best corner-exit speed.

Fig. 12-5. Track surfaces can become highly polished as the surface irregularities are worn down by constant use. Here, the dry line approaching the uphill at Lime Rock shimmers in the late-afternoon sun.

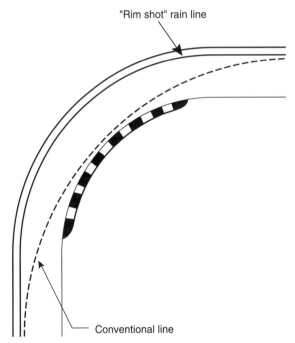

"Rim shot" rain line

Conventional line

Fig. 12-6. The "rim shot" takes advantage of the superior grip available outside the polished dry line.

Your Line Options

There are two parallel concerns in trying to decide on the best rain line. One is that, as we covered above, you want to keep speed as high as you can while in the corner. You do this by finding the grippiest pavement, staying away from the slippery stuff down around the normal apex. In our Lime Rock experiment, the cornering force available on the dry line was in the neigh-

borhood of .6 Gs. On the outside, the G readings were in the vicinity of .85 Gs, some 42% better. By using the outside route, you started accelerating down the following straight from a higher speed and, given more total grip, you could use more throttle earlier than you could on the dry line

The rim-shot technique works especially well in long, sweeping corners where you'll spend a lot of time cornering. The more time spent cornering, the longer you have that 42% grip advantage and the bigger the lap time advantage. Even though the radius of the dry line is bigger, the limited traction still means a loss in speed. In West Bend, a long sweeper at Lime Rock, the speed around the outside was 6 m.p.h. faster than the dry line. You also carry that 6 m.p.h. advantage onto the straight.

Another phenomenon that has bearing on your approach to rain lines is that tires lose more of their cornering ability in the wet than they lose either braking or accelerating grip. Relative to the dry, our tires lose about 36% of their dry weather traction in braking or accelerating. The cornering ability, however, falls 50%.

In light of these facts, you can decide to focus on the tires' strengths when it rains and try to minimize the time spent turning. You would do this by trying to square off the corners—that is, turn later at a slower speed and get the car pointing as straight as possible as early as possible, using aggressive acceleration early in the corner. It's like turning the racetrack into a series of dragstrips and braking zones, connected by low-speed turns where you get the car's angle changed over a short distance and time (see Figure 12-7).

This technique works really well on courses with tight short corners but not so well on racetracks with

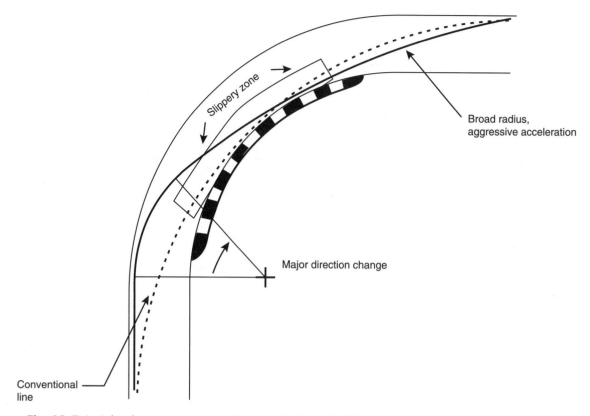

Fig. 12-7. In tight, short corners, one option is to do the bulk of the car's change of direction early in the turn, allowing a much straighter acceleration path at the corner exit. This does require passing over the slippery dry line and the throttle will have to be modulated to account for the changes in grip on this path.

long sweepers and hairpin turns, where the rim shot is generally more effective.

With either approach, you have to cross the dry line at some point, so expect that you may have to modulate the braking pressure on the way into the corner and breathe out of the throttle at the corner exit as you pass over the more slippery pavement.

The Makeup of the Circuit

Your choice of line and approach will vary from track to track, even corner to corner, based on the layout of the course and what the road surface is like. At Lime Rock, a circuit with three fast sweepers, two long hairpins and one banked medium-speed corner, the rim shot technique is the way to go, as you've seen. This is especially so because the track surface is all asphalt and polished from years of racing.

At a place like the Sebring test circuit, there are four short, slow corners where the track surface is made of porous, abrasive concrete. The concrete drains well and the water seeps into the surface pores; consequently, the apex area of these four turns isn't any worse than the rim as far as traction is concerned. In these four corners, you can square off the turn by using a late apex and get a good straight run off the

> *"I spun a car once in the rain at Watkins right on the pit straight. I hit a puddle with the right side of the car—I couldn't see well enough to realize where the water was deep. I'd have never hit it knowingly with one side of the car. The car did a 360 and kept going, and I didn't lose a half-second. I didn't have anything to do with the fact that I ended up going in the right direction—it just happened."*
>
> *—Skip Barber*

corner even thought you're crossing the dry line. The other fast corners at Sebring have an asphalt surface and driving off-line, much like you do at Lime Rock, creates some grip advantage in these corners.

Straights

In dry weather, the path down the straight is obvious. You track out of the corner leading onto the straight, then use the straight to position your car for the entry of the next corner. In the rain, it's possible to get wheelspin down the straight, even in relatively low-

Fig. 12-8. Over time, ruts form in the braking zones, then fill with water when it rains. Braking is much better by keeping the tires on the dryer crown adjoining the ruts.

> *"At New Orleans, in the Lights car with Essex Racing, it rained and stopped, rained and stopped, and we changed tires so often in that race that I forgot what tires I was on—which ultimately led to our demise. We were leading with 20 minutes to go when I went off-line to pass a backmarker and, just as I went to the brakes, it dawned on me that he was on rain tires and I was on slicks. I slid right past him, right out of the lead and into the tire barrier.... I got caught out on that one just a bit."*
> —Jim Pace

powered cars, if you run on the wettest part of the track. Your approach to the straight is to find the driest path, and that may not be in the accustomed place. You certainly want to avoid hitting puddles, especially hitting them with only one side of the car. Hitting deep water at speed has a formidable braking effect. Ask anyone who has done a belly-flop off a bridge.

Hitting a puddle with one side of the car can spin it right out from under you. If there's no way around it, like when it extends from one verge of the track to the other, try to hit it square so that the car will skim over the top and arrive on the other side pointing the same way it started.

In the braking zone at the end of the straight, don't lock into the idea of using the same part of the racetrack as you do in the dry. Many corners have ruts worn into them at the approach to corners and these little hollows fill up with water, robbing you of braking traction. Often just straddling these ruts, placing your tires on the crown rather than the trough, will improve the car's braking potential.

Once the race has settled down and drivers find a workable line, it will tend to get drier unless you're faced with a continual downpour. You have to keep in mind that when you pull off of this drier line to pass another driver in the braking zone for a corner, you'll be back on the really wet stuff. Outbraking in the wet can be dicey, especially in drying conditions where the off-line can be considerably more slippery than the path most drivers are on.

COMMON-SENSE TIPS

In the rain, little things can catch you out. With the limited traction, any of the mistakes that you normally make in your dry-weather racing are magnified. The mismatched downshift that you got away with in the dry can get the rear of the car sliding in the wet. Ditto for trailing throttle oversteer. You have to try to be as smooth as you can with all the controls.

Always look for drier or more abrasive asphalt. If the track surface looks glossy, it's probably slippery. If it's dull gray in appearance, there's probably some grip there. Look for patches in the racetrack surface. Some, like Mid Ohio's dreaded epoxy sealer, are like ice. Concrete patches, especially if they are freshly poured, have great grip.

A lot of your competitors will spin in the wet. Just going the distance without going off the road can allow you to finish well. If you do spin, try to be cool. We've seen so many people do a second spin in an effort to hurry back onto the track that you'd think it's required in the rules. If you think the track is slippery, grass raises "greasy" to another level of magnitude.

If you prepare for the wet, it really shouldn't be any more intimidating than racing on a sunny day. It has its own special requirements, but if you have good driving gear, a good car, and an experimental attitude, you can consistently out perform the many other drivers who just want to get it over with.

Part IV

The Role
of Hardware

CHAPTER 13

TIRES

ULTIMATELY, YOUR RACE-car is just a fancy accumulation of expensive parts that keep the tires in contact with the road. The maximum cornering capability of the car is a reflection of the tires' cornering grip. The car's maximum ability for braking lies with the tires' potential for braking traction and, once you have an engine big enough to need all the acceleration traction of the tire, the grip the tire provides you defines how well your racecar will accelerate. In other words, tires make the racecar.

It would seem, then, that all you need to do to optimize the car's abilities is to bolt on the grippiest set of tires available, and that's that for the tire issue. Well, it's not that simple, but there is an element of truth to the sentiment. Many drivers over the years have had a chassis-engine combination that looked like a world-beater, only to be saddled with a brand or type of tire that made the car uncompetitive.

Today, in most forms of racing, the choice of tire is either mandated by the rules of the particular series or is a clear and obvious choice—the tire that the front-runners use. There's more, however, to know about tires than that.

TRACTION BASICS

Tire technology is a subject about which volumes have been written: we make no pretense of covering the subject from A to Z in this book. Our interest is in helping you to acquire knowledge you can use as a driver to improve your performance. If, however, you have a deeper interest in how tires work, there are sources listed in the bibliography which will go into much greater detail.

Racing today uses a wide variety of tires, from the over-the-counter street radials used in showroom stock racing to the qualifying slicks which have unearthly grip and a useful life of barely one flying lap. Despite their obvious differences, all of them have some basic properties in common.

> **Ultimately, tires provide the forces that define a racecar's performance, so each type of tire has different implications for driving technique.**

face and the actual interlocking of thousands of tiny bits of the tire rubber with the microscopic irregularities in the road surface. To resist the tire's motion relative to the road, this bonding action requires shearing off these points of contact from the body of the tire, which takes considerable force.

This type of friction between a tire and asphalt is different than the father of physics, Isaac Newton, would have predicted. Newton formulated laws which predicted that the force it took to move an object sideways across a smooth surface would not be larger than the downward force it exerted on the surface upon which it rested. Newton never anticipated the inventiveness of tire manufacturers.

A race tire, and indeed some street tires, can exert a braking, accelerating or cornering force greater than the force pushing down on the tire. When this force is used to displace the car sideways, as in cornering, we say this force is being used *laterally*. In braking or accelerating, this force is being used in the fore-and-aft direction, *longitudinally*.

Levels of Grip

The pneumatic tire grips the road with a combination of molecular bonding between the rubber and the road sur-

Coefficient of Friction

It would be easy to assume, once the tires are bolted onto the car, that their maximum level of grip stays constant but, of course, it never does. The amount of traction available from a tire is determined by a number of factors: some you can't control, but some that you have the power to manipulate.

Don't worry, we won't go too high-tech on you. *CF*, or *coefficient of friction*, is simply a number you can use to quickly compare one tire's ability against another. CF is a ratio of the maximum force a tire can generate relative to the load pushing down on it. A tire with a CF of 1, for example, can create a usable force equal to the vertical load on the tire. A CF of 1.5 means that the tire would be capable of creating a force one and a half times the force pushing down on it. CF is simply a handy way of describing the relative grip of a tire without having to take into account the particular car or corner the tire is mounted on. A tire with a higher CF will give greater grip than one with a lower CF.

Inflation Pressure. Back in the old days, when there was precious little else a driver could adjust to improve the handling balance of a car, adjusting tire pressures was a popular way of trying to get the front and rear ends of the car to slide at the same point. The fact that a tire, especially a street tire, changes CF with inflation pressure allows you to change the relative grip of the front or rear end of the car.

Increases in inflation pressure increase the CF up to a point, and then it falls off again. There is a particular pressure where the CF is at its maximum and, of course, this is the point you'd like to find in order to maximize the car's cornering force.

Adjusting the front and rear pressures up and down isn't the best way to adjust cornering characteristics, since you often end up reducing the traction capability of one end of the car to get its cornering close to neutral. When you do this, the car may feel better, but it will have less overall traction than it would have if both front and rear tires were at the pressure that yielded the best traction. Once you had both fronts and rears at their optimum pressure, you would then trim the car's cornering balance by mechanical means—by adjusting sway bars, spring rates, ride heights, etc. But if you're driving a car that is non-adjustable, juggling tire pressures, within reason, will work to trim its cornering balance.

There are a number of racecars for which, even today, tire pressure is an important handling adjustment. In cars which produce a good deal of aerodynamic downforce, it is necessary to fit very stiff springs to the car to keep it off the surface of the road at high speed and to keep it from changing its pitch attitude, thus preventing dramatic changes in the balance of downforce. In such cases, the tires' inflation pressure has a pronounced effect on the handling of the car since the tires themselves are functioning as springs to a greater extent than on a soft-spring car.

Since most true racecars are adjustable, the role of inflation pressure has less to do with trimming its cornering balance than with finding the pressure which delivers the best CF. You start with the cold pressures recommended by the tire manufacturer technicians, who invariably know better. When the car comes off the course, you note the hot pressure of each tire and see how much each gained from cold. You try to adjust the cold pressure so that the pressure rise from cold to hot is the same on the front and rear tires of the side of the car doing the most cornering work— the outside pair in the majority of corners.

With racing slicks, the trick is to adjust pressures to keep an even tire footprint across the contact patch. Too much pressure will put a crown in the center of the tire, thus under-utilizing the edges, and too little pressure will over-use the edges while also making the tire feel squirmy and imprecise. This effect is somewhat dampened with modern radial race slicks, but it is still there.

Camber. When a tire is standing straight up, perpendicular to the road surface, it has zero degrees of camber. If you tilt the top of the tire in toward the center of the car the tire goes into negative camber. Tilt it the other way, top away from the car, and you've created positive camber.

The CF of the tire varies with changes in camber. It increases as you go from zero camber into negative camber and decreases as you go into positive camber. From a design standpoint, you would like to have a suspension system on the car which keeps the most heavily loaded tires in a range of camber where the CF is at its highest value. It is important to remember that braking and accelerating forces tend to decrease with increasing negative or positive camber settings. The best static camber setting is the one that offers the best overall balance of cornering, braking, and accelerating traction.

How You Can Adjust CF

It is interesting to see how CF changes with changes in inflation pressure and camber, but these are mechanical adjustments that are out of your hands once you take to the circuit. True enough, these are good examples of how CF is variable, but there's not much you can do when underway to improve the car's performance by affecting tire pressure or camber. There are, however, parameters which affect CF that a driver can control when behind the wheel.

Download. Earlier in this book, we said that the harder a tire presses down on the pavement, the better it grips. To see this principle in action, you can graph the CF of a particular tire as the download increases (see Fig. 13-1).

In this graph, the CF starts out at 1.75 at light loadings in the 150 lb. range. As the download on the tire increases, the CF gradually *falls* to 1.25 at 450 lbs. of download. The key is to separate total grip from CF. For example, if the tire has 200 lbs. of download on it, you can see that its CF at that point is 1.7. To see how much *force* this converts to, multiply the download (200 lbs.) by the CF (1.7). With this tire, 200 lbs. of download will create 340 lbs. of tractive force.

If, however, you increase the download to 400 lbs., the CF goes down to 1.35 from 1.7. Multiply the CF of 1.35 by the download of 400 lbs. to get the total grip and you'll find the traction has increased to 540 lbs.

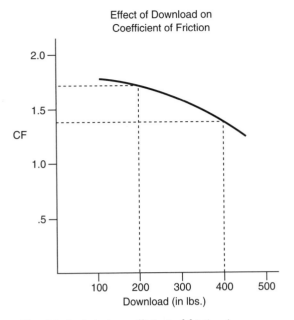

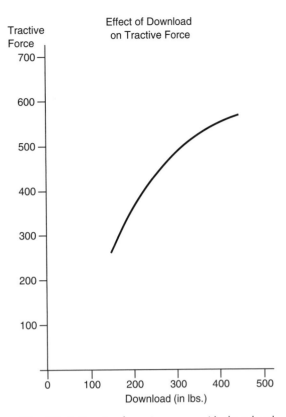

Fig. 13-1. A tire's coefficient of friction is a representation of its ability to convert download into traction. The CF declines with increases in download.

Fig. 13-2. Tractive force increases with download but its rate of increase declines as the loading gets higher.

This phenomenon of diminishing CF as downloads get higher is one of the foundations behind the fact that lighter cars can attain higher cornering, braking and acceleration forces than cars with greater mass. It also explains why designers try to keep the center of gravity of racecars as low as possible in order to minimize the amount of load transfer from the inside tires onto the outside tires under cornering. The greater the load transferred to the outside, the more the CF of the loaded tires will suffer. Less load transfer means a higher overall CF for all four tires and, consequently, greater traction and cornering speed.

Fig. 13-2, which shows download vs. traction, is more applicable to what drivers can do to affect a car's traction and thereby its potential performance. As the loading goes up, so does the traction; but you can see that the rate at which the grip increases slows down at higher loadings.

All of this data simply reinforces what you learned in the chapter on car control. The way you drive—how you move the controls—affects the loadings on the tires and consequently adjusts the handling characteristics of the car.

Producing Peak Cornering CF. We've dealt with slip angle before and hinted at the fact that a tire's cornering force varied with the slip angle. Now we can put it in terms of a changing CF to try to clear up just how much sliding delivers the best cornering grip.

When we talk about a tire with a CF of 1.5, we mean a *peak* CF of 1.5. The graph of slip angle vs. CF in Fig. 13-3 is an example of how the grip will vary. At

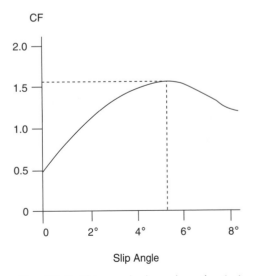

Fig. 13-3. This graph shows how the tire's peak CF comes at a particular slip angle. Above or below this optimum angle, the tire will be operating below its peak potential grip.

low slip angles the tire's CF is small, but as you increase the slip angle, it gets better and better. In this graph, the CF gets very close to its peak value of 1.5 at about 5 degrees.

> *"Any racecar that's handling well is going to have a little bit of yaw in it—but it varies. The Formula cars on street tires liked a reasonable amount of slip angle. The Dodge GTU car went best when you kept it on rails. The GTS car, you had to be aggressive, but patient, because with all that power if you got in it too early you were just laying rubber and in a couple of laps you'd just burn the tires off the car."*
>
> *—Jeremy Dale*

Up to this point, the tire is not necessarily sliding across the road. Because of the elastic properties of a tire, the angular difference between the way the rim is facing and the direction the contact patch is facing is accommodated by the pliant nature of the inflated tire. At some point, the tire has deformed as much as it can to accommodate this angle and any increase in the angle will mean that part of the contact patch will begin to slide. If the angle continues to increase, a greater and greater percentage of the patch slides until at some angle the entire contact patch has some lateral motion across the asphalt. Somewhere between the slip angle where the sliding begins and where the entire contact patch is sliding lies the point of maximum CF—in this example, at about 5 degrees.

In terms of cornering speed, in a 200-foot radius corner, tires operating at the peak range of 5 degrees will allow a car (without aero downforce) to corner at 67 m.p.h. At a CF of 1.35, the limit cornering speed is down to 63.6 m.p.h. At 1.3, it's down to 62.4 m.p.h. Clearly, the fastest driver would operate the car in the range of 5 degrees of slip: not over, not under.

Exceeding the optimum slip angle of the tires not only puts you in a range where the CF is lower but greater slip angles also create more heat, another factor which varies the CF of tires.

Tire Temperature. The traction of the tires varies with heat. A tire's CF is lower than the peak at cooler temperatures but rises to a maximum at a particular temperature range. It then falls off again as the tire temperature exceeds its design range. The driver that has the most grip runs tires at their optimum range, running them hard enough to create tire temperature but not so hard that they overheat and "go off."

This optimum temperature range stays in the same ball park for a surprising variety of cars. The temperature ranges that most slicks like fall into the realm of 200 to 240° F. The tire designers stir together a combi-

nation of tire construction and the type of rubber compound to come up with a tire that will live in this range on the type of car its being used on. It is then up to you, the driver, to use the tires in a way that keeps them in this range. This usually means finding a handling balance that equally stresses both the front and rear pair of tires. Over use the fronts and they'll overheat, turning a car that might have been balanced into one that wants to plow straight on at every corner. Over use the rears and you end up with a car that wants to spin every time you turn the steering wheel.

> *"In general, particularly with higher horsepower cars, the rear tires go away first. The first place you notice it is on exiting the corner. You start picking up more and more wheelspin and you can't get the power down. You really notice it on an oval where you're leaning hard on the rear tires, especially the right rear, and if you lean on it too hard and use it up, it goes away and you get a loose car. With a loose car on a fast oval, you're miserable.*
>
> *"Sometimes if you just go a little easier on them, if you consciously really try and concentrate on not sliding the tires as much—not spinning the tires coming off the corner—you can help them a little bit, but they'll never come back to the way they were."*
>
> *—Bryan Herta*

Compound Choices. When choosing which tires to run, you have to consider the different rubber compounds that are available. The idea is to come up with a tire on race day that will get to its optimal temperature range given the conditions. If the racetrack is especially abrasive or the track temperature is high, or there's a combination of the two, the tire compound for the day may be a hard one. At the other extreme, if the racetrack is slick and the temperature is low, a softer compound would have a higher CF and be faster than the hard tire.

At the entry level end of the sport, most of us are spared these decisions. You run the tire that is available for sale or the tire mandated by the rules of the series you're running. Sometimes, if your budget is stretched, you run the ones you have on the car.

Percent Slip

Changes in CF change the potential of the car. We've been focusing on cornering force changes but as the grip of the tires change, so does the car's ability to brake and accelerate. A parameter that comes into play when we're talking about longitudinal forces like braking and accelerating is "percent slip." Percent slip is the longitudinal equivalent of slip angle.

As a tire is freely rolling across the surface of the road, its contact patch—that portion of the tire in contact with the road surface—is stationary relative to the road surface. At this point, there is 0% slip. In the brief moment when the rubber of the tire meets the asphalt of the road surface, they meet in a one-to-one relationship like a chain passing over a sprocket.

> *"The GTO car has big tires—a 14-inch tire width—and until they scrub, they lock incredibly easily with no feel whatsoever. It's so easy to flat-spot a tire in the first two laps. In the middle of the race when you pit, the next two laps after you leave the pits, it's just so easy to lock up a tire that you can't believe it—and not feel it. Instant. I did a bunch of them.*
>
> *"A flat-spotted tire will do the shake. Every time you brake from then on, it will stop again on the flat spot and grind off more rubber. If you keep doing it, it will grind it to the point where it will blow it out. If you flat-spot it once and then behave, it will, over some time, round itself back out, but you're stuck not being able to brake real hard for a long time."*
>
> —Dorsey Schroeder

If you graph the proportion of the tire's potential peak traction against percent slip (see Fig. 13-4), you find that the maximum value comes not at 0% slip as you might expect, but at around 15% slip. This fact, of course, has implications for how you think of using the car when you want to maximize either braking traction or acceleration traction.

In your everyday street driving, you would seldom (unless you're a real yahoo) use any slip under braking or accelerating, but if you want the lap record on the racetrack, you need to be able to flirt with percent slip under braking for the corner and on acceleration away from the turn.

In braking, you'll be looking for the level of pressure on the brake pedal that will make the tires continue to turn, but turn at a rate 15% slower than if the tires were freely rolling over the surface of the road. Push on the pedal too lightly and the slip rate is less than 15%, thereby using less traction than is available. No surprise: it will take longer to decelerate from straightaway speed to corner-entry speed than it would if you've developed the skill to use percent slip to optimize braking traction.

Of course, you can over use percent slip under braking. Push too hard on the brake pedal and the percent slip rate goes higher than 15% and traction is lost. The grossest error is pushing so hard on the

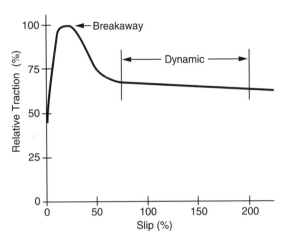

Fig. 13-4. Under braking or acceleration, the tire delivers its optimum traction at a certain range of % of slip and falls off on either side of the peak.

brake pedal that the tires stop rotating altogether. As "lockup" occurs, the tire loses 30% to 40% of its peak traction and a few nasty side effects occur. One is that with the tires locked up, you lose all lateral traction so that if you decide to turn the car, you're out of luck. The other major down side of lockup is that the road surface will grind a flat spot in the tire as it scrapes across the road. The flat spot may be minor on a hard street tire, but on a soft racing slick, it won't be long before that flat spot starts to make the tire feel square.

At the corner exit, where you're trying to use all the power and grip available to the car to accelerate down the following straight, you need to develop the skill to coordinate your right foot pressing down toward the floor on the throttle pedal with your hands unwinding

> *"When the tires go away, luckily, it's gradual and it's like the track going away from you. It's something that you have to experience over and over. At our level in Indy Car, the tire companies are always coming up with something new and they handle the temperature differently. Some are not so good when it's hot and sunny; some are good when they're cold, some not. When they start to go off, it's a general sensation of loss of grip and it usually shows up on the end of the car that's your weakness. If your car has a little bit of understeer or a little bit of oversteer, it usually goes that way first. The experience comes in really learning how to deal with that and how to nurse it."*
>
> —Danny Sullivan

the wheel—you want to drive the car away from the corner with a combination of optimum slip angle and optimum percent slip from the driving wheels. Big wheelspin at the corner exit defeats both aims.

CARING FOR TIRES

It's not a hard sell convincing drivers that tires are their important link to the racetrack and that the tires' grip ultimately determines how well their car will brake and corner, as well as—given enough horse-power—how well they accelerate. But they tend to forget. Before long, the latest suspension gimmick or hot engine tweak distracts their attention and the tires get taken for granted.

Let's look at some practical tips on how to keep the best rubber on your racecar while it's on the track.

Slicks

There are only two major types of tires that you are go-ing to have to deal with when you go racing. Show-room stock racing aside, most conventional road racing classes allow the use of slicks. In dry condi-tions, a slick tire allows the greatest amount of rubber to be in contact with the road surface at the contact patch, thereby creating the greatest grip.

We have no intention here of stepping on the toes of team managers, crew chiefs or race mechanics by filling their driver's heads with impractical ideas. However, there are facts about tires that drivers should know and, since many beginning drivers are also their own crew chief, the team will benefit by the sharing of knowledge.

Tires' Enemies

Time. A brand new race tire, fresh from the manufac-turer, is as good as it's ever going to be. Its ultimate traction will be available within the first few laps it is brought up to temperature, then its traction will fall back to a slightly lower level for the rest of its life.

The implications of this fact are scary. To try to put a car on the pole would require warming up the tire and putting in your blistering lap in the first three laps. Clearly, this type of activity is not the province of be-ginners. Even if you've practiced on used rubber, the traction—and the speed potential of the car—will be at a new limit. To take advantage of it, you'll need to take some risks guessing at the car's new potential.

A professional race driver *has* to take the risk and go for it since, at the professional level, the potential differences between drivers and teams is within a win-dow where the traction advantage of a new set of tires can make an important advantage in grid position. To not try to take the traction advantage in qualifying would be a major failing on the driver's part and would represent a real weakness in the driving part of the team effort. Below this level, since it's your hide at

> "In the Indy Light car, as soon as you went out in qualifying, you had about five good laps on the tires—boom—that's when you have to get with the program cause that's when they're the best."
>
> —Robbie Buhl

risk, you should decide whether a three-lap-flyer should be attempted.

U.V. Light. Once the tire has been run, care should be taken to keep the tire out of direct sunlight as much as possible. If you're in a racing situation with the appro-priate budget to discard a set of tires on the same weekend you purchased them, don't rush around try-ing to cover them up between sessions. But if you'll use the set the following race, don't leave them out-doors on the trailer rack for a month, letting the U.V. light eat away at the traction.

Debris. Many (probably most) drivers mount a set of slicks on the racecar and then drive them through the paddock all weekend through an incredible amount of junk—stones, safety wire, oil, gas— none of which does the tire any good at all. If you can, use a old worn-out set of tires to drive around the paddock, es-pecially if it's an unpaved paddock. The worst situa-tion is coming off the racetrack with the tires still hot. Everything sticks to them. Change back to the oldies before going back to your paddock area if you can.

Heat Cycles. Much has been made in amateur racing about the number of heat cycles—the cycles of tire heat-up and cool-down—a race tire can endure with-out a noticeable loss in traction. There isn't any hard data to support any definitive measure of how much (or if, for that matter) a tire loses traction when it's heated and cooled repeatedly. The general feeling is that a tire wears out before it gets heat cycled enough to matter, but remember that this information is based on experience with top amateur and professional teams which use tires once and chuck them.

Flat Spots. Tires are meant to be round. By storing your car on the tires you intend to run in the next event you are creating a flat spot on the contact patch side. Take the good rubber off between weekends and store the racecar on junk tires. Some people go so far as to take the race-rubber off between sessions, a de-fensible practice.

Leaks. Pressures should be checked again just before you go out on the racetrack—in other words, they should be checked an hour before the scheduled start of your session and *again* a half-hour later. Compar-ing the pressures can give you an indication of wheth-er you have a leak.

STREET TIRES

More and more types of racing are done on street tires. Why the move away from a pure racing tire? In the case of the SCCA showroom stock classes, it's in keeping with the concept of the class—competition between cars in highway trim. For many manufacturers, the rationale is to be able to showcase their products and carve out a niche in the profitable performance tire market.

For the Spec Racer and Skip Barber Formula Dodge 2000 series, there are multiple reasons for preferring street tires to slicks. Safety and durability are high on the list. If you take a tire that was designed for a 4000-lb. car and use it on a vehicle with only 1/3 to 1/4 of this mass, you can safely say that the tire is overdesigned for the application. The street tire is invariably made of a less hysteretic (less energy-absorbing) rubber compound than the slick and is consequently less prone to destructive overheating, especially when run on lightweight cars. The peak traction of a street radial won't approach that of a slick, but if all the cars in the field have essentially the same traction, the competition remains fierce, regardless of the lap time.

The cost advantage is real, especially for Spec Racer and Barber Formula Dodge 2000. Although the heavy showroom stock cars will go through street tires as fast as an all-out racecar will go through slicks, the lighter cars can run a set of tires in race after race without any deterioration in traction. The end result is less-expensive racing.

Street vs. Slick

The most noticeable difference between a racing slick and a street tire is its ultimate level of traction. A racing slick as used on the rear of a Formula Ford has a

peak CF of 1.75. The street tire used in the Formula Dodge series has a peak of 1.3. In a 200-foot radius corner the slick-shod racecar could go 72.4 m.p.h. at the cornering limit, whereas the same car with street rubber on would be at its limit at 62.4 m.p.h.—a 10-m.p.h. difference.

For the most part, a tire's rubber compound determines its grip. Pure racing tires are generally much softer than street radials since they have an intended life, at most, of a few hundred miles. Street tires that last over 40,000 miles have become common, and that longevity comes from a harder, more durable rubber compound. What you gain in longevity you lose in ultimate grip. A secondary advantage of a harder compound tire is that its traction doesn't vary as much over the course of its life as it would for a pure racing tire.

Ultimate grip is the most obvious difference between street tires and racing tires, but there are several other important aspects of variable CF which make a big difference in the way the car will behave at its cornering limit.

Size of the Optimum Slip Angle. Fig. 13-5 shows how the CF of a tire responds to changes in slip angle. The curve for a racing slick shows that it has its peak traction at a very modest 5 degrees of slip; but a street radial's traction peak comes at greater slip angles. This means that the car with the street radials can be driven at higher yaw angles in cornering than the car with slicks.

The general rule is that the narrower and taller the tire, the greater the slip angles that provide maximum traction. Your sense of the correct amount of yaw to use when cornering has to vary with the type of tire used on the racecar. The driver of a car on slicks would try to be more tidy with the yaw angle of the car under cornering than if he or she were driving the same car on production tires.

Range of Good Grip. Looking again at the graph of the slick, Fig. 13-5, you can see that its best CF range is very narrow—between 3 and 6 degrees—before it loses more than 10% of its grip. You need to be very accurate and consistent in the amount of cornering yaw you use with this type of tire. The tire is good, but demanding. The street radial, however, has a wider range of usable slip angle and is more forgiving of inconsistencies in the degree of slide you use. Its slip angle range goes from 2.5 degrees to 9.5 degrees before you lose 10% of the grip available.

Peakiness. The fact that the traction falls off when the best slip angle is exceeded affects the drivability of the tire. A gentle, gradual fall-off of traction makes it easier to exceed the limit and not lose control. Typically, a slick racing tire has a more gradual loss of grip past its

> "When tires 'go off,' you can definitely feel it and it depends on the tires and it depends on the type of car. The Barber Formula Ford cars with the street radial tires—I've never felt the tire go off. They're very consistent. I think, generally, the harder the compound the more consistent the tire is.
>
> "Even in Barber Saab I never felt that the tires really went off during a race. There were certain tracks like Mid Ohio where it was very hot one year, where in qualifying if you would cool your tires for a lap you could get a little extra grip until they heated back up—that usually took about 3/4 of a lap. In those instances, where they're fairly hard compounds, it makes for a nicer, more consistent car. I think drivers always like consistency in tires."
>
> —Bryan Herta

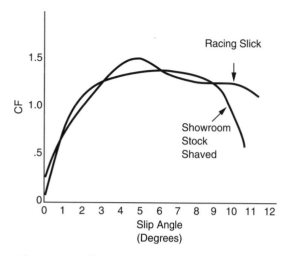

Fig. 13-5. Different tires respond to changes in slip angle in different ways. Here, in a comparison between a slick and a shaved street tire, you can see that the peak traction and the range of the peak vary.

peak than a street radial, making it more forgiving as you exceed the peak slip angle.

A tire with a sharp decline after the peak in its curve will yield plenty of traction at the peak but, as the slip angle increases, the grip falls off dramatically. Today's high-performance street radial tires are not all that peaky, but as a rule they're worse than slicks.

In Fig. 13-5, you can see how the CF of the street radial falls off much more dramatically than the slick. Early on in our Formula Ford series, we used a radial street tire that had terrific grip—up to a point. At 7 to 10 degrees of slip, it was a fast, grippy tire, but get a little too sideways coming into the corner and you were history. The tire operated in a narrow range of optimum traction and also had a sharp dropoff. Today's Michelin Pilot series of street radials, for example, has a much broader range of workable slip angles but the phenomenon of a steep dropoff in CF at higher slip angle ranges still exists.

Feel. The feel of the tire involves more than just the angle where it reaches its peak CF. Your perception of how responsive a tire is has much to do with how quickly the tire transmits steering wheel input into a change of direction. Relative to a slick, a street radial creates forces more slowly, partially because of decisions made by the tire manufacturer. Tire designers can spice up the responsiveness of a street radial to make an enthusiast happy but, for the average driver, such a tire would make their car feel nervous and darty. The end result is that most street radials will give you a smooth and progressive buildup of cornering force which, to a driver used to racing on slicks, feels relatively sloppy—kind of like driving a racecar injected with novocaine.

Another reason for the difference in feel is a difference in aspect ratios. Aspect ratio is the ratio between the height of the tire's sidewall and the width of the tire's tread. Tires with a high aspect ratio, like the 78s your grandmother used on her '48 Dodge, had a lot of sidewall which could deflect when you turned the steering wheel, making the car respond very slowly—turning was like changing the course of a glacier.

A tire with a low aspect ratio has less sidewall relative to the tread width and therefore transmits forces from the wheel rim to the contact patch more directly and faster, making the tire feel more responsive to your commands.

Percent Slip. Under braking or under acceleration the typical street radial reaches peak grip at smaller percentages of slip than slicks.

In showroom stock racing the limiting factor in braking is usually the braking system of the car and not the tire's hold on the road. Threshold braking in showroom stock is limited to qualifying or the well-timed outbraking maneuver executed after conserving the brakes. In cars with durable braking systems, drivers should expect that they will have a narrower window of acceptable brake pedal pressures which will keep the car near its peak performance; but because of the street tires' lower traction, relaxing brake pressure to get a locked wheel turning again will take a greater change than it will for a slick-shod car.

Durability. Street tires have a lot of advantages in the durability department. They are much more resistant to damage from debris than slicks, hold air much longer, and, especially on light cars, don't flat-spot as easily. Also, because they are treaded, a sudden rain shower isn't as disastrous as it can be on slicks.

Tread. Obviously, a major difference between street tires and slicks is that street tires have tread and slicks don't. The tread on a street tire is there because of the real-world possibilities of rain or snow. When you're running on slicks and the road surface starts to get wet, the tires still grip for a while—as long as they can squeegee enough water out of the way so that part of the still-warm contact patch can touch asphalt. But as you saw in Chapter 12, when the volume of water becomes great enough than it can't get out of the way of the descending contact patch, it forms a barrier between the tire and the road instead. By that time, the party's over—you're hydroplaning and your tires have no grip at all. Even driving slowly down the straight becomes an adventure.

Cars running on slicks will change to rain tires under these conditions and, on the surface, racing rain tires have the familiar tread patterns you're used to seeing on street tires. Although racing rain tires *look* like street tires, they share little more than the fact that they use tread to evacuate water from ahead of the contact patch.

Given the lubricating and cooling affect of water on the tire, a much softer compound can be run on a rain tire; and even in the limited friction of wet conditions, it will reach an optimum temperature of 200 degrees Fahrenheit or more. The problem with a soft compound rain tire is that the friction between the road surface and the tire can get too high, creating excess heat just like the full depth street tire in the dry.

Clearly, you want your street tires to still have grip when the weather gets crummy, so you're committed to having tread on the tire. Most new tires are delivered with a tread depth of between 15/32 and 13/32 of an inch. In the rain, these deep grooves leave plenty of room for even deep water to be channelled away from the contact patch, and in a showroom stock rain race, they would be the tire of choice.

The problem is that this depth of tread allows the individual tread blocks to move around a lot, especially when subjected to the large side forces generated in racing. This motion of the tread blocks produces enough heat to start breaking down the bonding of the tread blocks to the body of the tire. Given enough abuse, the most highly-stressed tread blocks begin to part company with the body of the tire—a phenomenon called chunking. Very bad, but not the tire company's fault. After all, you're using the tire in an application it wasn't designed for. One way to reduce the motion of the tread, and the heat generated, is to reduce the size and compliancy of the tread blocks by shaving the tread depth down from 13/32 to, say, 5/32 before using the tire on the racecar.

Shaving the tire not only reduces the temperature of the tire and eliminates chunking, but it increases the CF of the tire. Showroom stock tires are typically run at tread depths between 5/32 inches and bald. In our testing we have found that the CF differences from 5/32 inches on down are inconsequential.

THE BASIC RULES FOR TIRES

We have by no means covered all there is to know about tires, but the following key points apply as a general set of rules for tires and their usage.

- A tire's grip responds in direct proportion to how hard it is pushing down on the road surface. The driver, through manipulation of the controls, can change the loading on the corners of the car.
- A tire is temperature-sensitive. Run it too cold or too hot and it will have less than optimum grip.
- A tire's grip deteriorates with time and exposure to ultraviolet light.
- Under cornering, a tire's peak traction occurs at a particular slip angle. Corner the car at this angle and cornering speed can be maximized. Use too much or too little slip angle and you will have less available traction.
- Under braking and acceleration, the tire's peak traction occurs at a particular percentage of slip. Keeping the tire at this threshold allows you to maximize braking and accelerating forces.

Although all tires follow these general rules, the optimal temperatures, slip angles, and percentages of slip of various types of tires will vary from application to application. A technique or style of driving that may be the best for one type of tire may not be the best for another.

CHAPTER 14

CHASSIS ADJUSTMENTS

THERE IS A HUGE AMOUNT of confusion in the air about chassis set-up and tuning. While there are admittedly many aspects of set-up that vary from car to car, there are some basic facts that are universal; they're a good starting point for understanding the types of simple adjustments that can be made to help improve your racecar's performance.

> **Common chassis adjustments can result in a better, faster car if you know the difference between reality and myth when it comes to racecar set-up.**

LOAD TRANSFER

First, some basic facts about grip. The most fundamental rule for you to remember is that the amount of grip generated by a tire varies with how hard it is pushing down on the road's surface. More download delivers more grip. Where the download comes from doesn't matter. If the tire is loaded by air flowing over wings, for example, it gets more potential grip which you use to create more cornering force, braking force, or, if the tire is on a driven wheel, more accelerating traction.

The tire can also be loaded by the effect of inertia as you decelerate, accelerate or corner. Under braking, for example, deceleration transfers load off the rear tires onto the fronts. The fronts, since they are more highly loaded, have more traction than they did under acceleration. When the braking system of a racecar is designed and adjusted, a key consideration is the increased grip available to the front tires because of the increased download. Brake bias adjustments are an attempt to adapt the braking system of the car so that the braking effort is proportioned correctly to use the different levels of grip available to the front versus the rear tires.

METHODS OF CHANGING BIAS

The mechanical means by which you can change brake bias fall into two major categories. One method works by limiting the pressure available to the rear brakes, the end that typically requires less braking force. An adjustable pressure-limiting valve is in-stalled in the hydraulic line that feeds the rear brakes; and by adjusting the pressure, you can assure that the rear tires are doing a level of braking that is consistent with the amount of download on the tires under heavy deceleration.

The more common method uses separate brake master cylinders for the front and rear pairs of calipers. Each master cylinder is independently attached to the brake pedal: one on the left side of center, one on the right side. The attachment points are at the ends of a threaded bar, called the bias bar, which runs through the center of a metal tube attached to the lower end of the brake pedal. A spherical bearing at the center of the bias bar is in sliding contact with the inside of the tube; and it is at this point where the pressure from the ball of your foot on the brake pedal gets transmitted to the bias bar, then out to each master cylinder.

If the bias bar is adjusted so that the bearing is exactly in the center of the tube, 50% of the pressure on the brake pedal goes to the front master cylinder and 50% goes to the rear. By turning the threaded bias bar and moving the position of the bearing relative to the center, you change the proportion of pedal pressure that goes to each master cylinder.

Setting Bias

Since setting the brake bias is one of the first mechanical adjustments you will make to a racecar, you should know how brake bias works. The routine for preparing the car before setting bias is to first run it for a few laps, getting to the point where the tires are up to temperature. If you set the bias when the tires are cold and the grip is less than you'd experience under racing conditions, there will be less download on the fronts than there will be when everything is warm. Then you are likely to have too little braking at the front and too much at the rear when things finally heat up. This rear-bias situation can get overly exciting, so it's something you should avoid.

Once everything is warm, you should do a series of straight-line stops, off-line, after carefully checking the mirrors to avoid being run over. From high speed, squeeze the pedal on and continue adding braking pressure until either a front wheel or rear wheel gets just to the edge of lockup. In an open-wheel car, you should be able to notice the strobe-like effect of the tires slipping across the road and relax some pressure to keep them from locking. If, however, they lock anyway, modulate out of lockup as quickly as possible to save flat spots.

In open-wheel cars, feel free to use your eyes to confirm what you're feeling through the seat of your pants. Seeing front bias is easy—usually a car will have a slight tendency to lock either the right or left side slightly before the other and, after a stop or two, you can focus on that tire to see what it's doing. With rear bias, focus the mirrors on the rear tires while doing the brake testing to confirm the physical sensations of rear bias (the rear darts around during braking). In closed-wheel cars you have to trust your sensitivity and back it up with evidence of puffs of smoke out of the wheel wells.

With either type of car, you are aiming to get the brake bias adjusted so that the fronts begin to lock marginally sooner than the rears. You would rather have a little excess bias toward the front because it is the more stable of the two extremes. Going too far to the front, however, will compromise the overall braking ability of the car.

Bias and the Clutch. When testing the brake bias, you want to be decelerating the car the same way you would under racing conditions. In most cases of threshold braking, the car will be decelerating in gear with the clutch engaged, except for the moments when you dip the clutch for the downshifts. In this case, the brake bias should be set by braking the car with the clutch engaged. In most cases, the engine compression, especially with a high compression motor with a light flywheel, is contributing to the braking effort of the rear pair of tires. If you set the brake bias with the clutch disengaged, you'll end up with too much rear bias if you slow the car with the help of the engine during the race.

Some drivers, however, choose to threshold brake their cars with the clutch in or with the car in neutral. A common example of a car appropriate for this technique is a Formula Atlantic car, which has over three Gs of braking capability. It slows down *fast*—so fast, in fact, that many Atlantic drivers find that they can't move the gear lever fast enough to keep up with the car's changing speed. In these cars, you often skip gears, popping the gear lever into neutral when the braking begins and completing the downshift just before turn-in. If, under racing conditions, you decelerate *without* the engine's help, then the brake bias should be set under the same conditions.

Brake-turn Bias. Once the bias is close in straight-line stops, it's time to try it under simultaneous braking and turning conditions. If there is any possibility that the bias is too far to the rear, it will show up here. You may find that a bias that was perfect for straight-line braking will be biased a little too much to the rear for comfort under brake-turning. Under the combination of pitch and roll, which takes place while braking and turning, the inside rear tire is substantially unloaded and the drag of the rear brakes contributes to the rear losing cornering traction, allowing the rear of the car to slide slightly more than the front.

It is better to discover this problem in a test situation than on the first lap of the race. Anticipate that if there is a lot of aggressive braking and turning needed at a particular racetrack, the bias may end up a turn or two more toward the front.

Driver-Adjustable Bias. Setting the bias with a system where the mechanic has to adjust the number of turns of the bias bar will require a number of trips in and out of the pits, warming up the tires each time you go out. A better system for setting bias, and one found on more and more cars, is a driver-adjustable knob on the dash that is connected by cable to the bias bar. You can then do your own bias adjustments in one trip out onto the racetrack.

If you're running race tires that lose a portion of their grip for each cycle of heat-up and cool-down, this driver-adjustable bias can save many sets of tires over the course of a season. Another advantage of the driver-adjustable system is that you can readjust the bias if conditions change during the course of the race. Of course, there are crew chiefs who think that this system is as much a liability as an asset.

LONGITUDINAL LOAD TRANSFER

Longitudinal load transfer occurs when loads transfer fore and aft. Under acceleration, load transfers rearward. Under deceleration, load transfers to the front. Contrary to popular belief, you can't change the amount of load transferred by adjusting shocks, springs, anti-rollbars, or by varying anti-dive or anti-squat geometry. The amount of load transferred to the front under braking is determined by three things: 1) the height of the car's center of gravity (a car with a high CG will transfer more load than one with a low CG), 2) the wheel base of the car (a short wheelbase car will transfer more load than a longer wheel base car), and 3) how fast the car is decelerating (a car decelerating at 3 Gs will transfer more load than one decelerating at 1 G).

Center of Gravity

First, a quick definition of CG (Center of Gravity): think of it as the balance point of the car, the one point in space where if you lifted the car with a cable it would remain perfectly level, not falling off to the front or rear or from side to side. In the illustrations in Fig. 14-1, we hung the car three different ways from the rafters by a cable attached to the CG. The car doesn't roll or sway, even when you flip it on its side and hang it, as long as the cable is attached to the car's center of gravity.

In technical terms, the CG represents the point where the mass of the car is concentrated. The importance of the CG is that all the inertial forces you create in cornering, braking and accelerating act through this central point.

Let's look at the effect of CG on braking load transfer when the wheelbase and the level of deceleration are kept constant. Both cars in Fig. 14-2 have the same wheelbase and are decelerating at, for the sake of example, 1 G. In both cases the deceleration exerts a 200-lb. force acting on the CG.

In the car on the top, with a high CG, the vertical lever arm from the ground up to the CG is equal to the distance from the CG to the front tire contact patch. 200 lbs. of force at the CG creates 200 lbs. of download on the front tires. In the car on the bottom, where the CG height is half the height of the other car's CG, 200 lbs. of force at the CG only results in 100 lbs. of download on the fronts.

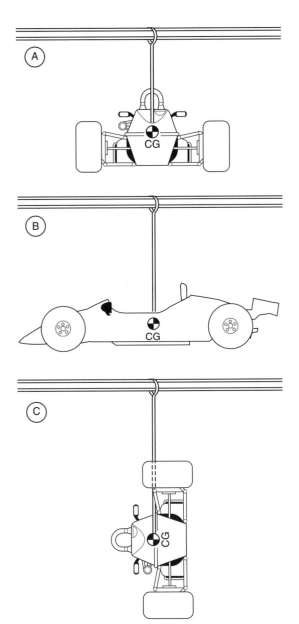

Fig. 14-1. Picture the CG as the balance point of the car where its mass is centered (A) right to left, (B) fore and aft and (C) top to bottom.

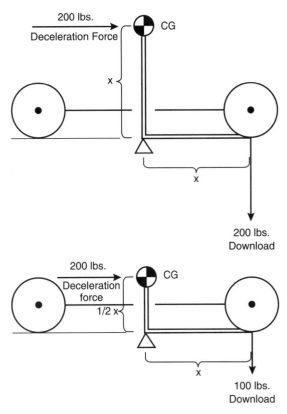

Fig. 14-2. If the level of deceleration is constant, the amount of load transferred under braking will vary depending upon the height of the CG.

The Wheelbase

Now, let's freeze the CG height and vary the wheelbase. In Fig. 14-3, the car on the top with a short wheelbase has a lever arm from the ground to the CG equal to that of the distance from the CG to the contact patch. 200 lbs. of force at the CG results in 200 lbs. of load on the front tires.

In the car on the bottom with a wheelbase twice as long as the car on the top, the distance from CG to

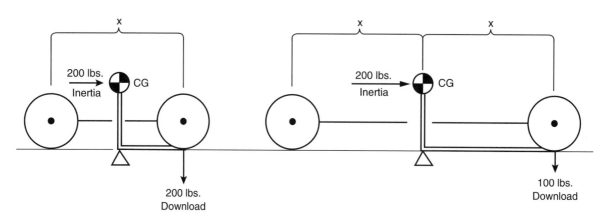

Fig. 14-3. The second variable determining the amount of load transfer under braking is the length of the wheelbase.

contact patch is twice the height of the CG so that a 200-lb. force at the CG converts to 100 lbs. of download on the fronts.

Rate of Deceleration

My old physics professor used to begin each class by saying, "Old Newton he say, F equals M A" (Force = Mass x Acceleration). A car braking at 2 Gs creates twice as much inertial force as one braking at 1 G. You could reduce the amount of load transferred by using less deceleration force, but that's shooting yourself in the foot. You'll have to take as a given that you're trying to maximize the rate of deceleration.

ADJUSTMENTS UNDER BRAKING

The most common misconception about chassis adjustments is that you can change the *total* load transfer under braking with adjustments other than CG height and wheelbase. You can't.

But you do want to reduce load transfer because although grip increases with load, as a tire gets more heavily loaded, it gets less and less efficient at making this conversion (the technical measurement of a tire's ability to convert vertical load into grip is called the tire's coefficient of friction, or CF). Although modern race tires have improved steadily in this area, it is still a good rule of thumb that you would like to minimize, if you can, the transfer of load created by inertia. You do it in the fore and aft direction by making the CG low and the wheelbase as long as is practical.

You can't easily change the *amount* of load that goes from rear to front under hard braking. You *can*, however, change two aspects of the load transfer: 1) how much the suspension moves in response to the change in loading, and 2) how quickly the load gets to the tire contact patch.

Springs

With soft springs on the front of the car, transferring 200 lbs. to the front under braking might lower the

nose, let's say, 2 inches. Installing stiffer springs in front may limit the change in ride height to 1 inch. The load is the same, it's just the reaction to the load that changes—the front moves down less. If you wanted to keep the front from dipping at all, you could weld the front suspension solid and there would be no ride-height change in response to the 200-lb. load. The load still gets there no matter what you do. The springs determine how much the suspension moves in response to the load.

Shocks

Shock absorbers or, more properly, dampers, have the primary function of helping to control the energy stored up by the springs. A spring is a remarkable depository of energy. When the spring is compressed by a bump or a change in the load on the spring, it stores the energy of the initial motion and feeds much of it back in the opposite direction. Without control, the spring would go through a number of cycles of compressing and extending in response to its first deflection, losing a little energy with each cycle. In a racecar, just picture the motions of the suspension and the changes in load at the tire contact patch if the springs were allowed to go uncontrolled (undamped) every time they encountered a bump or a change in inertial loading. The car would be bouncing all over the place and be, for the most part, uncontrollable.

Shocks Resist Motion. Shocks on their own don't support weight as a spring does. Springs are commonly described as having a "rate": that is, a particular force that it takes to compress the spring a given distance. A 200-lb. per inch spring, for example, requires 200 lbs. of force to compress it one inch. In contrast, shock absorbers take relatively little force to compress or extend—if you do it slowly. When the velocity of the motion goes up, the shock absorber's resistance to motion increases.

Now, adding a shock absorber to a spring suspension doesn't support any additional load while the car is standing still. The car will settle to the same ride height as it did without the shock in the system. But when the suspension is set into motion, the way the shock resists being extended or compressed has a substantial effect on the car's handling.

Bump and Rebound. The shock has resistance to motion in two directions. It resists compression (making it shorter), and it resists extension (making it longer). When some force acts on the suspension system to compress the spring, it also compresses the shock. When the shock compresses, it's called "going into bump." If a load is removed from the suspension, the spring gets longer and the shock extends—a state known as "going into rebound." On many racing shock absorbers, both the bump and rebound resistance of the shocks are adjustable.

Speed of Load Transfer and Motion. With a shock absorber in the system, if there is very little resistance to compression, the load gets to the tire relatively slowly, more like the way it did without a shock in the system. If the shock has a lot of resistance to compression, the load gets to the tire quicker, essentially bypassing the spring and going directly through the shock. Ultimately, the shock setting doesn't determine *how much* load gets to the tire or how much the suspension moves in response to the load. It alters the *speed* with which the load gets to the contact patch and the speed with which the suspension moves in response to loads fed into it.

A stiffer bump setting slows down the motion on its corner and speeds up the load transfer. A softer bump setting does the opposite—it allows the suspension to move faster and spreads the changes in loading out over a longer period of time.

The same is true in the rebound mode. Stiff rebound settings will force the suspension system to move more slowly when loads are removed from its corner of the car, but the unloading of the contact patch will be more abrupt. Softer rebound settings allow the suspension to move more quickly and the unloading of the contact patch happens more gradually.

LATERAL LOAD TRANSFER

When a car generates cornering force, it is actually accelerating the car sideways (laterally). When this happens, inertia resists the car's change of direction and exerts a force toward the outside of the turn through the CG. You can control the force and with it the amount of load transferred off the inside tires and onto the outside pair, but not in ways that you might think. Just as in braking, the amount of load transferred depends upon the height of the CG, the track width of the chassis (rather than the wheelbase), and the force exerted at the CG (cornering force).

CG Height

In Fig. 14-4, both cars have the same track—they're both the same width, tire center to tire center. The one on the top has a higher CG. In this case, the CG height is equal to the distance from the centerline to the contact patch (x). If 200 lbs. of force is exerted at the CG, 200 lbs. of force pushes down on the outside tire.

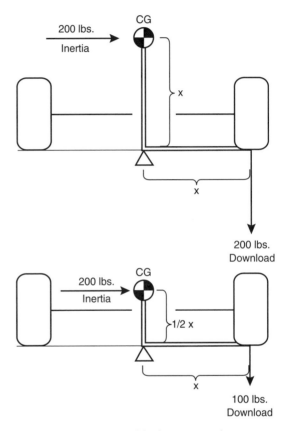

Fig. 14-4. One variable determining the amount of load transfer under cornering is the height of the car's CG.

The car on the bottom has a lower CG height, in this case half as high as the other car. When 200 lbs. of force is exerted by inertia at the CG, only 100 lbs. of force loads the outside tire. The effect on the inside tires is the opposite—they are unloaded by inertial force exerted at the CG.

Track Width

If you keep the CG constant and change the track width, you can alter the load transfer. The car on the left (see Fig. 14-5) with the narrow track would transfer all 200 lbs. of inertial force into the tire, since the lever arms are equal.

Widen the track so that, in the case of the car on the right, the distance from the centerline to the con-

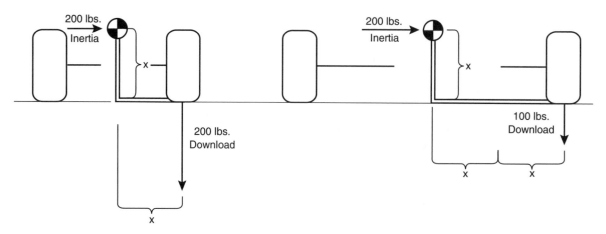

Fig. 14-5. The second variable affecting lateral load transfer is the car's track width.

tact patch is twice the CG height (x), and the same 200-lb. force results in only 100 lbs. of load transfer.

Cornering Force
You can also alter the lateral load transfer by reducing the inertial load at the CG, using lower cornering forces. You'd *never* do that, though—lower cornering force means lower cornering speed.

Why Make Changes?
The key is that, short of changing the track width, wheelbase, or the height of the CG, there's nothing you can do to change the total amount of load transferred due to deceleration, cornering or acceleration. What you *can* do is adjust the car to accommodate the loading change, so that it gives the car its best performance potential. In braking, this means having both the front and rear tires do their appropriate share of the braking effort by getting the brake bias right. "Right" means that you avoid asking the front or the rear pair of tires to do more than their fair share of the work. If the rear tires are asked to provide braking force all out of proportion to their download and grip, the car won't decelerate as well as it could.

In cornering, the same concept is true. The front and rear pair of tires have to contribute to the car's change of direction in proportion to the loads they have to absorb.

If either end of the car has to provide more than its fair share of the effort, the car's handling will suffer. If the outside front tire has to deal with the bulk of the cornering load transfer, its grip will be overtaxed and the car will understeer. If an undue proportion of the load transfer is dealt to the rear tires their grip will be compromised and the rear of the car will slide excessively—the always-entertaining state of oversteer. You want to limit the car's overall load transfer by running a low and wide car to keep the tires in the best CF range, giving you the best performance.

Still, no matter what you do to the car's design, it's going to transfer load from inside to outside during cornering. You can try to minimize it, but you can't eliminate it. And, since you're always going to try to maximize the cornering force, the only real variables when it comes to designing the car are track width and CG height.

CORNERING ADJUSTMENTS

After the designer is through with the car, you can still easily lower the CG by lowering the car's ride height, front or rear. The lower CG would reduce the total load transfer, but you only want to run the car low enough so that, throughout its normal range of pitching and rolling motions, you don't have the chassis itself slam down onto the racetrack. If this happens, the download on the tires will suddenly fall and awful things happen to the handling, so you keep the chassis as low as possible without bottoming out.

Let's look at a hypothetical car and see what's happening load-wise in cornering at the limit. Sitting still in the pit lane, the car in Fig. 14-6 weighs 1000 lbs.: 400 lbs. is supported by the front tires and 600 lbs. by the rear tires. This particular car happens to be symmetrical. Its left side weighs as much as the right side. Its total 1000 lbs. is distributed evenly: 500 on the left and 500 on the right.

At 1 G of cornering force, the CG and the track width are such that 200 lbs. of load is going to be transferred off the inside tires onto the outside tires. On the right in Fig. 14-7, the outside tires under cornering are now loaded with 700 lbs. of download while the inside pair have only 300 lbs. of download on them.

You can, by making some simple adjustments, determine which tire—the outside front or the outside rear—absorbs more of this transferred load. There are three areas of adjustment: spring rates, anti-roll bars,

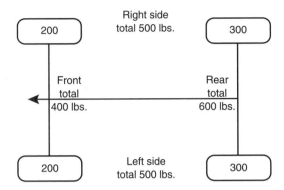

Fig. 14-6. In a symmetrically set-up racecar, both front tires will have equal load, as will both rear tires. The total load on the right side of the car equals the total load on the left.

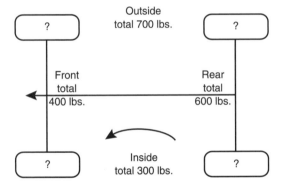

Fig. 14-7. In this hypothetical situation, the height of the CG and the track width are such that at maximum cornering to the left, 200 lbs. of load are transferred off the left pair of tires onto the right pair.

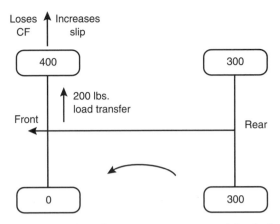

Fig. 14-8. If the front suspension were solid, all of the 200 lbs of load transfer would be absorbed by the right front tire. The front suffers a loss in CF and the car understeers.

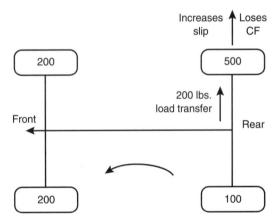

Fig. 14-9. If the rear suspension were solid, all of the 200 lbs. of load transfer would be absorbed by the right rear tire. Consequently, the rear suffers a loss in CF and the car oversteers.

and altering the roll center by raising or lowering the car's ride height at either end.

Springs

To illustrate how spring rates affect the cornering balance of the car, let's go to an extreme and see what happens. In Fig. 14-8, the front springs and shocks were removed and replaced by solid bars, essentially making the front suspension solid.

As you can see in Fig. 14-8, when the car corners and the load transfers, all of the 200 lbs. of extra load will be absorbed by the outside front tire (assuming an infinitely rigid chassis), since the front end resists all the rolling motion of the car. The outside rear tire doesn't contribute to any of this and consequently retains 100% of its original grip. The outside front, because of all this extra load, suffers a loss in CF relative to the rear and as a result operates at higher slip angle than the rear tire will. The car goes into understeer—in this case, probably pretty gross understeer—as the outside front is hopelessly overtaxed.

Now, let's put the shock/spring unit back on the front of the car and make the rear suspension solid. Under cornering, as you can see in Fig. 14-9, all the load transfer goes to the outside rear tire, causing the rear end to operate at higher slip angles—the definition of oversteer.

What you're seeing here is the world's stiffest spring, one with a spring rate of a million pounds per inch, or so. Nobody would really do this to a poor car, but it helps to illustrate the principle. All other things equal, a stiffer spring will increase the resistance to roll and absorb more of the load transfer at the end of the car on which it is installed. At the front, going to a stiffer spring (higher spring rate) will increase understeer. Going to a softer spring (lower spring rate) will decrease the roll resistance of the front, moving the cornering balance away from understeer.

At the rear, a stiffer spring increases the tendency toward oversteer, while a softer one goes in the opposite direction, decreasing the oversteer tendency and increasing the tendency toward understeer.

A quick caution about springs: while a softer spring should increase the relative grip of that end of the car, you have to keep in mind how the additional roll allowed by the softer spring affects the grip of the tire. Some suspension designs will be more sensitive to roll than others, and beyond a specific point, will start doing bad things to the contact patch. In an effort to improve grip by softening the spring rate, you might result in losing grip due to the suspension's inability to deal with roll.

These guidelines also don't take into account the effect of aerodynamics which is so critical to many high-tech modern cars. In cars and speeds where downforce plays a predominant role in the cornering balance of the car, the springs play a major role in keeping the attitude of the bottom of the car in a range that creates balanced downforce.

Anti-Roll Bars

Most cars set up for racetrack use have anti-roll bars at both the front and back ends of the car. Adjusting the anti-roll bars has the same effect on the car as changing the springs—it alters the roll resistance at the end of the car at which you make the change.

The anti-roll bars have no effect on the car when it transfers load fore and aft (longitudinally) as a result of deceleration or acceleration. The bars are free to pivot and create no resistance when both the left and right sides of the suspension move in the same direction with the same force, as they do in straight-line braking or acceleration.

Anti-roll bars only resist motion when the car rolls. You can think of anti-roll bars as springs that only work when the car rolls. There are two major ways anti roll bars create this resistance to roll. The first is purely leverage-based. The round bar is mounted to the chassis so that it is free to move when the suspension moves. Under braking, a front bar will simply rotate up as the suspension compresses (goes into bump) and both sides of the suspension move equally.

When cornering loads are introduced, the car rolls to the outside. The inside suspension droops relative to the chassis and the outside compresses. When this happens, the bar is twisted. The outside portion of the bar bends up and the inside part bends down. The bar itself is acting as a torsion bar, resisting being twisted, thereby creating resistance to the roll.

Adjusting Anti-Roll Bars

You can change the amount of resistance the anti-roll bar gives by changing the diameter of the bar, but that's time consuming. The easiest way is to change the lever arm that's acting on the bar. The distance from the point where the bar pivots on its mount to

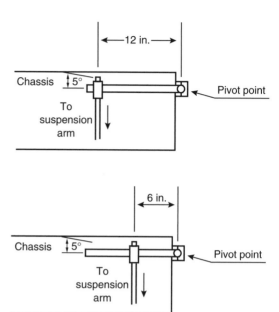

Fig. 14-10. The shorter the lever arm of a conventional anti roll bar, the greater the resistance to roll. This end of the car, front or rear, absorbs more load transfer and loses traction relative to the other end.

the chassis, to the point on the bar that is connected by a link to a suspension arm, determines its resistance. The greater this distance, the lower the resistance to roll. The smaller the distance, the greater the roll resistance.

For example, you can see in Fig. 14-10 that it will take half as much force to bend the bar 5 degrees if the force is exerted 12 inches from the pivot point than it would if you moved the adjuster to 6 inches from the pivot point. Moving the adjuster so as to make the lever arm smaller makes the bar stiffer, increasing the roll resistance and increasing the amount of load transfer that this end of the car must absorb. Moving the adjuster so that the lever arm is longer makes the bar softer, reducing the load transfer absorbed by the outside tire.

The effects are interrelated. Let's say that you have a car that understeers and you'd like to adjust it out by changing bar settings. You have two choices. You could adjust the front bar so that it creates less roll resistance or you could adjust the rear bar so that it creates more roll resistance. Lowered roll resistance in the front would force the rear to resist the roll motion more, putting more of the lateral load transfer on the outside rear tire. By lowering the roll resistance the car is going to roll more, given the same cornering forces as before. This may or may not be okay—problems can crop up. One such problem is the ride height: if the car is running very low, as you would like in order to lower the CG, extra roll would allow the outside front of the chassis to get closer to the ground, maybe even hit the ground. If it does bottom, any gain in grip from the bar adjustment might be lost by unloading the fronts when the chassis bottoms.

Harmful effects on the tire contact patch are another big problem. As a car rolls, the geometry of the suspension can be such that the camber stays within a range that the tire likes—up to a certain amount of roll. Past this point, however, the tire might suddenly lose traction. Allowing the car to roll more might also get you to the limit of the suspension's movement and when it goes solid, it washes out immediately. There are more considerations, but you get the idea—everything is more complicated than it appears.

With all these tales of horror, you may be thinking that you should never use a softer bar, but as long as the potential problems are recognized, there's no reason to avoid less roll resistance. In fact, a car that is allowed to have more suspension motion as load transfers laterally will load the outside tires more gradually since it takes time to move the suspension. The transitions will be less abrupt. The car will feel more like it bends into corners rather than darting into them. Also, if the racetrack is a bumpy one, any bumps encountered in the corner will act on a softer suspension than if the car had greater roll resistance.

Blade Adjusters

Many cockpit-adjustable anti-roll bars use a blade adjuster instead of a movable adjuster that slides along a round bar. Blade adjusters work by rotating a blade so that its cross section, and thereby its resistance to deflection, changes. The blade, or sometimes blades, are actually the lever arms of an ordinary anti-roll bar. The bar itself is mounted to the chassis the same way as an ordinary bar is mounted, and it resists being twisted when the car rolls.

When the blade lies flat, as in diagram A (see Fig. 14-11), the lever arm has less resistance to suspension

movement than it does when it is adjusted by rotating it as it appears in diagram B (see Fig. 14-11). The resistance varies as you adjust it between the two extremes. It's a slick system, but it's full of surprises.

Bars are the easiest adjustment you can make to the roll resistance of either end of the car and therefore are the devices most often used to trim the handling of the chassis in situations where aerodynamics don't come into play.

Roll Centers

The roll center for a suspension system is the point around which its end of the car rolls. It is determined by the suspension geometry—the lengths of the upper and lower arms, the location of the pickup points on the chassis, the track width—all kinds of geometric relationships between the tire contact patch and the chassis. For your purposes as a driver, you don't have to get involved in the details of this quagmire. It's enough for you to know that the height of the roll center also affects the roll resistance of the suspension system. Both the front and rear of the car have different roll centers and each moves as the suspension moves. All you need to know, for now, is that a higher roll center increases the roll resistance of the suspension and a lower roll center decreases the roll resistance. The simplest way to affect roll center is with ride height. The lower you run the ride height, the lower the roll center will be. Higher ride height raises the roll center.

In practical terms, if you were at the end of your range of adjustment with anti-roll bars and there wasn't time to change springs, adjusting the ride height (and thereby the roll center) could help you alter the roll resistance of either end of the car. Lowering the ride height on one end of the car would be the equivalent of softening the anti-roll bar or softening the spring rate at that end. Increasing the ride height

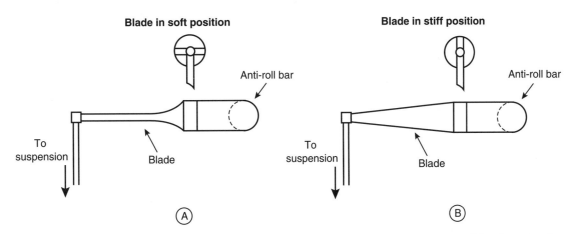

Fig. 14-11. A blade adjuster attached to an anti-roll bar changes the resistance to roll by changing the amount of force it takes to deflect the blade.

is akin to stiffening the anti-roll bars or going to a higher spring rate.

Shock Absorbers In Cornering

You can trim the cornering balance of the car by changing shock settings, but remember that shocks affect the car most in transition, when the suspension moves in response to new loads that deflect it. The relative resistance to motion of the shocks will affect the balance of the car most in the period of time when it's rolling into its cornering attitude. Once the cornering loads stabilize, the springs, bars and roll centers affect the balance to a greater degree.

For example, if the front shocks are much stiffer in bump than the rear, the outside front tire may be over-stressed relative to the rear and create understeer on the turn-in to the corner. Once the initial compression of the suspension takes place (assuming that aerodynamic download isn't the overriding factor), the bars, springs, and roll centers will establish the car's steady state balance.

It's best to think of shocks as a potential tool for adjusting the handling, if the car is changing its characteristics briefly when you make a change in the loading. Shocks are especially important in cornering situations where there are big differences between corner approach speed and the speed at the apex.

If the corner is slow, the change from decelerating and turning to accelerating and turning is going to happen over a shorter period of time. The loads are constantly going through transitions, shifting from rear to front, inside to outside, while reducing the deceleration; then, once acceleration starts, load transfers front to rear while the lateral load transfer reduces as the car exits the corner.

In any situation that is steady-state— that is, long braking zones, long sweeping corners, corners taken in a higher gear where acceleration is limited, racetracks that are very smooth—the shocks are less critical since they have essentially done their job once the loading change has taken place.

Bumps

The suspension system also reacts to track irregularities—namely, bumps. On a very smooth racetrack, you can get away with using stiffer bump and rebound settings, but remember that stiff settings slow down the suspension movement by having higher resistance to motion.

The down side of this maneuver is that if the suspension has to move fast to absorb a bump or a series of bumps, it may not be able to react fast enough to keep the tire in contact with the road. Tires that spend half their time in the air don't provide much grip. Expect that the shock settings for bumpy racetracks will have to be softer in order to allow the suspension to move fast enough to keep the tires in contact with the track surface.

WEIGHT JACKING

In road racing you are faced with corners that go left and right and in most cases you want a car that has the same ability to corner in both directions. Most of the time we want a car that is symmetrical, that is, its alignment and set-up are the same on the left side of the car as on the right. This isn't necessarily true on racecars that only turn left, as oval track racers do. As this book is primarily about road racing, we'll stick to what we know best and leave oval track set-up to the experts in the field.

We are going to leave experimentation with "wedge" to the guys that find a clear advantage in it. However, on racecars that use independent suspension systems sprung by coil over shock units, adjusting the loaded length of the spring has some effects which even a road-racing driver should know about.

First, let's look at how a coil/shock unit works. In Fig. 14-12, you have a typical spring/shock unit. The top eye (A) is bolted to the chassis and the bottom eye (B) is attached to the suspension. Sometimes it's attached to the suspension by a pullrod which transfers the motion at the wheel to motion at the shock eye. Sometimes the free end of the shock is connected to a suspension arm. It all depends upon the individual car's design. The key is that as the suspension moves into bump, the spring and shock unit gets compressed. When the suspension falls, the shock/spring unit extends.

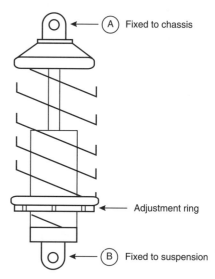

Fig. 14-12. A typical coil/shock unit includes the spring, shock, and an adjustment ring that changes the effective length of the spring.

Spring Rate vs. Wheel Rate

It is very rare when the spring compresses at the same rate that the wheel moves. If it did, you could very simply figure the resistance that the wheel has to being moved. If there were a one-to-one relationship here, a 1-inch motion at the wheel would compress the spring 1 inch. So, if you had a 200-lb.-per-inch spring installed, a 1-inch movement of the wheel would be resisted by 200 lbs. of force: thus the wheel rate would be 200 lbs. per inch.

As always, in real life, it's more complicated. In most cases, the wheel will move more than the spring will—sometimes at a ratio of 2 or 3 to 1. Let's look at an example of the wheel moving twice as far as our 200-lb.-per-inch spring does. If something moves the wheel 1 inch into bump and the spring compresses only a half inch, since a half inch compression of the spring takes 100 lbs., you might conclude that the wheel rate then is 100 lbs. per inch. You'd be wrong.

It's true that the spring resisted the motion with 100 lbs. of force but it did it with the wheel 's leverage advantage. Moving the wheel twice as far as the spring is like using a lever arm to multiply the force.

Look at the diagram in Fig. 14-13 to see what we mean. With this simple lever, the arm at the wheel side is twice as long as the length of the segment from the fulcrum to the spring. A half inch of motion at the spring results in 1 inch of motion at the wheel. The motion ratio is 2 to 1. It takes only 50 lbs. of force at the long arm of the lever to equal 100 lbs. of force at the short end. That's how levers work. You have to move the long arm of the lever more, but you multiply the force. To use an analogy we can all relate to, it works just like a bottle opener.

In this case, even though the spring compresses 1/2 inch, or 100 lbs. of resistance, it only took 50 lbs. of force out at the wheel to move it that half inch. Therefore, the wheel rate—with a 200-lb.-per-inch-spring—is 50 lbs. per inch.

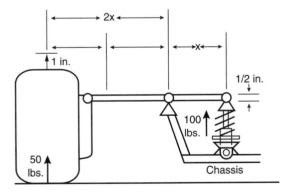

Fig. 14-13. The wheel rate is the key determinant of the wheel's resistance to motion. It is different than spring rate because, in most suspension systems, the spring moves less than the wheel.

Wheel rate is what really matters in cornering balance. Many people get very confused comparing the spring rates of their cars with spring rates of others, not taking into account that the other car's suspension design probably has a different motion ratio than theirs. Even though the spring rates may be different, the wheel rates may be the same.

A 500 lbs. per inch spring may sound stiff to you, but on a particular suspension system it may actually result in quite a soft wheel rate. It's important to distinguish between the two rates.

You can find the wheel rate by using the following formula: Wheel Rate = Spring Rate/(Wheel Travel/Spring Deflection)^2.

Corner Weights

Let's take a look at your hypothetical racecar again. When it's sitting still in the pit lane, your 1000 lb. car just happens to have 400 lbs. of its weight supported by the front tires and 600 lbs. supported by the rears. We could get more detailed and look at the load supported by each tire. A beautifully symmetrical race car would split the load up evenly. Each front tire would have 200 lbs. on it, and each rear tire would support 300 lbs. Now, you know that this isn't going to be the case the instant you put the car in motion. Every time you accelerate it, turn it, or brake it, inertia is going to act through the CG to move load around. This ideal distribution of load represents the *static* loading on the tires. Adjusting the spring perches can change this beautifully symmetrical loading.

In order to make this exercise easier, let's say that this car has a 1 to 1 motion ratio. A 1-inch motion of any wheel will compress its spring/shock unit one inch. In the diagram in Fig. 14-14, the outer end of each shock/spring unit is connected through the suspension to the wheel and the inner end is connected to the chassis. When you move the adjusters (spring perches) you can make the shock/spring unit longer or shorter. You can start with the front, noting what happens when you screw the adjustable spring perch up 1/4 inch on both left and right sides: if the motion ratio is 1 to 1, the front of the car rises 1/4 inch.

Nothing happens to the loading on the front of the car—it still has 400 lbs. of load at the front—but the front is just sitting higher. If you do the same thing to the spring perch on both rear springs, the ride height at the rear goes up. Pretty simple.

If you take one side of the car at a time, screwing the left front and the left rear perches up a quarter inch, your only result is that the car isn't level any more (see Fig. 14-15). The left side of the car will now have a ride height 1/4 inch higher than the right side.

You will find that if you adjust springs in pairs, the only thing that changes is the ride height at the end (or the side) where you made the change.

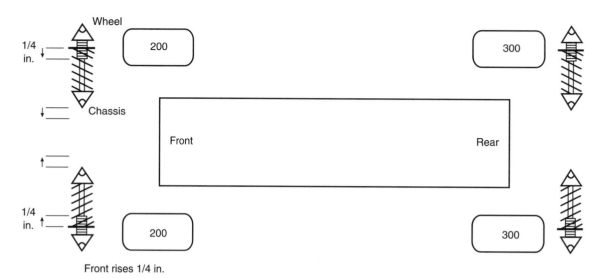

Front rises 1/4 in.

Fig. 14-14. At one end of the car, adjusting both spring perches the same amount changes the ride height, but not the loading.

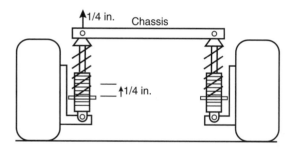

Fig. 14-15. At one side of the car, adjusting both spring perches the same amount changes the ride height of that side, but not the loading.

Static Load Totals

The other golden rule of corner weights has four corollaries: 1) the total of the static load at the front tires will remain the same no matter what you do with the springs, 2) the total of the static loads on the rear tires will remain the same no matter what you do with the springs, 3) the total of the left side static loads will remain the same no matter what you do with the springs, and 4) the total of the right side static loads will remain the same—you guessed it—no matter what you do with the springs.

Short of moving pieces of the car forward and backward, there's nothing you can do with adjusting the spring perches to change the weight distribution of the car.

Changing One Spring Perch

Let's take the left front spring perch and adjust it up, making the shock/spring unit longer, and see how it affects corner weights. When you adjust spring perch-

es, you always have to disconnect the front and rear anti-roll bars because you don't want the anti-roll bars to also contribute springing loads when the car isn't rolling. Trying to raise the left front introduces changes at every wheel. The first thing that happens is that the right rear spring will resist being rocked down toward the ground, and in doing so, loads its own corner and the opposite diagonal with additional tension through the spring. If the left front and right rear tire are now carrying more of the car's weight than they were before the adjustment, it makes sense that the left rear and right front are now carrying less.

Let's say that the left front has gained 25 pounds of static load as a result of this adjustment (see Fig. 14-16).Since the left front load plus the right front load have to add up to 400 lbs., the static load on the right front changes to 400 lbs. – 225 lbs. = 175 lbs. The left rear static load changes also. Since the total of the rear tire loads has to add up to 600 lbs, the left rear load is equal to 600 lbs. – 325 lbs. = 275 lbs. The car is now "crossweighted."

The ride height in this situation at the left front tire would certainly go up. The right rear with its new additional load would go down. The right front, with less load on it, goes up, and the left rear, with 25 lbs. less load on it, also rises. One little change wreaks all this havoc on a formerly symmetrical and perfectly level racecar.

A valid question to ask is why in the world would you want to adjust a spring perch so that you would dial in anything but identical static load on both front or both rear tires? A reason to do this intentionally would be to temporarily increase the grip of the tire, since download equals grip. Some folks work with crossweight this way but it's a bit advanced and of arguable value in road racing. Especially in situations where braking is important, you would like each of

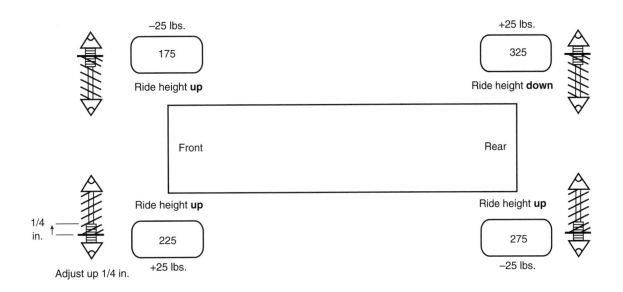

−25 lbs.

175

Ride height **up**

+25 lbs.

325

Ride height **down**

Front

Rear

Ride height **up**

225

+25 lbs.

Adjust up 1/4 in.

1/4 in.

Ride height **up**

275

−25 lbs.

Fig. 14-16. Changing only one spring perch affects the static loading and the ride height on all four corners.

the front tires, which do the largest share of the braking, to have the same grip so that one tire wouldn't lock up significantly before the other.

In road racing, you end up fooling with spring perches, for the most part, to fix a car which has a crossweight problem. For one reason or another, the symmetrical crossweight you had back on the shop floor has changed since you brought the car to the racetrack (and driven it off the track once or twice). You check the corner weights and, lo and behold, the right front corner has 25 lbs. more static load on it than the left front. Out come the shock spanners (special wrenches designed to be used to adjust spring perches), and you go cranking away jacking load around the car to try and keep the left front from locking every time you breathe on the brake pedal.

The fact of the matter, and you'll get arguments from legions of mechanics on this, is that, if the ride heights at each corner are where you want them, you have to adjust all four spring perches to alter the static loading without affecting the ride height. On the other hand, if you're dealing with a small crossweight—10 lbs. or so—your crew may be able to get it out with one turn of the adjuster (1/16 inch) and figure that the tiny change in ride height isn't worth the bother of doing three other changes.

Load Jacks Diagonally

Shortening the installed height of the spring, turning the perch so that it moves the adjuster toward the spring, will increase the static load on its corner and the corner opposite. Static loading will be reduced on the corners of the opposite diagonal.

To do this without changing the ride heights, you go up, shorter, on the diagonal where you want more load and simultaneously down the same amount, longer, on the opposite diagonal.

With this simple racecar with the same spring rate and motion ratio front and rear, all these up and down turnings would be the same amount. Let's say your car is okay on ride heights but the corner weight measurements are as you see in Fig. 14-17. The right front is 50 lbs. more loaded than the left front. You would go down (longer) on the right front and on the left rear.

Just doing this alone will do some of the load transfer, but will result in lower ride height overall—remember, the springs on the other diagonal were the right length to keep the car at the ride height you wanted at the lighter load. Put a higher load on them, as you do by lengthening the springs on the opposite diagonal, and they compress, allowing the chassis to get closer to the ground. In order to complete the adjustment, you have to turn the spring perch up (shorter) on the left front and right rear to get the ride height back given the new, higher load.

In a real-life racecar with different spring rates and motion ratios, front and rear, it's slightly more complicated and a topic better covered by the sources listed in the Bibliography. The theory here holds, but the specifics will vary from car to car.

The best approach for your specific car is to put the car on scales and experiment, so that at the racetrack, you'll know what's needed for 10–50 lb. adjustments. You'll also get a feel for how ride height around the car changes as you move the spring perches.

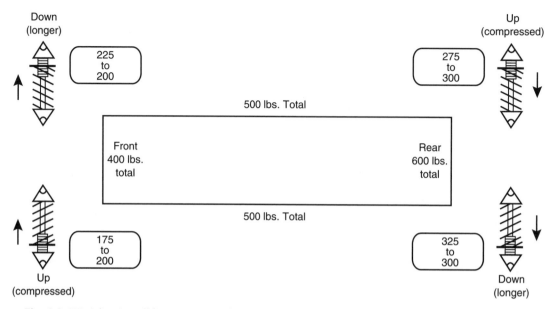

Fig. 14-17. Adjusting all four spring perches in the same direction diagonally can shift static load without changing the ride height at each corner.

AERODYNAMICS

So far, we've covered many of the simple adjustments you can make to alter the way the car works; and in many classes of car, especially the entry level classes, there are no aerodynamic devices to fool with to add an even greater level of complication to set-up. If you keep progressing, however, you'll end up in a racecar that creates additional grip by loading the tires with aerodynamic downforce. It's amazing that racecar designers took so long to discover the benefits of aero downforce, but since the late 1960s, if the rules of a class of racecar allow the use of downforce-creating devices, entrants use them.

The theory is simple. Wings are light and don't add to the overall mass of the car, but they create a downward load on the tires which creates additional grip.

One interesting piece of information is that the amount of downforce and drag produced by aerodynamic devices increases as the square of the speed divided by a constant. In other words, if your vehicle produces 50 lbs. of downforce at 40 m.p.h., it will produce not 100 lbs. of downforce at 80 m.p.h., but 200 lbs.(downforce = m.p.h.^{2} / 32). At 120 m.p.h., the downforce would be 450 lbs. In short, aerodynamic downforce is a considerable source of grip, especially in the higher speed ranges.

In some classes of cars like Formula Atlantic, Formula 1, Indy Car, and others, the effects of the aerodynamic downforce far overshadow the effects of any of the conventional chassis adjustments we have discussed so far. The car's cornering balance, especially in corners over 80 m.p.h. or so, is pretty much deter-

mined by the aerodynamic balance of front end downforce vs. rear end downforce. All of the chassis adjustments we covered earlier are frequently sacrificed in the name of creating more aerodynamic loading of the tires. A huge amount of engineering work is done in these classes to design the shape of the bodies and wings in an effort to distribute the appropriate proportion of the total downforce to the front and rear tires. If the design is wrong, often no amount of trimming wings or suspension adjustments will help. Over the years, many an innovative design has failed because the downforce created by the design was either too far to the front or too far to the rear or, worse still, moved back and forth unpredictably.

Angle of Attack

Less complicated are cars which generate downforce without benefit of downforce-producing underbodies. Instead, they have independently adjustable wings mounted on the front and rear which provide the downforce. Classes like F/F 2000 and Barber Dodge use externally mounted and easily adjustable wings, front and rear, which can be adjusted to create varying levels of downforce and drag. Increasing the angle of attack of the wings (their angular direction to the air flow) increases the downforce and drag.

Increasing the angle of attack of the front wing creates more grip at the front and will tend to decrease understeer or increase oversteer tendencies. Increasing the angle of attack of the rear wing increases grip at the rear of the car, decreasing oversteer tendencies or increasing the car's tendency to understeer.

Stall

You can't increase the angle of attack indefinitely. The downforce of a wing is created by the difference in air pressure between the upper surface of the wing and its lower surface. At some specific angle of attack, the airflow over the wing becomes turbulent and the wing stalls. At this point, the wing loses some downforce and creates gobs of drag.

Also, the downforce it creates has to be matched so that the front and rear tires gain proportionately. Too much front relative to the rear creates high-speed oversteer. Too much rear relative to the front creates high-speed understeer.

You also have to consider how much overall downforce, and its detrimental flip side, drag, is best for lowering lap time at a particular circuit. In the high speed ranges where the wings are most effective, the aerodynamic drag of the car uses greater and greater percentages of the power available to accelerate until all the available power is being consumed. At that point, the car won't go any faster.

Racetracks with long, high-speed straights and a majority of low-speed corners, where the wings will be relatively ineffective, will require a low drag/low downforce set-up. On a racetrack with many fast sweepers and short straights, a lot of balanced downforce should help the speed through the corners, yet not be a liability for too long. Street circuits, with typically short straights and a mix of high- and low-speed corners, usually find the field running maximum downforce, since not much is lost to drag down the short straights, while reasonable grip is available in mid-speed corners.

A point worth remembering is that the angle of attack of wings varies as the car pitches. Changing the ride height of one end of the car in order to effect the mechanical chassis set-up will also affect the aerodynamic balance of the car. Lowering the nose of the car increases the angle of attack of both wings, while raising it goes the other way.

Wings and Turn-In Response

The response to turning the steering wheel into a fast corner can be easily tailored by using wings. In a car without wings, the front/rear loading and the cornering balance of the car is going to take a bit of time to reveal itself and stabilize the balance that you'll feel in the middle of the corner. With aerodynamic loads on the tire at the end of the straight, the balance of the car at the turn-in and up to the point where the car has rolled into its cornering set will be largely determined by the front/rear balance of the wings. A car with an aerodynamic understeer (too little front wing relative to the back) might understeer only until the roll resistance of shocks, springs roll bars and roll centers take over to establish a different balance.

DESCRIBING CAR BEHAVIOR

You will find that increasingly, especially with cars where aerodynamics affect the handling, you will need to be more specific with your analysis of how the car is handling. "Okay" is probably not the answer the professional crew chief is looking for when you're asked to describe the car's handling at a test session. It's not useful to describe the car's handling characteristics with one catch-all phrase like "understeer"; to fix the problem, the crew needs to know where and how the understeer is occurring.

Test Driving

You have to use a slightly different mind set when you're testing. Let's face it—any good race driver is competitive in nature, not only against others but against himself or herself. Given 20 laps, alone, without a specific purpose, a driver will try to get faster and faster, competing to do better and better. In testing, this can obviously skew the results in favor of whatever changes come last.

You have to drive fast—there's no use having a racecar that's perfect a half second off the pace and awful at the lap record—but consistently. You want to settle into a range where there is only a tenth or two variation over five laps. Then your team can start to make changes and have some hope of identifying what works and what doesn't.

> "[In testing,] you really have to drive 9 1/2 to 10/10ths because that's where these cars are used to operating and that's the data you're looking for—how the car performs in that range, so that's how you've got to drive. You don't go test at a race track where you've never been to before and expect to learn a lot, because the driver himself is going to be learning the track throughout the day so that will skew the data.
>
> "I think the other thing you have to do is you get your control and then you measure everything else against the control and then the last thing you have to do in the test is go back to the control and see how accurate that still is. That kind of gives you a beginning and an end to look at and then you can compare everything in the middle."
>
> —Brian Till

Trust yourself. Identifying car behavior is based on sensations that can sometimes be very subtle. A good testing and development driver has to learn to be perceptive. If you feel the car doing something odd or something that doesn't make sense, don't let your logic get in the way of what you're feeling. Tell the crew chief what you felt, and where you felt it, without self-censorship. This is especially true when you suspect that something is going wrong. If it feels like the car is going bad on you, trust your perceptions. Overruling your better judgement can get you in big trouble fast.

> "Your instincts are right. If it feels like it's wanting to get loose, it's about to get loose, even if it hasn't yet. You have to trust yourself 'cause that's all you've got. Your instincts are the right instincts. Whether your crew chief says, 'That's the way we ran it in 1956 or 1992,' doesn't mean shit. It's you."
>
> —Dorsey Schroeder

Work With Good People

To be a valuable asset to racecar testing and development, you also have to work closely with a good crew chief or race engineer. Many people in the mechanical end of racing are just as confused as drivers about chassis dynamics, only they're more adamant that they're right. As you've learned, racecar set-up is full of compromises. One change often results in multiple effects; on the other hand, it's rare for a crew to make one change that makes the car better everywhere.

If you latch onto one principle alone and let it overwhelm the thinking about set-up, you'll miss the boat more often than not. An extremely valuable person is one who takes the existing knowledge and theory about vehicle dynamics and tempers it with experience and an open mind.

There is, admittedly, a lot to adjusting racecars and improving their performance—we've barely begun to scratch the surface. We're assuming that your primary interest is in driving racecars, not designing, engineering or sorting one. For the sake of general understanding, we have taken liberties by simplifying some very complicated subjects, but there are plenty of books out there which are more technically complex and accurate. Most of the best books on the subject are contained in the Bibliography, most notably the Carroll Smith series on racecar preparation and Van-Valkenburg's *Racecar Engineering and Mechanics*.

> "Different engineers have different approaches. I don't think there's a right and a wrong, necessarily. It's just like driving. Drivers have different approaches to things and so do engineers. I know engineers who like to go out on the racetrack during the session and watch the car because they feel they can see things on the set-up that they can adjust for. Other guys will base it strictly on what the computer information is telling them.
>
> "The trick is the chemistry between you and your engineer, making sure that you can work with the person that you're dealing with, so that your approach is similar and that you compliment each other.
>
> "You have to develop a good rapport and you have to believe in each other. If the engineer doesn't believe what you're telling him or you don't believe the engineer is doing a good job, then it's a bad situation. You have to find the right person. Engineers are like drivers. Some are good and some are not so good."
>
> —Bryan Herta

It's also a good idea to learn your engineer's individual perspective on each of the areas of adjustment we've covered. Every class of racecar has its own set of adjustments that are more critical than others, and it will be useful for both the driver and crew to agree on their perspective before testing begins.

The Ultimate Tweak

The fact remains that, especially at the start of your racing career, you are the component of the mix that can suddenly pull a one or two percent lap time improvement out of thin air. You need to try to be as perceptive and as critical of your own performance in the car as you are about the car's handling. The car could have a problem, but then again, it might be you. Get used to looking inward for speed. As amateur athletes, we're normally far from perfect. It's sometimes a good idea to get a driver who is more experienced and accomplished in your particular class to work with you on a test day. It's one way of settling the issue of whether it's the car or you.

Part V

Becoming a Race Driver

CHAPTER 15

COMPARING CARS

W E ARE OFTEN ASKED whether the techniques taught at the Skip Barber Racing School are the same ones you would use in faster cars. The basics are the same but the problems you'd face in an Indy Car are vastly different from those you'd encounter in a Formula Dodge. These differences will certainly have an effect on the way you drive the car and how you build on the fundamentals.

In order to move up in the world of racing, you have to learn to adapt the basics of race driving to suit the special demands of various types of racecars. You need to take into account the increases in force and speed that you'll deal with as you compete in more and more powerful machinery. To get a quick basis for comparison of the acceleration, braking, and cornering forces available in different racecars, take a look at the graph in Fig. 15-1.

> **As you compete in increasingly powerful, faster machinery, you adapt the basics of race driving to suit your specific type of racecar.**

You can see that different types of racecars have different strengths and weaknesses, which will affect the technique used to extract the most performance from the car.

As you progress up the ladder through increasingly sophisticated and powerful cars, the limits of the car's

> *"Ultimately we start at the same point which is pretty much the same for all cars and all situations and then you learn, and you fine tune it and you end up learning tricks. That can't be taught on a blackboard. The tricks are different with each new situation. That's what makes everybody go a different speed."*
>
> —*Dorsey Schroeder*

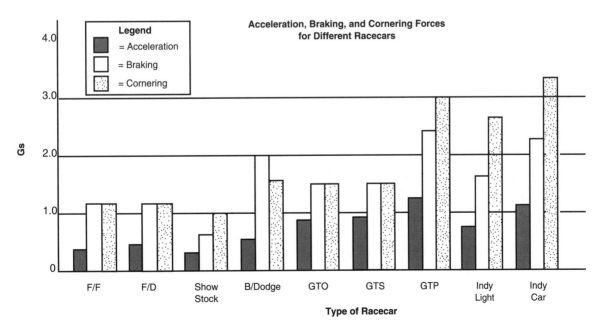

Fig. 15-1. This comparison between different racecars shows a marked difference in potential acceleration, braking, and cornering forces as you move up the racing ladder into faster, more powerful machinery.

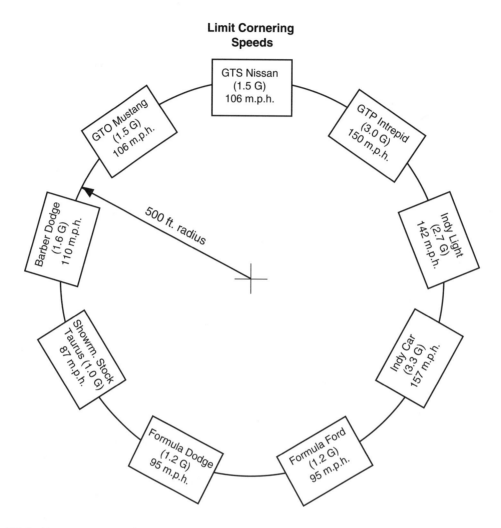

Limit Cornering Speeds

Fig. 15-2. Here, you can see how the potential cornering forces of different racecars affect their top speeds at the cornering limit.

ability to accelerate, brake, and corner increase. In acceleration, the car will gain speed more quickly—having sufficient grip to handle the horsepower becomes a factor. Once you transition to cars where aerodynamics become important, cornering and braking grip increase at an astounding rate. It's quite an adjustment to be able to drive through a corner 50–60 m.p.h. faster than you could in a car without aerodynamic aids.

For the sake of comparison, look at Fig. 15-2, where we have computed the limit-cornering speeds around a 500-ft.-radius arc for racecars ranging from the Formula Dodge 2-liter car on Michelin Pilot radial tires to an Indy Car in the 160-m.p.h. range.

We will start our comparison with a school Formula Dodge and move up through the variety of racecars that you'd most likely drive on your way to the top. This includes Showroom Stock, Barber Dodge Pro

"I think it is different from car to car, but I think the basics are the very same. I learned how to drive in a Formula Vee as opposed to a Can Am car and all the stuff I learned in Formula Vee stood with me throughout my career. It taught me all good habits.

"At the same time, I really don't think there's any real black and white to driving racecars. There are rules which we sort of abide by, or learn by, or use, but there are a lot of different people that do it a lot of different ways. You have to teach people black and white at the beginning but you also teach them that, as you move up, you can improvise."

—David Loring

Series, High-Powered Sedans and Trans Am, Indy Lights, Sports Prototypes, and Indy Car.

This is by no means the definitive list of racecar types and racing series in which drivers can compete. A detailed look at each SCCA class (and indeed there are many where the racing is hot and heavy and the competition top-notch) would fill a volume in itself. We've concentrated on the types of cars we're most familiar with and those in which our past and present instructors have had the most first-hand experience.

For each type of racecar, we'll take a quick look at its makeup and its performance potential. Then we'll go into the nitty-gritty details, explaining factors that affect your driving technique for each car. We agree with our drivers that the basics are the basics when it comes to racing just about any car, but we also know that every car has its own little quirks, and the technique considerations for one type of racecar are not necessarily applicable for the others.

FORMULA DODGE

Formula Ford racing in the United States exists in three major categories: SCCA National and Regional F/Ford; Club Ford as it is raced in the SCCA and other, more regional groups; and, from 1976 to 1994, the Skip Barber Formula Ford Series.

In 1995 the Barber Series Formula Fords were converted to use modern Dodge 2000 cc four-cylinder powerplants, upping the horsepower of the cars some 25%. The chassis remain essentially unchanged other than modifications to accommodate the new engines and some shock and spring changes to keep the handling similar to the previous race car.

Both SCCA F/Ford and Club Ford are run on slicks, while the Barber Dodge Series cars compete on Michelin street radials.

The Barber Series—East, Midwest, Florida and California—are "Rent-a-Ride" series and the company provides the cars and organization for its thirty annual events.

Driver Technique Considerations

1) Drafting. Between 80 and 100 m.p.h., aerodynamic drag cuts the car's accelerating ability to less than 40% of its maximum. Minimizing the aerodynamic drag by drafting another car has a significant effect on the car's acceleration and top speed in the over-80 m.p.h. range. On racetracks where the cars spend a majority of their time running at over 80 m.p.h., it is possible for drivers of varying ability to stay together because of the draft effect, even though their cornering speeds may vary significantly. Strategy in using the

Fig. 15-3. The author (left) consults with Jeremy Dale during testing for the Formula Dodge Race Series.

Fig. 15-4. The Formula Dodge, powered by modern Dodge 2000 cc four-cylinder powerplants, may have more horsepower than the Formula Ford, but it's good racing technique, not horsepower, that gets results in the Barber Dodge Series.

> *"I'm always impressed by the drafting in the Formula Dodges. It seems like if you gain two miles per hour in the draft, you've got that two m.p.h. all the way by, or at least all the way alongside. It's a reliable passing tool. In many other cars, it's not that way. You might get two or three m.p.h. directly behind the other car, but as you pop out, it drops down."*
>
> —Brian Till

> *"The Skip Barber Formula Dodge is one of the harder cars to learn to adapt to driving quickly. They always like to have a little rotation to them to help point them out of the corner so that they don't understeer off the track at the exit. The way you accomplish that is having a phenomenal feel of the brake pedal. Just having the right amount carries you in there and creates just the perfect level of rotation....You don't come into the corner and snap off the brake pedal and over-rotate the car. You carry a lot of entry speed but you're still pointed in the right direction in the middle of the corner to get on the throttle. Many guys slow the car down more at the entry than they need to, but if they're not balancing it on the brakes, it feels too fast when they turn in. It's not as much an issue in fast corners, but in medium- and slow-speed corners, it's all in the brakes."*
>
> —Robbie Buhl

> *"...[I]n a Formula Dodge, with street radial tires, you can get away with a lot of slip angle in the tire without scrubbing as much speed as you would on slicks. If you were to put slicks on the car, you would have to use a lot less slip angle, or yaw, through the corner. Still, even though you can slide them a lot, you have to be careful of scrub, even with the street tires.*
> *I never used big angles on the car—I just don't throw the car around a lot. I haven't changed what I do much. I've stuck with that approach and I think it's been more of an advantage as I've moved up."*
>
> —Bryan Herta

draft advantage at the right time often determines the race winner.

2) Braking. Weighing less than 1100 lbs. including driver and fuel, Formula Dodges decelerate quickly and reliably. You can work on increasing corner entry speed by moving brake points progressively closer to the corner, safe in assuming that the mechanical part of the braking mix is relatively constant—not true in many other types of racecars.

3) Use of Street Radial Tires. Running a racecar on street radial tires has many advantages, especially for an entry-level series. Admittedly, the tires deliver less peak grip than slicks, but still, maximum cornering and braking forces are in the 1.2 G range. The beauty is in the slip angle range where the tire delivers its best cornering grip. It's not only higher than a slick but, as the slip angle increases beyond optimum, the tires' loss of grip is more subtle and happens over a wider range of slip angle. This allows the average driver to get a feel for car control and yaw angles while at the same time allowing a bit of a safety net for the overachievers. Slide the car too much and it just goes slower, not off the racetrack.

4) Sensitivity of Controls. With its light weight and small-scale components, the Formula Dodge's steering, throttle, brakes, and gear lever don't need to be moved much or very forcefully to result in peak performance. This doesn't put significant demands on the driver in terms of strength and endurance, but rewards deft and subtle input.

5) Hewland Mark-9 Dog Ring Gearbox. The smallest of racing gearboxes is an excellent starting ground to learn double-clutch downshifting. With its lightweight internal components, it is forgiving of poor technique and produces smooth, effortless shifts when the driver matches the revs well.

Fig. 15-5. A light touch on the controls is necessary for peak performance in the Formula Dodge.

"There is a degree of laziness that goes along with driving any high horsepower car. Maybe not laziness but a bit of complacency. In any car you're trying to maximize every last tenth, but I think a lot of guys who drive high horsepower cars fall back on the horsepower. When I get back into a Formula Dodge, it kind of fine tunes you, it brings you back. It's a little reality check, because it's good technique that makes it faster than some one else, not more horsepower."

—Jeremy Dale

6) Competition. A very difficult aspect of entry-level racing is to separate how the driver is doing from the car's potential. Often, a better car driven poorly can beat a poor car driven brilliantly. In "Spec Car" competitions like the Formula Dodge Series, the cars are essentially the same and it's superior driving that nets winning results.

SHOWROOM STOCK RACING

The Taurus SHO we tested for this book, run by Woodstock Motorsports, competed in the Firestone Firehawk Endurance Series, a tour of 11 professional race events sanctioned by IMSA. Showroom stock racing in many forms and classes exists in professional form in both IMSA and the SCCA and at the amateur level in SCCA National and Regional races. Class rules and the level of modification allowed vary from series to series, but the fundamental concept is to race cars in essentially their showroom configuration, on street tires. Roll cages and other safety modifications are generally allowed.

Driver Technique Considerations

1) Front-Wheel Drive. This is the only form of racing where drivers have to deal with front-wheel drive. FWD racecars have one universal disadvantage compared to a rear-wheel drive configuration. At the corner exit, load is transferring off the front tires as the car accelerates away from the corner. This reduces the traction of the front tires just when it is needed most to provide grip to accelerate the car onto the following straightaway. This biases the car's cornering balance toward understeer in the second half of corners—the more impatient the throttle foot, the more gross the understeer. The most common line adaptation for these cars is to apex corners later than you might in a conventional racecar, in order to get a higher proportion of the direction change done early in the corner, allowing a straighter line—and thereby greater acceleration levels—coming out.

At limit cornering, there are similarities and differences in how a driver cures understeer or oversteer. Understeer is handled just like it is in a rear wheel drive car—reducing throttle to transfer load onto the front tires. In the FWD car, reducing throttle also relieves the front tires from some of their acceleration duties, providing more cornering grip at the front.

In FWD cars, there are plenty of options to handle oversteer. Oversteer can be handled with a correction in the direction of the slide and an application of power which drives the front of the car to the outside of the slide, reducing the yaw angle. More and more drivers are discovering that you can neutralize the oversteer with power—without a steering correction—keeping the front tires pointed at the apex and accelerating toward the apex, dragging the rear tires behind. If you apply too much power, the front tires will lose cornering grip and slide out to match the arc of the rears.

Drastic oversteer can sometimes be solved by booting the throttle, totally upsetting the front end grip and allowing the front to slide to match the rear, again reducing the car's overall yaw angle. The throttle boot is an emergency spin-avoidance technique.

Fig. 15-6. The Taurus SHO put extreme demands on the braking system, especially in endurance races. The turtle in the back seat offers encouragement.

It is very easy in a FWD car to get into a downward spiral of worse and worse understeer. Impatient throttle application will heat the fronts from a combination of tire scrub and front wheelspin. As the tires overheat and lose traction, it gets easier to spin them, which increases the temperature more, which increases the scrub and wheelspin . . . on and on until the car plows every time the steering wheel is turned.

2) Drafting. The draft can be a significant advantage, especially to a car in a slower class that can follow in the wake of a more powerful car. Using the draft-by pass depends upon the aerodynamic shape of your car—a slippery one will carry its drafting speed advantage longer than a boxy design.

> *"The draft works just like our classic passing talk. When you pull out from behind, there's a boat wake of air—you lose a bit of speed pulling alongside and the other car slows a bit because you're not behind him anymore. With three cars in line, the third guy would go by every time."*
>
> —Terry Earwood

3) Brakes. Brakes designed for street applications are seldom up to the task of the racing environment, where they are used frequently and very hard in order

> *"There was a night Dorsey Schroeder and I drove at Mid Ohio for five hours without front brakes—so you just set the handbrake as you came up to turn seven and it left your hands free to do the downshifts. Then you dropped the handbrake as you turned into the corner.*
>
> *"The flip side of the braking understeer at the entry to the corner is rotating too much at the turn-in and having the scrub from the yaw be too much—it just slows the car down more than you intended. If you wind up with too much rotation, you have to sort of tap the throttle with the correction in and the car kind of duck-walks away from the apex. When it does that, your first reaction is to turn the wheel back in toward the apex and you crack in power understeer again.*
>
> *"I've started to not dial my steering correction in and literally try to let the car rotate and keep the fronts pointed at the apex and feed in the power and tug the car, tail and all, down to the apex. If you overdo the power, even that'll let the front slide out a little wider which fixes the oversteer. As far as correction is concerned, I now try to use it only to really save a spin."*
>
> —Terry Earwood

to decelerate heavy cars. Brake fade—some times even complete brake failure—is a routine part of showroom stock racing. The Taurus, for example, can decelerate at .8 Gs—twice. In racing conditions, the typical deceleration level which will allow the brakes to live is more in the .4 G range and the level of braking pedal pressure is 35% less than the typical purpose-built racecar.

> *"When I first went to showroom stock cars from Formula Fords, I hated not being able to see the tires under braking. I found it more difficult to sense the limit, but if you work on it, it fine tunes you to that feeling of deadness that you get when you lock a wheel. I think a lot of the feel comes through the steering wheel. It's tougher to sense in a car with power steering but still doable.*
>
> *"In the Dodge showroom stock cars that we drove with Paul Rossi, we were allowed to use the brakes at about 60% of their potential—otherwise we would just burn the brakes off the car."*
>
> *—Jeremy Dale*

In showroom stock racing, it is more critical to arrive at the turn-in point of the corner at exactly the maximum speed the cornering arc will allow than it is to try to save lap time by using a higher rate of deceleration. Another technique which has been shown to work is to continue light brake-turning past the turn-in point of the corner and to allow tire scrub from cornering to take off the speed needed to make the apex.

Should the brakes seriously deteriorate or go away all together, you have to improvise ways to slow for the corners. Using the handbrake, downshifting early and often, shutting off the ignition between shifts, exaggerating tire scrub into the corner, or using the back bumper of a car with good brakes are all part of the racer's repertoire.

4) Tires. Street radial tires are used in showroom stock racing and all are shaved prior to racing use to prevent overheating and chunking. Tire companies, of course, like to promote the fact that their tires win on the racetrack; and more and more "off the shelf" tires are being constructed specifically for racing but look like stock tires. Since most of the tires are taller and skinnier than racing slicks, they operate at higher peak slip angles and have a broader range of angles that will deliver competitive grip. Cornering yaw angles will typically be higher than slick-shod racecars.

Fig. 15-7. Terry Earwood on his way to victory in the relative comfort afforded by a working windshield wiper and defroster.

5) Control Sensitivity. The number of turns lock to lock in a showroom stock car is much greater than that of a lightweight formula car. In many true racecars, you very seldom have to move your hands from the 3 and 9 position to get as much steering lock as you will ever need. Not so in a street sedan—frequently, you have to reposition your hands in the middle of a steering correction to get enough lock to save the day. It pays to practice shuffle steer to ensure that you can get the size of correction you need when the time comes. Shuffle steer involves being prepared to quickly relieve whichever is the top hand on the steering wheel so that you can pull downward with the help-

> *"When you drive a sedan car I call the steering technique "the granny method," where one hand pushes the wheel up turning into the corner up to the 12 o'clock position and the other hand is sliding up to meet it. Then the other hand takes over and pulls down to six o'clock. They're always diametrically opposed. They meet at twelve and at six. While one is turning the wheel the other is sliding to meet it.*
>
> *"The only time I don't do it this way is when I've got the car in a full lock skid and that first recovery is so important to do quickly that I'll do one full turn back around with one hand, then pick up the shuffle for the rest. The other exception is if I've dialed some correction in and at the last minute realized I've got to go over twelve o'clock for the last two degrees, then I'll do that instead of switching grip."*
>
> *—Terry Earwood*

ing hand to add more lock than you could by crossing your arms.

The brake pedal can feel different every time you touch it. Universally, a street car brake pedal will have more travel than an unassisted multi-master system. Sometimes, with a cold set of hard brake pads, the pedal will feel "brick." You push hard and the pedal doesn't feel squishy—it's rock hard—but the car just doesn't seem to slow down. Sometimes it feels good—

progressive with good stopping power. Sometimes it travels most of the way to the floor and feels spongy. Sometimes it goes all the way to the floor with practically no resistance, but can be pumped back into life if you move your foot up and down quickly enough. Sometimes it goes easily to the floor and can't be pumped back and after a while you stop bothering with it. If you like surprises, you'll love showroom stock braking.

"Terry [Earwood] and I drove together for the longest time in Dodges with Paul Rossi and all kinds of terrible things would happen to you but nobody would ever believe you because we were winning....Terry's on the radio one night while I'm driving along in the 24 Hours, and all of a sudden we broke a strut. When I tried to turn right, the strut would separate and it wouldn't turn right because everything would become disconnected.

"At first it was a symptom that was just developing, but it was getting worse and worse and I didn't want to say much about it because you know the response you're going to get when you call the crew. You call 'em and you say, 'I ain't got no brakes.' They say, 'Well, you wore 'em out. If you want to fix 'em, c'mon in. The tools will be on the pit lane wall.'

"So I'm not going to tell them that the steering is out, but finally I couldn't hold out any more because it just wouldn't turn right, at Watkins Glen. So finally, I called Terry on the radio and said, 'I got a problem— the car won't turn right.' He comes back and tells me, 'Don't turn right.' So I thought, okay, I should have known that. Okay, I won't turn right. I guess I'll just get down to the end of the straightaway and fake it.

"So I got to the end of the straight and I thought, okay, I'll try and use the handbrake and it will help me turn toward the right if I can get any steering at all. So I went click, click, click on the handbrake and turned the wheel to the right, but this time, instead of turning like a normal wheel, it kind of moved like an eccentric, and the car said, 'Not today.'

"What had happened was that all the bolts had fallen out of the steering wheel, on the hub, except for one. So when I turned the wheel, I was just turning it around that last bolt. And that created an increase in the heartbeat—the heart worked good just then and I got strong—real strong.

"And when you really need to, you can turn. And I turned. I pushed that wheel on and somehow made it through the corner.

"I realized that something bad was wrong. I was grabbing the hub and trying to turn—I made it back onto the straightaway and I tried to assess the situation. I reached down onto the floor and found another bolt and put it in and when I just got it under control again, I called and got Terry on the radio and said, 'Hey, Terry, you know how I can't turn right? I'm dealing with that, but something real interesting just happened. The steering wheel just fell off.' He said, 'No it didn't.' And I said, 'Yes it did.'

"He said, 'So far, you've told me that you've got no brakes, you can't turn right, and the steering wheel's falling off. What more are you going to start bitching about next?'

"Now, this car was going down the straight at close to 140 m.p.h., almost as fast as the GTU car, and I see that when I screw one bolt back in, the vibration is screwing the other one out, so I'm just barely keeping even here. So I started holding the palm of my hand on the hub to keep them from screwing out and when I get to the straight, I'm fishing around on the floor to find another bolt.

"I figured I couldn't drive the rest of my two hour stint like this so I looked around and realized that the roll bar padding was put on with racer's tape. I said, 'Aha, that will work.' So I rip off a little piece of tape, screw one bolt all the way in and tape it. It's not goin' nowhere.

"This is the last stint of the 24-hour race, and I guess we came in fourth or fifth. I get into the pits and I'm livid, shaking the steering wheel, kicking the tires, but Terry comes up, wagging his finger, saying, 'No, no, no. We're on T.V. There's people here. Don't make an ass out of yourself. We'll talk about it later.'"

—Dorsey Schroeder

"Scrub, from yaw angle, is a big plus. Since you can't late brake like you can in a real race-car, I brake early just to start settling the weight up on the nose—then we can go ahead and get it in the next lower gear, if it's a downshift corner, so that the engine does just as much of a fair share of slowing the car down as the brakes. The deceleration rate stays the same from when the brakes first come on right up to the point where you get back on the throttle.

"In a formula car you start out with a number 10 pedal [on a scale of 1 to 10], then bleed off to an 8 or a 7 in order to turn the car. In a showroom stock car you're approaching the corner at a 6 or a 7 and you bend it into the corner at a 6 or a 7, so now we're going to use that bending-in to start scrubbing off speed cause in a big heavy car it starts wallowing the tires over and knocking the speed off. You also start to get some rotation hopefully and the yaw of the car creates more braking drag.

"You want to go into the corner on the brakes but just short of brake understeer TBU—trailing brake understeer.

"Like the toe of the boot at the Glen, you've got to turn so much because of the steering angle alone—it's such a sharp corner—at a number 5 brake pedal the car just takes off on you and TBUs. For the steering angle you want, you're using up too much of the contact patch with the brakes. You either have to give up entry speed or make a gentler turn out of it, and since you can't change the turn, the only thing to do is to start slowing down sooner."

—Terry Earwood

"Gearboxes [in showroom stock]...aren't as tough these days as they were when we were growing up with the Muncie 4-speeds and such. Now we knock synchronizers out instantly—and gears, too. I use double clutching as a way to try to save the car. And just for timing—it's the only way I shift, so to change away from the double clutch is harder to do than to just stick with the routine. I also try not to rush the upshift and do a slight pause in neutral—the wrist ought to feel the position of neutral. You can see guys going straight through the gate, and there's a little crunch on every upshift which is just wearing the transmission out, especially in a 24-hour race."

—Terry Earwood

"I had come out of doing open wheel sprint races, so my time in Firehawk was well spent because it taught me the discipline necessary to succeed in endurance racing. That's one of the best things about Firehawk because it teaches you so much about that stuff.

"Probably the most fun I've had in racing were the two years I spent with Paul Rossi, because there was very little pressure on us. We were just having a good time. We had good race cars and we knew we were in contention for the win every weekend. There were always four or five team cars on the racetrack and we were all on the same radio channel. We'd all have a good time and we really enjoyed racing, and that probably helps your level of success. Those two things do go hand-in-hand."

—Jeremy Dale

6) *Gearbox.* Since showroom stock cars have synchromesh gearboxes, you don't have to double clutch downshifts, but you still need to blip the throttle before engaging the next lowest gear to smooth the transition—unless, of course, the brakes are gone and you need the engine compression to slow the car down. Double clutching does, however, save wear on the synchronizers—very important in an endurance event. Besides, most drivers we know do it anyway out of force of habit.

7) *Competition.* An ordinary production car is not designed to endure the kind of punishment an endurance race will dish out. Often the winner of a race will be driving a cripple that's just a shell of its former self, but the name of the game is to keep going and drive around the car's limitations.

The race pace is a function of keeping the competition in sight without beating up the car any more than necessary. Passing loses the immediacy found in a sprint race and the driver can be more conservative when contemplating a risky passing maneuver.

Being part of a team also takes on added importance. In order to do well, the mechanical crew frequently has to perform magic and the drivers can best show their appreciation by bringing the car in for its next pit stop more or less in the same condition it was in when it left the pit lane.

BARBER DODGE PRO SERIES

The Barber Dodge Pro Series (formerly the Barber/Saab Pro series) is a series of professional races held concurrently with NASCAR, SCCA, or CART events before large crowds and a television audience. All cars are owned, prepared and tested by the Skip Barber organization; entrants pay an entry fee and are awarded prize money relative to their finishing position. The annual series champion, in addition to the season's winnings, receives a $100,000 Career Enhancement Award to help finance the next step up the professional racing ladder.

In 1995, the cars, which were powered by Saab 4-cylinder turbo-charged engines from 1986 through 1994, were re-powered by Dodge 3.5 Liter V6 power-plants. Other than modifications to suit the new engine, the chassis remains essentially unchanged from the earlier version. Horsepower and driveability are both improved by the new, normally aspirated engines. For the 1998 season, a new Reynard/Dodge racecar will be the Series standard, bringing a new level of sophistication to the championship.

> *"One of the things guys notice when they go from the Formula Dodge to the Pro Series is that the slingshot by another car that you get in the Formula Dodge just doesn't seem to work in the Pro cars. You can run in the draft behind somebody and get a good tow, but when it comes time to make the move out into the dirty air, now that speed doesn't stay there as much."*
>
> —Brian Till

> *"The biggest step up for me was from the Formula Fords to the Pro Series car. That was because I was coming out of a low horsepower, street radial-shod car into a higher horsepower car with slicks and wings. The slicks and wings were as big a change to me as the horsepower was."*
>
> *"Once you get used to it though, horsepower's not hard. Going fast is not hard—anybody can drive 200 m.p.h. down a straightaway. Its what you do in between the straightaways that's the challenge."*
>
> —Bryan Herta

Fig. 15-8. 1992 Barber/Saab Champion Bryan Herta found the horsepower of the Pro Series cars an easier adaptation than dealing with the added grip afforded by slicks and wings.

Driver Technique Considerations

1) Drafting. The initial design of the racecar took into consideration a major concern for keeping the turbo-charged Saab engine adequately cooled. As a result, the car uses oversized radiators and air inlet ducting, sacrificing aerodynamic slipperiness for engine reliability. Although there's clearly a drag advantage to following another car down high-speed straights, this advantage is instantly negated once the following car pulls out of the draft to pass and runs into the wall of air at high speed. This virtually eliminates the draft-by pass which is such a staple of more slippery cars such as Formula Dodges.

2) Power. With 225 hp on tap, the first adaptation for the driver is to become familiar with the level of acceleration and the short time period between shifts, relative to a slower-accelerating car. With more power available, you might think that power oversteer would become a big problem. Offsetting the additional power, however, is the additional grip available from the 12.5-inch rear slicks. Don't misunderstand—there's power oversteer available, but since the engine makes considerable torque down low in its rev range, the car's initial reaction to an abrupt throttle application is to squat and bite at the rear, unloading the front of the car and causing power understeer. You can maintain a power oversteer balance with the throttle but not without progressive throttle. A sudden jab to the gas consistently induces understeer.

3) Brakes. With four puck calipers and ventilated disks, brake reliability or fade is not a problem. Cockpit adjustable brake bias allows drivers to tailor the bias to the racetrack and conditions, but it's the most frequently misadjusted setting, often contributing to corner entry balance problems.

4) Tires. The cars are fitted with 8.5-inch slicks on the front and 12.5-inch on the rear and, relative to a street radial, they require less yaw angle in cornering. The compound, however, is relatively hard in modern terms and more yaw can be used than appropriate in, for example, a WSC car on softer tires. The harder compound allows the tires to be safely clear of overheating and going off, in all but the very worst hot weather and abrasive racetrack conditions. The problem becomes generating sufficient heat to provide maximum grip. The harder compound wears longer and has less variation in grip over its useful life than a softer tire.

The tire is also more resilient than softer slicks in its ability to come back to a standard level of grip if it

"Driving in the Barber Pro Series is the first time for a lot of guys on an oval and probably the first time many of them are tempted to experiment with left foot braking.

"If you could brake as well with the left foot as the right, you'd be better off to do it with the left because the time segment between [throttle off and brake on] is shorter and since you're doing it in the corner it doesn't upset the car as much.

"You can actually use both, which I do on the ovals. I mean, I do that here on [the New Hampshire International Speedway]. I'll get out of the throttle to brake for the corner but I'll get back on the throttle without releasing the brake. I'll go down on the throttle a lot to get the turbo spooled up and, as the nose gets where I want, I'll start releasing the brake for my acceleration curve. That works awfully well on an oval—it really does. And there's no reason it wouldn't on a road course—if you were efficient. The only reason I use it on an oval and don't use it on a road course is that at threshold level braking, my left foot isn't as sensitive. Yet, for a slow down deal like here where you're not doing a maximum stop— you're just slowing up—the left foot is fine. It works good. Not a problem."

—Dorsey Schroeder

"The compound that the Pro Series cars run is harder than most of the guys in GTS run—for a little 1500-lb open wheel car. You just can't hurt those tires. As a matter of fact, often you have a tough time getting them up to temperature and that's why often in qualifying, the quick times are set at the end because the tires are just getting there.

"The most intriguing thing about that to me is that it makes the opening lap or two very interesting. It's so difficult to get heat in the tires. It's always good to watch a guy who's really good on cold tires. It's really difficult to drive a blistering first lap on cold tires."

—Jeremy Dale

5) Sensitivity of Controls. The horsepower to weight ratio is up substantially from the Formula Dodge but the mass of the car is higher, requiring higher input forces on the controls. The contact patch of the front slicks, for example, is much greater and its also loaded with downforce from the front wings, making the steering wheel much harder to turn. Additionally, the design of the front suspension requires more caster, adding again to the force required. When transitioning to the Pro Series cars, most drivers adjust their normal seating position so that they have a greater bend in their arms, making it easier to exert force on the steering wheel.

Drivers are free to adjust the wing angles and rear flap angle, and the shock absorber bump and rebound settings. The drivers also have cockpit adjustable brake bias, and front and rear anti-roll bars. The cars can always be reset to baseline settings determined by test drivers (top level professionals such as Dorsey Schroeder, John Paul Jr., and Robbie Buhl). The baseline settings produce a car with the potential of being within the same second as the pole time. At baseline, the car's characteristics approximate neutral cornering balance yet driver technique variations can pro-

Fig. 15-9. The Barber/Dodge Pro Series racecar provides the driver with adjustable front and rear anti-roll bars and cockpit adjustable brake bias.

is inadvertently overheated. All it takes is a relatively easy lap or two to cool the tires a little and get the car back in the competitive ballpark.

Unlike softer compounds, the tires require more laps to get to their peak traction temperature. Each car is fitted with one set of new tires for the race weekend and since at least 30 minutes of practice are run before qualifying, there is no need to attempt a three lap qualifying charge as you would if a new set were fitted for qualifying.

Fig. 15-10. Robbie Buhl (car no. 7), the 1989 Barber/Saab Champion, found a rhythm and momentum that led to dominance.

"In testing the Pro cars, I've found that 70% of the drivers use too much front brake bias. They'll run lots of front brake bias because it gives them stability and the car never wants to get loose. It gives them a rock hard brake pedal but not a good stop. You're pushing like hell and there's a lot of resistance in the pedal, but there's not a lot of stop. But if they haven't felt a good stop, they don't realize it. They are happy with the pedal feel and they say, 'Okay, this is the best the car has got,' but it's not. You can wind it to the back a little bit and pick up the efficiency of the rear wheels. And the bias is going to change as you go through the race—if you wear rear tires more than the fronts, it's not going to want as much rear bias. It's hard to deal with."

—*Dorsey Schroeder*

"When I first go back to doing the testing for the Pro Series, I find myself, when I first get in them, over-driving them a little bit. And then I just back it down a notch. Get to the basics. Make sure you're not over-slowing the entry. Find the fine line of just trailing off—just picking up the throttle at the right time and at the right speed. You know when you hit it right—it's just a great sensation. And then you just try to duplicate it. Once you get back in the car, if you back down a bit and find the rhythm, you usually end up going a little bit quicker."

—*Robbie Buhl*

voke both understeer and oversteer. The range of chassis adjustments provide subtle changes in the balance, helping the drivers trim the handling to their liking while avoiding going drastically too far in any one direction.

The variety of adjustments can tailor the car's behavior in each of the three phases of a corner, corner entry, steady state cornering, and the corner exit.

6) Gearbox. The Ft-200 five speed works much like the Mk-9 Hewland, but each gear inside is roughly twice the weight of its Mk-9 counterpart. It takes more strength to move the gear lever.

Another complication is the location of first gear. When the gearbox was originally designed, first gear was meant to aid the car in getting out of the pits. It seemed reasonable to separate first from the other four gears and have the driver engage it in a two step motion: down to the left against a spring loaded plunger, then back to engage first. The recent proliferation of street courses and slow chicanes now forces drivers to use first in racing situations. Drivers frequently struggle to select first until they learn that it takes more time than the other gears, and a double motion.

Any shortcomings in downshifting technique will show up immediately in your performance. If your footwork is lazy or sloppy, causing fumbling with the gears, the mistake, even a small one, will typically cost you a position because of the closeness of the competition in the series.

7) Competitiveness. Although it doesn't necessarily affect the driving technique you use, the level of competitiveness in the series can profoundly affect your attitude. Drivers entering the Barber Dodge Pro Series have been successful in other forms of racing and it can be rough on a driver's confidence to finish 11th when they are accustomed to winning. Drivers need to keep in mind that as they reach higher levels in the sport, the standard of skill of the front runners is at a higher plane than the less professional levels. Typically, the closest competition takes place in the fifth through tenth positions as drivers make small mistakes and recover. It's not that they are bad drivers—it's just that there are five drivers in front of them who are not making any mistakes.

The key is to keep a positive attitude, stay with it and keep learning and improving.

FRONT-ENGINE SEDANS AND SCCA TRANS AM

There are numerous venues of professional races for closed wheel sedans based on production cars. The cars are thinly disguised all-out racecars—funny cars, if you will—which use exotic materials and the highest technology available. There has been heavy factory involvement by auto makers such as Nissan, Mazda, Ford and General Motors, which in turn makes the budgets astronomical.

SCCA sanctions the Trans Am series for cars similar to GTS but with tighter restrictions on modifications and tire size. Manufacturers are also heavily involved in Trans Am, but since the rules are more restrictive, a team without factory support has a greater chance of success in Trans Am than in GTS.

Both types of cars are very powerful and typically have engines mounted in front of the driver, which creates problems in getting their tremendous power to the ground.

Driver Technique Considerations

1) Power. The GTS car, with 800 hp available, is strikingly fast; and with the engine mounted forward of the driver, it suffers from a relative lack of grip from

Fig. 15-11. Trans Am cars like Dorsey Schroeder's Mustang Cobra (right) have access to their incredible horsepower throughout a wide RPM range.

the rear, driving tires. This has a tremendous effect on the way the throttle is applied at the exits of corners. While many lower-powered cars are able to go at full throttle around the apex of a corner and out to the track-out, these cars are rarely at full throttle until the corner is completed—especially true of slow corners.

Fig. 15-12. Most competitive GTS cars use turbo-charged engines, calling for a delicate touch on the throttle and a flawless sense of timing when it comes to acceleration out of corners. Here, Jeremy Dale races in his Nissan 300ZX Turbo.

"I think, acceleration curve-wise, a Trans Am car is in the same league as a Formula car like Barber Dodge in acceleration, but the difference with the Trans Am car is that you have such an incredible amount of torque and power on the low end.

"I think that all of the guys that came after me in the Roush gong show that came out of a formula car background were really taken off by the fact that when you first go to power in the corner, when you first make the transition from brake to throttle, you've go so much more than you ever had before, so much more torque, so much more power. When you first go to power you go to way too much.

"The big factor is not only horsepower but torque. A GTU motor, like a Mazda rotary, is a motor that puts out tremendous horsepower but not tremendous torque; and the management of what you have is not as big a factor. They like to be kept in the upper ranges of their RPM because the hp falls off below a certain RPM level, unlike my car, where I've got a workable range from 4,500 RPM up to 8,000 and [the rotary] has a range of 6,500 to 8,000, maybe higher. That peakiness is a different problem that has to be dealt with."

—Dorsey Schroeder

Complicating matters further, the majority of competitive GTS cars used turbo-charged engines, where there is a great difference in the motor's horsepower output between low and maximum boost. This calls for great delicacy of throttle application and an accurate sense of timing so that the boost comes on as the car enters the straight, not while in mid-corner.

GTS cars are capable of speeds exceeding 180 m.p.h., roughly 40 to 50 m.p.h. faster than the next slowest class of car. A tenth of a second delay in applying the brakes carries the car close to 30 feet closer to the corner, calling for consistent accuracy in brake points. Adapting to high speed is a requirement for all of the cars from this class onward.

"In moving up to a GTS car, the biggest thing is the combination of power and lack of downforce in a fairly heavy car. I came out of the lightest, most agile, best handling, underpowered GTU car there was into the heaviest, most powerful, worst handling GTS car there was—with tons of turbo lag.

"The higher closing speed was particularly a problem in IMSA racing—a huge problem. There are so many cars with such diverse abilities. The speeds of the cars are so different and the abilities of the drivers are so different. You get into big problems in traffic, especially in the one hour sprint races."

—Jeremy Dale

"I drove the GTS Nissan with Geoff Brabham and Dominick Dobson, and it used a lot of road. We sent Brabham out in it first and he came in after eight laps and said 'This thing is ****ed.' Something was wrong with the car.

"We put Millen in the car and he came back and said there was nothing wrong with it. What it was, was that Geoff was so used to the amount of downforce generated by the Nissan GTP car—I guess it was planted all the way around and that's what he expected.

"The GTS car floated a lane to 3/4 of a lane on the banking. We ran so little downforce on it to get the speed on the banking—it's only a two-liter, four-cylinder motor—that it was weird. It took you four or five laps to realize that it was just going to go places unpredictably. It wasn't vicious or snappy—it just went where it wanted.

"I thought it was terribly unpredictable, but I got used to it. I hated traffic. You just had to leave a lot of room. You come up on a guy in an old GTO car and you're going 'Here I come! Don't do anything stupid!'"

—David Loring

Fig. 15-13. The Nissan 240SX GTU car with which David Loring won his 1992 GTU Championship was considerably less brutish than Jeremy Dale's 300ZX GTS rocket.

> *"The toughest thing in an S car is the heat. The temperature of the pedals gets up to 180 to 190 degrees and that comes through your shoe. You feel that.*
>
> *"I remember at Sebring, we made carbon fiber inlays for my shoes to insulate my foot from the pedal. It's amazing. The whole chassis gets hot. You couldn't touch a chassis tube in the cockpit, it was so hot. The heat soaks through the whole car.*
>
> *"It's not something you would normally think about, but you don't take your gloves off before you get out of the car because you're probably going to grab a chassis tube on the way out."*
>
> —Jeremy Dale

cially on hot race days, it is important that the driver be in peak physical condition in order to deal with the wilting effect of high temperatures.

2) Braking. Both Trans Am and GTS cars are at least 1000 lbs. heavier than any single-seat car. While the brakes are for the most part consistent and reliable, they are more prone to fade than those on lighter cars. When the car is set up in sprint race mode, with softer brake pads, the pedal effort is reasonable. In an endurance race, however, the teams try to maximize pad life by going to a harder pad and a lower friction rotor, which can put the maximum brake pedal pressure over 300 lbs. Strong legs are required.

> *"A big change was braking and the fact that it took so much effort to get the car to stop. The car felt like it was never going to stop. The G-forces generated under braking were not sufficient for as fast as you were going."*
>
> *"It's so bad in the 24-hour that by the next morning I was using both feet on the brake pedal. The first few years I did it, you'd push so hard on the brake pedal that your foot would wrap around the pedal and you'd bruise the bottom of your foot 'til it was painful...300 lbs. of pressure is a lot when you only weigh 160!"*
>
> —Dorsey Schroeder

A special speed-related adaptation required in GTS is that their races are frequently made up of two or more classes of car, some of which are 50 m.p.h. slower, and driven by racers within a wide range of talent. Lapping situations frequently call for a new level of risk taking that isn't found in races with a single class of car where there aren't the huge differences in speed potential.

With the engine mounted ahead of the driver, much more heat finds its way into the driver's compartment than in a rear-engined formula car. Espe-

"I use brake bias a lot. I've learned to use it because of the cars I've had to drive—like the Trans-Am car. They only allow you to build in 52% rear weight maximum.

"Now, when you look at 32 gallons of fuel—almost 7 lbs. per gallon—and it's located behind the rear axle in the fuel cell, and during the course of the race you get over 220 lbs. of weight off, the car's going to get wicked loose at the back. So you end up having to change sway bars and brake bias as you go.

"You had to dial that out, toward the front, as you ran out of fuel. In any braking zone, if you started to feel the back start to go, you quickly turn the adjuster. The difference was, like, two full turns from full fuel to empty. If you were in a 24-hour race like Daytona, and that was basically a Trans-Am type car, then you had to go back when you refueled."

—Dorsey Schroeder

"98% of the time in a GTS car you can use the brakes as hard as you want. The cars have huge brakes and they never really have any big brake problems. The biggest potential problem is when you pit and there's no more cooling air going over the brake. They tend to heat soak and boil the fluid. That's why we had water-cooled calipers on the Nissan. When you pitted, you turned on the circulating pump and it would take the heat out of the calipers and keep the fluid from boiling. It's pretty slick."

—Jeremy Dale

"Conserving the tires is a big factor in GTS. I reckon that no matter what tire you put on a GTS car, in ten laps, if you wanted to, you could run the tires off the car. You could run the car that hard.

"We test at a race pace. You try and be consistent but it burns through tires so quickly that it's tough to keep one set of tires on the car long enough to get a real read on what the car's doing.

"Once the tires start to go away, the car doesn't have grip entering the corner or exiting the corner. You end up going through a phenomenal number of tires just because the car is so heavy and so powerful.

"The car will tolerate a pretty solid brake level and pretty hard cornering levels, but as soon as you start to slide the car, whether it's on entry or exit, you're going to start to burn the tires off the car. It's easier to do that on exit with throttle, but it's just as doable on entry."

—Jeremy Dale

"The gearboxes are getting so good. Double-clutch downshifting, I think, is still the right thing to do. It never unloads the car—it keeps your balance—but the gearboxes have gotten so good that you don't have to do it....

"The good [racers] will blip, because dumping it in gear without the clutch, just cramming it in, you can't brake at more than 60% efficiency without locking the rear wheels."

—Dorsey Schroeder

"The gearboxes were very durable as long as you took care of it, didn't abuse it. It's very important in any racecar not to abuse the gearbox. A lot of guys do.

"I do the traditional double clutch (going down). I always upshift without the clutch because I find it smoother. Any time you push the clutch you potentially damage it. If you never push in the clutch you're probably not going to wear it out or break it.

"There are certain corners where I'll just go down one gear with a light brake application and not use the clutch—just nick it into neutral, give it a blip and go down a gear. Going down more than one gear, I'll do the traditional double clutch downshift."

—Jeremy Dale

3) Tires. Power oversteer is available any time the car is turning, and while the most obvious drawback is the possibility of spinning because of aggressive throttle application, your greater concern is ruining the grip of the rear tires. In these cars, you could do that in three laps of over-aggressive throttle application.

4) Gearbox. The gearboxes in these cars are able to take quite a bit of wear and tear, but you still have to be careful. The best route is to consistently use the double-clutch method of shifting. Technically, you don't have to double-clutch with these cars, but if you want to be able to get through an endurance race, you want to conserve the gearbox as much as possible.

5) Competition. Although drivers coming in to GTS or Trans Am will have had some experience testing in lower formulas, professional teams invariably have a team engineer who works closely with the driver on testing new modifications to the car and in deciding on the optimum set up for each racetrack. The rapport between driver and engineer can be extremely important to the team's success. The best relationships are based on free and open communication, mutual understanding, and respect. Drivers who cultivate this relationship do better than those who can't.

For the driver, new responsibilities come along with factory involvement. Your on-track performance has to be above reproach. There are hoards of drivers waiting in the wings to take your place should the team begin to think that you're not getting everything that you could possibly get out of the car. The manufacturers are supporting the effort in order to win, and their interest is to use the racing results to sell more cars. There can be considerable pressure on the driver to meet these goals.

Beyond the behind-the-wheel skills, drivers at this level will be required to take part in promotional events, give speeches and presentations, and function as the company's representative—both at the track and in any public place. Frequently, you'll be scheduled fully by the company during race week to spearhead their marketing and promotional efforts. Social skills as well as public speaking ability become an important part of your role as a racer. It can be difficult to keep your focus on racing when you have to wear so many hats.

SPORTS PROTOTYPES

Sports prototypes encompass a wide range of specific car types, but all share some common configurations. Essentially, they are purpose-built racecars where, if you stretch your imagination, there is seating for two. The most obvious difference relative to Formula cars is that the wheels and tires are covered by bodywork.

The specifications to which the cars are built change frequently—often annually—but even with all the variations, there are basically three major categories of prototypes: Group C cars, GTP, and WSC.

Group C Cars
The sports prototype equivalent in Europe is Group C. Occasionally, Group C cars have been allowed to compete in endurance races such as the 24 Hours of Daytona and the 12 Hours of Sebring.

GTP
The primary prototype in the United States was the GTP car, which evolved from 1981 through the early 1990s. This was IMSA's premier class—exotic machines with enclosed driver compartments and, as time went on, phenomenal downforce and mind-numbing performance.

World Sports Car
Starting in 1993, IMSA reacted to the escalating costs of fielding GTP cars by mixing in a new classification called World Sports Car (WSC), open-top versions of

"From a GTS car to a GTP car—in this case, to a Group C car—was a big jump. The cornering and braking forces, even with modest tunnels, was a lot higher. In the chicane at Daytona, for example, in the GTS car, you're taking a lot of speed off and going down a couple of gears; but in the Group C car, you barely brake, go down one gear and you're gone. I mean, you're flying.

"In terms of top speed it was very quick—it would go 215 m.p.h., where the GTS car wouldn't go above 185 or 190.

"From a handling standpoint, it was the least responsive car to drive. It was also the heaviest, at 2,100 lbs. You could really feel the weight of that car. It felt heavy and kind of cumbersome to drive. Of course, it had 800 to 850 horsepower, so it was very, very quick. It was quicker in corners than the WSC car, but it wasn't light on its feet. The weight difference between the two wasn't enormous but it was the combination of downforce and tire and weight that made it feel ponderous.

"I enjoyed the challenge of driving the car. For me, at the time, it was a great experience to drive that car."

—Jeremy Dale

"I had been used to Road Atlanta in the Pro Series car and the turn at the end of the straight, after a while, felt sort of routine. In the GTP car you're still braking at the same point but you're going 35 m.p.h. faster and everything, the braking, downshifting, and turn-in all happens that much faster. Challenging the brake zone was a big step....It wasn't the top speed that was the big thrill as much as holding it as late as the car was capable of going."

—Jim Pace

"The first time I drove a GTP car, I drove a Chevy Spice for Jim Miller for a couple of races, and I raced it for the first time at Miami. It was a fast car and I didn't have my speed converter up to snuff and I had to consciously think too much about what I was doing. It's a matter of time in the car—testing. It was an experience. We only had two test days in it before we went."

—David Loring

GTP cars where both the horsepower and the downforce-creating bodywork were restricted from earlier levels. Presently, WSC has replaced GTP as road racing's top-line closed-wheel racecar.

Fig. 15-14. GTP cars had more than enough horsepower—so much so that racetracks like Lime Rock had to modify the course to keep the cars on the ground.

> "In a GTP car, you sit pretty far forward, and it's hard to read the back end of the car a little bit when you come into a slow corner....That's where the heaviest stuff of the car is.... But it has a lot of opportunity to build momentum before you as a driver ever feel it."
>
> "All of the cars I've driven, from Barber/Saab on up, will tolerate the same kinds of slip angle, the same amount of rotation. There will be a degree or two difference here or there, but they'll all tolerate close to the same amount. The thing that makes a difference is when you can go to the throttle and either carry that rotation with power or settle the rear end back down. That depends on the power plant in the back of the car."
>
> —Brian Till

> "In the WSC car, you really have to pay attention to how you put on the power. It has more downforce than a GTS car so it's a little better about burning the tires off. You can still do it but you have to work a little harder at it. In cornering, they never really get set and settled because they don't have a lot of downforce. They are always moving around.
>
> "I don't have a lot of experience in high downforce cars so, to me, it doesn't bother me as much. It's funny to hear a guy who's used to high downforce get out of that car. Their comments are always the same. 'This sure is unstable in cornering.' To me, it's not a big deal because it's kind of what I'm used to. I never got spoiled by a lot of downforce."
>
> —Jeremy Dale

> "I've found the World Sports Cars to be more challenging to drive than the GTP cars. You have to be a lot more sensitive with the throttle. It requires a lot more from the driver—'What's the car telling me? Can I squeeze a little more throttle yet? Oops, that's too much, I got wheelspin, got to ease back a little—don't snap, just breathe—just lift your big toe.'
>
> "...They don't require as much physically to hold on in the corners as a full-on GTP car, but as far as driving the car, I think it takes a lot more sensitivity. Much more."
>
> —Jim Pace

Driver Technique Considerations

1) Power. The power of different prototypes varies widely and each has its own little wrinkle. In GTP cars, the standard problems of delivering a tremendous amount of horsepower without using up the rear tires can be further complicated by the type and state of development of the powerplant. In V8 powered cars like the Intrepid, the power band is relatively wide and torque in the lower RPM ranges is formidable. In the Toyota GTP car, universally admitted to be the most highly developed of the type, the engine is comparatively small and relies on the effect of turbocharging to make horsepower. The power comes on suddenly with some lag between the throttle application and the sudden rush of power.

Fig. 15-15. World Sports Cars require more throttle sensitivity than GTP cars due to the lower grip available without downforce-producing tunnels. Jim Pace drove this car to victory at both Daytona and Sebring in 1996.

"The Toyota GTP that I test-drove at Sears Point was tough to drive, not just because of the power, but the way it came on. You come in to the hairpin and the car would rotate, and you'd add all the opposite lock you could, then try to go to the throttle and drive it on off the corner. You'd go from 200 to 750 horsepower just instantly. It was the design of the motor—4 cylinders with a turbo charger that was probably as big around as a 15 gallon drum and you go to the throttle and nothing...nothing...everything! That made it difficult."

—Brian Till

"In the GTP Spice, you had to make a big adjustment in the way you put the power on. The torque available in a big Chevy V8 was such that you had to roll into the throttle. If you did a stab and steer it would sometimes go into big understeer but most of the time get big oversteer—light the tires up."

—Jim Pace

"When I first drove the Toyota GTP car at Daytona—we were going 210 m.p.h. on the banking—I came in after the first run and said 'What the hell happened to all the straights?'

"This car was so fast that there was no time between any of the corners. In a Camel Light car, a GTO car, a GTU car, you had days between corners. The speed itself never seemed different, but you have to adjust to the closing rate. There was a car at Daytona we lapped every four laps—for 24 hours.

"What a neat race car! It was the fastest car in the world at that time. It took me four or five laps to go through the banking flat, because it uses a lot of road."

—David Loring

Top prototype cars are capable of speeds over 200 m.p.h. and while most drivers adapt to the increased velocity in time, an additional problem is that they frequently are racing with cars of significantly lower speed potential. The closing rates in passing situations, especially high speed passing situations where the car can't be placed precisely, can be tricky.

2) Traction. All prototype race cars, even if the rules preclude using the huge underbody tunnels which gave GTP cars such formidable downforce in their heyday, still have a large area of underbody that can be used to create downforce.

The downforce created can vary greatly with changes in the car's ride height and rake. To control changes in rake and to support the aerodynamic loads, the cars often are very stiffly sprung. This complicates matters on undulating or bumpy racetrack: here, a compromise has to be made between ultimate grip in high speed corners and driveability in low

"In the Toyota GTP car we trimmed the thing out a lot at Daytona, but still it had gobs of downforce. The bus stop (the chicane) was 4th gear. You'd come down into it, go from fifth to fourth, turn it in, go back to throttle—it would spool up by the right hander, then you're just hanging on—Whoooooah! Turn it back up into the banking and then get fifth. It was unbelievable. Wicked fast."

—David Loring

"[T]he first time I drove a 700 hp GTP car, it impressed me a lot. That night I got on the phone and called some of my buddies from med school. Said, 'Hey, you would not believe the way this thing goes around the last turn at Savannah. Both my cheeks wind up on the same side of my helmet.' It is wonderful."

—Jim Pace

"At a test session you have specific pieces that you want to test and a particular way you want to do that. The engineer is the best guy to put that program together. He'll brief me and the crew chief and the team manager so that we're all in sync. Between sessions we talk about what we're going to do next session and we share ideas of how to accomplish what we want and we figure out between us the best way to do it. We're deciding from session to session what the strategy is going to be. It's worked out pretty well.

"The first place we ever tested the [Spice WSC] seriously was at Daytona in '94. We put the car on the racetrack and it was like dragging a rock through the air. We decided by just looking at the nose that it didn't look like the best piece for what we wanted to do so we evolved away from it. It started like that and for the first five months of the season it never saw a wind tunnel. Initially, it was just trial and error. But when you throw a different nose on and you gain 5 m.p.h., that's a pretty good indication that you're headed in the right direction."

—Jeremy Dale

speed turns where aerodynamics don't have as great an effect on the car's grip.

Downforce and grip are usually a big step up from lower classes of cars. The driver stepping into a prototype car for the first time has to reacclimate to just how fast the car is capable of cornering.

3) Competition. Unlike other series, there are often a wide variety of cars under the sports prototype umbrella, each uniquely designed within broad parameters set up by the sanctioning bodies.

The closest prototype racing came to having a one-design series was in the days when the Porsche 962 was the dominant package. Even then, many teams would take the stock 962 and modify it in pursuit of an advantage over the competition.

With unique designs come many potential pitfalls. Unlike a car like the 962, which was a highly developed car, slightly modified and improved over a 10 year history, a new prototype is designed and developed over a short period of time. It's normal that new designs have teething problems. A successful racecar is made up of thousands of parts, and many interrelated systems, any one of which can deteriorate or fail.

The sorting and development of a prototype and the access to facilities to continually create new parts, engine configurations, and body work is a key factor in your success as a competitive racer. Your ability to test and be an active and helpful partner in the development of the car is invaluable.

Prototypes often compete in 12 hour and 24 hour endurance races as part of their year-long schedule. To remain competitive, you have to adapt to the con-

"What's happening more and more with real racecars like GTS and WSC is that the endurance races have become sprint races....The philosophy now is that you go out and you run about as hard as you can and if you don't break, you're going to win.

"The WSC car we run in an endurance race like Daytona is pretty much the same car as we run in sprint races. A couple of details will change, but it has all the same parts as in a sprint race. The biggest difference is the RPM limit you use. That's the biggest change. The V 8's weakest link is the valve train and that's directly related to RPM. You have to run an RPM that you feel the valve train is going to live with for 24 hours. We've had good luck with that for the last two years. I felt that the motor was just as strong at the end of the race as at the beginning. Maybe that means we were too conservative, but we've hit the nail pretty solidly on the head for two years now. It also reflects well on the guys that we had in the car."

—Jeremy Dale

ditions these kinds of races will impose. The requirements in terms of logistical support are vastly different than what is required of a two hour sprint race. Refueling, driver changes, race strategy, and long stints behind the wheel are all variations drivers will have to adapt to.

Sharing a race car with another driver or two complicates matters. Driver size and seating positions will vary as will individual driver's preferences on car set up. Lap times are also sure to vary from driver to driver and presents a sometimes delicate problem of preventing bruised egos from over extending the car.

In both long and short events, some prototypes are better than others in terms of the strength and endurance required of the driver. Some of the most stiffly sprung GTP cars were murder on a driver, even in a relatively short sprint race. One team racing on a particularly bumpy circuit had to fabricate a restraining device in the footwell of the car that ran across the top of the drivers ankles so that his feet could stay in some proximity to the pedals as the car violently bounced down the straight.

Heat inside a closed prototype can also be a problem and many teams resort to fitting cool suit devices for their drivers to keep their body temperatures under control.

INDY LIGHTS

Indy Lights are almost like the farm system in baseball, in that top talent in this class of racing tends to move up to Indy Cars. As you can imagine, the competition at this level is incredibly fierce, since every racer in Indy Lights is out to prove they can make it to the pinnacle of racing.

> *"I had raced both the GTU event and the Camel Lights race at Portland. I had just done the GTU race. so I was in that car for two hours, then I had an hour out of the car, then I got in the Camel Light car. It was 105 degrees and, wouldn't you know it, they plugged my cool suit in backwards. We're well into the race and I was dying. I had already taken my gloves off, unzipped the top of the driving suit, tried to rip the cool suit off. Then the radio broke so I couldn't tell them what was going on. I was weaving back and forth as I went by the pits trying to let them know I had a problem and needed a replacement. Finally at the end of the front straight at Portland everything went black and white and I knew I'd better come in. They dragged me out of the car. I had a body temperature of 104.9."*
>
> —David Loring

> *"The Indy Lights car is a car you have to drive. No question about it. I think an okay driver in an Indy Lights car is going to be at the back of the pack because you've got to be willing to really drive the car 110% all the time. If you're not, there are people out there who are....You're just on the edge all the time—a controlled edge, but on it. That's where you're figuring out what the car's doing and being able to give the feedback to your crew guys. It's definitely a series where you have to figure out what the car's doing and where it's doing it so that...[the crew] can make a change. It's not the type of series where a driver can carry a car."*
>
> —Robbie Buhl

Driver Technique Considerations

1) Drafting. In higher horsepower cars, the draft effect becomes less pronounced since they are using proportionately less of their horsepower to overcome aerodynamic drag. Still, the draft, especially on long straights, can be an effective passing tool.

On high speed ovals, however, following closely in the draft can upset the aerodynamic downforce of the car, substantially affecting its grip and handling.

2) Power. The Buick V-6 in an Indy Lights car delivers 425 hp and, without a turbocharger, its power is more progressive than a turbomotor where once you're off the boost the power is reduced dramatically then tends to come on suddenly once the turbo spools up. The torque of the Buick is a key ingredient.The motor pulls well, even lower down in its RPM range, and getting the power to the ground, especially in the lower gears, requires sensitivity on the throttle.

> *"The Indy Light car would draft fairly well and you could use it to pass. It [also]decelerated a little bit, you know, when you popped out, but it would maintain a pretty good draft."*
>
> —Brian Till

> *"When I moved up from Barber/Saab to Indy Lights, there was a little more grip, but the biggest difference then was mainly just horsepower. It affected everything, because you arrive at the corners quicker and your timing has to change. It changes your timing on everything—brake points, downshifts."*
>
> —Bryan Herta

Fig. 15-16. The team aspect of racing takes on more prominence at the higher levels of the sport. After a successful season in Indy Lights, including a victory at Mid Ohio, the RAL team with driver Brian Till took the big leap to Indy Car.

> *"Being in an Indy Lights car, which is 420 hp, I'm not hardly as smooth as I used to be in a Barber/Saab... I really have to be hard on myself to keep that smoothness because you can get away with a little bit more aggressiveness...you use the horsepower more to steer the car.*
>
> *"Lots of times you have to get off the power in the middle of the corner to get it to point and come down toward the apex. But every time you do that, you're killing your exit speed. It doesn't hurt you as bad as in a turbo car like the Barber/Saab, where getting off the throttle dumps the boost, but still, you'd rather not be lifting. Theoretically, you brake, come back off the brakes, turn in, squeeze to power and keep squeezing all the way through—when the car is right."*
>
> —Robbie Buhl

may be a new experience. Smooth braking transitions from the straight into a fast sweeping corner may require developing the new talent of braking with the left foot so as to minimize the sharp transition of load that occurs with a full throttle lift to get over to the brake pedal.

> *"I never used left foot braking until I ran Indy Lights. I ran my first year of Indy Lights braking with my right foot and there was nothing wrong with it, but I decided that I wanted to try left foot braking, especially on ovals. I had to spend a whole day with it but by the end of the day I felt comfortable and confident with my left foot. I probably had a lot of sensitivity in my left foot from having raced Karts where you use your left foot on the brake.... [But] I don't use my left foot on road courses."*
>
> —Bryan Herta

3) Brakes. Brakes on Indy Lights cars are powerful and consistent. There is, however, a wide choice in the type of brake pad available from various vendors, and each driver can choose the pad type that suits his preference of level of effort, feel and stopping power.

For drivers who cut their teeth on road race courses, both the car setup and the driving strategy of ovals

4) Tires. The Firestone racing slicks have no special quirks, but it is important not to get carried away with accelerating away from corners with wheelspin. The rear tires will go off from overheating and it's easy to get into the downward spiral of increasing oversteer.

The level of competition in this series is intense and the fact that the tires have their ultimate grip in

Fig. 15-17. Patience and timing with the throttle is a key aspect of conserving tires in Indy Lights. Here, 1992 Champion Robbie Buhl deals with one of the toughest corner exits on the circuit: Mid Ohio's Keyhole.

"An Indy Light car is a car that doesn't respond to trail braking as well as a Formula Ford because it's almost more important to get the car settled down before you get into the corner so that you can think about getting on the power coming out.

"The Indy Light cars will encounter fade. I had horrible brakes at the end of the races last year. We just had problems reading our temperatures on our brakes. We weren't cooling them properly. We thought they could last at a certain temperature the whole race but even though they were in the window of operating temperature they developed a fade. Now we duct both front and rear on all road courses and that's made the problem go away."

—Robbie Buhl

Fig. 15-18. Indy Lights are just one step away from the top rung on the US road-racing ladder, as Bryan Herta proved after winning his championship in 1993.

their first few laps of life has a great effect on qualifying technique. To take advantage of the extra grip afforded by fresh tires, you have to get in your best lap within three or four laps of leaving the pit lane.

5) *Adjustability.* An Indy Lights car has all the standard adjustments available on any sophisticated race car—bars, springs, front and rear wings, and shock absorbers. It would be all too easy to treat these flat-bottomed cars as if the wings were the only adjustment affecting aerodynamic balance. Not so. Even

though the cars are not fitted with downforce producing tunnels like Formula Atlantic or Indy cars, maintaining the proper angle between the road surface and the flat bottom is key to creating downforce and grip, especially in fast sweepers and on oval tracks. Top teams focus particular attention on shock absorber adjustment and development.

It is especially important, since the cars behave quite differently with different setups, that the driver be able to communicate accurately with the crew.

6) *Gearbox.* The Weismann 5 speed is much like any other dog-ring racing transmission but with a light weight car and lots of horsepower the car accelerates quickly and doesn't stay in any one gear for very long. Shifts have to be precise and quick and since the car accelerates so quickly, a missed or slow shift is going to cost proportionately more than in other cars.

7) *Competition.* This class of racing is one step away from Indy Cars and the level of talent and motivation is extremely high. It is not a place for dilettantes or the faint of heart.

> *"The first day the biggest transition from Barber/Pro to Indy Lights was the horsepower. As you move up there's a lot more people around you and your job changes. In Barber/Pro I was my own Engineer. I drove the car, thought about the set-up, and made changes to it after discussing it with my mechanic and with the series personnel. In Barber/Pro maybe you knew what you wanted, you knew what you meant and you could make the changes, but later on, if you can't relate what the car is doing to other people, you're not going to be successful."*
>
> *—Bryan Herta*

> *"Indy's not like any other racetrack, that's for sure. The car is extremely sensitive to input. You have to be very smooth with things. It's very fast. What you do with the car at the corner entry—whether you lift off a little bit, or lift off early then go back to power—all dictates the attitude and the set the car takes through the corner.*
>
> *"It's an amazing place because the car is so sensitive to the smallest change because you're going so fast. You can read it instantly but you have to be very consistent with your driving. If you go into the corner a different way, it affects the car all the way through the turn, so you have to be consistent with that before you start getting crazy with changes."*
>
> *—Robbie Buhl*

> *"With the Indy Car, handling from the turn-in point down toward where you start putting the throttle on is so good that you don't have to necessarily give up that part. The Indy Car has 700 horsepower, so you want to take advantage of that down the straightaway; but it also has good handling—if you set it up right—so you want to take advantage of that, too.*
>
> *"In a Formula Atlantic car, you can afford the extraneous thought. In an Atlantic car you can come out with 240 horsepower, light up the rear tires, slide it sideways through the turn and go (yaahooooo!). In an Indy Car, that same throttle movement controls 700+ horsepower so the small adjustments in the throttle are that much more effective on the car. So you just have to concentrate just that much more—it's imperative."*
>
> *—Brian Till*

INDY CAR

In the United States, Indy Car is the absolute top of the heap. Even sports fans who don't follow racing can name at least a half-dozen Indy Car drivers. To drive one of these cars is to have arrived at the pinnacle of your profession.

Driver Technique Considerations

1) *Power.* An Indy Car, depending upon the specific powerplant (and who you believe), has between 700 and 1,000 horsepower available to push a 1,550-lb. car. Like many other high powered cars such as GTS, GTP, and World Sports Car, getting this power to the ground is a major concern, especially when you con-

sider the potential of using up the rear tires with excessive wheel spin.

All of this power is available at a price. The engines are highly stressed and complicated and, consequently, their reliability varies widely. Although most are fitted with rev limiters, it is still relatively easy to damage the motor by over-revving, especially in the lower gears, where the car accelerates so fast that shifts come quickly and the acceleration of the motor is at its most rapid. The easiest way to blow up an Indy Car is to over-rev the engine on downshifts.

All this power on tap also affects the reliability of the drive train components, and making it to the end of a race is an accomplishment in itself.

With Indy Cars, lots of horsepower and light weight equal speed—real speed. 230 m.p.h. speeds on

Fig. 15-19. Above, Brian Till competing in Indy Car in 1992. The driver who makes it to Indy Car has reached the peak of the racing profession, and competition is fierce to stay at the top of the heap.

"The hardest time to adjust to the speed is when you've had a winter off and you've done primarily road course testing. The first time you go to Indy or Michigan the speed gets your attention. You go charging down into Turn 1 for the first time doing about 230, and you know last year it was flat . . . for a while you're thinking, 'Whoa, am I going fast!' Then what invariably happens is that, once you settle in, you find yourself trying to push the accelerator pedal through the bulkhead trying to get it to go faster. It's always that way."
—Danny Sullivan

Fig. 15-20. Robbie Buhl, here in the 1996 Phoenix IRL event. Oval track racing calls for some adaptation of classic road racing techniques, particularly at corner entry.

the straights are routine, but more intimidating is the cornering speed. Many racedrivers find this a difficult adjustment from slower racecars. A 100 m.p.h. drift is one thing. Balancing a sliding racecar at a speed 130 m.p.h. faster is a very different story.

Again and again, drivers new to Indy Cars note that things happen fast—so fast that they don't have the luxury of analyzing problems that crop up, as they could in slower classes of car. A deep background of racing experience is needed to react instantly—almost unconsciously—to the unexpected.

2) Traction and Braking. The ground effects design of Indy Car underbodies creates tremendous downforce at high speed; the implications for the driver involve a great deal of finesse in braking and controlling the car.

One of the problems is that the car's grip is speed-variable. In low speed corners where aerodynamic downforce is low, the mechanical setup of the suspen-

"In practice and qualifying at Long Beach this year, I think I hit the wall six times, only doing damage once. In practice and qualifying you drive 100% the whole time...no, in qualifying you pick it up a little. As soon as we go out in qualifying—we have about five good laps on our new tires—boom—that's when you have to get with the program 'cause that's when they're the best. Basically, at both Long Beach and Detroit, the two street races, I turned in, went to power, and biffed my front steering rod because I hit the inside apex wall. The car on new tires didn't start washing away as soon as I anticipated.

"Lots of times you brush the wall on the way out, but that hasn't caught me out yet. You're just using all the road—if you've got a big power oversteer when you do it, obviously you're going to snap something.

"At the Indy Light level of racing, with the seriousness of the competition, if you're not doing that stuff, you're not going to be on the front row. If you're leaving four inches from the edges during qualifying, you're not going to do it—unless your car is way, way hooked up or you're cheating.

"I think that with any of the top drivers in Indy Lights, if you give them the proper equipment and the proper test time, they're going to go out and be competitive in an Indy Car. We want to show ourselves and we're willing to go wheel to wheel with a Michael or an Al, given the proper circumstances."

—Robbie Buhl

"In a slow corner, following another car makes little or no difference. As speed increases, the closer you get to the car in front, the more you lose grip on the front of your car and the front end starts to push out. Unless you have a strange imbalance in your car, it almost exclusively affects the front. At Indy, you can be running behind someone and as you catch him, all of a sudden the steering will go light and the front just starts to slide. At that point, your only option is to gradually come out of the gas and wait as the car slides wide of the other car— you'll start to pick up some of the grip again and get the front end back. You have to be very subtle with the throttle change.

"Brake points are almost identical in every kind of car you drive. It's really funny. Your brake point at Mid Ohio at the end of the back straight is almost the same in an Indy Car as it is in a Barber Pro Series car. The difference is that in the Barber Pro car, you're braking from 150 to 70 where in the Indy Car you're braking from 185 to 100. The timing changes because you're going through the process a lot quicker. At that point your basics have to be good...better than that, they have to be second-nature. If you can't shift the car properly and brake and all the other basic skills of driving the car, then you can't concentrate on finding the maximum speed through the corner."

—Bryan Herta

"The thing about an Indy Car is that the car creates so much down force that down a 180 mile an hour straightaway, the car now theoretically weighs so much that it's almost impossible to get brake lockup. It requires such effort because you're not driving a 1,500-lb. car, you're driving a 5,000-lb. car. Yeah, you can get the wheels to lock up, but it requires such gargantuan effort on your part to do that it's not likely to happen accidentally.

"On a road course where the car is going very fast, you'll normally see the lockup occur in the second part of the braking zone because that's when the car weighs less. A ground effects car requires a different braking technique than a flat-bottom car. The braking effort required to slow the car down at its limit from 180 miles an hour is different than the braking effort that is going to be required at 60 miles an hour. You have to come out of the brake pedal. Not a ton, but there's a certain amount you definitely feel."

—Brian Till

sion—springs, sway bars, shocks, roll centers, etc.—determine the balance of the car. At higher speeds, the downforce masks the effect of mechanical suspension adjustments purely by the magnitude of the downforce on the tires created by airflow. At racetracks with both low speed and high speed corners, the car's behavior can be vastly different in each type of turn. In testing and practice, the game for the team is to come up with the best combination of low speed and high speed handling that results in the best overall lap time. The car, however, may be beautiful in one part of the course and a handful in another. You have to adapt and drive through a problem, even though the car is, in places, evil.

Naturally, the variability of grip with speed affects braking. In a high speed to low speed braking area, such as the approach to the hairpin at Long Beach, the braking traction decreases as the speed of the car decreases, meaning that the driver has to be prepared

Fig. 15-21. Danny Sullivan at the Long Beach Grand Prix, 1995. Sullivan epitomizes, for racers and fans alike, the notion that experience and determination combined with teamwork make for a successful run in racing.

to relax the level of pressure on the brake pedal as the car slows to adjust to the changing rate of speed loss.

Cornering and braking forces frequently exceed 3 G's, and these forces put considerable strain on your body. Simple things like an ill fitting seat can become extremely painful and detract from a driver's performance. Great care must be taken to make the driving environment as comfortable as possible.

3) Competition. A major aspect of competing in Indy Car is the fact that, with 3 Gs slamming you around for hours at a time, your physical condition toward the end of a race can be a major factor in the success of the team. Short of Trans Am, GTS or GTP cars, no race car is more physically demanding.

Pit stops are a standard issue in Indy Car racing, and often the team which does the best job in the pits and makes the best decisions on when to stop finishes first. Also, with a racecar that is so sensitive to setup, your analysis of changes that can be quickly made to improve its performance can be a definite advantage over others.

Indy Cars also race with a finite amount of fuel available for the event. Changing the level of turbocharger boost changes the power and fuel consumption; and monitoring fuel consumption versus power is an additional complication you have to deal with during the course of the race.

Like many of the professional series, the stakes are high in Indy Car, and teams struggle for the slightest advantage over the competition. This means continual testing and modification of the car to suit different racetracks and to seek gains in lap time. To make progress, you have to be able to function as a tester as well as a racer. Sometimes the two skills don't come in the same package. Testing requires consistency at the limit so that changes can be measured. The consistency can't be at the expense of speed, since the job is to find modifications that work at a race pace, not at a slower speed. You also have to develop a close relationship with the crew chief and/or the team engineer so that you all can communicate freely and accurately. With the proliferation of on-board computer data collection systems, you had better be straightforward and honest about what you're doing behind the wheel, since data that doesn't support your oral feedback can undermine the crew's confidence in your analysis of what the car is doing on the racetrack.

It takes much more than the driver to make an Indy Car work. The skill and motivation of each member of the team has to be at a peak for the team to have success. Any weakness in a subsystem of the car, chassis, gearbox, motor, suspension, areo devices, brakes, can mean failure of the entire effort. There is very little a driver can do to carry a car that has weaknesses in fundamental setup. The level of driver skill

"I had some trouble with some cramping in my right leg last year. I thought it was a problem with the amount of pressure you have to push on the brake pedal....It turns out that the cramping was because my seat wasn't entirely comfortable. When we changed my seat that eliminated all those problems.

"You don't ever want to finish a race and say, 'I might have done better if...,' anything. Especially if it's something as dumb as, 'If I had only been more comfortable.' You get a seat that's poking you in the back, it's going to take away because it's going to distract you."

—Bryan Herta

"It's amazing what they're doing now. They're developing simulation programs that are getting pretty scary. They're probably a year or two away from being able to change shock settings, load it into a computer, and, without even taking the car on the track, seeing what it does. We can set ride heights almost exactly. The laser ride height stuff often doesn't work right—you get dust in the optics that changes it. Now we have a system that takes into account tire squash numbers, suspension deflection, shock travel, and plugs it into an equation that solves for ride height. There's other stuff I can't even tell you about—I'd have to kill you."

—Bryan Herta

Fig. 15-22. Bryan Herta in the Team Rahal Reynard in 1996. Little things like an ill-fitting seat can distract from peak performance and, in this league, details make a big difference.

"It sounds silly, but not thinking about how tired you are really helps. Physical trainers will tell you when you're lifting weights, that the more faces that you make and the more grunts you do, [the more you] take away from the strength that you should be putting into that lift, and it's really true.... Concentration is the key. If you let things bother you and your concentration goes off, then you're in trouble."

—Brian Till

"I would say the biggest thing that I learned as you go up the racing ladder is that more and more the people around you are crucial to your success. The closer to the top you get, there's a much greater premium on the equipment you're in and the personnel that run the car. I don't think there's any mystery to doing well in an Indy Car—you've got to be in a position to be able to have the equipment capable of doing it, and good people running it."

—Robbie Buhl

is so high at this level of the sport that precious little skill separates the driving ability of 2/3 of the field. The best driver with the best car wins. The best driver with the second best car doesn't.

The importance of teamwork goes beyond the mechanical aspects of the car. Finances and logistical concerns have just as much an effect on success as the nuts and bolts.

An aspect of team-building that is often underrated in the racing world is the human relations side. Successful teams have chemistry. On the winningest teams, each team member knows their job and is good at it. Just as important, they like doing the work despite the fact that an Indy Car season is long and hard. Team members spend a lot of time together (often in a highly-charged atmosphere) and the team is at a definite advantage if the team members like working with each other and have a high degree of mutual respect. Many teams have a combination of talent that, on paper, should be a winning formula, but if the chemistry is missing, the results will suffer. It happens all the time. You have to realize that, although you carry the banner, you are as much, if not more so, a member of a team; and you can have a significant effect on the team's morale and chemistry.

CHAPTER **16**

INSIDE THE WORLD OF RACING

IF YOU'RE TEMPTED TO TRY driving racecars or you're ready to make a serious professional commitment to racing, you have a tremendous number of choices ahead of you, from the type of racing to the kind of car you'll race.

But choices aside for a moment, let's get one thing straight. Racing is racing. It doesn't matter if you're racing a Kart, your own street car, a Bomber on a local dirt oval, a vintage sports car, a Legend car, or a Formula Dodge. Racing is challenging, exhilarating, and just plain fun, no matter how you choose to get active in the sport.

We've drawn up a list in the Appendix to provide you with contacts and information sources for all

> Whether you're inclined toward amateur racing or you aspire to a professional career, it pays to get a clear picture of auto racing's realities.

types of racing. At the Skip Barber Racing School, however, our orientation is road racing—it's the branch of the sport we know best. That being the case, we can't and won't claim to be experts on where and how to start racing Karts or Ovals. But whichever path you choose up the racing ladder, we can give you a bit of general advice and a few reminders as you set out to become a participant in the sport.

BE REALISTIC

Racecars cost money. Getting involved on a shoestring is possible but potentially very frustrating. You have to be honest with yourself on the financial front.

Fig. 16-1. No matter how or where you choose to move out of the sidelines and into the driver's seat, racing is just plain fun.

Determine how much you're willing and able to spend per season on this hobby. No wishes or fantasies here. How much of your own hard-earned money are you willing to have disappear in exchange for the challenge and excitement of being on the racetrack? If the thought creeps into your head that you'll pick up some sponsorship to supplement your budget, get over that fantasy quick. No matter how far you hope to go in the sport, get it through your head right now that you'll be spending a lot of your own money for some time. If you can talk someone out of some of theirs, more power to you, but don't count on it.

Once you arrive at a brutally honest budget figure, keep in mind that a good portion of that budget is going to go for non-racing expenses like travel, lodging, food, etc. If you're going racing in your own car, there will be weekly expenses for equipment, preparation, tires, fuel, entry fees and such. Far too often we have seen beginners spend 95% of their budget on acquiring the car, quickly running out of money to run it. You want to drive, not admire how the car looks in your garage.

Also, be honest with yourself about the risk, both to yourself and to your car. Both can be hurt in the racing environment. It's certainly not inevitable, but the possibility is there and you have to be willing to accept that.

What Do You Want From Racing?

There are lots of potential answers to this question. Is it thrills that you're looking for? The challenge of learning a new, difficult skill? Do you want, someday, to be a famous professional racer?

Regardless of your initial answer to this question, you'll have a lot more success, and enjoy it more, if you decide that you're choosing to race because you want to do it well. Make it your mantra—*Do It Well.*

Give Yourself A Break

The ultimate success on the racetrack is winning, and it's far too easy to get impatient about being fast and winning races. Take it easy. You've seen how complicated race driving can be and the variety of skills you have to master to be able to do it right. Allow yourself the time to learn. You'll learn better if you take some of the pressure off yourself. Allow yourself the time to develop. It is not unreasonable to spend three years in the same type of car to learn and perfect the fundamentals of racing.

By all means, try hard. Now, when we say, "Try hard," every new driver leaps to the conclusion that trying hard means driving the car hard. Not so. Trying hard means applying effort to the skills you'll need to get better. Having trouble putting the car perfectly on line lap after lap? Try harder to find reference points, be accurate with car placement, and read the symptoms of early and late apexing. Try harder at developing your ability to concentrate on the task at hand.

> *"Anybody can drive a racecar—it just takes practice, like playing a violin. The only problem in this business is that it's not like your mom buying you a glove and a bat and a ball and sending you out in the back yard to practice. So, to be a racecar driver, you have to practice like anything else and the unfortunate thing about racecar driving is that it costs a phenomenal amount to go practice. I was very lucky when I was a kid because I spent $50 every Tuesday or Wednesday and drove all day at Thompson, Connecticut. $50 was all it cost to run all afternoon. I ran my tires down to the second ply—they were four ply tires—and it didn't matter how fast I was going. It mattered that I drove, and drove, and drove, and drove, and encountered experiences and filed them away."*
>
> —David Loring

Keep at it. The biggest mistake you can make is to blow off the fundamentals and make errors in your impatience to go faster.

Get Experience

The key is getting experience. To get good, you have to drive a lot, concentrate on what you're doing while you're at it, and be self-critical about your abilities. There are many levels of racing, and it takes experience and hard work to move through each level to the next. In the first few years of your experience on the race track, reduce the pressure on yourself to win races. Instead, increase the desire to perfect all the details which will eventually equip you to consistently finish toward the front and will allow you to step up to a higher level of racing.

Where Do You Want to Go?

The vast majority of beginning race drivers get involved without aspirations to a professional career. Still, for anyone who drives a race car, way back in the corner of your mind there's a voice that says "If not Indy, maybe Daytona or Sebring." Then there are those who are determined to get to the professional ranks.

Many beginners, especially those with career aspirations, hurt their development by putting way too much pressure on themselves to win right away. This sometimes comes from the mistaken notion that your racing résumé has to consist of win after win, championship after championship, in order to impress potential sponsors. The truth of the matter is that at the entry level of the sport you're racing in anonymity. Although you may think everyone is watching, the fact is that your immediate family and a few friends are probably the only people who really give a hoot where you finish. You can use this to your advantage to learn the craft without being in the spotlight. Someday you may have to call on all the skills you've developed and all the experience you've gained to take advantage of a big opportunity. Early on, you're preparing yourself for this day.

> "You have to go through the steps. Nobody can go from a Formula Ford to an Indy Car and be successful without spending the time it takes to learn to handle it. There's things beyond just learning about horsepower that you have to go through at each of the levels. Each stage is important.
>
> "If you're successful at your level and comfortable, you're probably ready to step up to the next one. If things are happening quick or you're still not able to anticipate what the car is doing, you have to stay where you are. If you're not successful at the level you're at, stay there. I'm a firm believer that you should have some level of success at the level you're in before you move up to the next step."
>
> —Bryan Herta

Some drivers are so intent on their goal for the future that they waste the here and now. We see this a lot with the younger drivers who are determined to make a career of racing. It happens all the time in the Three Day Racing School. On their first day in a racecar they're asking about what they have to do to get in a Pro Series car as soon as possible.

For every beginning race driver, the hardest part to swallow is that progressing from the fundamentals takes time. Racing is no different from other sports in this respect. How long does it take to become a scratch golfer? How long must you practice to become a good enough ball player to progress as far as the minor leagues? How many years of training, dedication and practice to qualify for the olympic team? Why should becoming an excellent race driver be any different? Well, it isn't.

RACING IS DIFFERENT

You can plot out your journey through the world of auto racing all you want, but eventually you have to face the hard, cold fact that this sport is different from other professional sports in the way it treats talent. If you're a minor league baseball player and you bat .420, hit the ball 400 feet, and have an arm like a bazooka, someone will likely pay you handsomely to play for their team.

> "The greatest driver in the world, when he first sat in a Kart or a Formula Ford, couldn't have been capable of jumping right into an Indy Car at a place like Michigan. At 230 to 240 m.p.h., things will be coming at you too fast. It took me many years to realize that, even when I got to the big powerful cars, how little experience I had and how easy it was to get caught out. And it wasn't getting caught out about the power—it's just the situations.
>
> "I remember the first year at Indianapolis— crashing. Afterward, Rick Mears said, 'Oh, you got caught by the wind between the grandstands over at Turn 4.' There was a gap between the grandstands and the wind would come through the gap and pin the nose of the car; and I spun the thing around late in the race. The other thing was that I hadn't done 500 miles before and I wasn't as alert as I needed to be late in the race. It's all experience. All the things that happen to you. You can't teach that. You can tell people about it but you have to have it happen to you to really learn it."
>
> —Danny Sullivan

> "People ask, 'What do I have to do to turn pro?' The answer is to enter a pro race. You don't have to do anything. It's just a change in attitude. I didn't enter pro races because I never had the kind of situation where I could win—I had old cars, didn't have any budget, just did things out of pocket. I knew I could do well if I ever had those things but I didn't pursue it like these guys pursue it now. I wanted it to come to me—'I'm winning everything, somebody's going to recognize that' was the attitude. Doesn't work that way. It took me way too long to realize that. But being in it year after year, you meet people and opportunities present themselves. When my opportunity came, I had a tremendous amount of experience and I was able to make good on the chances I got."
>
> —Dorsey Schroeder

The minor leagues of racing, however, are filled with drivers with as much, or more, raw talent than the drivers at the top of the professional heap. What they lack is the opportunity to drive a top-rank car, and the years of experience needed to deal with that car's peculiarities.

"If you are going to be serious about it, you have to race against the best at your level. That's why I went to Europe in 1971. On the same day when there's 140 of us racing at Brands Hatch for the BOC championship, there's 95 guys up at Snetterton for the Sunbeam Electric Championship. That to me was real racing; if I was going to be a race driver I had to race with real people. You are forced to raise yourself to the level of competition.

"The BOC championship, which was the championship I was after over there, you could do 25 races a year—more than I could do in a year and a half in this country. Sullivan and I raced together. Between Formula Ford and Formula Three he did sixty races a year. You can't do that here—never mind the intensity—that's the big thing. All of those guys are there to win the championship and get into the next step—to get into Formula Three, to get into Formula Two, to get into Formula One."

—David Loring

"I think other than the ability to drive the car, the most important ingredient isn't a skill, really. It's a character trait: tremendous perseverance. Being able to represent a sponsor and stuff is way down the line. I think there are more guys that have the skill to drive the racecar than have the perseverance and the good luck to end up in the right situation.

"I think it's being willing to do all the suffering and not give up. I can think of many drivers who, to them, thought they were giving up a lot to get where they wanted to go, but gave up before the guys that ultimately made it. I think it's traits of personality rather than being attractive or a good entertainer or cultivating the kinds of things that might matter when you drive at the Roger Penske level. He's still, first and foremost, picking the guy who can, as they used to say, stand on the gas."

—Skip Barber

"One of the most important things is desire. I wanted it and still want it so badly that it is a very single-minded focus for me. It runs over into every other aspect of my life. I see a lot of other guys out there with a lot of desire too that don't get there. You have to have that, but it's not enough. You have to be able to work hard at it, and take some chances.

"For example, when I won the Barber/ Saab championship, I won $178,000 worth of prize money. Although I won the championship, nobody was offering to pay me to drive in Indy Lights. The only way I could continue was to take that money, which I had in a bank account, and invest it back into my racing career. For someone 20 years old, that was a lot of money. I had to believe in it, that it would pay off in the long run.

"I was lucky too in that my family was supportive and they helped out whenever they could. Ability is the last ingredient. Some people have it and some don't.

"There may be five guys out there who are good enough to win, but only one of them can. Your determination, and your intelligence and a little bit of luck, is what determines who wins and who doesn't.

"You look at Indy Car: there are guys like Michael Andretti who win races which they shouldn't have won just because they want it so badly they find a way. There are others who are fast but don't know how to win. It's as simple as that: some people know how to win, will find ways to win. It's a war out there."

—Bryan Herta

Talent

In becoming a professional racedriver, talent is a requirement, but it's not enough to guarantee success. You have to be able to put yourself in a car year after year to develop that talent, and gain experience.

In chemistry, there are two conditions which determine whether a chemical reaction will take place. One is the "Necessary Condition"—that is, the combination of ingredients and environment which are absolutely necessary for the reaction to take place. They don't guarantee that it will take place, but they have to be there if there's any chance of the reaction happening. There is also the "Sufficient Condition," which is a recipe for the reaction to actually take place. In racing, talent is a "Necessary Condition" but not "Sufficient Condition." The talent has to be there when the opportunity comes, but it doesn't guarantee that opportunity will knock.

Even if you get to the point where you are considered a talented professional by your peers, the struggle to put your butt in a good car continues. Race driving is not a career for those who value job security.

Money

Staying in a racecar year after year takes money and, if you aspire to being a professional, you have to accept that fact from the start. That money can be your own money or someone else's—it really doesn't matter—money is money.

The comedian Steve Martin does a skit where he holds a seminar on "How to Become a Millionaire." He starts by saying, "First, get a million dollars." The easiest way to finance your racing career is to take this approach, because you'll certainly need the money.

The reality is that before someone is going to pay you to drive their racecar, you'll have to develop the talent, gain the experience, and, unless you're extremely resourceful or you're the world's best deal maker, you're going to foot the bill for the early stages of your career.

Demonstrating your talent behind the wheel will not be enough. You'll need to hustle up the resources to do the next season, or the next fastest class of car, every season. If we knew a sure-fire way to accomplish this feat, we'd be in the sponsorship brokerage business. There simply is no foolproof strategy which is guaranteed to work.

SPONSORSHIP

Major corporations contribute large sums of money to fund racing teams through their marketing and promotions departments, but since their managers are doing this in the best interests of the company and are answerable to a higher authority, they tend to go with established racing teams and drivers who have established their credentials as players in the professional ranks.

Advertising

In many cases, especially at the lower levels of the professional ladder, it's hard for a company to justify spending advertising money on a racing sponsorship. This is not to say that there can't be some economic justification to sponsoring a racing team: if there weren't, you wouldn't find the depth of corporate sponsorship found in NASCAR, for example. At that level of the sport, however, there is substantial television coverage, getting the sponsor's logo to millions of viewers. For smaller teams running local races before a small crowd that pays admission to the racetrack, it's difficult to make the argument that the money spent on a race team reaches as many potential customers as conventional advertising will.

Helping A Company

An important part of any sponsorship of a race team or driver is putting together a program that satisfies the sponsor's needs. Simply thinking that the name

"The one piece of advice to someone who wants to go racing? Don't give up. Short of someone's ability to buy ride after ride, they will have to experience the disappointment and hardship of what racing's all about. I don't know anybody who's been in this thing long term that hasn't suffered ten years of disappointment to the one good year they finally got. The ones that stuck it out, that kept that point of interest, that focal point as the single thing they wanted to do more than anything else in the world, that never gave up, are the ones that achieve what they wanted—the others never did. It's probably the most unrewarding, unjustified, cruel sport there could ever be. Only those that really want it bad enough will ever really make it because they will have had to give up everything else to stay focused on the one thing they want. You can't give up."

—Dorsey Schroeder

"I went to a dinner for the induction of Dan Gurney and Don Prudhomme to the Motorsports Hall of Fame a couple of years ago. There was a great story about Prudhomme when he was a kid, bothering Dan Gurney, saying, 'How do I get into the sport?' Gurney wasn't trying to brush him aside but he said, 'Son, where there's a will there's a way. If you love it bad enough you'll figure out a way to do it.' And I think that does apply. Obviously times are changing a little bit because the sport has become fueled by corporate dollars, more so than a driver with talent getting a break. But I still think that there are possibilities out there if you're willing to work at it."

—Robbie Buhl

plastered on the side of the car is providing a useful advertising function doesn't do it. The most useful function of having a company associated with a racecar is that the participation can be used as a device to generate enthusiasm, excitement, and brand loyalty for that company.

In addition to the direct sponsorship of the costs of running the car, there will often be an additional part of the racing budget which goes to at-track hospitality tents to entertain the company's staff, clients, and potential clients. An additional part of the budget may

"Racing is becoming—already is—big business. It costs millions and millions of dollars to run Indy Car teams. It costs hundreds of thousands of dollars to run lesser teams. That money comes usually from sponsors, which means it's big business and you need to have an understanding of big business. Whether that's a college degree, whether that's advertising, marketing or finance classes at a community college—whatever—there has to be some kind of understanding of business.

"The deals that are now being structured sponsorship-wise, a lot of these deals aren't straight money deals—they're product trade-out deals and deals where you use one company or one sponsor to leverage off another. You marry companies together so that they can benefit from each other's involvement and that, in turn, sponsors the racing team.

"You have to have some kind of understanding of how those propositions work or you'll never have an understanding of how to get the money to go racing.

"You try to make yourself as a driver the most complete package that you can. That means certainly understanding the racecar, understanding set-up, understanding how to race, but also understanding the business side of the sport."

—Brian Till

"The biggest thing I've learned in 20 years of running a business that I wish I appreciated when I was racing is patience. I just loved driving a race car and not being able to do it for a whole year was unthinkable. Getting organized, making money, saving money, working on trying to raise money, doing that kind of thing instead of driving—no way I would do that. Every year I had to somehow, some way, go racing, often very little. Constantly broke, constantly trying to catch up. I never had a plan. I never thought drive this, then move up to that—I drove anything I could as soon as I could, and ended up always being broke.

"Patience. And I would have learned how to promote myself. I think that now I'm a reasonably good marketing guy, but as a racer I was too shy. I remember once, when I had just won my first National race at Lime Rock, an official saying to me, 'Do you want to meet the fellow who owns the racetrack?' No, thanks.

"I believed that if you were good enough, someone would come to you. It wasn't that I was arrogant—I was afraid. I wouldn't even go around asking guys to drive their cars. If I had it to do over again I sure as hell would do it differently and, I have a feeling, with a much greater result. You have to learn to go banging on doors."

—Skip Barber

go toward hooking an ad campaign to the racecar. In short, hooking a corporate sponsor involves answering the question, "What are you going to do for *me*?"

At the lower levels of the sport, there are all kinds of sponsorship arrangements ranging from the $100 worth of parts from the local auto parts store to the local eccentric who always wanted to own a racing team. In any case, you have to identify what the potential sponsor wants from the arrangement and deliver it in spades.

Something to Show

It used to be that an important aspect of securing support was to have something concrete to show to a potential sponsor. You would have much more success if you could show a potential supporter a shop, a car—an existing operation. While this is still true, more and more racers are carrying their helmet (and the money necessary to support a team's effort) to an existing team that has the experience and knowledge to field a competitive car in a particular class. The driver is essentially buying the ride and the team isn't particularly concerned with where the money comes from. It could be the driver's own money or the driver could

"Guys have to quit the fantasy that Roger Penske is going to call and offer a contract. More likely is that there's a guy over there who has a trucking company, and another guy over here that sells electrical fittings and maybe if you can put the two together and they like you and see how helping you go racing can help them, then maybe you can put together a program that has a chance to grow over the next few years. That's a much more likely deal than waiting for somebody to sign you up and you're going to be the next Danny Sullivan."

—Jim Pace

have rustled it up from a personal sponsor—it doesn't matter to the team as long as they get, for example, the $600,000 or more a year it takes to run a Formula Atlantic team.

The same is true for a spec car series like the Barber/Dodge Pro Series, where the series operator owns all the cars and the drivers are responsible for finding the financial support to enter the season's races. The

> "If you've got a surgeon working on you, you'd rather that he cut up twenty or thirty cadavers before he gets into you. That's the thinking that team owners have when approached by rookies. If you're a car owner, are you going to put an untested rookie in the car or a guy who's raced for twenty years—and doesn't crash—and goes as fast as anyone else?"
>
> —David Loring

> "I struggled for years until I met Garvin Brown. I didn't have any money and my partner, Frank Faulkner, who got me involved in racing, was an academic: he didn't have any money. Garvin saved my career. When I came back from Europe, my career was stalled, and there was nothing bright on the horizon. Garvin helped me and then my career took off, but if he hadn't I might not have gone any farther. It's a fine line."
>
> —Danny Sullivan

> "Advice for someone who wants to become a pro? Go out and make a lot of money. You know the old line, 'I know there's a fortune in racing, because I put it there.'
>
> "On the driving end a really good way to start is with Karting. I think that almost applies to anyone because I think it's just invaluable—and it's so cost-effective.
>
> "Definitely go to racing school and do a series like Skip's, because you learn so much in such a short time. Learn about marketing. Learn about business. Learn about presentation. Learn about communicating with people. It's a very difficult thing to succeed in because you have to wear so many hats. Unfortunately the thing you can't do is to focus on nothing but your driving. You can't do that. That will just get you depressed.
>
> "It's not a sport that is based on ability alone like so many other sports are. You have to be brilliant in the car and out of the car. You need to get the experience in the car but you also need to have the other part of the package....[T]here are people who know how to go out and sell a program. You're best off aligning yourself with someone with those talents. Some drivers are successful at wearing that hat—Kenny Bernstein is probably the best example—but for the most part, it's much easier to have someone else sell you than to sell yourself."
>
> —Jeremy Dale

cars can be painted in your sponsor's colors and logos and, although you don't have your own shop and car to show them, there's a good deal of security for the sponsor in getting involved with an professional organization with a long track record, in-house public relations and marketing people, and a television deal.

A Patron

A number of racing teams have been established over the years by a single person who can make the decision to spend personal or corporate money to get involved in big-time racing. Jim Trueman, Garvin Brown, and Ted Field, for example, were the men behind the important phases of the careers of Bobby Rahal, Danny Sullivan, and Danny Ongias, respectively. They began their racing teams around the driver, and to do this, the personal relationship between the team owner and the driver was the key to making it happen. Also, team owners weren't saddled with justifying the decision to others who held the purse strings. They did it because they wanted to and there didn't have to be any economic justification to continue.

MONEY ISN'T EVERYTHING

Aspiring to being a professional racing driver involves more than just money. You can buy time in a racecar so that you can keep driving and gain experience, but you can't buy talent, determination, and motivation. You have to supply these on your own. You'll notice that the top professional drivers, when asked what

the most important ingredient for a successful racing career is, tell you time and time again that perseverance and dedication to the sport are key.

THE JOB

There are common illusions about the reality of being a professional race driver. It's not all T.V. interviews and fast-lane lifestyles. If you go to a professional event like the Daytona 24 Hours or an Indy Car event, the scene is highly charged and, in a way, glamorous. On the inside, however, it's less glitzy. For the drivers, a big race event is business first, and the job is not without its down side. Although you would get few

> "Concentration and seriousness is what it takes. I mean if you want to do it, really want to try and do it, and you concentrate on it, it is a 24 hour a day job, 370 days a year."
>
> —David Loring

drivers to admit it out loud, there is an undertone of risk at every race event.

At the entry levels of the sport, the speeds are relatively low and, when bad things happen, your chances of walking away unscathed are pretty good. At the top levels of the sport, real danger is ever-present. Drivers seldom talk about it and perform in a perpetual state of denial about the obvious risks.

UPS AND DOWNS

For someone who is passionate about racing, it's hard to imagine that there could be any serious down sides to having a top-level ride. Most drivers, while privately wishing they could just drive the car, realize that the driving is the reward for all the background work that allows them to be in the driver's seat.

"When you get to within the last second in any car, it gets hard. The last few tenths are really, really, hard. That holds true across the board, no matter what you're driving. I think each time you step up into another type of car, at first you think it's really good because the performance is better. But when you try to make it go as fast as the best guys do in that car, you've got to find that new limit, and that's the tough part.

"You drive in as deep as your mind says you can go and still live—and the car can be a lot better than that. So you sneak up on it. Try deeper and you say, "Well, that wasn't so bad." But when you get to where it has to be, 10 tenths driving, it is that bad. The designers raise the limit, then we have to counter by learning to cope with that."

—Dorsey Schroeder

"The higher closing speed was particularly a problem in IMSA racing...a huge problem. There are so many cars with such diverse abilities. The speeds of the cars are so different and the abilities of the drivers are so different. You get into big problems in traffic especially in the one hour sprint races. You're just taking unbelievable risks but you have no choice. If you're chasing a guy and he gets through the traffic and you don't you're cooked. You kind of reevaluate, at least I did, what you think is a prudent driving style. Prudence is a relative thing but that changed for me.

"The first place I ever drove the GTS car was at Riverside, which I had never seen. It isn't exactly an easy racetrack. It can be pretty intimidating racetrack...it's very quick. I'm in this car that I don't know much about and all I know is that it will go about a buck eighty and I don't know this racetrack, and it's real fast. I had some moments...I never spun the car but it took me a while to get comfortable with it and get up to speed."

—Jeremy Dale

"The approach we were taking in my rookie year at Indy was to keep everything comfortable. I was just trying to have a maintenance throttle all the way around the track and when things got comfortable to bump it up a bit. I went round and round just building the comfort level of turning in without lifting. We went from 213 to 214 to 216 that way, not using full throttle or maximum boost.

"Everything was comfortable and then—I don't know what happened—we crashed. The crash happened so early in the corner...I was spinning before the apex. That's why a lot of people think that something must have broke, but we couldn't tell because so much of the car was destroyed. Maybe it was something I did, but I don't remember because I was knocked out. I didn't know if I was coming or going for about four or five days.

"Four days later I got back in the spare car and did four laps in the car and the transmission got stuck in two gears, locked up the rear end, and we hit the wall again at over 200 m.p.h. At least we know for sure that was the car breaking. Still, four laps, after having the biggest crash of your life. Mentally, it's like, Oh, shit, shit. "

—Robbie Buhl

"I love it and I wouldn't trade it for anything. You'd have to be an idiot to complain about it. I feel really lucky to be able to do what I always dreamed of doing and be fortunate enough to make a living at it and to be able to concentrate full time on racing.

"Maybe one of my biggest frustrations is trying to explain the sport to people who don't understand. I love it so much and derive so much personal satisfaction from it that I want everyone to see in it what I see and you just can't get that."

—Bryan Herta

"When you're being paid to drive...the hard part is keeping your sense of humor. A lot of people suddenly take it more serious. I try to keep it light. If everyone on the team is enjoying their work, you have a much better chance of finishing on the podium.

"I feel like the luckiest man alive. I've been blessed with good teams and good owners and good co-drivers. When the day of reckoning comes, I'm going to thank everybody I was involved with. I might have won a race or two on my own but, boy, I can't remember it. It was always a group effort."

—Terry Earwood

"I've tried being big-time intense and it didn't work for me. I went from being the most footloose and fancy free person to taking it too seriously. When I took it really seriously, my performance went way off. I wasn't having any fun.

"Over a period of time things got to be work. Too much work, too much pressure. I wasn't acting like me. I was trying to act like everybody wanted me to and I just didn't do as well. I wasn't as happy doing what I was doing. You've got to be yourself...He's the person who got you there."

—Dorsey Schroeder

"Race drivers are a little like circus dogs. You're out back practicing jumping through the hoop, hoping you'll get your chance to audition and move your act out to the big ring. That chance might not ever come but you've got to keep jumping through that hoop so that, if it does, you're ready.

"In the car, you're prepared to accept the car breaking, not finishing the race, not winning the championship, the motor blowing up. You have to accept that.

"The bigger frustration is all of the people that say they're going to deliver, then don't. It's such an interesting study of personalities. You hear it time and time again. 'We're really interested. We want to get involved. We're going to do big things and put together a great program.' Then they don't return a call, and a month later the phone number is changed. You think, 'If you had just said no a couple of months ago it would have saved us both a lot of aggravation.' Everybody in racing has their own stories about those situations.

"But you can't let deals that fall through make you skeptical about everything that comes down the pike. You have to keep motivated for every dinner you have with a group of people who say they're interested. You have to have your selling shoes on every time the opportunity presents itself. You know it's a long shot. You know the odds are against you but you still do it anyway.

"It's easy to think, 'same song, different verse,' a different set of guys, a different year. But you have to be just as optimistic as the first time, every time. You can't afford to be bitter. One of my big goals is not to be old and bitter about the sport. There are too many guys who never got the hoop to come around that are bitter about it, and worse, bitter toward the guys who did get the opportunity.

"What keeps you going is that there's lots of up sides to racing. The competition, not only against others, but with yourself. The people that you meet. There's a wonderful group of people who share the same interests in perfecting the cars and doing a good job at the racetrack. One of the things that is the hardest to attain but the most cherished is the respect of your peers. To have the respect of people in your field, the people you work with, I think, is the greatest reward."

—Jim Pace

Appendix

Racing Resources

Karts: Schools

Jim Hall Kart Racing School
1555-G Morse Ave.
Ventura, CA 93003
(805) 654-0227

Road Atlanta Driver Training Center
5300 Winder Hwy.
Braselton, GA 30517
(404) 967-6143

Michiana Raceway Park
120 Stone Ave.
Lake Forest, IL 60045
(708) 234-6357

START!! Racing
2721 Forsyth Rd., Suite 466
Winter Park, FL 32792
(800) 243-1310

Performance Motorsports Kart Racing School
P.O. Box 12571
Columbus, OH 43212
(614) 294-5020

Karts: Sanctioning Bodies

International Kart Federation
4650 Arrow Highway, #C-7
Montclair, CA 91763
(909) 625-5497

World Karting Association (WKA)
P.O. 294
Harrisburg, NC 28075
(704) 455-1606

Car Club Time Trial Events

National Speedway Directory (Cost: $10)
P.O. Box 448
Comstock Park, MI 49321
(616) 361-6229

Aston Martin Owners Club
(USA/East)
Robert Burt, Secretary
204 Penn View Drive
Pennington, NJ 08534

Alfa Romeo Owners Club
Glenna Garrett, Exec. Sec.
2468 Gum Tree Lane
Fallbrook, CA 92028
(619) 728-4875

BMW Car Club of America
2130 Massachusetts Ave.
Cambridge, MA 02140-9850
(800) 878-9292

Miata Club of America
P.O. Box 920428
Norcross, GA 30092
(770) 368-8002

Porsche Club of America
P.O. Box 30100
Alexandria, VA 22310
(703) 922-9300

Porsche Owners Club
P.O. Box 9000-277
Seal Beach, CA 90740

VINTAGE RACING: ORGANIZATIONS

Chicago Historic Races
P.O. Box 1159
Chicago, IL 60690
(312) 563-0495

Vintage Auto Racing Association
Megan Collins
2925 Denison Ave.
San Pedro, CA 90731
(800) 280-VARA

Classic Sports Racing Group
Mark Mountanos
1361 Lowrie Ave.
South San Francisco, CA 94080
(415) 978-2490

Vintage Auto Racing Association of Canada
Steve Bodrug
87 Troy St.
Mississauga, Ontario,
Canada L5G 1S6
(905) 274-8754

Corinthian Vintage Auto Racing Corp.
Bradley Balles/ Steven Torrance
P.O. Box 232
Addison, TX 75001
(214) 661-9030 or 931-3183

Sportscar Vintage Racing Association
P.O. Box 489
Charleston, SC 29402
(803) 723-7872

Daytona Antique Auto Racing Association
Doug Howard
2525 Volusia Ave.
Daytona Beach, FL 32114
(904) 248-1606

Historic Motor Sports Association
Steve Earle
P.O. Box 30628
Santa Barbara, CA 93130
(805) 966-9151

Historic Stock Car Racing Group
Carl Jensen
5418 Reeve Rd.
Mazomanie, WI 53560

Historic Sports Car Registry, Ltd.
Joe Pendergast
3005 Peacock Lane
Tampa, FL 33618
(813) 931-5642

LEGENDS CARS

600 Racing Inc.
5725-C Hwy. 29 North
Harrisburg, NC 28075
(704) 455-3896

SCCA

Sports Car Club of America
9033 E. Easter Place
Englewood, CO 80112
(303) 694-7222

MAJOR PROFESSIONAL RACING SCHOOLS

Bob Bondurant School of High Performance Driving
Firebird International Raceway
20000 Maricopa Road, Gate 3
Chandler, AZ 85226
OR
P.O. Box 51980
Phoenix, AZ 85076
(800) 842-7223

Skip Barber Racing School
29 Brook St.
P.O. Box 1629
Lakeville, CT 06039
(800) 221-1131 or (860) 435-1300

Russell Racing School
Sears Point Raceway
Hwys. 37 & 121
Sonoma, CA 95476
(707) 939-7600

Bridgestone Racing School
Box 260 RR2
Shannonville, Ontario,
Canada K0K 3A0
(613) 969-0334

PROFESSIONAL SCHOOL RACING SERIES

Skip Barber Racing School
29 Brook St.
P.O. Box 1629
Lakeville, CT 06039
(800) 221-1131 or (860) 435-1300

Russell Racing School
Sears Point Raceway
Hwys. 37 & 121
Sonoma, CA 95476
(707) 939-7600

Bridgestone Racing School
Box 260 RR2
Shannonville, Ontario,
Canada K0K 3A0
(613) 969-0334

MAJOR OVAL RACING SANCTIONING BODIES

Automobile Racing Club of America (ARCA)
P.O. Box 5217
Toledo, OH 43611-0217
(313) 847-6726

United States Auto Club (USAC)
4910 West 16th St.
Speedway, IN 46224-0001
(317) 247-5151

NASCAR
P.O. Box 2875
Daytona Beach, FL 32120-2875
(904) 253-0611

American Speed Association (ASA)
P.O. Box 350
202 S. Main St.
Pendleton, IN 46064-0350
(317) 778-8088

ROAD RACING SANCTIONING BODIES

International Motor Sports Association (IMSA)
3502 Henderson Blvd.
Tampa, FL 33609
(813) 877-4672

Sports Car Club of America (SCCA)
9033 E. Easter Place
Englewood, CO 80112
(303) 694-7223

PUBLICATIONS

Autoweek Magazine
1400 Woodbridge Avenue
Detroit, MI 48207-3187
(311) 446-6000

National Kart News
51535 Bittersweet Road
Granger, IN 46530
(219) 277-0033

National Speed Sport News
79 Chestnut St.
P.O. Box 608
Ridgewood, NJ 07451-0608
(201) 445-3117

On Track
128 South Tryon St.
Suite 2275
Charlotte, NC 28202
(704) 371-3966

Racer
1371 East Warner Ave., Suite E
Tustin, CA. 92680-6442
(800) 999-9718 or (714) 259-8240

SportsCar: The Official Publication of the Sports Car Club of America
9033 E. Easter Pl.
Englewood, CO 80112
(303) 694-7222

Victory Lane
2460 Park Blvd. #4
Palo Alto, CA 94306
(650) 321-1411

BIBLIOGRAPHY

Alexander, Don, and John Block. *The Racer's Dictionary*. Santa Ana, CA: Steve Smith Autosports, 1980.

Bedard, Patrick. *Expert Driving*. Cincinnati, OH: Valentine Research, Inc., 1987

Bentley, Pat. *Stalking the Motorsports Sponsor*. Santa Ana, CA: Steve Smith Autosports Publications, 1979.

Bondurant, Bob. *Driving With Car Control*. Chicago, IL: Science Research Associates Inc., 1980.

Bondurant, Bob, with John Blakemore. *Bob Bondurant on High Performance Driving*. Osceola, WI: Motorbooks International, 1982.

Fittipaldi, Emerson, and Gordon Kirby. *The Art of Motor Racing*. New Haven, CT: Nutmeg Productions. 1987.

Frère, Paul. *Sports Car and Competition Driving*. Cambridge, MA: Robert Bentley, Inc., 1963, 1992.

Holbert, Al, Holbert, Bob, and Al Bochroch.*Driving to Win*. Tucson, AZ: AZTEX Corporation, 1982.

Hunter, Harlen C., and Rick Stoff. *Motorsports Medicine*. St. Louis, MO: Lake Hill Press. 1992.

Jenkinson, Denis. *The Racing Driver*. Cambridge, Ma: Robert Bentley, Inc., c1997.

Johnson, Alan. *Driving In Competition*. Newport Beach, CA: Bond/Parkhurst Publications, 1972.

Miller, Butch, with Steve Smith.*Short Track Driving Techniques*. Santa Ana, CA: Steve Smith Autosports Publications, 1989.

Prost, Alain, and Francois Rousselot. *Competition Driving*. Richmond, Surrey, England: Hazleton Publishing, 1990.

Puhn, Fred. *How to Make Your Car Handle*. Tucson, AZ: H.P. Books, 1976.

Scott, Peter. *Racing: The Drivers Handbook*. Berkeley, CA: Northwind, 1986.

Smith, Carroll. *Prepare To Win*. Osceola, WI: Motorbooks International, 1975.

Smith, Carroll. *Tune To Win*. Osceola, WI: Motorbooks International, 1979.

Smith, Carroll. *Engineer To Win*. Osceola, WI: Motorbooks International, 1985.

Taruffi, Piero. *The Technique of Motor Racing*. Cambridge, MA: Robert Bentley, Inc., 1959, 1991.

Turner, Richard H., and J. B. Miles. *Winning Autocross/Solo II Competition: The Art and Science*. Hutchins, TX: National Academy for Professional Driving, Inc., 1977

Turner, Richard H. & Shelton, David T. *Accident Avoidance and Skid Control*. Hutchins, TX: NAPD Publishing Company, 1979

Van Valkenberg, Paul. *Race Car Engineering and Mechanics*. New York: Dodd, Mead & Co., 1976

GLOSSARY

Aero
Short for aerodynamic. Aero adjustments on a race-car are those which affect the behavior of the car in the speed range where the flow of air is fast enough to affect the downforce on the tires.

Aglet
The little plastic piece that holds the end of your shoe-lace together.

Angle Of Attack
The angle relative to the air stream at which a racecar wing is set. A high angle of attack creates more down-force and drag than a low angle of attack.

Apex
The point during the corner where the car comes clos-est to the inside edge of the road.

Aspect Ratio
The relationship between the sidewall height of a tire relative to its tread width. Smaller aspect ratios de-scribe a tire which is wide and squat vs. thin and tall.

Balaclava
A hood, made of nomex or other fireproof material, frequently worn under a helmet.

Balance
The mix of front vs. rear end grip. In cornering, the aim is to get a balance of front and rear cornering trac-tion. In braking, it is a matter of having the front and rear ends of the car do their appropriate share of brak-ing in proportion to their different downloads.

Bedding Pads
The friction material of a brake pad is bonded to its backing plate with adhesives which boil out when the pad is first heated. "Bedding pads" is a process of heating up the pads in a non-race situation so that all of the solvents which reduce the pad's friction are boiled away, making the pad perform at its peak with-out fade.

Bind
The car is bound when the driver holds excessive steering angle while the car is turning and trying to ac-celerate. The excess steering angle creates more resis-tance against the road, hurting the car's accelerating ability.

Blip
In order to do a proper downshift the engine revs must be increased to allow smooth engagement of the next lowest gear. The "blip" is a sudden jab of the throttle pedal, usually done with part of the driver's right foot, to temporarily increase the engine revs.

Brake Bias
The proportioning of braking effort toward the front or rear of the car to accommodate the differing tire loading brought about by deceleration. In most mod-ern racecars, brake bias is cockpit-adjustable.

Brake Pads
The easily replaceable, consumable portion of the braking system. Brake pads rub against the brake ro-tor when the brakes are applied, creating friction, which slows the car. The pad is made of friction mate-rial which can withstand high temperatures. The fric-tion material is bonded to a steel plate against which the pucks in the brake caliper exert their force.

Brake Point
Each corner which requires speed loss at its entry has a point beyond which it is impossible to slow the car enough to make the corner. The brake point is a spe-cific reference on or next to the track which drivers use to trigger the application of brakes. Smart drivers

start with a conservative brake point and work it closer to the corner as they progress.

Brake-Turning
Using the car's braking and turning abilities simultaneously in the area between the turn-in point and the apex of a corner.

Breathing The Throttle
The slightest of lifts from full throttle.

Caliper
Calipers convert hydraulic pressure into a force which squeezes the brake pads against the brake rotors, slowing the car.

CF
Coefficient of friction. A convenient way of comparing the grip of different tires. It is a measure of the ratio at which a tire converts download to traction.

CG
Center of gravity. The point in space where the car's mass is centered. At this point there is as much mass forward of it as behind it; as much mass above it as below it; as much mass to the right as to the left.

Constant Radius Corner
A corner which can be defined by a single radius throughout the course of the corner.

Correction
The first step in handling a tail-out slide is the "correction" phase: the driver turns the steering wheel toward the direction the rear of the car is sliding.

Corner Entry
Corner entry includes the area where deceleration for a corner begins, up to the throttle application point.

Crab
Gradually leaving the outside edge of the road on the approach to a corner. Uses up road width at the turn-in point, making the corner tighter and sometimes causing an early apex.

Damper
The technically correct term for a shock absorber. A device that damps motion without necessarily supporting load.

Decreasing Radius Corner
A corner where the first section of the turn has a larger radius than the second.

Deep. Also "Going Deep."
"Going deep" is driving as close as possible to the corner before braking.

Dump Shift
Skipping gears when downshifting, typically going directly from fourth gear to first rather than going through each gear.

Early Apex
In a corner, an early apex occurs when the car touches the inside edge of the road too soon, which will cause the car to run out of road at the corner exit unless the driver increases the amount of direction change in the second part of the turn.

Exit Speed
The speed a car can attain at the track-out point of the corner and consequently the speed carried onto the following straight.

Flat Out
Never lifting off of full throttle. Also, driving absolutely at the limit, leaving no margin for error.

G
G is the force which gravity exerts on earth. It is used as a reference point to compare the acceleration forces which cars can generate. The force of gravity will accelerate a body at 32 feet per second, or 22 mph per second. A car which accelerates at 1 G would do the same.

Hairpin
Arbitrarily defined by the Racing School as a corner with more than 120 degrees of direction change. In conventional use, a hairpin is a relatively slow corner which comes back on itself as in the shape of the round end of a hairpin.

Heel-And-Toe
The process of blipping the throttle in order to synchronize gears while downshifting, and at the same time continuing to have consistent pressure on the brake pedal. It involves using the left side of the right foot for braking while rotating the foot around the ankle and tapping the throttle with the right side of the foot.

Increasing Radius Corner
A corner where the radius of the early section of the corner is tighter than the radius of the later section.

Kink

A jog in the road, normally found on part of a straight, which can be taken as fast as the car can go, or nearly so. Often hair raising.

Late Apex

In a corner, a late apex occurs when the car touches the inside edge of the road further around the corner than necessary, leading the to car to use less than the full road width at the exit of the corner unless the driver, by relaxing steering effort, decreases the amount of direction change in the second half of the turn.

Lift

Reduction of throttle.

Limit

The absolute maximum of the car's capability.

Line

The optimum path around the racetrack. In corners, this path is usually the largest radius arc which can be fit into the confines of the turn. The line can vary with track conditions and the type of racecar being driven.

Load Transfer

The change in tire download that results from accelerating, turning, or braking a car.

Lockup

Lockup occurs when, under braking, a tire stops rotating. Smoke, loss of steering control, flat-spotted tires, and decreased braking traction are the results.

Loose

Synonymous with oversteer.

Master Cylinder

A hydraulic cylinder which converts force on a brake or clutch pedal to hydraulic pressure, which actuates the brake or clutch system.

Modulation

Changing the pressure on the brake or throttle in an effort to keep the tires near, but not over, their traction limits.

Monocoque

A type of racecar construction in which the body is integral with the chassis.

Neutral Handling

A car which, when cornering at its limit, has both front and rear sets of tires operating in the same slip angle range is a neutral handling car.

Oversteer

If, at the cornering limit of the car, the slip angle of the rear tires is greater than the slip angle of the front tires, the car is in oversteer.

Pause

In a tail-out slide, the "pause" is the moment when the movement of the rear of the car toward the outside of the turn stops and the movement toward the inside is about to begin.

Pinching

Adding steering lock to a car when it's cornering. Most frequently used in the second half of the corner to make up for an early apex.

Pitch

Movement of the car which changes the ride height of the car front or rear is known as a "pitch" change.

Recovery

In an oversteer slide, the "recovery" phase starts when the rear end of the car begins coming back toward the inside of the turn. Recovery is the act of taking back the initial steering correction that stopped the motion of the rear end of the car toward the outside.

Reference Point

Any point on, or beside, the racetrack which a driver uses as a visual device to trigger some action: turning in, apexing, brake application point, etc.

Road Camber

Road camber is the angle of the road surface relative to the horizon. Positive road camber is when the angle of the road surface helps the car's corner force. Negative road camber reduces the cornering force of the car. Synonymous with "positive banking" or "negative banking."

Roll

Movement of the car which changes the ride height on the left or right of the vehicle's centerline.

Rotor

The "disc" in disc brakes. A circular plate against which the brake pads squeeze, creating friction which slows the car.

Shaved Tires

Tires used in racing which were originally designed as normal road tires would quickly overheat in racing applications because of their deep tread. These tires are shaved before racing use so that their tread depth is greatly reduced, often down to a few 32nds of an inch, in order to reduce their potential for overheating.

Sight Picture

A visual template drivers use to locate themselves precisely on the racetrack. After using concrete reference points to find the proper placement of the car around the course, drivers then frequently develop a visual feel for whether the car is on the proper line. If what they are seeing doesn't match up with their template, they have to adjust their driving to accommodate this new path.

Skidpad

Any piece of asphalt large enough to contain a circle of at least 200 feet in diameter; it is used to test a car's limit cornering capabilities. Also used to develop drivers' ability to handle cars cornering at the limit of adhesion.

Slicks

Racing tires which have a slick, treadless surface, allowing the greatest amount of rubber to be in contact with the road surface at the contact patch, thereby creating the greatest grip. Used in dry conditions.

Slip Angle

When tires are cornering, there is a difference between the direction the wheel rim is pointing and the direction the tire is traveling. This difference is referred to as the slip angle. Tires have a range of slip angle where they deliver their maximum level of cornering traction.

Steering Lock

The amount the steering wheel is turned. To add steering lock is to turn the steering wheel more toward the inside of the corner.

Straight

The straight portions of a racetrack. Notable exceptions are the portions of the circuit which can be driven as fast as the car can go, but are not necessarily perfectly straight: those portions are to be considered part of the straightaway.

Sweeper

A fast corner, usually taken in either top gear or, at most, one gear lower than top.

TTO

The abbreviation for Trailing Throttle Oversteer, the tendency for a car to develop oversteer if the throttle is lifted, or "trailed," while the car is near its cornering limit.

Turn-In

The point at the start of a corner at which the driver first turns the steering wheel, transitioning the car from the straight into the corner.

Track-Out

The point at the exit of a corner at which the car touches the outside edge of the road.

Threshold Braking

Using 100% of a car's braking capability while braking in a straight line. At the "threshold" point, the tire will be revolving some 15% slower than it would be if freely rolling over the road.

Trail-Braking

A term used to describe the general process of combining the car's straight line braking capability with its braking and turning ability at the entry of corners.

Tight

Same as understeer.

Throttle Application Point

The point in a turn where a driver begins to apply power to drive through and away from the corner.

Understeer

If, at the cornering limit of the car, the slip angle of the front tires is greater than the slip angle of the rears, the car is in understeer.

Yaw Angle

The angle between the centerline of a car and the direction the car is travelling when cornering.

INDEX

A

ability, 250

accelerating and cornering, 8-9
  forces, 80-82

acceleration
  for different racecars, 219
  on straights, 5
  point on the corners, 10-11
  zone, 7

acceleration-limited car, 53-55

accident-causing errors
  early apexing, 172
  failure to warm up, 174
  going deep, 173-74
  jerking car back on track, 172-73
  mismatched downshift, 173
  passing, 174-75
  stackup, 174-75
  trailing throttle oversteer, 173

accidents, 254
  anecdotes, 178
  common errors, 172-75
  other people's, 175-76
  risks, 169
  spins, 169-72

accordion effects, 160-61

adjustability in Indy Lights cars, 241-42

adjusting anti-roll bars and cornering, 208-9

advertising in sponsorships, 251

aerodynamics, 214-15

all-wheel drive, 72

analysis, post-race, 168

Andretti, Mario, 76, 120

Andretti, Michael, 250

angle of attack, 215

anticipation, 14

anti-roll bars and cornering, 208-9

apex, 21, 24-25, 38-44

arc and speed, 19-21

arc radius, 9

arc reference points, 21-22

assumptions (brake-throttle transition), 88-90

attitude at apex, 38, 39, 60

autocross, 70

B

bad downshifts, 15

banking, 45-48

Barber, Skip, xiv
  accordion effect, 161
  defensive driving mode, 152
  early apexing, 38
  patience, 252
  perseverance, 250
  rain racing, 180, 186
  recognizing mistakes, 58
  speed at trackout, 87
  on spinning, 58
  on teaching, xiv

Barber Dodge Pro Series, 103, 227-31, 252

Barber Dodge wings, 215

Barber Formula Dodge 2000, 197

Barber Formula Ford, 197, 221

Barber Saab, 172, 197, 239-40
  Championship, 228, 230, 250
  Pro Series, 227
  race, 157

basic racetrack, 4, 12

basic skills, 244

becoming a race driver, 247-55

Beetle engine, 53

Bernstein, Kenny, 253

biased braking system, 61

"Big Horsepower Blow-By", 141, 148

big rotation, 69-70

blade adjusters and cornering, 209

bleed-off braking, 88

blip in downshifting, 93

blip the throttle, 13

blocking, 153

BOC Championship, 250

Bohren, Walt, 141, 181

Brabham, Geoff, 232

brake application point, 29

brake bias, 31-33
  adjustments for wet weather, 182
  settings, 201-3

brake lockup, 170-72

brake modulation, 31, 79

brake pedal pressure, 30, 74-75, 83-84

brakes
  Barber Pro Series, 228
  Indy Lights, 240

brake slamming, 73

brake system force, 29-30

brake-to-throttle transition, 33, 87-90

brake-turning, 33, 82-86

brake-turn vs. corner type, 86

braking
  control, 61, 71-72
  costs of lighter, 77
  different racecars, 219
  experience, 11
  Formula Dodges, 222-23
  front wheel drive, 71-72
  fundamentals, 29-30
  gaining time, 75
  hard, 77
  Indy cars, 243-45
  last minute, 76
  left foot, 85, 229, 240
  lighter for smaller speed losses, 79
  lightly, 77
  margin, 90
  markers, 14
  modulation, 74-75
  pedal pumping, 74
  performance, 29
  Procedure, The, 76
  reference points, 75-76
  at Sebring, 111, 113-16, 118-19
  short, sharp, 77
  showroom stock, 224-25
  skill (*see* braking and entering)

265

WARNING—
• Racing and driving are in-
herently dangerous—both to
yourself and others. Drive conservatively and responsibly on
public roads. Do not race or
practice race driving except on a
designated race track. There is
no substitute for attending qualified driving schools and learning to drive and race under
controlled, safe conditions.
• Before using this book,
thoroughly read the Warning on
the copyright page.

ART CREDITS

Art courtesy of David Allio: Introduction, p. xv.

Art courtesy of D. Burns: Introduction, p. xi.

Art courtesy of Doyle Racing: Introduction, p. xvi.

Art courtesy of Richard Dole: Fig. 15-20, 15-21.

Art courtesy of Terry Earwood: Introduction, p. xv.

Art courtesy of Exxon Motorsports: Introduction, p. xvi.

Art courtesy of Rick Graves: Fig. 15-9.

Art courtesy of Geoffrey Hewitt: Fig. 15-16.

Art courtesy of Carl Lopez: Introduction pp. xii, xiii, Fig. 1-1, 1-14, 1-15, 1-17, 1-18, 1-19, 1-20, 1-21, 1-22, 1-23, 1-24, 1-25, 2-14, 4-6, 4-7, 4-8, 5-1, 5-8, 5-10, 5-11, 5-14, 5-15, 5-16, 5-17, 6-1, 6-2, 6-3, 6-4, 6-5, 6-6, 6-7, 6-8, 6-9, 6-10, 6-11, 6-12, 6-13, 6-14, 6-15, 6-16, 6-17, 6-18, 7-1, 7-2, 7-3, 7-4, 7-5, 7-6, 7-7, 7-8, 7-11, 7-12, 7-16, 7-19, 7-21, 7-23, 7-25, 7-26, 7-27, 7-28, 7-29, 7-30, 7-31, 7-32, 7-33, 7-34, 7-35, 7-36, 7-37, 7-38, 7-39, 7-40, 7-41, 8-1, 8-2, 8-3, 8-4, 8-5, 8-6, 8-7, 8-8, 8-9, 8-10, 8-11, 8-12, 8-13, 9-1, 9-2, 9-3, 9-4, 9-5, 9-6, 10-1, 10-2, 10-3, 10-4, 10-5, 10-6, 10-7, 10-8, 11-3, 11-4, 11-5, 11-6, 11-7, 11-8, 11-9, 11-10, 11-11, 12-1, 12-2, 12-3, 12-4, 12-5, 12-8, 13-1, 13-2, 13-3, 13-4, 13-5, 14-1, 14-2, 14-3, 14-4, 14-5, 14-6, 14-7, 14-8, 14-9, 14-10, 14-11, 14-12, 14-13, 14-14, 14-15, 14-16, 14-17, 15-1, 15-2, 15-3, 15-4, 15-5, 16-1.

Art courtesy of Carl Lopez and Cathy Earl: Fig. 1-2, 1-3, 1-4, 1-5, 1-6, 1-7, 1-8, 1-9, 1-10, 1-11, 1-12, 1-13, 1-16, 2-1, 2-2, 2-3, 2-4, 2-5, 2-6, 2-9, 2-10, 2-11, 2-12, 2-13, 3-1, 3-2, 3-3, 3-4, 3-5, 3-6, 3-7, 3-8, 3-9, 3-10, 3-11, 3-12, 3-13, 3-14, 3-15, 3-16, 3-18, 3-19, 3-20, 3-21, 3-22, 4-1, 4-2, 4-3, 4-4, 4-5, 4-9, 4-10, 5-2, 5-3, 5-4, 5-5, 5-6, 5-7, 5-9, 5-12, 5-13, 6-7, 7-9, 7-10, 7-13, 7-14, 7-15, 7-17, 7-18, 7-20, 7-22, 7-24, 9-7, 9-8, 9-9, 9-10, 9-11, 9-12, 9-13, 9-14, 9-15, 11-1, 11-2, 12-6, 12-7.

Art courtesy of Charles Loring: Introduction, p. xiv.

Art courtesy of Randy McKee: Fig. 15-14.

Art courtesy of Nissan Motorsports: Introduction, p. xv, Fig. 15-12.

Art courtesy of PacWest Racing Group: Introduction, p. xvi.

Art courtesy of RAL Group, Inc.: Introduction, p. xvi, Fig. 15-19.

Art courtesy of Randy's Photos, Salisbury, CT: Fig. 3-17

Art courtesy of Shell Motorsports: Introduction, p. xv, Fig. 15-22.

Art courtesy of Sidell-Tilghman: Fig. 15-10, 15-11, 15-13, 15-15, 15-17, 15-18.

Art courtesy of Skip Barber Racing School: Introduction p. xiv, Fig. 2-7, 2-8, 15-8.

Art courtesy of Mark Weber: Fig. 15-7.

Art courtesy of Woodstock Motorsports: Fig. 15-6.

Art courtesy of Wright Enterprises: Introduction, p. xv.

AUTHOR'S ACKNOWLEDGMENTS

I NEVER THOUGHT OF MYSELF as a medium; however, early in the process of writing this book, I realized that my role was to be a link between a bevy of experts and those who would like to make use of their experience and avoid having to learn about racing by trial and error. I have many people to thank.

At the top of the list is Skip Barber. Skip provided the opportunity for me to become an author, which was more than a small leap of faith. This considered faith is typical of Skip's approach. He has always encouraged members of his organization to grow—to take on new responsibilities and tasks and invent solutions to problems. I am extremely grateful for this, the latest of a long string of challenges. Thanks, Skip, for the chance and for your patience.

The ten professional drivers who submitted to my grilling have given this book special character. Thanks to Skip Barber (again), Robbie Buhl, Jeremy Dale, Terry Lee Earwood, Bryan Herta, David Loring, Jim Pace, Dorsey Schroeder, Danny Sullivan, and Brian Till. All have freely and enthusiastically offered their hard-earned lessons so that the rest of us don't have to plow the same row.

In addition to specific driving techniques, I have learned about courage from these men—a special kind of courage. Not, as you would think, the kind required to take calculated risks in the car, but the courage to pursue the profession in the face of seemingly insurmountable odds against success, and to face and overcome the emotional and physical setbacks dealt to them.

Behind the scenes are the dozens of others who have contributed in sometimes small, sometimes profound ways. Our instructing staff, a combination of race drivers, friends and colleagues, all influenced the content of this work. I want to thank Walt Bohren, Harry Reynolds, Capt. Bud Dotson, Jim Clark, Kelly Collins, Larry Grabb, Duck Waddle, Bob Green, Bil Prout, and Don Kutchall.

Thanks to my Connecticut neighbors, Mike and Tracy Rand, R. B. Stiewing, Candy Stiewing, Todd Snyder, Linda Snyder, Jason Holehouse, Brett Rubinek, Nick Longhi, and especially Bruce MacInnes for his willingness to wade through early manuscripts and offer very useful criticism and suggestions.

In this same vein, Rick Roso was a tremendous help with valuable input along the way as well as encouragement when things looked dark. Others who read early versions and helped refine the text include David Durnan, Bob Ziegel, Larry Blades, Carroll Smith, Kevin Doran, and Drew Kesler. Thanks.

My appreciation also goes to race drivers such as Divina Galica, David Murry, Nick Nicholson for his sanding and varnishing, Steve Debrecht, Carl Liebech, Vic Elford, Kris Wilson, Randy Buck, Chris (Stanley) Menninga, and Will Pace. As always, special thanks to Barry Waddell for his consistently thought-provoking and lengthy conversations. I'm also indebted to Barry, as well as to Jim Pace, Peter Argetsinger, and Greg Borland for their patient help in photo shoots in Sebring. Thanks also to Sid Brenner for his invaluable contribution to the glossary.

Racecar data collection played a key role in defining and analyzing racing skills and, since I'm no computer whiz, I've been led through bits and bytes by the likes of Chris Wallach, Kurt Roehrig, Bruce (Twister) McQuiston, Kenny Johnson, Todd Snyder, Jeremy Dale, and Michael Zimicki. Keith Hermle deserves special thanks for his help in constructing and trouble-shooting the in-car hardware.

Many people made it possible to take a close look at top-level racecars, in most cases complicating their lives in an already pressure-packed schedule. Folks like Willy Lewis, Gary Blackman, Lee White, Max Jones, and Steve Sewell. Skip Williamson, Bill King, Frank Resciniti, Peter Kuhn, Steve Cole, and Jeff Braun helped provide insight into the awesome capabilities of various professional-level types of cars.

We relied heavily on experts to both provide and confirm various technical details. Special thanks to the people at Michelin for shedding light on tire technology, to Carroll Smith and Kurt Roehrig for their input on chassis adjustments, and to Dave Reilly for helping build the framework of my understanding of mechanical setup.

The administrative staff at Skip Barber Racing School provided help in a variety of ways. In the final stages of the book, Nancy Comstock-Smith managed to put a few more balls in the air by clearing my instructing schedule so that I could concentrate on the final edit. I owe you. Melinda Agar freed me up by taking over, and improving on, a time-consuming project. Thanks go to Louise Richardson, who, way-back-when, championed my writing, leading to this opportunity. Georgia Blades displayed patience and support in what seemed, at times, to be an interminable project.

A number of talented people contributed to the art in this book. Thanks to Sidell Tilghman, Michael Browne, Rick Dole, Paul Pfanner and Keith May of *Racer*, Rick Graves, Anne Hogg, Randy McKee, and Dan Burns. I have a new appreciation of the impact of design and layout provided by the folks at Robert Bentley, especially Lee Ann Best, John Kittredge, and John Koenig.

I'm terrified that I've forgotten someone, and I'm sure I have since so many people have helped along the way. Please forgive me for any oversight—it's unintentional.

I'd also like to thank my mother and father who, with no particular justification, patiently endured a directionless college kid bouncing from major to major over an extended university career. What practical use could come from combined studies in engineering, English literature, business administration, journalism, and communication? As it turns out, you never know.

A life in racing means that your work is often away from home and your family has to deal with this reality, picking up the slack created by your absence. Many relationships have failed under the strain. My wife, Rosemarie, and my son, Max, have dealt patiently with my frequent absences and in doing so, have allowed me to enjoy a career that follows my passion and still have a home to return to when the work is done. Thank you both for your understanding and support. What's that, Rose? Pass the mashed potatoes?

ABOUT THE AUTHOR

CARL LOPEZ HAS BEEN ASSOCIATED with The Skip Barber Racing School since 1977, and over the past twenty years has played a wide variety of roles for the organization, among them Competitor, Teacher, Test Driver, Operations Manager, Data Collection Guru, Instructor Coordinator, and presently Director of Program Planning. He was directly involved in the infancy stages of racecar data collection and its application to coaching race driving, as opposed to its more common use as a racecar tuning device. He wrote and co-directed the 90-minute race-driving training video, "Going Faster," part of the Racing School's constant effort to refine and clarify its curriculum. He has also developed his own racing site on the Internet (http://www.ThinkFastRacing.com).

Carl lives in Canaan, Connecticut, with his wife Rosemarie and son Max.

ABOUT THE SKIP BARBER RACING SCHOOL

THE SKIP BARBER RACING SCHOOL is the world's largest and most comprehensive driver training organization. The company began humbly in 1975 when an acquaintance convinced Skip to lend his name to a little racing school in Thompson, Connecticut. Skip had recently retired from the driver's seat after a 17-year career as a champion amateur and professional race driver, one of a handful of Americans in the history of the sport to compete in the Formula 1 World Championship for Drivers. By 1976, Skip acquired the assets of the school and set out on his own.

The seasonal school was a success. As the number of graduates grew, the pool of trained drivers with nowhere to practice reached critical mass, so Skip decided to offer a Race Series the following spring. The idea was simple: acquire a fleet (originally a total of eight) identical racecars which drivers would share, thereby driving down the cost of participation. By design, what was created was a level playing field where driver talent, not a superior racecar, made the difference. The Skip Barber Race Series was born, and 1998 marks the 22nd consecutive season of this hotbed of entry-level racing.

The next evolutionary step was to make the business a year-round enterprise by acquiring racecar transporters, making any racetrack in North America a potential site for a Skip Barber event. The first schedule of schools in the south began in the winter of 1978, followed by the first Southern Race Series in 1979. Through the years, the expansion of the Racing School and the Race Series continued, including a Midwest base at Road America in Wisconsin and a Western base at Laguna Seca Raceway in California.

For the first ten years of its existence, the focus at Skip Barber was on race driving, but it became more and more apparent that there were auto enthusiasts out there who were interested in improving their driving skills but not necessarily keen on participating in races. By taking many of the skills that race drivers use to go fast and applying them to the street environment, Skip created what is now called the Dodge/Skip Barber Driving School. In this program, anyone whose interest is in better, safer, more proficient driving can learn and practice the skills that could save their life—and have the time of their life doing it.

Soon after creating the Driving School, Skip embarked on yet another dramatic expansion: the formation of a professional open-wheel championship based on the same equal-car premise as the entry-level Race Series. Created in 1986 using thirty Mondiale-designed space frame chassis, what is today called the Barber Dodge Pro Series is a 12-race, $800,000, internationally-televised championship using state-of-the-art carbon-composite racecars called Reynard Dodges. Up-and-coming professional drivers from around the world use the Barber Dodge Pro Series as a stepping stone into CART Indy Lights or FIA Formula 3000, hopefully on their way to Indy Cars or Formula 1.

The four facets of the organization—the Skip Barber Racing School, the Dodge/Skip Barber Driving School, the Skip Barber Formula Dodge Race Series, and the Barber Dodge Pro Series—are today augmented by the Special Projects Group. This branch of the organization designs and conducts product introduction and sales training programs for the auto manufacturing industry as well as custom-tailoring driving and racing programs for corporate customers and groups.

Conducting more than 700 separate programs in any given year, today the Skip Barber Racing organization trains well over 10,000 people annually between its racing, driving, and special projects operations. It has base operations at Lime Rock Park in northwest Connecticut; Sebring, Florida; Elkhart Lake, Wisconsin; and Monterey, California; and operates at more than 20 of America's finest motorsports venues. In addition, racing's most comprehensive scholarship ladder system, a ladder that starts with Karts and continues up through the Racing School, the Formula Dodge Racing Series, the Barber Dodge Pro Series, CART Indy Lights, and CART Indy Cars, and is funded to the tune of nearly $1,000,000 annually, is now in place thanks to Skip Barber.

Automotive Books From Robert Bentley

ENTHUSIAST BOOKS

Unbeatable BMW: Eighty Years of Engineering and Motorsport Success *Jeremy Walton* ISBN 0-8376-0206-8

Volkswagen Beetle: Portrait of a Legend *Edwin Baaske* ISBN 0-8376-0162-2

Small Wonder: The Amazing Story of the Volkswagen Beetle *Walter Henry Nelson* ISBN 0-8376-0147-9

Glory Days: When Horsepower and Passion Ruled Detroit *Jim Wangers* ISBN 0-8376-0208-4

Think To Win: The New Approach to Fast Driving *Don Alexander with foreword by Mark Martin* ISBN 0-8376-0070-7

Maximum Boost: Designing, Testing, and Installing Turbocharger Systems *Corky Bell* ISBN 0-8376-0160-6

Sports Car and Competition Driving *Paul Frère with foreword by Phil Hill* ISBN 0-8376-0202-5

The Racing Driver *Denis Jenkinson* ISBN 0-8376-0201-7

The Technique of Motor Racing *Piero Taruffi with foreword by Juan Manuel Fangio* ISBN 0-8376-0228-9

Race Car Aerodynamics *Joseph Katz* ISBN 0-8376-0142-8

The Scientific Design of Exhaust and Intake Systems *Philip H. Smith and John C. Morrison* ISBN 0-8376-0309-9

The Design and Tuning of Competition Engines *Philip H. Smith, 6th edition revised by David N.Wenner* ISBN 0-8376-0140-1

The Sports Car: Its Design and Performance *Colin Campbell* ISBN 0-8376-0158-4

Volkswagen Sport Tuning for Street and Competition *Per Schroeder* ISBN 0-8376-0161-4

Volkswagen Inspection/Maintenance (I/M) Emission Test Handbook: 1980-1997 *Volkswagen of America* ISBN 0-8376-0394-3

Harley-Davidson Evolution V-Twin Owner's Bible™ *Moses Ludel* ISBN 0-8376-0146-0

Jeep Owner's Bible™ *Moses Ludel* ISBN 0-8376-0154-1

Ford F-Series Pickup Owner's Bible™ *Moses Ludel* ISBN 0-8376-0152-5

Chevrolet & GMC Light Truck Owner's Bible™ *Moses Ludel* ISBN 0-8376-0157-6

Toyota Truck & Land Cruiser Owner's Bible™ *Moses Ludel* ISBN 0-8376-0159-2

Alfa Romeo Owner's Bible™ *Pat Braden with foreword by Don Black* ISBN 0-8376-0707-9

The BMW Enthusiast's Companion *BMW Car Club of America* ISBN 0-8376-0321-8

BMW SERVICE MANUALS

BMW Z3 Roadster Service Manual: 1996–1998, 4-cylinder and 6-cylinder engines *Bentley Publishers* ISBN 0-8376-0325-0

BMW 5-Series Service Manual: 1989–1995 525i, 530i, 535i, 540i, including Touring *Bentley Publishers* ISBN 0-8376-0319-6

BMW 5-Series Service Manual: 1982–1988 528e, 533i, 535i, 535is *Robert Bentley* ISBN 0-8376-0318-8

BMW 3-Series Service Manual: 1984–1990 318i, 325, 325e(es), 325i(is), and 325i Convertible *Robert Bentley* ISBN 0-8376-0325-0

AUDI OFFICIAL SERVICE MANUALS

Audi 100, A6 Official Factory Repair Manual: 1992–1997, including S4, S6, quattro and Wagon models. *Audi of America.* ISBN 0-8376-0374-9

Audi 80, 90, Coupe Quattro Official Factory Repair Manual: 1988–1992 including 80 Quattro, 90 Quattro and 20-valve models *Audi of America* ISBN 0-8376-0367-6

Audi 100, 200 Official Factory Repair Manual: 1988–1991 *Audi of America* ISBN 0-8376-0372-2

Audi 5000S, 5000CS Official Factory Repair Manual: 1984–1988 Gasoline, Turbo, and Turbo Diesel, including Wagon and Quattro *Audi of America* ISBN 0-8376-0370-6

Audi 5000, 5000S Official Factory Repair Manual: 1977–1983 Gasoline and Turbo Gasoline, Diesel and Turbo Diesel *Audi of America* ISBN 0-8376-0352-8

Audi 4000S, 4000CS, and Coupe GT Official Factory Repair Manual: 1984–1987 including Quattro and Quattro Turbo *Audi of America* ISBN 0-8376-0373-0

FUEL INJECTION

Ford Fuel Injection and Electronic Engine Control: 1988–1993 *Charles O. Probst, SAE* ISBN 0-8376-0301-3

Ford Fuel Injection and Electronic Engine Control: 1980–1987 *Charles O. Probst, SAE* ISBN 0-8376-0302-1

Bosch Fuel Injection and Engine Management *Charles O. Probst, SAE* ISBN 0-8376-0300-5

VOLKSWAGEN OFFICIAL SERVICE MANUALS

Eurovan Official Factory Repair Manual: 1992–1999 *Volkswagen of America* ISBN 0-8376-0335-8

Passat Official Factory Repair Manual: 1995–1997 *Volkswagen of America* ISBN 0-8376-0380-3

Jetta, Golf, GTI, Cabrio Service Manual: 1993–1997, including Jetta/// and Golf/// *Robert Bentley* ISBN 0-8376-0365-X

GTI, Golf, and Jetta Service Manual: 1985–1992 Gasoline, Diesel, and Turbo Diesel, including 16V *Robert Bentley* ISBN 0-8376-0342-0

Corrado Official Factory Repair Manual: 1990–1994 *Volkswagen United States* ISBN 0-8376-0387-0

Passat Official Factory Repair Manual: 1990–1993, including Wagon *Volkswagen United States* ISBN 0-8376-0378-1

Dasher Service Manual: 1974–1981 including Diesel *Robert Bentley* ISBN 0-8376-0083-9

Super Beetle, Beetle and Karmann Ghia Official Service Manual Type 1: 1970–1979 *Volkswagen United States* ISBN 0-8376-0096-0

Station Wagon/Bus Official Service Manual Type 2: 1968–1979 *Volkswagen United States* ISBN 0-8376-0094-4

Fastback and Squareback Official Service Manual Type 3: 1968–1973 *Volkswagen United States* ISBN 0-8376-0057-X

Beetle and Karmann Ghia Official Service Manual Type 1: 1966–1969 *Volkswagen United States* ISBN 0-8376-0416-8

Cabriolet and Scirocco Service Manual: 1985–1993, including 16V *Robert Bentley* ISBN 0-8376-0362-5

Volkswagen Fox Service Manual: 1987–1993, including GL, GL Sport and Wagon *Robert Bentley* ISBN 0-8376-0340-4

Vanagon Official Factory Repair Manual: 1980–1991 including Diesel Engine, Syncro, and Camper *Volkswagen United States* ISBN 0-8376-0336-6

Rabbit, Scirocco, Jetta Service Manual: 1980–1984 Gasoline Models, including Pickup Truck, Convertible, and GTI *Robert Bentley* ISBN 0-8376-0183-5

Rabbit, Jetta Service Manual: 1977–1984 Diesel Models, including Pickup Truck and Turbo Diesel *Robert Bentley* ISBN 0-8376-0184-3

SAAB OFFICIAL SERVICE MANUALS

Saab 900 16 Valve Official Service Manual: 1985–1993 *Robert Bentley* ISBN 0-8376-0312-9

Saab 900 8 Valve Official Service Manual: 1981–1988 *Robert Bentley* ISBN 0-8376-0310-2

Robert Bentley has published service manuals and automobile books since 1950. Please write Robert Bentley, Inc., Publishers, at 1734 Massachusetts Avenue, Cambridge, MA 02138, visit our web site at http://www.rb.com, or call 1-800-423-4595 for a free copy of our complete catalog, including titles and service manuals for **Jaguar, Triumph, Austin-Healey, MG,** and other cars.